The Judicial Tug of War

Why have conservatives decried "activist judges"? And why have liberals – and America's powerful legal establishment – emphasized qualifications and experience over ideology? This transformative text tackles these questions with a new framework for thinking about the nation's courts, "the judicial tug of war", which not only explains current political clashes over America's courts, but also powerfully predicts the composition of courts moving forward. As the text demonstrates through novel quantitative analyses, a greater ideological rift between politicians and legal elites leads politicians to adopt measures that put ideology and politics front and center – for example, judicial elections. On the other hand, ideological closeness between politicians and the legal establishment leads legal elites to have significant influence on the selection of judges. Ultimately, the judicial tug of war makes one point clear: for good or bad, politics are critical to how judges are selected and whose interests they ultimately represent.

ADAM BONICA is Associate Professor of Political Science at Stanford University.

MAYA SEN is Professor of Public Policy at Harvard University's John F. Kennedy School of Government.

POLITICAL ECONOMY OF INSTITUTIONS AND DECISIONS

Series Editors
Jeffry Frieden, *Harvard University*
John Patty, *Emory University*
Elizabeth Maggie Penn, *Emory University*

Founding Editors
James E. Alt, *Harvard University*
Douglass C. North, *Washington University of St. Louis*

Other Books in the Series

Alberto Alesina and Howard Rosenthal, *Partisan Politics, Divided Government, and the Economy*
Lee J. Alston, Thrainn Eggertsson, and Douglass C. North, eds., *Empirical Studies in Institutional Change*
Lee J. Alston and Joseph P. Ferrie, *Southern Paternalism and the Rise of the American Welfare State: Economics, Politics, and Institutions, 1865–1965*
James E. Alt and Kenneth Shepsle, eds., *Perspectives on Positive Political Economy*
Josephine T. Andrews, *When Majorities Fail: The Russian Parliament, 1990–1993*
Jeffrey S. Banks and Eric A. Hanushek, eds., *Modern Political Economy: Old Topics, New Directions*
Yoram Barzel, *Economic Analysis of Property Rights (2nd edition)*
Yoram Barzel, *A Theory of the State: Economic Rights, Legal Rights, and the Scope of the State*
Robert Bates, *Beyond the Miracle of the Market: The Political Economy of Agrarian Development in Kenya*
Jenna Bednar, *The Robust Federation: Principles of Design*
Charles M. Cameron, *Veto Bargaining: Presidents and the Politics of Negative Power*
Kelly H. Chang, *Appointing Central Bankers: The Politics of Monetary Policy in the United States and the European Monetary Union*
Tom S. Clark, *The Supreme Court: An Analytical History of Constitutional Decision Making*
Mark Copelovitch and David A. Singer, *Banks on the Brink: Global Capital, Securities Markets, and the Political Roots of Financial Crises*
Peter Cowhey and Mathew McCubbins, eds., *Structure and Policy in Japan and the United States: An Institutionalist Approach*
Gary W. Cox, *The Efficient Secret: The Cabinet and the Development of Political Parties in Victorian England*
Gary W. Cox, *Making Votes Count: Strategic Coordination in the World's Electoral System*

(Continued after the Index)

The Judicial Tug of War

How Lawyers, Politicians, and Ideological Incentives Shape the American Judiciary

ADAM BONICA

Stanford University, California

MAYA SEN

Harvard University, Massachusetts

CAMBRIDGE
UNIVERSITY PRESS

University Printing House, Cambridge CB2 8BS, United Kingdom

One Liberty Plaza, 20th Floor, New York, NY 10006, USA

477 Williamstown Road, Port Melbourne, VIC 3207, Australia

314–321, 3rd Floor, Plot 3, Splendor Forum, Jasola District Centre, New Delhi – 110025, India

79 Anson Road, #06–04/06, Singapore 079906

Cambridge University Press is part of the University of Cambridge.

It furthers the University's mission by disseminating knowledge in the pursuit of education, learning, and research at the highest international levels of excellence.

www.cambridge.org
Information on this title: www.cambridge.org/9781108841368
DOI: 10.1017/9781108894005

© Adam Bonica and Maya Sen 2021

First published 2021

A catalogue record for this publication is available from the British Library.

ISBN 978-1-108-84136-8 Hardback

This book is dedicated to Silvia Blackwell-Sen and Jenny Shen.

Contents

III RAMIFICATIONS OF THE JUDICIAL TUG-OF-WAR

Figures

Tables

Acknowledgments

This book is the product not just of our own efforts but also of the valuable input, constructive criticism, and generous feedback provided by dozens of colleagues, judges, and attorneys. First, we are grateful to many academic colleagues who have been generous with their time and their feedback. The list is long and includes colleagues such as Alberto Alesina, Michael Alvarez, Arthur Applbaum, Michael Bailey, Matt Baum, Matt Blackwell, Adam Chilton, Tom Clark, Dara Kay Cohen, Gary Cox, Jeff Frieden, Jacob Goldin, Jake Grumbach, Andy Hall, Alexander Hertel-Fernandez, Jeffrey Jenkins, Stu Jordan, Asim Khwaja, Jonathan Ladd, Jane Mansbridge, Greg Mitchell, Michael Peress, Vincent Pons, Eric Posner, Bob Putnam, Dani Rodrik, Howard Rosenthal, Carrie Roush, Kyle Rozema, Ben Schneer, Kenneth Shepsle, Barbara Spellman, Arthur Spirling, Abby Wood, Richard Zeckhauser, and many others. We are also grateful to our team at Cambridge University Press, including Robert Dreesen, Jackie Grant, and Linsey Hague.

Members of the Harvard Kennedy School faculty, which draws deeply from an interdisciplinary mix of economists, historians, political scientists, and philosophers, helped us shape the broader arguments about representation and its importance. Members of the Stanford University Political Science Department gave us substantial feedback on the methodology and framing, and our colleagues Avi Acharya, Johanna Dunaway, Justin Grimmer, Josh Goodman, Mike Henderson, Josh Kertzer, Quinton Mayne, Clayton Nall, Danny Shoag, Ryan Sheely, and Daniel Smith provided additional help, support, and informal feedback. Melissa Kappotis, Sarah Merchant, Amanda Pearson, and Carolina Ramirez provided valuable research and logistics assistance.

This book has also benefited from feedback generated at multiple conferences and presentations at academic departments. We are grateful to workshop or conference participants at Georgetown University, Harvard Kennedy School, Harvard Law School, Massachusetts Institute of Technology, New York University, University of Southern California Law School, University of California-Irvine Law School, the University of Virginia Law School, and the University of Michigan. We received excellent feedback at Harvard's Political Economy Seminar. In addition, we are also grateful to participants at academic conferences, including at the Political Methodology Conference at the University of Rochester, the 2015 Midwest Political Science Association Conference, the 2014 Political Economy and Public Law Conference, and the 2014 Conference on Empirical Legal Studies. Additional joint work with Adam Chilton, Kyle Rozema, and Jacob Goldin – some of which explicitly relates to the research we present in this book – helped us more sharply hone the arguments and evidence we present here. We are especially grateful to these colleagues. We also benefited from generous research support from Stanford's Institute for Research in the Social Sciences (IRiSS).

We are also grateful to the journalists who have, over the years, covered our research, in turn generating even more useful feedback for us to consider. This list includes Adam Liptak, Christina Pazzanese, Peter Weber, and others. We have also been contacted by members of the public, who have helped shape and push our arguments about representation in a more nuanced and, we think, more valuable direction. This list includes various retired judges, attorneys in private practice, interested readers of various newspapers and journals, and blog post and Twitter interlocutors.

Lastly, we are grateful to our personal friends and family for their support of our research. We are especially grateful to Jenny Shen, Matt Blackwell, Hugo Blackwell-Sen, Silvia Blackwell-Sen, Joe and Diane Bonica, Nuo "Mack" Shen, Li Jiang, and Peli Learned Paw.

A. B.
Stanford, CA
M. S.
Cambridge, MA

Introduction: The Tug of War Over the American Judiciary

"One of my proudest moments was when I looked at Barack Obama in the eye and I said, 'Mr. President, you will not fill this Supreme Court vacancy.' "

Senator Mitch McConnell[1]

On February 13, 2016, Justice Antonin Scalia, the conservative intellectual anchor on the US Supreme Court, died unexpectedly while on a hunting trip in Texas. Attention immediately turned to President Barack Obama and how he would respond to a vacancy on the nation's highest court. Although Scalia was not a pivotal member of the Court by any means, his absence left behind a 4-4 balance in terms of justices appointed by Democratic presidents and those appointed by Republican ones. Obama's appointment of a liberal-leaning successor would immediately shift the balance of power on the Court toward a 5-4 liberal majority, possibly for decades.

These ideological ramifications led to an explosion of political fighting, strategizing, and defensive and offensive maneuvers. On the one hand, Republicans – who at that point controlled the US Senate[2] – demanded that the vacancy go unfilled until after the 2016 presidential election, seven months away. Weighing in, a group of eleven Republican Senate Judiciary Committee members wrote an open letter to Majority

---

[1] McConnell (2016).
[2] As of Scalia's death, Republicans held fifty-four seats in the US Senate as opposed to the Democrats' forty-four. Two New England senators – Bernie Sanders (VT) and Angus King (ME) – were independents but caucused with the Democrats.

Leader Mitch McConnell (R-KY) informing him that they would not hold any hearings on an Obama nominee.[3] Egging on these efforts, then-candidate Donald Trump said in a televised debate that it was incumbent for Republican leadership to "delay, delay, delay" the consideration of any nominee until after the 2016 elections.[4] Adding support to these arguments was the fact that, in 1992, Obama's vice president, Joe Biden, had called for then-president George H.W. Bush to delay filling any vacancy until after the 1992 elections. This led Republicans to mockingly call for the application of the "Biden Rule" to block any potential Obama nominee.[5]

On the other hand, Democrats urged Obama to fill the vacancy, arguing it was his constitutional duty to do so. Senate Minority Leader Harry Reid (D-NV) warned Republicans that "[f]ailing to fill this vacancy would be a shameful abdication of one of the Senate's most essential constitutional responsibilities."[6] Senate Judiciary Committee member Chuck Schumer (D-NY) cited constitutional principles, demanding that Republicans "show me the clause that says president's only president for three years."[7] These arguments found support in a letter from thirty-three constitutional law professors from across the country, who wrote in support of Obama's executive authority to appoint (and have confirmed) a successor to Scalia.[8]

The overwhelming force of partisan reactions complicated Obama's strategy. With an ordinary vacancy, Obama could have nominated someone substantially younger and more liberal to fill the seat. The circumstances made that path more precarious. On March 16, about a month after Scalia's death, Obama nominated Judge Merrick Garland, then aged sixty-three, to the seat. Garland came with the highest academic and professional qualifications: A high school valedictorian, a distinguished graduate of both Harvard College and Harvard Law School, an editor of the *Harvard Law Review*, and a former Supreme Court clerk to William Brennan, Garland had also served as a well-regarded federal prosecutor. Later on in his career, Garland served on the prestigious US Court of

---

[3] Grassley et al. (2016). McConnell agreed, publicly stating, "This nomination will be determined by whoever wins the presidency in the polls. I agree with the Judiciary Committee's recommendation that we not have hearings. In short, there will not be action taken" (Herszenhorn 2016).

[4] Corasaniti (2016).

[5] See Davis (2016).

[6] Reid (2016).

[7] ABC News (2016).

[8] Andrias et al. (2016).

Appeals for the District of Columbia, with a number of years as its chief judge. In addition, he had a reputation for being ideologically center-left – hardly a firebrand liberal.

Obama's gambit put Republicans in a defensive position. Given Garland's impeccable qualifications, they could hardly argue that he was too inexperienced or unqualified to be on the Supreme Court; neither could they credibly argue that Garland was too much of an ideologue or simply too young. Nonetheless, Republicans held firm, avoiding direct attacks but claiming that voters needed to have a voice.[9] Under McConnell's leadership, they refused Garland a hearing in the Senate Judiciary Committee. Eventually, with Donald Trump's victory in the 2016 presidential election, the issue came to an end: Garland was forced to return to his position on the federal appeals court and President Trump went on to nominate conservative federal appeals judge Neil Gorsuch, who was quickly confirmed by the Senate mostly along party lines.[10]

The example of Merrick Garland illustrates how the process of nominating and appointing judges has become a partisan battleground. For conservatives, the concern has been about trying to limit the influence of "activist" judges and ideologically liberal courts.[11] In 2016, for example, then-presidential candidate Trump loudly complained about "political" and "incompetent" Justice Ruth Bader Ginsburg. He complained more the next year about the "terrible record" of the California-based Court of Appeals for the Ninth Circuit and its "ridiculous rulings."[12] The accusations of judicial activism have even been levied at judges who were appointed by Republican presidents. For example, also in

---

[9] The political gravity of the situation was not lost on voters. According to a Pew Survey on issue importance in the 2016 election, 65 percent of voters viewed Supreme Court appointments as a "very important" consideration in deciding how to vote in the 2016 presidential election. The percentages of liberal Democrats and conservative Republicans stating that Supreme Court appointments were "very important" was even higher at 69 percent and 77 percent, respectively (Pew Research Center 2016).

[10] Gorsuch was confirmed on April 7, 2017, with fifty-four senators voting in favor and forty-five against, with three Democrats voting to confirm. He was invested onto the Court later the same day, in time to join the Court before the end of the 2016–2017 term.

[11] As we discuss in later parts of this book, it was not always the case that the charge against "activist" judges was led by conservatives. The early twentieth century, and in particular the New Deal era, saw substantial pushback against conservative judges by liberals, including by Franklin D. Roosevelt and other progressive supporters of economic regulation. We discuss this further in Chapter 2.

[12] See https://twitter.com/realdonaldtrump/status/753090242203283457, https://twitter.com/realdonaldtrump/status/857182179469774848, and https://twitter.com/realDonaldTrump/status/857177434210304001.

2017, then-presidential candidate Ted Cruz lambasted Chief Justice John Roberts for upholding the Affordable Care Act in a 2013 Supreme Court ruling. "The Court's brazen action undermines its very legitimacy," he wrote in a furiously worded editorial for *The National Review*. "[T]his Court has crossed from the realm of activism into the arena of oligarchy."[13]

The conservative ire at "activist" judges has translated into broader attempts to keep liberal-leaning judges off the courts. As an example, in 2015, Republicans in the Oklahoma Senate filed dozens of bills that would have changed the way state judges were selected; these included a mandatory retirement age, having the governor select judges himself, and changing the composition of Oklahoma's nominating commission away from a nonpartisan group of attorneys to individuals selected by the governor.[14] In 2018, Republicans in Pennsylvania, stinging after an unfavorable ruling on a redistricting case, briefly considered impeaching the majority of the state's supreme court judges;[15] and, in 2017, Republicans in North Carolina, reeling from an election of a Democrat to replace a key Republican swing justice on the state supreme court, proposed to limit judges' tenure and to change the way state supreme court judges could hear cases.

Liberals' response to the Merrick Garland nomination was different yet also predictable: Those on the left grew increasingly vocal and critical about what they perceived to be the increasing disregard of legal experience and qualifications and of the increased politicization of the courts. This politicization, those on the left have since argued, has fundamentally eroded public support in the judiciary and threatens to make the judiciary no different than other political branches of government. For example, in a widely publicized opinion piece in the *Wall Street Journal*, then-president Barack Obama warned that the Republicans' handling of "the Supreme Court like a political football makes the American people more cynical about democracy. When the Supreme Court becomes a proxy for political parties, public confidence in the notion of an impartial, independent judiciary breaks down. And the resulting lack of trust can undermine the rule of law."[16]

---

[13] Cruz (2015).

[14] Lewis (2016).

[15] Manno (2018).

[16] Obama (2016). Garland himself never expressed criticism or public regret about his failed nomination, but his former clerks and colleagues did. One former clerk said about him that he "did everything right – he never said a cross word, he never made a joke about it, he never politicized it" (quoted in Lyall 2017).

SUMMARY OF OUR ARGUMENT

In this book, we tackle the underlying puzzle raised by these prominent partisan conflicts over the nation's judiciary. Why have Republicans blasted "activist judges"? Why do they support attempts at "reforming" the judiciary – even as it risks public criticisms of interjecting partisanship and politicization? On the other side of the spectrum, why have Democrats decried Republicans' tactics, choosing to focus instead on ostensibly nonpartisan characteristics such as pedigree and experience?

We also address a question even more fundamental to these partisan fights. The coveted status of the American judiciary has led to contentious fights between political factions on the right and those on the left – fights that have ultimately shaped the composition of the judiciary and determined who becomes a judge. Thus, partisan fights speak not only to how conservatives and liberals approach judicial appointments but also to why choosing judges is so important. That is, why has the American judiciary remained at the center of the political process rather than at the bureaucratic periphery as is typical in other advanced democracies?

To answer these intertwined puzzles, we step back to consider the key players in what we refer to throughout as the **tug of war** over the nation's judiciary. Not only are conservatives and liberals locked in a battle over the nation's courts but the partisan sides operate within a broader landscape of judicial selection. Here, American history points us to a pivotal and often-overlooked player: lawyers. As we document in Chapter 2, since the nation's founding, lawyers have occupied politically outsized roles. For example, more than half of the men who signed the Declaration of Independence in 1796 were lawyers or trained in law (twenty-nine out of fifty-six),[17] while twelve out of the first sixteen presidents were lawyers. In contemporary times, lawyers – a group that today comprises just 0.4 percent of the voting-age population – are extraordinarily overrepresented in Congress and the Executive Branch, with nearly 42 percent of congressional representatives as of 2018 coming from the legal profession. To say that the story of American politics has been written, acted, and directed by the legal profession is no exaggeration.

---

[17] The remaining four – George Washington, William Henry Harrison, Zachary Taylor, and James Madison – were military officers and landowners. Madison studied law but did not consider himself a lawyer.

Yet how have lawyers specifically shaped the tug of war over the American judiciary? As we explain in Chapter 3, all members of the judiciary – which itself occupies a third, coequal branch of government – are former lawyers. All nine justices of the US Supreme Court are lawyers, as are the nearly 200 judges on the US Courts of Appeals and the nearly 700 judges on the US District Courts. Among the states, all high court judges are former lawyers as are most lower court state trial judges. (Several states actually make this a formal requirement.) These facts, as we document throughout the book, mean that lawyers form the candidate pool from which judges are drawn. Moreover, because of this, bar associations have lobbied for a highly unusual regulatory structure that grants the exclusive power to regulate lawyers and the legal profession to judges.

This symbiotic arrangement has paid off handsomely and put the courts squarely at the center of American politics and policy. As we show in Chapter 3, the courts have been an effective tool for nullifying or blocking legislation that would subject lawyers to regulations not of their own making, fending off unwanted reforms to the legal system, and exempting the legal profession from antitrust statutes. From the perspective of the tug of war over the judiciary, the benefits work both ways: The bar has worked to expand the scope of judicial authority and to position the courts at the heart of the political and regulatory process. Thus, lawyers' efforts have amplified the political power of American courts relative to other advanced democracies. All the while, lawyers have developed a strong interest in the composition, organization, and authority of the judiciary, serving not just as its core constituency but also as its primary font of candidates. We refer to this control over the judiciary as **the captured judiciary**. This helps explain the answer to one of our questions: American courts are a singularly important political prize in the US political system in large part because of the political power of the American legal profession.

However, the interests of lawyers often conflict with those of political actors, a tension that further defines the tug of war. As sophisticated, ideologically motivated individuals, politicians have their own preferences over important policy outcomes; they also have their own strongly held interests when it comes to what the judiciary should look like and how it should function. Politicians, after all, seek to appoint judicial candidates that will further their policy interests and uphold their legislative agenda (and, if possible, strike down or undermine those they oppose, including possibly those of their political opponents). Quite simply, conservative politicians prefer conservative judges and liberal politicians prefer liberal judges.

The relationship between conservative and liberal politicians and the legal establishment establishes the basic tug of war that frames this book. This tug of war, in turn, explains our question of how different party factions fight over the political prize that is the courts. Specifically, as we show using one of the largest data sets ever amassed on lawyers' and judges' political ideologies, as long as the interests of lawyers and those of the party in political power are in harmony – and the bar and politicians see eye to eye with regard to the role, composition, and ideology of the judiciary – then political elites will welcome the involvement of the bar in the process of selecting and vetting judges. The interests of the lawyer class and those of political elites are, however, often in conflict. Sometimes the bar is more liberal and powerful politicians more conservative (as is generally the case today); at other points in US history, the bar has been more conservative than those in political power (e.g., in the 1930s when Franklin Roosevelt was attempting to push through his New Deal legislation).[18] When this mismatch happens – that is, when the bar is at odds with the preferences of the party in power – partisan conflicts over the judiciary will arise.

Importantly, our tug-of-war framework not only describes the current state of judicial politicization but also helps predict where fights and attempts at judicial "reform" will emerge.[19] Widening ideological gulfs between the bar and politicians in power will exacerbate tensions, thereby leading political elites to adopt measures to limit the bar's influence. More concretely, this will manifest in increased attempts at shifting judicial selection toward partisan systems, including partisan elections, appointments by politicians (e.g., by governors), and other kinds of systems that allow for the explicit consideration of ideology and party membership. These attempts will also deemphasize traditional qualifications such as prestige, legal training, or experience. The

---

[18] The pattern of a conservative bar (and a comparably more liberal political class) was evident through much of the twentieth century, as evidenced by seminal early works such as Eulau and Sprague (1964).

[19] Throughout this book we refer to attempts at changing how judges are selected as attempts at "judicial reform." We use this phrase largely because political actors advocating for such changes tend to use this terminology. However, as we discuss in later chapters, reform attempts can have either positive or negative outcomes, depending on one's ideological preferences.

more ideologically distant politicians are from the bar, the greater the
tension. The example of Merrick Garland – and more broadly of today's
Republican Party – illustrates this tension.

On the other hand, ideological congruence between the bar and politicians will result in the opposite; political actors who are ideologically
proximate to the lawyerly class will be inclined to adopt selection systems that allow the bar a significant amount of influence and input into
the selection of judges. After all, both share a vision about what the
judiciary should look like in terms of ideology and potential rulings,
making these politicians more inclined to favor the involvement of the
legal establishment in the selection of judges. This could include reliance
on merit-oriented commissions, pre-vetting of possible candidates, qualification ratings, and nonpartisan elections. As we show in the pages
that follow, American history is replete with examples of this, with the
current-day Democratic Party being a clear example.

In sum, our argument is one where at a fundamental level the relevant
actors (political elites and lawyers) are jostling and fighting over an enormous political prize: the American judiciary. Our framework explains
not just these fights but also the nature of the courts in the United States.
In so doing, we seek to help explain another component of American
exceptionalism.

THE POLITICAL POWER OF THE AMERICAN LEGAL PROFESSION

More detail helps put our book into broader scholarly context and helps
frame the chapter summary that follows in this Introduction. Our argument – in departure with much of the literature on judicial politics –
focuses significantly on the political importance of the American legal
class.[20] Indeed, in our framework, "the bar" – the nation's attorneys,
organized via professional trade organizations such as the American Bar

[20] Important works focusing on the role of the legal class include Barton (2010) and
Fitzpatrick (2009), which we discuss throughout. In addition, we note the extensive literature at the intersection of law, sociology, and history that has documented the impact of
the bar on American institutional and social development. This includes broader works,
such as Kagan (2009) and Kessler (2017). However, very few studies in contemporary
political science – including works in American political development or judicial politics
– have looked at the political importance of the bar and the outsized influence wielded
by lawyers. (An important early study in this regard is Eulau and Sprague (1964), which
documented the impact of lawyer-legislators.) We discuss the history of the bar and of
the legal profession in Chapter 2.

Association (ABA) and other state bar associations – is among the most important political classes in the country. While many other developed democracies relied on the nobility to populate their elite classes earlier in their histories, the United States relied on "men of letters." These men of letters – nearly all of whom were lawyers – were instrumental in declaring American independence, writing the US Constitution, establishing early federal and state laws, and setting the tenor of domestic political life. In sum, the legal profession has historically had immense influence over the nation's political landscape, and this influence extends downstream to all facets of state and national government, including in their compositions.

An argument that we develop and demonstrate through empirical evidence is that the political power of the bar has allowed it to extract benefits for itself. This has been accomplished by several means. The first mechanism is via legislation in line with the legal profession's professional and political interests. As we show in Chapter 2, the United States, exceptional among peer countries in the number of lawyers in state and national legislatures, has one of the most litigation-focused regulatory states,[21] one of the largest populations of incarcerated people, one of the most favorable climates for medical malpractice lawsuits, and one of the most profitable markets for law firms. This is all evidence that the legal profession has been effective in creating a political environment very favorable to its interests. These components have, in turn, contributed to the United States' outlier status among advanced democracies along a number of economic and political indicators. This American legal exceptionalism is both the product and the protector of lawyers' interests and has, in turn, allowed the bar to enjoy and hold on to its political power.

The second mechanism is that the bar has been effective in rebuffing attempts at government oversight or regulation, a topic we address at length in Chapter 3. As we show in that chapter, efforts to regulate the legal profession have invariably failed, often as a result of lawyers in elected assemblies or on the bench (i.e., judges) opposing these measures. This is not for lack of precedent. Other professions (such as medical doctors) are highly regulated by state and federal agencies. The legal profession is, by contrast, largely self-regulated. The bar operates mostly independently in regulating law schools, administering the bar exam, and, with the support of state and local governments, determining who can and who cannot practice law within a given jurisdiction. Despite

---

[21] Our arguments here are consistent with the important argument of "adversarial legalism" advanced by Kagan (2009).

outside pressure, the legal profession has remained far more loosely regulated by the government compared to other equivalent white-collar professions.

As we show in both Chapters 2 and 3, this arrangement has generated extremely favorable outcomes for the legal profession despite its cost to the public welfare. Compared to other economically developed nations, the legal services industry in the United States is far larger and more lucrative. In addition, many functions that would be performed in other countries by government agencies are instead litigated via the courts – a phenomenon termed "adversarial legalism" by the legal scholar Robert Kagan.[22] Although many have attributed this adversarial legalism to America's political culture, we think that it is actually the product of interest group politics and this historical institutional development. In other words, it was not the public's demands for legalistic solutions that empowered the bar; rather it was the bar's political influence that shaped American political institutions in ways that advanced the interests of lawyers and judges. The result, as we argue in Part I of the book, is a highly litigious and lawyer-dominated legal system that caters to the high-end of the market while leaving much of the public unable to afford or access legal services.

THE CAPTURED JUDICIARY

Our argument is not simply one about the legal profession's political power on its own or within a vacuum. This power wielded by the legal profession has had real consequences. Specifically, as we argue in Chapter 3, the legal profession has used the courts to further its political advantage. Indeed, although the US Constitution includes no eligibility requirements for judges, in practice all judges in the United States are lawyers.[23] In fact, thirty-two states actually require by law that all individuals sitting on their high courts be members of the bar.[24] Judges are

---

[22] See Kagan (2009).

[23] All federal judges in recent memory have been lawyers, and all state high court judges are lawyers as well. This includes all justices on the US Supreme Court, who have always been lawyers. As we more fully document in Chapter 2, historical practice admitted to the bar individuals who did not necessarily complete a formal legal education but who instead completed an apprenticeship. This practice has been phased out, but a number of early judges (and political actors) were trained in this fashion. We therefore consider these early individuals members of the legal profession.

[24] Barton (2010, p. 30).

trained in the same environment as members of the bar; they are intimately familiar with the conduct, ethical codes, and professional norms of lawyers. They share a common professional culture, and they even share a professional national-level advocacy organization (the ABA) to lobby on behalf of their shared interests. One of our arguments is that, given this close relationship, leaving the regulation of the legal profession to courts is tantamount to self-regulation.[25]

The bar's control of the judicial branch, we argue in Chapter 3, actually represents an extreme form of "capture," a term from the literature on the bureaucracy. By "capture," we refer to instances where a regulated industry has managed to gain influence over a regulatory agency or commission. This capture is usually partial. However, in the case of lawyers and the courts, the capture is complete: By controlling the path by which lawyers are trained, how lawyers are admitted to the bar, and the kinds of qualifications judges need to have, the bar essentially has a monopoly over who can aspire to become a judge. In some jurisdictions, moreover, the bar plays an active role in deciding which lawyers can become judges. Through this professional capture, the bar has developed both its own policy interests and its own form of regulation and policing of judges. Because of this, as we discuss in Chapter 3, we refer to this as "constitutional capture" – the capture of an entire branch of government and its constitutionally mandated powers.

What does this mean from the perspective of the nation's judges? Quite simply, the captured nature of the judiciary means that the judicial branch will closely reflect the bar's professional membership and much of its professional and ideological interests. In terms of membership, for example, the bar formally excluded women, Jews, and African Americans for much of the twentieth century; these people were thus unable to become judges, retaining judicial power in the hands of more conservative protestant white men. This policing of boundaries of the legal profession has served – and still serves – as a well-organized and highly effective gatekeeper for the judiciary.

The judiciary also reflects the bar's professional interests, as well as its ideological ones (although the latter perhaps less perfectly). On this

---

[25] See Barton (2010) for more on the relationship between the courts and the bar; his argument is that the bar's influence has resulted in what he calls a "lawyer-judge bias" in courts' decision-making. Our focus is not on this specific bias in judicial decision-making, but we do provide additional evidence of this in a comparative context in Chapter 2. That chapter also focuses on the development of lawyers' political power.

professional dimension, judges tend to represent the narrow economic interests, values, thinking, and approaches to problem-solving of the legal profession, of which they are members. For example, for much of the nation's history, the bar – the "Men of Letters" – exclusively represented the interests of the well-educated, moneyed elite. Thus, for most of the nation's history, the bar was a financially conservative force in American society, pushing policy and legislation rightward in an attempt to maintain lawyers' status and to promote professional priorities and business interests. The judiciary, as we document in Chapters 3 and 7, largely mirrored these more conservative policy interests.[26]

Today, as we document in Chapter 4 and through the remainder of our analyses, the bar actually leans in a more liberal direction, not just in terms of professional interests but more broadly in terms of lawyers' partisan and ideological preferences. This move to the left reflects both a legal profession whose membership is more diverse and well-documented generational trends, with younger lawyers being more likely to identify as Democrats. As we show, these ideological shifts strongly shape the candidate pool for judges (particularly at the elite level) and create significant challenges for conservative politicians. The judicial tug of war, in other words, is one where the legal profession is now pulling leftward.

THE INCENTIVES OF POLITICAL ELITES

The bar has succeeded in making the judiciary a "captured" branch of government, a case that we develop throughout Part I of the book. However, an important point for our broader argument is that, even so, the bar never has had absolute control over whom from its ranks will be selected onto the nation's courts (even as it has a firm monopoly over the candidate pool). The power to select judges is one that is shared – sometimes reluctantly by the bar – with politicians and, in some contexts, voters.

The important role played by elected officials in determining the final composition of the judiciary is well established and deeply embedded

---

[26] An early study on the impact of lawyer-legislators, Eulau and Sprague (1964, p. 22) notes the widespread view that lawyers are "'conservative' and that their numerical superiority serves through this trait to give one-sided direction to public policies." They note in their analysis (using data from the late 1950s), however, that lawyers and non-lawyers are roughly equivalent in terms of the ideological breakdown (see Eulau and Sprague (1964, table 1.1). This mid-century pattern comports with what we see in our data, which is a shift in lawyers' preferences leftward.

in the separation-of-powers framework of American government. At the national level, the US Constitution calls for federal judges to be chosen by the president with the "advice and consent" of the US Senate. At the state level, too, political actors play important roles in deciding which lawyers become judges. As of 2018, six states select judges via executive appointment or legislative elections, while another twenty-four states use an "assisted appointment" system whereby the executive chooses from a slate prepared by a nonpartisan merit commission.[27] Thus, even though lawyers represent the constituent class from which judges are chosen, the other key players in the selection process are politicians – including legislators, executives, and other nonelected party players.[28] Our framework therefore must take politicians' preferences and incentives into account.

How do politicians influence the composition of the judiciary? An obvious way is by appointing judges who share their policy and ideological preferences. For example, many papers have examined the interplay between the president and the Senate in trying to shift the pivotal median justice on the Supreme Court,[29] while others have focused on state-court appointments and elections.[30] This scholarship takes as a starting proposition that politicians will seek to shape the judiciary in ways that serve their strategic political and policy interests; that is, liberal politicians will prefer liberal judges, while conservative politicians will prefer conservative judges.

Less well studied is how the interplay between the interests of politicians and the bar could influence the judiciary. This is a key question, however; given the nature of the "captured judiciary," politicians do not have unfettered control over the judiciary. They must deal with the reality that the legal profession exercises a great deal of control over the judiciary; they must also confront the fact that all judges must be lawyers and, therefore, the bar exercises an exclusive gatekeeping role over the candidate pool.

This makes the important relationship – or possible conflicts – between politicians and the legal profession a defining feature of our judicial tug of war. For most of US history, the interests of politicians and the

---

[27] See *Judicial Selection in the States* (2018).
[28] We take a broad view and occasionally refer to politicians or to the parties, but both refer to the key political players in a given jurisdiction. For the most part, we assume that the incentives faced by the parties are shared by the relevant political actors.
[29] See, e.g., Krehbiel (2007) and Moraski and Shipan (1999).
[30] See, e.g., Brace, Langer, and Hall (2000), which argues that state politicians' ideology can be a good proxy for the ideology of judges in those states.

bar were closely linked; as we noted, a large number of politicians were lawyers themselves or, at the very least, came from the same educational and socioeconomic environment. "Men of Letters" populated governments at both the state and the federal level and across political and career governmental positions. Because the ideological or policy preference divergence between the political and legal class (which often was one and the same) was limited, this incentivized politicians to delegate substantial authority over the judiciary to the bar; after all, if politicians and lawyers essentially came from the same social and educational strata, and if they shared similar views on policy and politics, then having an active bar involved in the judiciary was a win-win proposition for most politicians. Thus, for much of US history, politicians found it helpful to engage the bar in the selection of judges and in the policing of boundaries of who could – and could not – become a judge. These aligned political incentives thus helped foment the "captured judiciary," which, as we develop further in Chapter 3, has been a distinctive feature of American political development.

As we discuss in greater detail in Chapters 4 and 7, however, these interests of the legal and political elite have not always been in harmony. Not only have lawyers shifted ideologically over time (with greater force in certain jurisdictions), but the political class has also become more variegated in terms of its educational and professional composition. Even though lawyers still occupy prominent positions within government, the nation's political class has gradually expanded to include more business owners, physicians, educators, military veterans, and career politicians without formal legal training. In addition – and as we show in this book – the bar's political leanings have moved steadily to the left over the course of the past few generations, while the political class has moved more to the right. This has created a relatively new and important mismatch in the ideological and policy interests of the political parties – particularly the Republican Party – and the bar.

This mismatch has acted like an earthquake fault line, exacerbating the judicial tug of war over the nation's courts. On the one hand, politicians must contend with a well-established norm that judges must be drawn from the bar and, in some jurisdictions, the additional formal involvement of the bar in the judicial selection process. On the other, the ideological mismatch between the bar and elected politicians, who have themselves become increasingly polarized, means that the political parties cannot always trust the bar to ensure that members of the judiciary will be ideologically palatable. For that reason, a central component of our argument is that the greater the ideological and political distance between political actors and the bar, the greater the incentive political actors will have to politicize the judicial selection process by interjecting partisan and ideological considerations. This means that, increasingly, the personal politics of potential judicial candidates will be highly salient and that, when political actors have more discretion, they will attempt to shape the judiciary in accordance with their political interests. This also means that ours is a system in which tension builds for some time and then is released in a flurry of judicial reform efforts, which could include strategic departures from long-standing rules and norms for selecting judges or, at the very least, other compromises that result in otherwise ideologically suitable appointments.

There are several important caveats to this. The first is that this all plays out within the context of specific judicial selection systems. Some systems – such as those that rely on executive or legislative appointments – allow politicians significant influence over judicial composition. This is the case in the federal judiciary as well as in the judiciaries of several states (particularly those in New England). Other systems – such as those that rely on nonpartisan merit commissions – enhance the influence of the bar. As we show in Chapter 6, the type of selection mechanism does indeed influence the composition of the judiciary in important ways.

In addition, these selection mechanisms are themselves institutional arrangements that have emerged from more than two centuries of interactions and conflicts between the legal and political establishments. In some places, attempts at judicial reform have slowly changed the way judges are selected; in others, the ideological proximity between the bar and political actors has made reform attempts less common. As we discuss in Chapter 7, the institutional mechanism by which judges are selected is an important outcome of the tug of war between the bar and the political parties, as well as an important feature for predicting the ideological composition of the judiciary.

The second caveat concerns the American public's role in this tension between the bar and political actors. Our theoretical framework identifies the bar and political actors as the leading players in shaping the judiciary, relegating the American public to a secondary role. This may be surprising to some, but, we believe, it historically has been the case. For the most part, the American system is one where the selection of judges is actively shielded from the pressures of public opinion by design. At the national level, the Founding Fathers – including the authors of *The Federalist Papers*, who were themselves lawyers – fully intended for judges to be insulated from the incendiary vicissitudes of the public. In so doing, they created a federal system where judges are appointed by the president with limited public input.

Many states adhere to this federal model of executive appointments, but others have a mix of judicial elections (partisan or nonpartisan) and commission systems. Some of these – particularly judicial elections – allow for more public input. However, as we discuss in Chapter 6, even in states where judges are elected, the process is one that is carefully cultivated by politicians or by the bar; in other words, judicial elections are tolerated insofar as they result in the kind of judiciary that our two main players in the judicial tug of war would like to see.[31] Thus, although we extensively discuss the consequences of direct elections of judges in Chapters 6 and 7, the public is often on the sidelines in the tug of war between the bar and political elites. This is particularly so when it comes to the most politically important courts, including the nation's federal courts and many state high courts.

HOW DOES JUDICIAL IDEOLOGY MATTER?

A reader versed in the law and the legal system might express reasonable skepticism about our view of the judiciary as a political prize to be fought over. After all, if the purpose of a judge is to interpret the law pursuant to existing law and legal precedent, then why should the political beliefs of a judicial candidate matter? Doesn't the law dictate how judges decide cases? Put differently, why should it matter that ideology is interjected into the selection of judges at all?

These are important considerations that we take up throughout this book. Although we engage with the law and decision-making seriously, particularly in Chapters 3 and 8, our focus is on the way that competing interests influence the ideological composition of the courts. As roughly seven decades of empirical scholarship from across law, political science, and economics have documented, a judge's ideology and policy preferences are some of the most important predictors of how a judge will rule once on the bench.[32] The studies are numerous. One influential

---

[31] For example, as we discuss extensively in Chapter 7, conservative politicians have changed nonpartisan elections to partisan elections, attempting to shape the judiciary in more favorable ways.

[32] Putting it the most strongly, the influential "Attitudinal Model" of Segal and Spaeth (2002) confirms the strong relationship between ideology and judicial decision-making. Their argument is that the "Supreme Court decides disputes in light of the facts of the

study showed that federal appeals court judges appointed by Republican presidents are more likely to vote in a conservative direction on important cases, while judges appointed by Democratic presidents are more likely to vote in a liberal direction on the same sorts of cases.[33] This has been shown not just for appeals judges at the federal level but also for justices on the Supreme Court,[34] federal district court judges,[35] and judges across state courts.[36] In our view, these findings offer overwhelming support for the idea that judges, like political actors (such as legislators and executives), rely on their ideology and policy preferences in making decisions. The law, of course, serves as an important constraint on the full expression of policy preferences,[37] but we still can and do detect important differences in the behavior of judges according to their political affiliations and policy views, making the raw importance of ideology in shaping judicial decision-making very clear.

Recent conflicts within the judiciary showcase just how crucial this is to politics and policy. In recent years, the judiciary has ruled on some of the most polarizing and controversial issues in American politics – often along party lines. These include landmark rulings on abortion and reproductive rights, gun rights, religious freedom and the separation of church and state, federal regulation of marijuana, and same-sex marriage and LBGTQ rights – all topics that are highly important to conservatives and liberals. In addition, the courts have been active on issues relating to voting and elections, for example in the areas of campaign finance, partisan gerrymandering, voter identification laws, the legacy of the Voting Rights Act, and, most notably, the outcome of the 2000 presidential election. This highlights another reason why parties and politicians view controlling courts as a strategic imperative: Judges play a key role in shaping policy and in regulating the administration of elections. More

case vis-a-vis the ideological attitudes and values of the justices. Simply put, Rehnquist votes the way he does because he is extremely conservative; Marshall voted the way he did because he was extremely liberal" (Segal and Spaeth 2002, p. 86). For an overview of the extensive political science literature on this topic, which dates back to the 1940s, see Harris and Sen (2019).

33 Sunstein et al. (2006). The same study also found that judges influence one another; for example, a panel of three Republican appointees is more likely to reach a conservative-oriented decision than is a panel of two Republicans and a single Democrat.

34 E.g., Segal and Spaeth (2002). For a good overview of this large literature as well as additional convincing findings, see Epstein, Landes, and Posner (2013); Ruger et al. (2004).

35 E.g., Epstein, Landes, and Posner (2013).

36 E.g., Bonica and Woodruff (2015).

37 Epstein and Knight (1998).

broadly, a reactionary or originalist-leaning court might put a quick end to a progressive agenda; a liberal "activist" court might do the same for a conservative agenda. Although the parties cannot control what judges do with exactitude, they can try as much as possible to stack the deck with judges likely to rule in their favor.

Thinking otherwise – and assuming that the law and its interpretation are primarily what matter to judicial decision-making – is at odds with the reality of contemporary politics. Indeed, if judicial ideology was truly unimportant, we should see little partisan conflict in terms of appointments, not just to state courts but also to federal courts and possibly also to the US Supreme Court. Of course, we see just the exact opposite. At the Supreme Court level, Senate Republicans' unwillingness to even meet with Barack Obama's nominee to replace Justice Scalia, Merrick Garland, signaled a strong commitment to maintaining a conservative majority on the high court. Likewise, the Republican leadership's willingness to keep open dozens of federal lower court seats in the chance of a Republican presidential victory signaled the tremendous political importance of these seats. These highly strategic and political considerations – obvious not just in the US Senate but across all tiers of American government – would be rare in a world in which judicial ideology took a distant backseat to the letter of the law.[38]

We also note that our arguments bypass some of the normative considerations commonly raised by proponents of judicial reform, which tend to center on judicial independence, the "quality" of candidates to judicial office, and whether judges are unduly influenced by partisanship or electoral concerns. Although these are salient concerns from the perspective of the public good, we believe that invocations of these characteristics serve to mask the true objectives of the players involved; the concerns of the legal and political elite, we believe, fundamentally revolve around having their policy and ideological preferences reflected. For that reason, our arguments focus more on what kinds of selection mechanisms will benefit the various participants in the "tug of war" from a strategic perspective. That is, Democrats will tend to ally with lawyers and prefer selection mechanisms that lead to more liberal judges and Republicans

---

[38] On the other hand, as the example of Merrick Garland also shows, because judicial ideology is a key predictor of judicial decision-making, having an ideologically representative or balanced judiciary might be an important normative good – something desirable and worthy of consideration in its own right. We return to these themes in the pages that follow, particularly in Chapters 5 and 6.

will prefer selection mechanisms that rely more on ideological factors and that lead to more conservative judges. Indeed, our argument is that the ideology of the judiciary – as opposed to genuine concerns about "legitimacy" or "qualifications" – is what ultimately shapes how the parties approach judicial selection.

THE TUG OF WAR OVER THE NATION'S JUDICIARY

What is the result of these forces and of the relationship between political elites versus the legal profession? We argue, and we seek to explain in this book, that this fractious relationship between political elites and the legal profession is tantamount to a tug of war, one in which the judiciary not only is the prize to be won but is also caught in the middle. The more politicians pull on the "rope," the more the judiciary will shift to match the preferences of politicians; the more the bar exercises control over its "captured judiciary," the more the preferences of the judiciary will resemble those of lawyers.

This broad framework, and thinking about the judiciary as a political prize to be fought over, generates a host of implications. As we discuss in Chapters 2 and 7, the history of the nation suggests that the interests of the bar and of the political class were once much more closely aligned (and, indeed, that there were times that the political class was more liberal than the more aristocratic lawyerly class as a whole). Thus, for much of American history, political actors were content to "allow" the bar to win the tug of war over the judiciary; so long as lawyers were ideological allies, allowing lawyers control over judicial selection and judicial codes of conduct was entirely compatible with politicians' ideological incentives. Thus, the twentieth century saw a trend favoring the appointment of judges via merit commissions, which (as we discuss in Chapter 7) allowed the legal profession considerable leverage over the selection of judges. This, in turn, enhanced the power of the legal profession and its hold over the judiciary.

Today, however, the interests of the political elite and of the bar have diverged somewhat, not just in terms of their descriptive profile (as we will see in Chapter 2) but also in terms of ideology. This has meant that the political parties have an incentive to alter the composition of the judiciary and to shift it away from a "captured judiciary" and into one that looks more and more representative of a wider spread of political interests. That is, our theory predicts that the further the interests of the bar and of political actors diverge, the more the latter will have an incentive to interject more politics and more ideology into the selection of judges and to shift control away from the nation's lawyers and the legal profession. This is particularly the case where selection mechanisms afford politicians the opportunities to interject their policy preferences into the selection of judges. If, however, the preferences between political parties and the bar display even greater cleavages, and the selection mechanisms in place do not allow party leaders the power to alter the composition of the judiciary, then the selection mechanisms in place are likely to be challenged (as we explore in Chapter 7).

Our framework also has implications for the composition of the judiciary. If offered the opportunity (e.g., in jurisdictions with appointments systems), and with sufficient divergence between the bar and parties, judges will take more and more after politicians. In the absence of such an opportunity (e.g., in places with merit commissions), or in places where elite politicians are ideologically aligned with the bar, judges will take after the bar. Thus, in terms of whom the judiciary actually represents, our answer is that judiciary is not so much a meritorious group of elite lawyers – as perhaps many Americans think or hope – but rather that they represent the winner of a complicated and highly strategic contest of strength between political and legal elites. This tug of war determines whom judges actually represent.

ORGANIZATION OF THIS BOOK

We organize the book into three themes. Part I develops a novel argument regarding our first key player in the judicial tug of war, the legal profession. Here, we provide evidence regarding the political influence of lawyers and the bar, demonstrating how the American legal establishment has both been exceptional within the United States and also contributed to American exceptionalism globally. We then document how these historical forces have led to what is fundamentally a "captured judiciary." We explain how this captured judiciary has over time allowed the bar even greater power and independence, to the point where it has engaged in "constitutional capture," or the professional capture of a full third of American government.

This sets the stage for Part II of this book, which describes the incentives of our second key player in the judicial tug of war, political elites. Here, we plumb historical and contemporary accounts to explore what political elites hope to get from judicial appointments. In doing so, we document tensions between the political establishment and the bar, tensions that have led to ongoing and increasing attempts to interject politics into the selection of judges. We use this intuition to develop our key theoretical argument of the tug of war between the bar and political actors over the nature of the judiciary. Next, we introduce and explain our quantitative data; using these data, we apply our tug-of-war framework to two settings. The federal courts, as the nation's most prominent and most politically important courts, are the logical starting point. These courts rule on the most important national issues of the day, including on matters of US constitutional interpretation, separation of powers, and presidential power. Our second application is the state courts, which feature a substantially greater variety of judicial selection mechanisms. As we show in this discussion, how judges are selected is an important factor in shaping the judicial landscape, constraining or facilitating politicians' attempts to select judges on the basis of ideology.

Part III of this book explores the downstream consequences of this judicial tug of war and what it means for the judiciary to be a political prize. In this part, we also explore the implications of our theoretical argument for issues facing the nation's courts. First, we acknowledge the institutional mechanisms by which judges are selected – for example, via appointments or via elections – are themselves a product of the tug of war between the bar and political actors. We illustrate these policy implications via several case studies. Second, we show that a growing mismatch between the judiciary and the political branches can also lead to increased conflict and polarization within the courts. As American politics careens toward increased polarization and partisanship, we will expect to see more and more conflicts between political elites and the nation's legal profession – tensions that will result in more strife within the courts themselves.

Part I: The Legal Profession and the "Captured Judiciary"

We begin our substantive discussion in Chapter 2 by motivating why we consider lawyers to be a key player in the tug of war over the nation's courts. We start by discussing how the bar – the nation's attorneys – occupies a historically prominent place within American politics. As we show, the United States is quite unusual in this respect. Unlike European countries, where governments have (historically at least) been populated by members of an aristocratic class, the United States had no entrenched nobility; the bar emerged as an educated, wealthy class and, as some historical observers noted, occupied the role that in other countries had been assumed by the nobility. Over time, the organized bar emerged, and it developed fairly conservative policy interests and economic and regulatory interests. As we document via a series of novel empirical findings, this has contributed to American exceptionalism in several policy areas, most pronounced in those areas relevant to the bar and its interests.

How has a profession that has made itself so essential to the workings of every aspect of the political process – including the regulatory process – remained unburdened by government oversight and accountable only to itself? This is the question we address in Chapter 3. As we document in this chapter, the power of the bar led to an uneasy alliance with political actors; the bar sought more and more autonomy and, in line with a long-standing and natural connection with the judiciary, began to professionally "capture" the judiciary. It did so not only by monopolizing the candidate pool of potential judges but also by instituting rules about how lawyers (i.e., future judges) should be educated, codes of judicial conduct, and, ultimately, making binding recommendations on how judges should be selected. In turn, the government has entrusted the "captured judiciary" with regulatory power over the legal profession. As we show through both qualitative and quantitative evidence, this symbiotic arrangement furthered the bar's political and economic power.

Part II: Political Actors and the Incentive to Politicize

We pivot in this part to discussing the other key player in the judicial tug of war – political elites. Chapter 4 begins by considering how the interests of political actors and of the bar clash over the captured judiciary. Specifically, over time, political actors and lawyers have drifted apart ideologically, resulting in tension. This mismatch, we argue, sets the stage for contemporary fights over the politicization of the judiciary, over activist judges, and over the meritocracy of the judiciary – the judicial tug of war. We also note in this chapter that an increased interjection of "politics" into the selection of judges, although perhaps unappealing to many Americans, need not necessarily be undesirable; after all, having a judiciary that represents a greater variety of political and ideological interests (including conservative ones), and not just the bar's, might be the most desirable from a normative perspective.

We begin our data analysis in Chapter 5, which empirically links our broad predictive theory of the judicial tug of war to the nation's courts. This chapter examines the federal courts, the most politically important courts in the American judiciary. As we show in this chapter, fights over federal courts appointments illustrate the tense tug of war between the national bar and politicians. Given that federal courts appointments operate with advice and consent of the US Senate, an elected body whose political leanings do not dovetail with the bar's, we expect to see (and we document using empirical data) an ideological divergence. In the last decade, this divergence manifests itself in a federal judiciary that is substantially more conservative than is the national bar. As we show, this also creates supply-side incentives among legal elites. Specifically, conservative graduates of elite law programs have a much higher probability of becoming judges (of any kind); their relative scarcity in law schools and in the academy, furthermore, has increased the importance of conservative-leaning legal associations, such as the Federalist Society.

Federal courts only represent one kind of selection mechanism – appointment by the executive with the advice and consent of a legislative chamber. Because selection mechanisms vary across different jurisdictions, Chapter 6 explores how patterns may vary with regard to state courts. Indeed, part of our overall argument is that different selection mechanisms can both restrain and facilitate the incorporation of politics into judicial selection. As we show, appointments systems – like the appointments process used to name federal judges – are more sensitive to the needs and preferences of the political parties; by contrast, systems that are oriented toward merit-oriented criteria – including systems that are reliant on merit commissions, nonpartisan bodies, and local and state bar associations – are more sensitive to the needs and preferences of the bar. Thus, given the tension between political actors and the bar that characterizes the judicial tug of war, certain judicial selection systems may (or may not) be favorable to the different players. In other words, judicial selection mechanisms set the rules by which the tug of war is played.

Part III: Ramifications of the Judicial Tug of War

As our discussion in Chapter 6 makes clear, how judges are selected shapes the power dynamics of the judicial tug of war. This makes judicial selection itself a source of heated conflict, the subject we take up in Chapter 7. We use our judicial tug-of-war framework to explore how the parties respond or try to change existing judicial selection mechanisms. Specifically, as we show, the greater the misalignment between the ideological preferences of attorneys and politicians, the greater the incentives political elites will have to introduce ideological considerations into the judicial selection process. Understanding this dynamic, we argue, is key to both explaining and predicting attempts at judicial reform: Under current ideological configurations, conservatives will, depending on how liberal they perceive the bar to be, back reform efforts oriented toward partisan elections and executive appointments, while liberals will work to maintain merit-oriented commissions. We explore the contours of this predictive framework with three illustrative case studies: Florida in 2001, Kansas in 2011, and North Carolina in 2016.

In Chapter 8, we turn to a slightly different question but one that has occupied much public interest – the topic of judicial polarization. Looking at the federal courts, we document how our framework of the judicial tug of war can explain ideological polarization in the courts as politicians attempt to replace judges with ones who are more ideologically compatible. In addition, we show that greater polarization leads to greater judicial conflict, including more dissenting opinions and increased intra-court uncertainty. To this extent, the American judiciary has followed the general trend in American politics toward increased partisan conflict and polarization, facilitated by the tension between political and legal elites.

We conclude the book in Chapter 9 by describing what we see as current trends in law and politics and how these might shape the courts in years to come. Indeed, year after year, the political nature of the judiciary has, if anything, become increasingly salient – particularly given the highly polarized climate of American politics. We highlight two ongoing factors that are likely to exacerbate the judicial tug of war: (1) a rightward shift in the ideologies of pertinent political elites and (2) a leftward shift in the ideologies of the elite legal establishment and law graduates. These two forces are likely to create even more conflict over judicial appointments and more attempts at judicial reform. We do not see reason only for pessimism, however. Increased ideological diversity in the judiciary, even though a result of increased ideologically based selection, can help create a more ideologically diverse judiciary than we might otherwise expect.

OUR METHODOLOGICAL APPROACH

Before we conclude this Introduction, we note that our quantitative methodological approach makes our work different from previous explorations of judicial reform. We rely on some of the largest data sets ever amassed on American lawyers and American judges, which we then merge with the Database on Ideology, Money in Politics, and Elections (DIME). Our final data set includes information, including measures of ideology, on nearly half a million lawyers, judges, political actors, activists, and other members of the political and legal establishment. Using these data allows us to make comparisons between these various groups and test implications of the captured judiciary and the judicial tug of war.[39] Indeed, without the substantial advances of "big data" in the last fifteen or twenty years, addressing these issues might have been intractable. Thus, even though scholars before us have explored key questions of judicial ideology and selection, as well as of the importance of the bar and its composition in terms of the "capture" of the judiciary,[40] ours is among the first comprehensive, data-driven examinations.

Because our empirical work is primarily quantitative, we rely throughout on the presentation of statistical results. Our goal here is not to make the statistics the focus but rather to use the data and results to highlight the substantive points and implications of our argument. We therefore opt wherever possible for the graphical presentation of data and results and for findings that have a clear substantive interpretation. However, readers who are more familiar with data analysis and with statistical techniques might prefer our related papers, which offer a greater share of technical details. All of the data necessary to replicate our results are also available online.[41]

In addition, although our approach here is mostly quantitative, we rely extensively on qualitative information to provide additional context and to explore the implications of our inferences. In Chapters 2, 3, and 7, for example, we rely extensively on historical accounts to

---

[39] For a longer description of these data, see Chapter 4 and also our discussion in Bonica and Sen (2017c) and Bonica and Sen (2017a). Other papers that have used these data include Bonica and Sen (2017b), Bonica, Chilton, and Sen (2016), and Bonica et al. (2018).

[40] For example, see excellent work such as Fitzpatrick (2009) and Shugerman (2012), which we discuss in later chapters.

[41] See Bonica and Sen (2017c) and Bonica and Sen (2017a) and related replication archives.

distill examples of the captured judiciary and the judicial tug of war. In addition, because attempts at judicial reform are oftentimes not successful (thus meaning we lack reliable quantitative data on judicial reform efforts going back historically), we rely on detailed qualitative case studies of judicial reform. We present these in Chapter 7. Throughout, we discuss the normative implications of our analyses, linking our findings with the broader institutional concerns about the role of courts in American government and society.

CONCLUSION

We conclude this Introduction by drawing attention to the broader implications of our argument. The implications of a politicized judiciary in a polarized era of American politics have been a matter of considerable interest. Recent years have seen American courts issue rulings on some of the most politically charged controversies of the day, including campaign finance, affirmative action, health care reform, and same-sex marriage. Underlying these tensions are even more fundamental questions. Should we trust that judges are nonpartisan arbiters of the law? Are members of the judiciary insulated from partisan and political considerations? These questions not only are normatively important but have significant practical importance as well, with the business of selecting judges becoming increasingly ideological and driven by party politics.

We explore these questions through our theory of the judicial tug of war. We demonstrate the framework by bringing to bear one of the largest and most ambitious data sets on judicial ideology. These data enable us to provide a systematic exploration of how judges operate ideologically and how, and to what extent, ideology influences judicial selection. Indeed, the conflict over selecting judges has typically been understood as a battle between the executive and the legislature and fought mostly on ideological terms. As a result, theoretical models of the judicial selection have followed general separation-of-powers models of interacting and competing political institutions. This scholarly literature has, however, overlooked a critical player: the legal profession. As our framework shows, a primary conflict in the selection of judges is between politicians and the bar. Indeed, under our theory, the conflict between political branches (e.g., the executive and the legislature) has been largely secondary to efforts by politicians to wrest control of judicial selection from the bar.

Our tug-of-war view of what judges look like and whom they represent depends in large part on interactions between politicians (the selectors), lawyers (the candidate pool), and the method used to select judges. The more liberal the bar is, and the more conservative political actors are, the greater the conflict and the greater incentive political actors have to interject politics into the selection of judges. Their ability to do so, however, depends on the method of judicial selection. The hodgepodge of different judicial selection methods used at the local and state levels exhibits tremendous institutional variation and is prone to change. Moreover, judicial selection is not exogenous to these forces: The greater the ideological mismatch between political actors and lawyers, the more pressure there will be to reform the system in ways that amplify political considerations and scale back the influence of the bar.

Thus, our conclusion is that the judiciary represents the outcome of substantial ideological conflict, a conflict that shapes not only the ideological tenor of the judiciary but also the very mechanisms by which judges are selected. This might be construed as alarming, given the widely understood narrative of the courts as nonpartisan, nonideological institutions. However, another view on this is that the conflict that shapes the judiciary also serves the important purpose of interjecting more ideological diversity into the "captured judiciary." Ultimately, for good or bad, we show in the chapters that follow that politics is a key component of how judges are selected and which professional, political, and ideological interests judges ultimately represent.

PART I

THE LEGAL PROFESSION AND THE "CAPTURED JUDICIARY"

2

The "American Aristocracy"

"If I were asked where I place the American aristocracy, I should reply without hesitation, that it is not composed of the rich, who are united together by no common tie, but that it occupies the judicial bench and the bar."

Alexis de Tocqueville[1]

Traveling through the United States in the 1840s and 1850s, the Frenchman Alexis de Tocqueville made several important observations about the new American democracy, especially as it compared to existing European states. America's social order, he observed, appeared highly structured along occupational and racial lines, making them different from existing (and perhaps more rigid) European regimes. Particularly intriguing to Tocqueville was the fact that, in the absence of a birthright aristocracy, certain "men of letters" – specifically lawyers – had established themselves as the ruling political class. American lawyers, he wrote, "form the highest political class, and the most cultivated circle of society" and they "fill the legislative assemblies, and they conduct the administration; they consequently exercise a powerful influence upon the formation of the law, and upon its execution."[2]

---

[1] Tocqueville (1835).
[2] Tocqueville (1835, p. 279). This powerful influence of the bar also extended to the judiciary. As Tocqueville observed, "the courts of justice are the most visible organs by which the legal profession is enabled to control the democracy" (p. 279). After all, he wrote, "[t]he judge is a lawyer" and "his legal attainments have already raised him to a distinguished rank amongst his fellow-citizens; his political power completes the distinction of his station, and gives him the inclinations natural to privileged classes" (p. 280).

The bar's influence within American democracy and its overrepresentation among the political class are the themes of this chapter. How did the American bar come to constitute, to use Tocqueville's term, America's "aristocracy"? How does America compare to other countries in terms of the close relationship between its legal and political elite? More importantly, how did this influence impact the trajectory of US political norms and institutions? These questions speak not just to the importance of the proverbial "lawyer-legislator"[3] but also to the development of US public policy and the emergence of American exceptionalism. They also speak to the strong relationship between the legal establishment and the nation's courts, a relationship that is so strong that we refer to the courts as the "captured judiciary" in later chapters.

This chapter serves to explain the historical and political importance of the legal profession, laying the groundwork for why lawyers are a key player in our tug-of-war framework. Our argument in this chapter hinges on the fact that lawyers – as noted by observers such as de Tocqueville – have historically comprised the American political elite and that this massive overrepresentation extends far back in American history to the time of the nation's founding. Because this role was even more pronounced earlier in American history, this meant that lawyers played a significant role in structuring the institutions of American government, including participating in the Constitutional Convention and in being overrepresented in the crucial First Congress. In addition, through the nineteenth and twentieth centuries, the bar became more organized, and national-level organizations (such as the American Bar Association [ABA]) came to have more well-defined policy positions and policy influence. This influence has extended in the more modern period to the rise of the administrative state during the New Deal era, a politically important time period in which lawyers played a key role.

Throughout these time periods, lawyer-legislators have been hugely overrepresented in halls of power.[4] While at no point accounting for more than a sliver of the US voting-aged population, lawyers have held an average of 62 percent of seats in the House and 71 percent in the Senate since the time of the nation's founding.[5] Although this overrepresentation

---

[3] By lawyer-legislators, we mean elected representatives with a law background.

[4] For early works documenting the overrepresentation of lawyers in legislatures (and the downstream policy consequences of this overrepresentation), see Derge (1959), Eulau and Sprague (1964), and Green et al. (1973). A more contemporary exploration of these patterns is provided by Robinson (2015).

[5] These percentages are calculated based on our coding of congressional biographies, as reported by the Biographical Directory of the United States Congress.

has gradually lessened over the past century, the dominant presence of lawyers in political office sets the United States apart from other economically advanced democracies. Specifically, as we show in this chapter, America's high share of lawyer-legislators has influenced policy across a host of issues, from law and order to trade and commerce. Compared to other advanced democracies, the United States has higher law firm profitability, higher litigation costs, a higher share of its population incarcerated, and a distressing record in terms of the ability of working- and middle-class people to access and afford legal representation. In other words, the prevalence of lawyer-legislators in the United States has fundamentally shaped the nation's laws and politics, thus contributing more broadly to American exceptionalism. This leads to our discussion in Chapter 3 regarding the "captured judiciary."

We organize this chapter as follows. First, we provide an overview of the history of the national bar and its transformation from a loose collection of lawyers into a politically powerful professional organization. Here, we pay careful attention to the bar's presence among the political elite and how that translated into concrete policy outcomes favorable to the bar. Second, we discuss how lawyers currently populate corridors of power by looking at lawyer-legislators both in the US Congress and in a comparative perspective. This analysis shows how the United States is an outlier across a host of issues traditionally situated within the scope of the bar's interest. Our goal here is not to show a causal relationship (although we believe one might exist); it is instead to show that the decisions on how to structure the country's legal system in tandem with the bar's overrepresentation among political classes have led to the legal profession having tremendous influence on important policy questions. This has also strengthened the bar's ability to govern itself, a fact that sets the stage for Chapter 3, in which we address how the historically powerful American bar has "captured" the American judiciary.

HISTORICAL IMPACT OF LAWYER-LEGISLATORS AND THE BAR

It is difficult to overstate the influence that lawyers – and by extension the bar – have exercised over the development of American political institutions and norms. In the earlier days of US democracy, Tocqueville (himself a lawyer) wrote of an American legal class that was pervasive and operating on the body politic. Lawyers, he wrote, "constitute a power which is little dreaded and hardly noticed; it has no banner of its own; it adapts itself flexibly to the exigencies of the moment and lets itself be carried along unresistingly by every movement of the body social." Even so, he continued, "it enwraps the whole of society, penetrating each component class and constantly working in secret upon its unconscious patient, till in the end it has molded it to its desire."[6]

Lawyers' Influence in Early American Government

Tocqueville's commentary helps contextualize the early influence of the American bar. The early American colonies were, as scholars have noted, not necessarily ones where the bar had significant influence.[7] However, the legal establishment's influence grew significantly around the turn of the eighteenth century, propelled by both demand and supply. In terms of demand, growth in the colonies' economic and mercantile prominence encouraged local and colonial governments (and the bar) to establish more reliable practices of trade and commerce.[8]

In terms of supply, this time period saw an increase in educational opportunities within the colonies themselves, including the establishment of universities such as Harvard College (1636), the College of William and Mary (1693), and Yale College (1701). In tandem with these educational developments came more formalized apprenticeships, which pushed the legal profession toward having standardized requirements and which lessened the need to import British lawyers. Ultimately, it was this "superior education and training," as the legal historian Charles Warren argued, that propelled "the lawyer of the Eighteenth Century to become the spokesman, the writer and the orator of the people when the people were forced to look for champions against the pretensions of the Royal Governors and the judges and of the British Parliament."[9]

---

[6] Tocqueville (1835, p. 270).

[7] There were several reasons for this. First, as Charles Warren notes in his *A History of the American Bar*, the law failed to "touch popular life" in a meaningful way. Second, for many, the legal establishment was seen as reinforcing the status quo, including the American colonies' relationship with Britain. Most broadly, the law and lawyers came into conflict with the colonies' then existing "aristocratic" classes, which were either (in terms of politics and the economy) landowners and merchants – not surprising given the colonies' station as longtime outposts of trading and merchant activity – or, in terms of moral stewardship, the clergy. This was also reinforced by the fact that the most important judicial activity was handled not by the local elite but by colonial courts where cases were handled by British lawyers and judges (Warren 1980, p. 3).

[8] Warren (1980, p. 17).

[9] Warren (1980, p. 18).

Many Founding Fathers were trained in this environment – for example, Thomas Jefferson (who read law as an apprentice in Virginia), John Adams (who did the same in Massachusetts), and Alexander Hamilton (who had a successful Manhattan practice).

This privileged backdrop allowed the legal profession to take a starring role in fashioning the new institutions of American independence. Indeed, lawyers occupied some of the more prominent roles in the shaping of state governments as well as the federal government. Looking at the federal government, of the fifty-six men who signed the Declaration of Independence, twenty-five were lawyers or were trained in the law. Of the fifty-six signatories to the US Constitution in 1787, thirty-two were lawyer-legislators or had some sort of formal legal training.[10] Of the first sixteen US presidents, twelve were lawyers in some capacity.[11]

The tight-knit relationship between the legal and political elite extended to early congressional sessions, which relied heavily on lawyer-legislators. To see this, we used information from the Biographical Directory of the United States Congress, categorizing members based on their listed occupation, education, and professional training prior to serving in Congress.[12] Figure 2.1 shows the historical seat shares for lawyers and, for purposes of comparison for a similarly well-educated profession, physicians.[13] During the first few decades of Congress, lawyer-legislators accounted for about half of congress members. In terms of service on the First Congress (1789–1791), which enacted the Bill of Rights and other

---

[10] This historical statistic is based on applying the same biographical coding scheme we used for members of Congress, based on the Biographical Directory of the United States Congress (described in more detail in Note 12). The remainder of the signatories of the US Constitution were small business owners or merchants, while a small number were simply independently wealthy, mostly from land or slave ownership; George Washington is an example of this latter category.

[11] The early lawyer-presidents were John Adams, Thomas Jefferson, James Monroe, John Quincy Adams, Andrew Jackson, Martin Van Buren, John Tyler, Millard Fillmore, Franklin Pierce, James Buchanan, James Polk, and Abraham Lincoln. A notable exception is George Washington, whose occupation was that of a wealthy landowner.

[12] We code all legislators who have either studied or practiced law prior to entering Congress as "lawyers." Combining the two into one category is practically more important for the earlier time period, when many lawyers simply trained via apprenticeships (as opposed to attending a law school).

[13] Physicians provide a compelling historical and contemporary comparison for several reasons. First, like lawyers, the medical profession has always been highly educated. Second, doctors are targets of heavy regulation; in this sense, they provide a useful counterpoint to lawyers, who, although regulated, have managed to engage in self-regulation (a topic we explore in Chapter 3). Lastly, even more so than lawyers, doctors enjoy certain public trust.

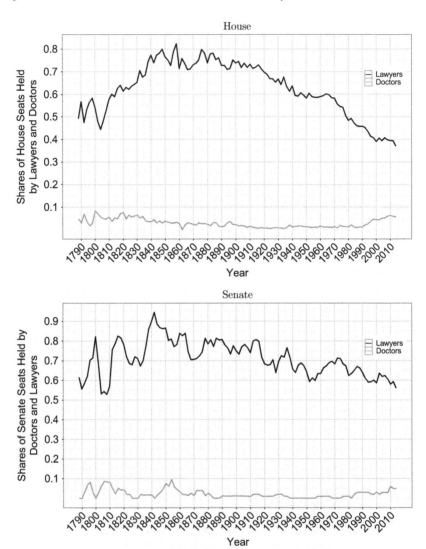

FIGURE 2.1 Historical trend for the share of US House (top) and US Senate (bottom) seats held by lawyers and physicians.
Source: Biographical Directory of the United States Congress.

important early legislation, seventeen out of twenty-eight senators (or 60 percent) and thirty-one of the sixty-four representatives (or 48 percent) were lawyers.

The relationship between legal and political class carried over to the nation's early courts, which were organized at the federal level by the

First Congress via the Judiciary Act of 1789. All of these early federal judges were trained lawyers and all had close connections with state and local bars – not to mention with the lawyers arguing cases before them.[14] This close connection was furthered by the tradition of judges traveling "in circuit," or around their jurisdictions. Writing in the late eighteenth century, one Massachusetts lawyer wrote of these "circuit" meetings that "[t]he manners of judges were not only decorous and the members of the Bar courteous and well-bred; but in their familiar intercourse there was little formality or restraint."[15] A custom in New England state courts was, for example, for hearings to be followed by a call "for both Bench and Bar to assemble at the tavern for a social meeting. On these occasions, they constituted a court among themselves."[16]

Ultimately, although the legal class was heavily overrepresented in the elected branches of government, it had full and exclusive representation in an entire branch of government, the judiciary (highlighting the concept of "judicial capture," which we develop in Chapter 3). As one commentator noted, "[w]ithout a monarch or a clearly defined aristocracy, with a practical utilitarian outlook, with little by way of competing professions, the new nation was almost inevitably bound to rely on lawyers to perform a wide range of functions. Lawyers became the technicians of change as the country expanded economically and geographically."[17]

Increasing Egalitarianism in the Legal Profession

The time period leading up to the mid-1800s saw the bar becoming more egalitarian and less elite. Two factors pushed the legal establishment in this direction. The first was the admission of a number of midwestern and western states into the union, which tended to have more egalitarian norms regarding otherwise elite professions. These states also had fewer elite universities and established law practices from which to draw trained lawyers.[18]

---

[14] For an overview of these early connections between lawyers and judges, including justices on the US Supreme Court, see Warren (1980, ch. 11).

[15] Warren (1980, p. 164).

[16] Warren (1980, pp. 204–205).

[17] Stevens (1967, p. 7). The close connection between the bench and the bar was a source of concern for some. Warren quotes one contemporaneous observer, who lamented that "[t]he profession of the law assumes in every State a political consequence, which considering the use which is made of it, has become truly a subject of the most serious concern" (quoted in Warren 1980, p. 222).

[18] Barton (2010); Kessler (2017); Pound (1953).

The second was a broader national movement in which populism and anti-elitism were the dominant political flavors. American democracy in the age of Andrew Jackson's presidency (1829–1837) embraced the idea that self-taught men – including self-taught lawyers – could accomplish the same as formally educated men.[19] In general, these movements toward reform came not from the bar or from judges but from state legislatures.[20] In 1800, for example, all but five states required a defined period of professional training before admission to the bar. By 1860, only nine of thirty-nine states did.[21] State courts also moved away from the appointment of judges and toward the more populist-friendly election of judges.[22]

Though the national movement toward populism encouraged an acceptance of apprenticed and self-taught lawyers, particularly so in newer states and in more rural areas, this did not undermine the legal profession's grip on positions of political power. There is perhaps no better example of this than Abraham Lincoln. Born in a log cabin in Kentucky and raised in Indiana and Illinois, Lincoln had limited access to education; like many of his contemporaries in what was then the frontier, his legal education consisted primarily of reading the legal classics such as *Blackstone's Commentaries on the Laws of England* and *Chitty's Pleadings*.[23] Even so, Lincoln was able to rise to national political prominence, a trajectory facilitated by the continued clout of lawyer-politicians.

We show evidence of this continued influence in Figure 2.1, which shows lawyer-legislators as a share of all congressional seats in the time leading up to the Civil War. As the figure shows, lawyer-legislators steadily consolidated their share of seats, reaching an astounding *82 percent of all seats* in 1858. To provide more context, Figures 2.2 and 2.3 disaggregate seats by region and party. Lawyer-legislators have

---

[19] Jackson did not attend university, instead studying law as an apprentice in North Carolina before moving to Tennessee; however, historians know little about his apprenticeship, instead focusing on "Jackson's propensity for horseplay" (Ely 1979, p. 422). For a broader context of this time period, see the discussion in Barton (2010, p. 111).

[20] Downes (2013); Pound (1953).

[21] Pound (1953).

[22] We discuss the movement toward judicial elections in further depth in Chapter 7. These movements were met with resistance from both practicing lawyers and judges. Barton (2010, p. 112) tells of one lawyer who wrote in 1847 that "[t]he voice of the multitude is against the legal community" and that "[t]he bar finds no favour at the ballot box."

[23] For example, in a letter dating to 1855, Lincoln wrote, "Get the books, and read and study them till, you understand them in their principal features; and that is the main thing. It is of no consequence to be in a large town while you are reading" (Lincoln 1865).

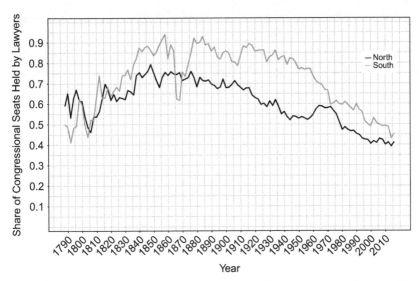

FIGURE 2.2 Historical trend for the percentage of US congressional seats held
by lawyers, by region.
Source: Biographical Directory of the United States Congress.

historically been more prevalent in the South, having held approximately 80 percent of seats from the mid-nineteenth century through well into the twentieth century. We believe that this speaks to the localized power of the bar as a gatekeeper to politics: Specifically, African Americans women, and religious minorities would be effectively excluded from pursuing a legal education, making a legal background an attractive prerequisite for political office from the perspective of southern white elites.[24] We discuss the legal profession's gatekeeping in greater depth in Chapter 3.

Rise of Organized Bar Associations

The second half of the nineteenth century saw rapid growth in the number of attorneys practicing in the United States. According to data from the ABA, the number of attorneys jumped by nearly 40 percent between 1880 and 1890 (from 64,137 to 89,630) and then again by nearly 30 percent between 1890 and 1900 (to 114,460), almost doubling over a period

[24] For more on the history of lawyer-litigators, see Eulau and Sprague (1964), Miller (1995), and Robinson (2015).

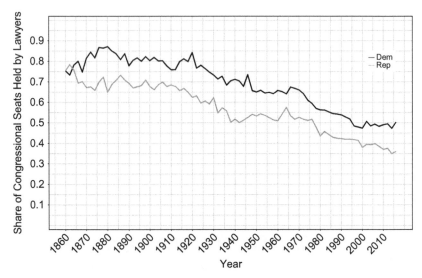

FIGURE 2.3 Historical trend for the shares of US congressional seats held by lawyers, by political party.
Source: Biographical Directory of the United States Congress.

of twenty years.[25] This rapid increase in the number of lawyers – and the relaxing of educational and professional standards – alarmed legal elites. In response, lawyers began to organize via formal bar associations, which first sprang up in large metropolitan areas and then expanded their reach into various states.[26] It was at a 1878 Connecticut state bar meeting that the topic of a national bar arose. This bar was envisioned to be "representative of American lawyers" and would "review the legislative work of the year, in this and other countries, and discuss matters of common interest."[27] The ABA was thus founded in 1878 as the legal profession's national-level trade organization.

[25] American Bar Association (2017).
[26] According to Baldwin (1917, p. 658), "[t]he first bar associations in the United States were naturally formed where it was easiest for lawyers to gather together, that is, in cities. The Galveston Bar Association was organized in 1868; the association of the Bar of the City of New York in 1870; and the Bar Association of St. Louis in 1874. In 1874 (May 14) was also formed the Iowa State Bar Association, followed in 1875 (June 2) by the Connecticut State Bar Association."
[27] Baldwin (1917, p. 659). Baldwin also has a collection of letters speaking to the early objectives of the ABA. These include a letter writer who noted that a national professional organization had the potential of being "extensively useful in perfecting and assimilating the laws of the several states; in improving and reforming our systems of jurisprudence; in advancing political science, and in giving higher character, and wider usefulness to the legal profession" (Baldwin 1917, p. 678).

The rise of bar associations helped cement and formalize the symbiotic relationship between the legal profession and the political elite, which would go unchallenged through the 1920s and 1930s. In terms of political representation, lawyers continued to thrive, comprising 52 percent of US state governors (from 1930 to 1940), around 60 percent of the US House of Representatives, and 68 percent of the US Senate. The number was even higher looking at southern governors, 72 percent of whom were lawyers in the period between 1939 and 1948.[28]

In terms of political leanings, these bar associations represented an affluent, well-educated segment of society who, in line with the class politics of the time, tended to be more conservative in their economic and philosophical outlook – an important point that shaped the bar's policy positions.[29] (Indeed, one of the ABA's first moves was to oppose the ratification of the Sixteenth Amendment authorizing Congress to levy an income tax on the grounds that such a tax represented an encroachment on private wealth.) Many of these policy positions concerned the selection of judges and the overall health and reputation of the legal system. For example, Roscoe Pound, dean of Harvard Law School, warned about the public's "dissatisfaction with the Administration of Justice," assailing the then widespread practice of electing judges.[30] These arguments spurred on attempts to bring merit-oriented criteria into the selection of judges, which had the effect of increasing the bar's influence over the judicial branch and placing more emphasis on pedigree. As we discuss in Chapter 3, this strengthened relationship between the bench and the bar was a key pathway toward the legal establishment's "capture of the judiciary" – in turn an important component of the judicial tug-of-war framework that we develop in later chapters.

---

[28] Cohen (1969, p. 569). This is consistent with our estimates based on entries from the congressional biographies as well as similar estimates from Miller (1995), Carnes (2013), and Robinson (2015). This confirms that the bar during this time period not only became more organized but also retained its political control over elected branches of government.

[29] Brockman (1962, pp. 271–272). To give an illustration of this conservative leaning, the ABA adopted a resolution in 1934 opposing a constitutional amendment to prohibit child labor, which read, "Resolved by the American Bar Association that the proposed Child Labor Amendment to the Constitution of the United States should be actively opposed as an unwarranted invasion by the Federal Government of a field in which the rights of the individual States and of the family are and should remain paramount" (Guthrie 1934, p. 405).

[30] Pound (1906).

The Bar, the New Deal, and the Rise of the Administrative State

The close policy interests connecting the American political and legal elite were tested during the New Deal era. The legal establishment – which at the elite levels tended to represent business and politically powerful interests – was a solidly Republican constituency. However, Franklin Roosevelt and the Democratic majorities looked to enact a progressive social and economic agenda that pushed against business interests. Unsurprisingly, then, the legal establishment – and in particular the ABA – was among the most vocal of critics of progressive New Deal policies, including the promulgation of new government regulations and new administrative agencies.

Although the most well-known conflict between the bar and the political leaders involved Franklin Roosevelt's infamous "court packing" plan of 1937,[31] the more profound conflict involved the development of the administrative state. Progressives were interested in establishing a robust governmental role in regulatory oversight of businesses, consumer protection, and labor relations. From the perspective of the legal establishment, however, this was unpalatable: Many lawyers perceived any growth in the administrative state as encroaching on roles traditionally filled by lawyers.[32] Roscoe Pound, who then chaired the ABA's Special Committee on Administrative Law, echoed these concerns, warning that unchecked administrative power would undermine the Anglo-American tradition of rule of law and that the erosion of judicial "powers which fifty years ago would have been held purely judicial and jealously guarded from executive exercise are now decided to be administrative only and are cheerfully conceded to boards and commissions."[33] His influential committee eventually urged the ABA to oppose the administrative state and to make sure it would not diminish the standing of the courts and, accordingly, of the legal profession. "[E]xcept as the bar takes upon itself to act," he wrote, "there is nothing to check the tendency of administrative bureaus to extend the scope of their operations indefinitely even to the extent of supplanting our traditional judicial regime by an administrative regime."[34]

---

[31] We discuss the court-packing episode in further detail in our introduction to Chapter 4.

[32] See Shamir (1995), which argues that the bar's resistance to the administrative state was rooted in a desire to protect the legal profession's privileged status and prestige, which was at that point rooted in its close relationship with the courts.

[33] Pound's report goes on to denounce Roosevelt's "administrative absolutism" and compare the New Deal to the doctrines of "Soviet Russia."

[34] Pound (1938).

In addition, many legal professionals also opposed the expansion of the administrative state on ideological grounds, being naturally skeptical of what they believed to be a left-leaning political enterprise. As the regulatory law scholar Nicholas Zeppos has argued, several agencies (such as the Interstate Commerce Commission and the Federal Trade Commission) had predated the New Deal but did not spark widespread professional concerns among elite lawyers, the implication being that the ABA's New Deal opposition may have been motivated less by a "shallow kind of professional opportunism" and more by the conservative political views of more prominent members.[35] Indeed, the ABA's fervent opposition to the New Deal led to a schism within the profession, with many lawyers leaving the ABA for rival bar associations such as the progressive National Lawyers Guild, founded in 1937.

The ABA's opposition crystalized with the introduction of the Walter-Logan Bill in 1939, described as "an extreme attempt on the part of the legal profession to judicialize administrative procedure."[36] The bill would have introduced courtlike proceedings into the agency decision-making process and would have required agencies to hold public hearings, present facts and evidence in support of their decisions, and be subject to judicial review.[37] Congress ultimately passed the legislation in 1940 but it was vetoed by Roosevelt, who called the bill "one of the repeated efforts by a combination of lawyers, who desire to have all the processes of government conducted through lawsuits."[38] Absent the ABA's determined opposition, Roosevelt may very well have been successful in his efforts to transform and establish a progressive, regulatory-based administrative state. As it turned out, the ABA's opposition helped secure the compromise passage of the Administrative

---

35 Zeppos (1997, p. 1133).
36 Woll (1963, p. 19).
37 Bertelli and Lynn (2006); Horwitz (1992).
38 Roosevelt (1940). In his veto message, Roosevelt further argued that conventional legal proceedings disadvantaged the average citizen and imposing them on administrative agencies would be contrary to the public interest:

> Litigation has become costly beyond the ability of the average person to bear. Its technical rules of procedure are often traps for the unwary, and technical rules of evidence often prevent common-sense determinations on information which would be regarded as adequate for any business decision. The increasing cost of competent legal advice and the necessity of relying upon lawyers to conduct court proceedings have made all laymen and most lawyers recognize the inappropriateness of entrusting routine processes of Government to the outcome of never-ending lawsuits (Roosevelt 1940).

Procedures Act (APA), which was signed into law in 1940 and which more narrowly drew the boundaries of a government-run administrative state.[39] The APA also achieved the ABA's primary objective of subordinating administrative agencies to the courts through the process of judicial review, thus meeting its twin goals of ensuring that the legal profession would remain free from rules and regulations not of its own making and that agency rulings would still be beholden to legal ones.

This episode illustrates the power of the bar in shaping a defining feature of contemporary American politics – closely related to what Robert Kagan has termed "adversarial legalism," or the idea that much of public policy (in particular regulatory policy) is shaped through litigation in the courts as opposed to administrative regulations.[40] Along these lines, the political scientist Francis Fukuyama has argued that the "judicialization of functions that in other developed democracies are handled by administrative bureaucracies has led to an explosion of costly litigation, slow decision-making and highly inconsistent enforcement of laws" and has linked the "decentralized, legalistic approach to administration" to "the other notable feature of the American political system: its openness to the influence of interest groups."[41]

LAWYER-LEGISLATORS IN THE UNITED STATES TODAY

The previous section highlighted the historical impact of lawyers on the development of US politics and policy. We now turn to examining the impact of the legal profession in today's political environment, starting

---

[39] As one scholar explained the difference, "whereas the Walter-Logan bill attempted to formalize the entire administrative process, the provisions of the APA applied primarily to the *formal administrative process*, the area where hearings are required by statute, or, more rarely, by agency rule" Woll (1963, p. 21).

[40] Kagan (2009). As Kagan has argued, "in the United States lawyers, legal rights, judges, and lawsuits are the functional equivalent to the large centralized bureaucracies that dominate governance in high-tax, activist welfare states" (Kagan 2009, p. 16). Several pieces of landmark legislation passed by Congress during the twentieth century included attorney fee-shifting statues that were designed to make private litigation the primary means of enforcement. Examples include the Equal Access to Justice Act, the Voting Rights Act of 1965, the Consumer Product Safety Act, and the Fair Labor Standards Act.

[41] Fukuyama (2014, p. 470). Farhang (2010) has likewise written about the consequences of the adoption of a highly legalistic approach to public administration, with conflicts that would typically be resolved in other countries through consultations between interested parties and the bureaucracy instead being litigated in the courts.

with its continued overrepresentation in politics and then examining downstream policy consequences.

Prevalence of Lawyer-Legislators

Today, lawyers account for roughly 3 out of every 1,000 US adults, or around 0.4 percent of the adult population. Even so lawyers are overrepresented in the White House, accounting for thirty-two of forty-five (or 71 percent) of all US presidents.[42] Members of the legal profession are also overrepresented in other parts of the executive branch.[43] Various components of the federal government – including the Justice Department, the Office of Legal Counsel, the Social Security Administration, the Department of Veterans Affairs, and the Department of Education – employ around 100,000 lawyers.[44] Lawyers are also extremely well represented among the ranks of lobbyists, particularly within Washington, DC–based law firms. Based on our data, we estimate that, as of 2012, 51,928 lawyers were practicing in Washington, DC, accounting for more than a tenth of the entire Washington, DC voting-aged population.

In terms of lawyer-legislators at the national level, Figure 2.1 shows that lawyers continue to be heavily overrepresented in Congress. In the 115th Congress (2017–2019), lawyers accounted for 39 percent of House seats and fifty-six percent of Senate seats. To help place this in context, lawyers elected to the House outnumber representatives from all twenty-four states west of the Mississippi combined. The overrepresentation of lawyers even exceeds even that of millionaires. Relative to the average citizen, millionaires are approximately ten times more likely to be elected to Congress;[45] lawyers, by comparison, are nearly *one hundred* times more likely to be elected to Congress.

---

[42] In total, twenty-nine presidents to date have practiced law. Three others – Warren Harding, Harry Truman, and Lyndon Johnson – attended law school but dropped out before graduating.

[43] As of September 2018, six out of fifteen cabinet members in the Trump administration were lawyers. (This is down from ten out of fifteen during the later years of the Obama administration.) These are Jeff Sessions, Alex Acosta, Robert Wilkie, Mike Pompeo, Alex Azar, and Kirstjen Nielsen.

[44] According to the ABA, "the federal government employs more than 93,000 attorneys" (Oliver 2009).

[45] Around half of all congressional seats are held by millionaires (Cody 2014), but they also draw from a larger share of the population (just less than 5 percent) compared to lawyers (around 0.4 percent).

Of note is that lawyers' dominance of political office has eroded somewhat, at least at the national level.[46] This is evident in Figure 2.2, which shows a decline in the relative share of lawyer-litigators in Congress through the twentieth century.[47] We see several reasons for this. The first is that candidates for state and federal offices used to be chosen by party leaders, among whom lawyers were no doubt heavily over-represented. This "old boy network" offered an ideal environment for lawyers to consolidate seat shares to the exclusion of other groups. The movement toward the adoption of direct primaries in the mid-twentieth century, however, meant that lawyers had to win the support of primary voters from diverse backgrounds, thus weakening their relative position and opening the door to other well-educated professionals (i.e., small business owners, financiers, military leaders, etc.).

Second, the early twentieth century saw a shift toward an increased professionalization and organization of the bar. As entry into the legal profession became more regulated and more expensive (in terms of both time and money), casually pursuing law as a means to enter into politics became more costly.[48] Lastly, a more recent phenomenon is the growing geographic concentration of the legal profession, which we examine in greater detail in subsequent chapters. Specifically, as of 2012, half of the nation's lawyers reside in just eighty congressional districts (18.5 percent of all districts). For example, California's rural 21st congressional district has less than 1/163th the number of lawyers per capita as New York's 12th congressional district.[49] The geographically representative nature of Congress makes this a significant hurdle.

One explanation we can rule out is an ideological one, or that lawyer-litigators have shifted overwhelmingly to one party or another, thus explaining the slight drop. This is confirmed by Figure 2.3, which shows the historical share of lawyer-legislators by political party. Democrats

---

[46] See Robinson (2015) for an excellent account of the relative decline of the lawyer-legislator compared to other professions.

[47] The decline also appears to reflect a more general pattern among representative democracies. For example, Franck (2013) documents a similar decline in France from 35 percent in 1876 to 20 percent in 1936, which he attributes to urbanization. However, the seat shares of lawyer-legislators in France have always been lower than in the United States.

[48] Robinson (2015) suggests that the pressures of a contemporary legal career, including increasing time demands and reduced flexibility (e.g., Fowler and McClure 1990), might discourage lawyers from entering politics.

[49] The populations of lawyers for congressional districts are calculated using geocoded address data from professional directories.

consistently have a higher share of lawyer-legislators, partly due to the fact that the South was controlled by the Democratic Party and, as seen in Figure 2.2, lawyer-litigators were particularly common among Southern delegations. More recently, as we will see in later chapters, lawyers tend to be left-leaning, which in theory should lead to a greater representation of lawyer-legislators by the Democratic Party. However, as Figure 2.2 shows, both Democratic and Republican party numbers look similar in a historical context.

Overall, despite a slight decline, lawyers have historically dominated the ranks of America's political elite and they continue to do so even today. These facts speak to the bar's direct and ongoing political power in terms of representation across all three branches of government.

Policy Consequences of Lawyer-Legislators

How does this overrepresentation translate into contemporary policy-making? If history is a guide, we would expect that professional biases, culture, and training carry over into a legislative setting, thus influencing the interests and goals of legislators. Some earlier scholarship has questioned this, however, noting the roughly even ideological split in terms of lawyer-legislators (certainly driven in part by the conservative nature of Southern Democrats).[50] However, with a few exceptions, none of the literature has looked specifically at legislation promoting or aiding the legal industry.[51]

To assess the helpful nature of lawyer-legislators to the legal industry, we examined the resolutions made by the ABA's House of Delegates, the ABA's policy-making body. The House of Delegates routinely adopts resolutions urging legislators to address a broad set of policies, including those of interest to the legal profession.[52] If the bar is indeed influential, and if the lawyer-legislator connection is well-established, we should see

---

[50] For more on this, see Eulau and Sprague (1964), Derge (1959, pp. 430–431), and Green et al. (1973). Derge (1959), does find that lawyers-legislators are more successful than nonlawyers in getting bills passed (p. 425) and a greater tendency for lawyer-legislators to act cohesively (p. 426).

[51] See Green et al. (1973, pp. 443–446), which explores "support for the judiciary" and finds no difference between lawyers and nonlawyers.

[52] According to the ABA's website, "The control and administration of the ABA is vested in the House of Delegates, the policy-making body of the association. The House meets twice each year, at ABA Annual and Midyear Meetings." See www.americanbar.org/groups/leadership/house_of_delegates.html.

that Congress will be receptive to these resolutions; if not, then we should see less interest in pursuing the ABA's goals.

We adopt an empirical strategy similar to the one used by contemporary scholars to estimate the influence of partisanship on representatives' roll call voting.[53] (By "roll call votes," we mean the formal votes of each senator or House representative.) Specifically, we try to predict each roll call vote cast in the House and Senate during the 100th–114th Congresses as a function of legislative ideology.[54] We then replicate the exact analysis but additionally include a term that captures whether a legislator was a lawyer or not. This allows us to compare whether the model that includes lawyer-legislator information does better in predicting support for legislation. In other words, we evaluate just how predictive being a lawyer is above and beyond ideology.[55]

These comparisons are given in Table 2.1, which lists the roll calls (out of 28,430 in total) ranked in the top ten by improvement in predictive power. That is, these are votes for which we can predict a representative's vote choice *better* using the additional information that the legislator in question is a lawyer (or not). Nine of the top ten bills listed in the table directly concern the legal profession.[56] Not only does this suggest that lawyer-legislators behave differently but that they are perhaps the most distinctive when it comes to policy issues of direct relevance to the legal profession.[57]

---

[53] See McCarty, Poole, and Rosenthal (2001); Snyder and Groseclose (2000); Clinton, Jackman, and Rivers (2004).

[54] Legislative ideology comes from the DW-NOMINATE scores. These scores place representatives on a unidimensional scale – from liberal to conservative – based on their roll call votes. See Poole and Rosenthal (1985); McCarty, Poole, and Rosenthal (2016).

[55] Specifically, for roll call j, restricted and unrestricted models are fit with a probit function,

$$\text{Restricted}: Y_{ij} \sim \beta_0 + \beta_1 dwnom_i \qquad (2.1)$$

$$\text{Unrestricted}: Y_{ij} \sim \beta_0 + \beta_1 dwnom_i + \beta_2 lawyer_i \qquad (2.2)$$

where $lawyer_i$ is a lawyer-specific fixed effect. We then use a likelihood ratio test to assess the improvement in model fit. The likelihood ratio statistic (LR) captures the relative importance of the lawyer-specific effects in explaining vote choices. β_2 has a similar interpretation but provides additional information on the direction of the effect.

[56] For example, the top piece of legislation, the Common Sense Product Liability Legal Reform Act, tried to limit manufacturer liability.

[57] Table 2.4 in the chapter's appendix reports on other notable roll call votes selected from the top 100. Many of these are similar in nature to the top-ten ranked votes, but several of them have implications that extend beyond matters directly impacting the bar. For example, the Violent Crime Control and Law Enforcement Act of 1994 and the North American Free Trade Act of 1994 might not have passed in the form they

TABLE 2.1 *Top ten congressional roll call votes (out of 28,430) ranked by improvement in model fit when including lawyer-legislator status.*

	Careong.	Bill	Title	Question	Description	LR	β_2	ABA
1	104	H.R. 956	Common Sense Product Liability Legal Reform Act	Passage	Enact comprehensive product liability reform; implement "loser pays" rule in product liability suits.	21.0	−1.01 (0.23)	−
2	107	H.R. 2563	Thomas Amdt.	Adopt	Limit personal injury claims in medical malpractice.	19.8	−1.14 (0.28)	−
3	100	H.R. 1054	Military Medical Malpractice Claims	Passage	Permit active members of the military to sue the federal government for malpractice occurring in US military hospitals.	19.3	0.85 (0.20)	+
4	104	H.R. 988	Attorney Accountability Act of 1995	Passage	Enact civil litigation reform; limit attorney fees; sanction attorneys for frivolous lawsuits.	16.5	−1.02 (0.28)	−
5	104	H.R. 956	Cox Amdt.	Adopt	Eliminate joint liability for noneconomic losses in civil lawsuits involving interstate commerce.	16.2	−0.79 (0.20)	−

TABLE 2.1 (continued)

	Careong.	Bill	Title	Question	Description	LR	β_2	ABA
6	106	H.R. 833	Conyers Amdt.	Adopt	An amendment to waive the provisions of title 11 relating to small business debtors where they result in the loss of 5 or more jobs; prioritize payment of legal fees in bankruptcy cases.	15.6	−0.79 (0.20)	−
7	107	S. 1052	Craig Amdt.	Table	Allow beneficiaries to bring personal injury claims against health insurers for damages resulting from a denial of claim for coverage.	15.2	−2.85 (1.12)	−
8	107	H.R. 956	Flake Substitute To Smith Amdt.	Adopt	Amendment to prohibit funding to administer the Cuban Assets Control Regulations with respect to travel.	14.8	−0.56 (0.15)	
9	113	H.R. 4660	Scott Amdt.	Adopt	Eliminate all funding to Legal Services Corporation.	14.5	−0.81 (0.22)	−
10	104	H.R. 956	Common Sense Legal Standards Reform Act	Recommit	Limit punitive damages in product liability suits to $1m.	14.5	1.10 (0.31)	+

Note: The column labeled *LR (D)* reports the likelihood ratio statistic. The column labeled β_2 reports the estimated coefficients and standard errors (in parentheses) of the lawyer-specific effects. The column labeled *ABA* indicates the implied directionality based on the ABA's stated legislative priorities.
Source: DW-NOMINATE, Biographical Directory of the United States Congress.

We can also examine the bar's official positions on these pieces of legislation. The rightmost column (titled "ABA") of Table 2.1 provides the directionality of the official legislative position of the ABA.[58] The estimated coefficients on the lawyer-specific effects consistently align with the ABA, indicating that lawyer-legislators' and the ABA's preferences align in every case. In terms of positions taken, this means that lawyer-legislators are significantly less likely to support legislation that would cap awards for damages, limit product or medical liability, or regulate attorney fees, but they are more likely to support legislation that would weaken constraints on filing law suits, increase funding for the Legal Service Corporation, or promote fee-shifting provisions in public interest suits. Lawyer-legislators are, in other words, more likely to vote in favor of positions supported by the nation's leading lawyerly organization.

These analyses provide compelling empirical support for the idea that the legal profession has leveraged its political influence to promote the bar's interests through its overrepresentation in Congress. They also show that lawyers are different from nonlawyers in how they view and interact with the legal profession. We build on these results in Chapter 3, in which we examine the "lawyer-judge" relationship and find strong evidence that this behavior carries over into judicial settings.

LAWYER-LEGISLATORS AND AMERICAN EXCEPTIONALISM

If the previous analyses are any indication, the influence of legislator-lawyers is significant and felt with particular force with regards to laws, rules, and customs governing the legal profession and structuring of the legal environment. However, the prevalence of lawyers in legislative assemblies and other political bodies is often explained as a natural consequence of the special relationship between law and politics.[59] In this section, we turn to investigating this question as well as what these patterns mean for American political and policy development. Is the United

---

did were it not for support from Democratic lawyer-legislators. Lawyer-legislators also disproportionately opposed the Lobbying Disclosure Act of 1995 and efforts to regulate political intelligence activities.

[58] The ABA positions are coded based on a 118-page document published by its governmental affairs office that details the ABA's official positions on hundreds of legislative issues and specific bills (American Bar Association 2016b).

[59] See, for example, Eulau and Sprague (1964).

States distinctive in these measures, or does the overrepresentation of lawyer-legislators contribute to broader policy differences between the United States and other advanced democracies?

Lawyer-Legislators in a Comparative Perspective

The legal profession's role in both the organization of markets and politics varies greatly across countries, translating into wide differences in how lawyer-legislators are represented across advanced democracies. We document this fact using the professional and educational backgrounds of members of national legislatures collected from the Inter-Parliamentary Union Chronicle of Parliamentary Elections.[60] This allowed us to calculate the proportion of legislators with backgrounds in law for twenty-five of the Organisation for Economic Co-operation and Development (OECD) member nations. To account for the possibility that the shares of lawyer-legislators are simply a function of the overall population, we calculate the number of lawyers per 1,000 citizens based on cross-national estimates of lawyer populations.[61]

More so than for other professions, there is tremendous variability in both the numbers of lawyers per capita and the number of lawyers elected to public office. For example, the number of lawyers per 1,000 people ranges from a low of 0.2 in Japan, to 0.7 in France, and a high of 3.7 in Greece. The United States, which alone accounts for nearly 21 percent of the global share of lawyers, has 3.3 lawyers per 1,000 citizens, ranking it behind only Greece and Spain in terms of lawyers per capita.[62] There are nearly seventeen times as many lawyers per capita in the OECD nation where lawyers are most common (Greece) than in the nation where lawyers are least common (Japan).

Figure 2.4 compares the proportions of seats in national legislatures held by lawyers as their share of the population rises.[63] The figure shows a clear relationship between lawyers per capita and the share

---

[60] Inter-Parliamentary Union: PARLINE Database on National Parliaments (2017).

[61] For this, we used data from Michelson (2013).

[62] By comparison, the size of the medical profession is much less variable, ranging from a low of 2.1 physicians per 1,000 citizens in Canada to a high of 4.9 in Spain.

[63] Data on lawyers in the US Congress are from our own calculations. The seat shares of lawyer-legislators for other countries are calculated from data on professional backgrounds of members published by the Inter-Parliamentary Union Chronicle of Parliamentary Elections. Cross-national estimates of lawyer populations are from Michelson (2013). These are then divided by population estimations from the World Bank to calculate lawyers per capita.

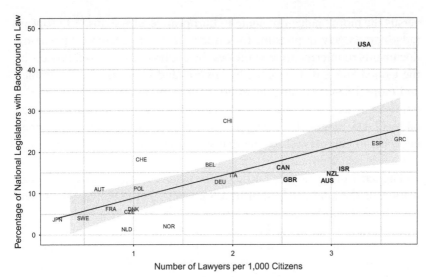

FIGURE 2.4 Relationship between lawyers per capita and the share of lawyers in a national assembly, for OECD member states.
Note: Nations with commonwealth legal systems are in bold.
Sources: Inter-Parliamentary Union Chronicle of Parliamentary Elections; Michelson (2013); World Bank.

of lawyer-legislators in national assemblies. To give some context, 13 percent of Members of Parliament (MPs) in the British Parliament have backgrounds in law, similar to other common law countries such as Canada, New Zealand, and Australia at 15 percent, 14 percent, and 13 percent, respectively. The percentages for France, the Netherlands, Sweden, and Denmark are lower, ranging from the low- to mid-single digits. Compared to all countries, the United States is an outlier, with *more than twice as many lawyer-legislators as would be predicted by the trend line for lawyers per capita.* Lawyers, in other words, are familiar to politics everywhere but nowhere as familiar as they are in the United States.

Policy Consequences of American Exceptionalism

Our findings in Table 2.1 suggest that lawyer-legislators are particularly sensitive to policy issues of interest to legal professionals. Could these differences extend to a comparative context? For example, many scholars have written about the "lawyer-dominated" American legal environment versus the more "judge-dominated" European legal systems.[64] European judges are largely responsible for evidence gathering, from subpoenaing documents to interrogating witnesses. By contrast, the pretrial process in the United States is dominated by lawyers and is substantially lengthier and more time-consuming. In addition, in many European countries, the paths to a judgeship and to a career in the law are distinctive career paths;[65] US judges, by contrast, are trained side by side with other lawyers, an educational regime that is so well accepted that many may not know that alternatives exist.

The legal profession in Europe is, moreover, subject to external regulation of the kind rarely seen by US lawyers. For example, the United Kingdom's Legal Services Act of 2007 sought to make a wide array of legal services more accessible and affordable for the poor and middle class. Class action lawsuits – in which parties pursuing legal action are represented collectively – are largely a US phenomenon; of the handful of countries outside the United States that allow such collective action, most adopted the practice relatively recently (within the past three decades). Other countries, such as Switzerland, considered proposals to adopt American-style class action lawsuits but ultimately rejected them.[66]

These possibilities lead us to consider that countries with greater shares of lawyer-legislators (such as the United States) are more likely to enact policies friendly to the legal industry, an analysis that is the logical extension of our earlier look at the distinctive voting behavior of US lawyer-legislators. To test this in a comparative context, the sections that follow present a series of cross-national comparisons for four key, law-related arenas: (1) law firm profitability, (2) liability costs, (3) accessibility and affordability of legal services, and (4) incarceration rates. We also link the relative national prevalence of lawyer-legislators to a fifth policy outcome: economic inequality. This speaks to a long-theorized

---

[64] See, for example, Kagan (2009). In writing on the subject of changes to the regulation of the legal profession, Semple (2017, p. 1) singles out the US for its resistance to reform:

> In common law Northern Europe and in Australasia, a wave of reform has been transforming legal services regulation since roughly 1980. Old structures and approaches, based on the principles of professionalism and lawyer independence, are being replaced in these jurisdictions by new ones that prioritize competition and consumer interests. In the United States, this has conspicuously not happened, leaving intact a regulatory approach whose broad outlines have changed little in the past 100 years.

[65] Abel and Lewis (1989).
[66] Baumgartner (2007).

(but largely untested) link between economic inequality and the alignment of the economic interests of the legal industry and that of their wealthy clients.

For each of the above, we briefly describe the source of the data and analyze its relationship with the proportion of seats in the national assembly held by lawyer-legislators.

LAW FIRM PROFITABILITY. Does the prevalence of lawyer-legislators allow the legal industry to tap into more markets and expand its reach? We might expect as much, at least if the financial robustness of the legal industry in the United States is any indication. According to *The American Lawyer*, 80 of the world's 100 largest law firms (by revenue in 2015) were headquartered in the United States.[67] Indeed, in 2015, while the top 100 firms in the United States had revenues of $83.2 billion, the top 100 law firms based in the United Kingdom had combined revenues of $25.7 billion.[68] Law firms in the United States are also more profitable on a per capita basis: The average profit per partner at the top twenty US law firms was $3.27 million; by comparison, among the top twenty non-US law firms, it was $1.12 million.

To investigate the relationship between the legal industry's political influence and law firm profitability, we gathered data on revenues per attorney at top law firms across fourteen countries in North America, Australia, and Europe, again comparing these to the share of national legislative seats held by lawyers.[69] Figure 2.5 provides this analysis, plotting the average revenues per attorney at top law firms (on the vertical axis) against lawyer-legislator seat shares (on the horizontal axis). The figure shows that, as the share of lawyer-legislators increases, law firm profitability also increases. It also reveals that (1) top law firms in the United States generate far more revenue per attorney than law firms based in other countries and (2) the United States has many more attorneys in its national legislature than any other country. Overall, the pattern here

---

[67] *The Global 100* (2016). Only in the United Kingdom, which is home to 18 of the top 100 global law firms, is the legal services industry comparable to that in the United States. The full effects of Britain's exit from the European Union are, however, not yet certain.

[68] For these figures, see *The UK 100* (2016) and *The US 100* (2016), respectively.

[69] *The Global 100* (2016). Although our outcome (revenues per attorney for top five firms) captures only a narrow slice of the legal industry, it does provide a good snapshot of revenues at the higher, more profitable end of the market.

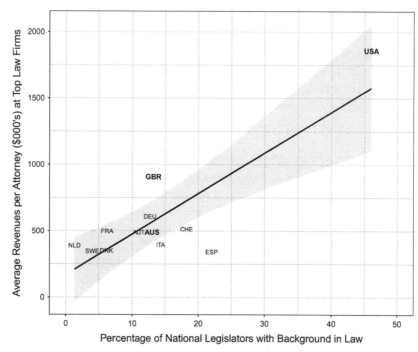

FIGURE 2.5 Relationship between share of lawyer-legislators in a national
assembly and law firm revenues per attorney at top law firms, by country.
Sources: Inter-Parliamentary Union Chronicle of Parliamentary Elections; *The Global 100*
(2016).

is clear: The political representation of attorneys is positively correlated
with law firm profitability.

COMPARATIVE LIABILITY COSTS. If lawyers wield significant influence
in politics, they might clear the way for more and more litigation and
regulation via the courts and the legal system – moves that would
naturally increase their spheres of influence. For example, the ABA
leveraged its significant political weight in the 1940s, when the federal government was considering administrative reform; ultimately, the
legislation that was enacted, the Administrative Procedures Act (APA),
created a compromise in which courts would be used as a primary
method of regulatory enforcement and the preeminent role of lawyers
in administrative regulation would be maintained.[70]

[70] Kagan (2009).

Does the prevalence of lawyer-legislators impact how much regulation is handled via the legal system? Analyzing this with quantitative data is challenging, since estimating the "level" of litigation in a given country is difficult.[71] We base our comparisons on general estimates of liability costs – described as the "costs of claims, whether resolved through litigation or other claims resolution processes" – as a fraction of GDP. The logic behind this calculation is that, if there is more litigation, litigation costs should occupy a higher share of a country's GDP. We calculate this measure for eleven countries using data from the US Chamber of Commerce's Institute for Legal Reform.[72] We expect to see a positive relationship between the political influence of lawyers and litigation costs (as a fraction of GDP).

Figure 2.6 plots liability costs as a fraction of GDP against lawyer-legislator seat shares. Here, we see a remarkably similar pattern to the one in Figure 2.5: The higher share of lawyer-litigators, the larger the share of GDP devoted to litigation costs. The United States continues to be an outlier in this analysis. Liability costs in the United States account for 1.66 percent of GDP, suggesting a legal industry that is large and powerful; this contrasts with 0.40 percent of GDP in the Netherlands and 0.30 percent of GDP in Japan.

AFFORDABILITY OF LEGAL SERVICES. While the American legal industry may rank first on overall profitability and impact on the national economy, vast segments of the consumer market for legal services remain poorly served, including the poor and middle class. This is, perhaps, unsurprising: We would expect that, as the political influence of the bar increases, lawyers become less likely to enter less lucrative practice areas (such as family law or immigration law). The inability of many people to afford effective legal representation has reached crisis levels, with some viewing it as a human rights issue.[73]

To investigate this, we make use of data from the World Justice Project (WJP) Rule of Law Index, which scores 113 countries along a number

---

[71] Experts in comparative legal systems have some measures. For example, in comparing litigation rates in the United States and Japan, Ramseyer (2013) notes that Americans file about 80,000 product liability cases per year; by comparison, the Japanese file around 100–300 cases per year.

[72] McKnight and Hinton (2013).

[73] Snyder (2016).

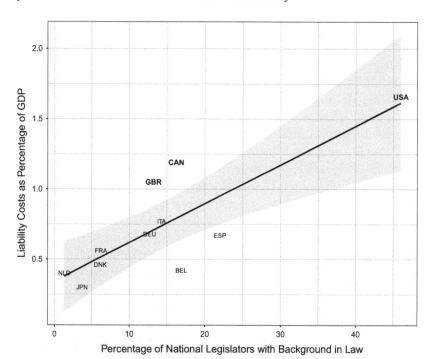

FIGURE 2.6 Relationship between share of lawyer-legislators in a national
assembly and liability costs as a fraction of GDP, by country.
Sources: Inter-Parliamentary Union Chronicle of Parliamentary Elections; McKnight and
Hinton (2013).

of dimensions.[74] These data include a measure of the accessibility and
affordability of the civil justice system, on which the United States
does especially poorly, ranking 94th out of 113 countries overall. This
places it immediately behind Myanmar (93rd) and Zimbabwe (92nd) and
well below the second-lowest ranked advanced democracy in our analysis, Canada (48th). Figure 2.7 plots this measure of legal accessibility
against lawyer-legislator seat shares, which shows a negative relationship. Specifically, greater political power wielded by the bar (via a higher
share of lawyer-legislators) is associated with reduced accessibility and
affordability of legal services.[75]

---

[74] The country rankings for the 2016 WJP Rule of Law Index "are derived from more
than 110,000 households and 2,700 expert surveys in 113 countries and jurisdictions"
(World Justice Project 2016).
[75] The United States also ranks poorly on several related dimensions, such as "Criminal
system is impartial" and "Civil justice is free of discrimination" (World Justice Project
2016).

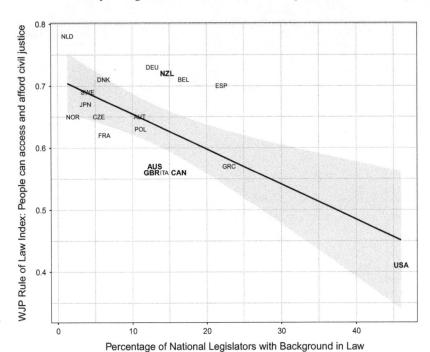

FIGURE 2.7 Relationship between share of lawyer-legislators in a national assembly and accessibility and affordability of the civil justice systems, by country.

Sources: Inter-Parliamentary Union Chronicle of Parliamentary Elections; World Justice Project (2016).

INCARCERATION RATES. We have so far discussed policy arenas that directly speak to the legal industry's profitability and market share. However, the power of lawyer-legislators could have either direct or spillover effects in other important policy areas.

One of these, we believe, concerns law and order issues. The United States is the Western world's leading jailer, with an incarceration rate that is nearly seven times the European average.[76] We suspect that the more concentrated power of the American legal profession may translate into greater use of incarceration. Indeed, several scholars have argued that self-regulation of the legal profession has led to the over-provision of legal resources to those at the top while largely ignoring the poor and middle class,[77] thus contributing to more and

---

[76] Walmsley (2013).

[77] Barton (2010); Hadfield (2008); Rhode (2004).

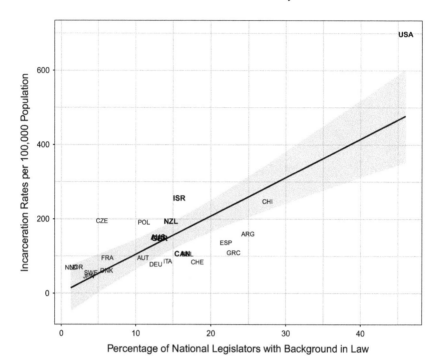

FIGURE 2.8 Relationship between share of lawyer-legislators in a national
assembly and incarceration rates, by country.
Sources: Inter-Parliamentary Union Chronicle of Parliamentary Elections; Walmsley
(2013).

more people being sent to jail. For example, one study finds that the
United States spends significantly less on indigent defense than other
advanced democracies.[78] Overall, lawyers and bar associations may tend
to favor legal solutions to social problems, relying more on criminalization as opposed to other remedies, thus driving up the incarceration
rate.[79]

Figure 2.8 plots countries' incarceration rates (per 100,000
residents) against the proportion of national legislature seats held by
lawyer-legislators. The figure shows a strongly positive trend, with

[78] Hadfield (2010), which estimates that the United States spends $86 on legal aid per case
compared to $148 in France, $322 in Germany, and $1,294 in England and Wales.

[79] For example, US drug policies have largely resorted to criminalization and incarceration
to deter usage, whereas other countries have treated addiction primarily as a public
health crisis.

more lawyer-legislators linked with a higher fraction of incarcerated citizens. The United States is again a notable outlier. (As reported in the appendix to this chapter, the relationship would still be positive – although slightly more modest in size – with the United States removed.) Overall, this analysis lends credence to the idea that lawyer-legislators push forward more law-and-order policies, while at the same time lessening the amount spent on defending low-income people.

ECONOMIC INEQUALITY. Going at least as far back as Theodore Roosevelt, critics of the organized bar have charged it with biasing the legal system in favor of the rich and corporations, in the process helping wealthy people avoid paying their fair share of taxes and circumvent regulations.[80] One example of this has been the ABA's public opposition to banking and financial regulation, such as the Bank Secrecy Act (1970) and Dodd-Frank Act (2010).[81] Such legislation was intended to prevent tax evasion and money laundering and impose fair accounting standards. The ABA's opposition, however, signaled an interest in higher-income business, possibly pointing to broader policy interests in wealth accumulation (and, accordingly, less interest in lessening income inequality). Spending on legal services in the United States today also remains highly concentrated among a small segment, with businesses and corporations accounting for 72 percent of total spending on legal services.[82] Given all of this, we suspect that more lawyer-legislators correlates with greater wealth inequality.

For this analysis, we use data on the top 1 percent's share of pre-tax income from the World Inequality Database.[83] (The top 1 percent income shares are among the standard measures of income inequality and are particularly sensitive to concentration among the wealthiest individuals.) Figure 2.9 plots the share of lawyers-legislators against top income shares and shows that the United States is again a noticeable outlier. While the nature of the relationship remains open to interpretation, the

---

[80] For example, as we noted above, the ABA's first public position was to oppose the Sixteenth Amendment to the US Constitution, which granted Congress the power to levy a national income tax.

[81] American Bar Association (2016a).

[82] Henderson (2015). These estimates are based on fees paid to lawyers and law firms. In addition to the fees paid to law firms, corporate spending on in-house legal departments has been estimated at $160 billion (Legal Executive Institute 2016).

[83] Facundo et al. (2016)

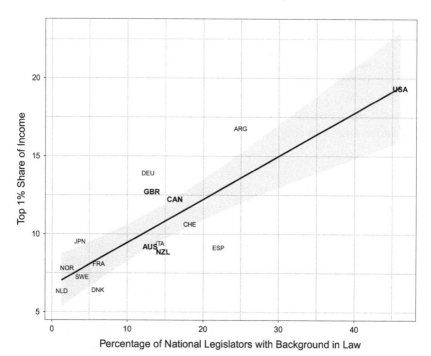

FIGURE 2.9 Relationship between share of lawyer-legislators in a national
assembly and top 1 percent income shares, by country.
Sources: The seat shares of lawyer-legislators are calculated from data on professional
backgrounds of members published by the Inter-Parliamentary Union Chronicle of
Parliamentary Elections. Top income shares are from Facundo et al. (2016).

overrepresentation of lawyers in national assemblies clearly goes hand in
hand with measures of inequality.[84]

Although we caution against interpreting this as a causal relationship,
it does offer an initial line of empirical evidence consistent with theoretical and anecdotal accounts that a legal system insufficiently aligned
with the public interest will exacerbate economic inequality. We suspect
that a self-regulated bar contributes to inequality but that it perhaps
has been more of a driver than an enabler. Indeed, as critics of corporate lawyering have long claimed, lawyers thwart efforts by democratic
institutions to counteract rising inequality,[85] an argument in line with the

[84] A surprising additional finding is that regressing top income shares on lawyers per capita
is actually not significant. This suggests the relationship derives from the structure of the
legal market and political power, not simply from the prevalence of lawyers.
[85] Bonica et al. (2013).

bar's historical role in blocking the development of a robust regulatory state.

In sum, these cross-national comparisons reveal that the US legal system is a consistent outlier on various dimensions, including in the share of lawyer-legislators in its national assembly. Despite the relative prosperity of the American legal profession, however, the United States lags behind the rest of the developed world in the ability of its citizens to access and afford legal services. Our findings here also build a case in support of the idea that the American bar has benefited, both economically and politically, from its position of political influence and has a strong interest in ensuring its continued capture of courts – themes that we pick up on in Chapter 3.

CONCLUSION

We conclude this discussion by emphasizing the strong – and comparatively exceptional – role that the legal profession has played in the development of law and politics in the United States. This influence has extended to three realms.

The first, most plainly, is that the legal profession forms the basis for America's political class, and it has done so since American independence. To give just one example of this intimate connection, Thomas Jefferson, who trained as a lawyer, wrote to a that the study of the law "qualifies a man to be useful to himself, to his neighbors, and to the public. It is the most certain stepping stone to preferment in the political line."[86] This close relationship between lawyers and the political class was, however, not limited to the eighteenth and nineteenth centuries. In his 1910 address to the ABA, future president Woodrow Wilson credited lawyers for the very crafting of the American system of government. In his words:

[l]awyers constructed the fabric of our state governments and of the government of the United States, and throughout the earlier periods of our national development presided over all the larger processes of politics. Our political conscience as a nation was embedded in our written fundamental law ... Public life was a lawyer's forum. Laymen lent their invaluable counsel, but lawyers guided and lawyers framed the law.[87]

[86] Jefferson (1790).
[87] Quoted in Wilson (1910, p. 606).

Even more recently, Justice Sandra Day O'Connor, introducing a volume celebrating America's lawyer-presidents, wrote that "[l]awyers have played a pivotal role in the shaping of the political and civic life of this country" and that "[l]egal education continues to provide the training grounds of significant numbers of our nation's leaders."[88] Thus, a theme that emerges – not just from these quotes but from US history itself – is that lawyers have been foundational to the development of American democratic institutions and norms.

The second is that the legal profession has had a significant influence on politics and policy more broadly. It has done so not just via its direct influence over the composition of the American political class but also via its role as one of the largest, richest, and politically powerful lobbying organizations. Both of these have worked in tandem to create a policy and legal environment highly favorable to the legal profession (and perhaps less favorable to the general public's interests). One example of this, as we have discussed, is the creation of the American administrative state. Indeed, the United States is unusual in having a weak government regulatory system, instead outsourcing much of its regulatory oversight to the legal profession and litigation (particularly tort, malpractice, and administrative litigation).[89] This shift places the legal profession at the heart of the American system of regulatory oversight and consumer protection. Other examples include the relationship between lawyer-legislators and (1) law firms being more profitable, (2) increased spending on litigation and attendant legal transactional costs, (3) poor access to justice and decreased affordability of legal services, (4) extreme incarceration rates, and (5) a legal market geared toward wealthy clients. The United States, with its extremely high share of lawyers in Congress and other political positions, is exceptional across all of these measures, lending to the idea that the outsized political power of the legal profession may very well help to explain some part of American exceptionalism across important issue areas.

A third theme, which we develop more fully in Chapter 3, is that the bar has always wrestled with the dueling conceptions of the practice of law as a civic-oriented profession versus as a business. The influential justice Harlan Fiske Stone was highly aware of this tension, once writing that "'[n]o tradition of our profession is more cherished by lawyers than

that of its leadership in public affairs" but that the bar's financial interest "has made the learned profession the obsequious servant of business,
and tainted it with the morals and manners of the market-place in its
most anti-social manifestations."[90] In the end, the legal profession has
embraced both roles – a trade organization concerned with the bottom
line as well as a civic-minded group with an elevated place within the
political class. These dual interests have meant that the legal profession
has shaped government into what we know today and also, at every
step along the way, has fought to make sure the government would not
encroach on the profession's financial well-being. As we argue in Chapter 3, much of this has been achieved through its capture of American
courts.

CHAPTER APPENDIX

In this appendix, we provide additional analyses exploring the relationship between the share of lawyer-legislators in national assemblies and
various outcomes that we explained in the chapter. These include (1)
law firm revenues per attorney, (2) litigation costs as a share of GDP, (3)
access to justice, (4) incarceration rates, and (5) income inequality. Specifically, we present the results from linear regression analyses in which the
outcomes are regressed onto the share of lawyer-legislators in a country's
national legislature. In addition, because common law countries could
differ from civil law countries in both the share of lawyer-legislators
and the various outcomes, we include a simple control for whether the
country is a common law country.

Table 2.2 presents these analyses. The coefficients for the lawyers' seat
share are standardized. (That is, a one-unit increase corresponds to a
change in seat shares of 0.087, or 8.7 out of every 100 seats.) For each of
the seven models, the estimated coefficient on lawyer seat shares is in the
expected direction and highly significant, meaning we can rule out that
each of these relationships is due to chance alone.

However, a challenge in interpretation is that the United States is
an extreme outlier across many dimensions. This makes determining
whether the political influence of the bar is what sets the United States
apart or whether it is yet another way in which the country is highly
unusual. We address this using the results presented in Table 2.3, which

[90] Stone (1934, p. 7).

TABLE 2.2 *Lawyers per capita, liability costs, incarceration rates, income shares, and access to justice as a function of lawyer-legislator seat shares and common law systems.*

	Lawyers per 1,000	Law Firm Revenue per Atty ($000's)	Liability Costs as % GDP	Incarceration Rates (per 100,000)	WJP Access to Justice	Top 1% Income Share
(Intercept)	1.60***	521.33***	0.59***	127.23***	0.65***	10.87***
	(0.18)	(75.77)	(0.05)	(19.74)	(0.02)	(0.69)
Lawyers Seat Share	0.55**	237.33**	0.16**	90.46***	−0.04*	2.73***
	(0.16)	(64.51)	(0.04)	(17.79)	(0.02)	(0.57)
Commonlaw System	1.01*	326.37	0.53***	79.93	−0.07	−0.20
	(0.36)	(168.89)	(0.10)	(40.42)	(0.04)	(1.34)
R^2	0.62	0.79	0.93	0.67	0.48	0.66
Num. obs.	22	12	11	23	20	17

***p < 0.001, **p < 0.01, *p < 0.05

Note: The effect for lawyers' seat share is standardized. A unit increase corresponds to a change in seat shares of 0.087, or 8.7 out of every 100 seats. Model is OLS, with standardized effects.

TABLE 2.3 Lawyers per capita, liability costs, incarceration rates, income shares, and access to justice as a function of lawyer-legislator seat shares and common law systems.

	Lawyers per 1,000	Law Firm Revenue per Atty ($000's)	Liability Costs as % GDP	Incarceration Rates (per 100,000)	WJP Access to Justice	Top 1% Income Share
(Intercept)	1.69***	445.09***	0.59***	117.52***	0.66***	10.90***
	(0.16)	(53.10)	(0.05)	(12.43)	(0.02)	(0.75)
Lawyers Seat Share	0.88***	24.25	0.14	37.28*	−0.02	2.78**
	(0.19)	(71.22)	(0.07)	(14.50)	(0.02)	(0.87)
Common Law System	1.12**	256.21*	0.53**	51.97	−0.06	−0.19
	(0.32)	(110.67)	(0.11)	(25.67)	(0.04)	(1.39)
R^2	0.69	0.42	0.84	0.39	0.20	0.45
Num. obs.	21	11	10	22	19	16

***$p < 0.001$, **$p < 0.01$, *$p < 0.05$

Note: The effect for lawyers' seat share is standardized. A unit increase corresponds to a change in seat shares of 0.087, or 8.7 out of every 100 seats. (Excludes the United States). Model is OLS, with standardized effects.

TABLE 2.4 *Top 100 congressional roll call votes (out of 28,430) ranked by improvement in model fit when including lawyer-legislator status.*

	Cong.	Bill	Title	Question	Description	LR	β_2	ABA
16	112	H.R. 5	Protecting Access to Healthcare Act	Adopt	Provide improved medical care by reducing the burden the liability system places on the health care delivery system.	13.4	−0.86 (0.23)	−
18	104	H.R. 956	Product Liability Reform	Conf. Report	Limits the ability for consumers to sue for punitive damages over product liability.	13.1	−0.82 (0.19)	−
20	112	H.R. 1229	Hastings of Florida, Part A Amendment, No. 11	Adopt	Reinstates awarding of attorney fees to plaintiffs in off-shore drilling cases.	12.7	2.13 (0.82)	+
24	102	H.R. 3371	Violent Crime Control and Law Enforcement Act	Passage	Landmark legislation on federal crime.	12.6	0.52 (0.16)	+
28	104	H.R. 956	Product Liability Reform	Veto Override	Failed override of Clinton veto of product liability reform bill.	11.93	−0.76 (0.19)	−

						LR	β_2	ABA
34	106	H.R. 775	Year 2000 Readiness and Responsibility Act	Limit liability for Y2k related failures.	Passage	11.4	−0.55 (0.19)	−
35	105	H.R. 5	Protecting Access to Healthcare Act	Limit medical malpractice liability.	Passage	11.4	−0.68 (0.22)	−
46	102	S. 1745	McConnell Amendment No. 1282	Enact limits on attorney fees.	Table	10.9	1.27 (0.36)	+
51	112	H.R. 5326	Austin Scott of Georgia Amendment	Eliminate funding for Legal Services Corporation	Adopt	10.6	−0.39 (0.17)	−
64	112	S. 2038	Grassley Amdt. No. 1493, Lobbying Disclosure Act of 1995.	Require disclosure of political intelligence activities; ban Congressional insider trading.	Adopt	10.2	−0.83 (0.27)	−
65	103	S. 349	Lobbying Disclosure Act	Vote voice to require the disclosure of the names of persons who provide funding for lobbying activities.	Motion	9.8	0.63 (0.15)	−

Note: The column labeled *LR* reports the likelihood ratio statistic. The column labeled β_2 reports the estimated coefficients and standard errors (in parentheses) of the lawyer-specific effects. The column labeled *ABA* indicates the implied directionality based on the ABA's stated legislative priorities.
Source: DW-NOMINATE, Biographical Directory of the United States Congress.

estimate the same set of regressions but with the United States excluded. At least with respect to income concentration and incarceration rates, the estimated coefficients on the share of the national assembly held by lawyer-legislators remain significant. Substantively, this indicates that the relationship between lawyer-legislators' political power and these outcomes is more general, not just one driven exclusively by the United States' outlier status.

3

The Bar, Self-Regulation, and Judicial Capture

"A good lawyer knows the law. A great lawyer knows the judge."

Legal saying

In 2015, Global Witness, a London-based nonprofit with the goal of exposing international corruption, set out to investigate the role of US law firms in aiding international money laundering. Posing as a representative of a corrupt West African government official, an undercover journalist set up meetings with various New York law firm partners to ask for their help with money laundering and other unsavory practices. In a series of undercover interviews, lawyers from twelve law firms – including one who was then serving as the president of the American Bar Association (ABA) – candidly offered advice on how to set up anonymously owned companies or trusts to hide assets.[1]

The language used by the lawyers in advising the fake potential "client" illustrates the themes we explore in this chapter. One partner at one law firm explained, "They don't send the lawyers to jail, because we run the country." Lawyers, he said, are "still members of a privileged, privilege [sic] class in this country." The same lawyer continued that "[lawyers] make the laws, and when we do so, we make them in a way that is advantageous to the lawyers."[2] To emphasize his point, he boasted that he went to law school with "half" the judges on the New York state bench and knew many others from bar association events; judges may

---

[1] Global Witness (2016). Thirteen lawyers – all partners at their law firms – were contacted. Only one refused to provide advice.

[2] Kroft (2016).

not throw a case, he said, but they would "bend over backwards to be courteous."[3] The undercover interviews led to a review of the transcripts by respected ethics experts; despite finding a willingness to "assist corrupt officials to profit from betrayals of public trust," the report concluded that no lawyer had violated any laws or ethical codes.[4]

The Global Witness investigation – and the statements of the lawyers involved – highlights an important tension that we explore in this chapter. On the one hand, the bar takes on a public calling, with lawyers occupying the highest offices in the land – the ones who, in the words of the above mentioned attorney, "run the country." On the other hand, the example shows that lawyers, like other professionals, pursue the maximization of profits. How has the bar navigated this tension? Why and how has a profession that has made itself so essential to the political process remained so free from government oversight? After all, despite its political influence, the legal profession remains self-regulated, unusual for an industry so large and expansive. Even in such an egregious example as the Global Witness investigation, the lawyers involved went unpunished and, as of our writing, remain key players in the elite New York corporate law scene.

This chapter explores how the bar has used its special place within American politics to further its own interests – a key step in building our judicial tug-of-war framework. Indeed, one of the ways the legal profession has exercised power, we argue, is via a strong and intimate relationship with one especially important branch of government, the judiciary. As we explain, the rapid professionalized nature of the judiciary has meant that lawyers and judges increasingly began to be drawn from the same environment and had the same training; these close professional networks led to overlap in professional and business interests. These strong bonds – and the standardization of law school training – meant that the judiciary came to be seen by elite lawyers as among the most prestigious of legal career paths. For lawyers, the judiciary became the branch of government that was intellectually, spiritually, and professionally "theirs."

The close connection between the judiciary and the legal profession has meant that the interests of judges and the interests of the bar often overlap, creating strong incentives for both to guard the relationship. For the legal profession, to the extent that any government oversight

---

[3] Quoted in Klein (2014).
[4] Leubsdorf and Simon (2015).

must exist, lawyers prefer to entrust it to their elite colleagues – judges. Thus, as we describe in this chapter, the judiciary is the only governmental entity across many American jurisdictions that has the authority to regulate the legal profession. As for judges, their affinity with the legal profession means that they are more inclined to rule in favor of the legal profession, to promote the legal profession's interests, and to protect the legal profession against government regulation and oversight. This promotes bias in favor of the legal profession in court rulings, a phenomenon documented by legal scholars.[5] Thus, the legal profession has collectively come to exercise substantial control over the nature and membership of the judiciary and, in turn, judges are one of the few state actors that have regulatory control over the bar.

This intimate, close relationship between the bar and the judiciary – which we refer to as the *captured judiciary* – is one of the major themes of this book and serves to underscore the power that the legal profession has in the judicial tug of war. However, our theory of a captured judiciary departs in nature and extent from that of "bureaucratic capture" – or capture of regulatory agencies by industries that are themselves the targets of regulation. First and most importantly, the captured judiciary is by definition absolute in its overlapping professional membership: All judges are lawyers. This overlapping membership brings together the legal establishment's and the judiciary's professional interests in a way unlike any other kind of bureaucratic capture. Second, this capture represents a rare and unique instance of *constitutional* capture: Unlike other instances of bureaucratic capture, in which a single agency has been captured, judicial capture involves an entire branch of government. Third, despite the perfect overlap in membership (and thus professional capture), lawyers must deal with the competing interests of politicians in the course of judicial selection. Thus, although the capture of the judiciary is *professionally* complete, it is not *ideologically* complete.

The argument has broader implications for the judicial tug of war that we more formally introduce in Chapter 4. Specifically, the "captured" nature of the judiciary means that the bar has a strong interest in cultivating and promoting judges whose professional and political tendencies resemble the bar as a whole; after all, judges who are like-minded will be more favorable in terms of proposed regulation and oversight, not to mention rulings. Accordingly, the bar, over time, has developed a strong interest in the political leanings and policy goals of the

5 Barton (2010).

judiciary – evidenced by the bar's strong involvement in judicial selection, in promulgating judicial codes of conduct, and in issuing judicial qualification ratings. This sets the stage for our subsequent chapters, in which we investigate the nature of the bar's stake in its relationship to the judiciary and how it creates tension between the bar and political actors. As we explain, these interests cast the composition of the judiciary as a tense relationship between the bar and politicians who seek to shape the "captured" judiciary as best they can.

We organize this chapter as follows. First, we explore how the bar historically used the justification of quality and consumer protection to enact barriers on who could practice law; conveniently, these rules effectively insulated the legal profession from competition. Over time, this led to a norm of self-regulation, which helped the bar to police its boundaries more effectively. Next, we unpack more carefully the important question of why this self-regulation persists over time. The answer to this question leads us to the important idea of the "captured judiciary." Specifically, we explain how, to the extent that government oversight over the legal profession exists, it happens almost exclusively via the courts. We show this by documenting how courts frequently "rubber stamp" bar association proposals, grant immunity to bar associations, and broadly rule in favor of lawyers and bar interests.[6] Lastly, as a key part of this symbiotic relationship, we discuss the ways in which lawyers strongly influence the composition and behavior of judges, doing so via involvement in the selection process and also by having created a monopoly over the judicial candidate pool. This sets the stage for a broader theory about ideology in judicial selection – and the judicial tug of war between the bar and political elites – which we take up in Chapter 4.

THE IMPORTANCE OF A SELF-REGULATED BAR

The legal profession's history of self-regulation has been key in how and why it has come to capture the judiciary. Yet this history is complex. As we discussed in Chapter 2, the early legal profession was one that relied on a mix of apprenticeships and elite personal and business connections. By the early twentieth century, however, the profession was in crisis. The "old boy" network combined with an absence of professional and ethical

---

[6] For more on this last point, see Barton (2010).

standards created an image of a disreputable, corrupt profession, one driven by venality and the pursuit of wealthy clients. This sentiment of a "discipline in decline" was echoed strongly in a 1905 address at Harvard College by Justice Louis Brandeis:

[T]he lawyer does not hold as high a position with the people as he held seventy-five or indeed fifty years ago; but the reason is not lack of opportunity. It is this: Instead of holding a position of independence, between the wealthy and the people, prepared to curb the excesses of either, able lawyers have, to a large extent, allowed themselves to become adjuncts of great corporations and have neglected the obligation to use their powers for the protection of the people. We hear much of the "corporation lawyer," and far too little of the "people's lawyer."[7]

Thus, the legal profession at the turn of the twentieth century faced something of a public relations dilemma: It was greeted by skepticism and wariness by the public and, increasingly so, criticized on the political stage.[8] These crises threatened to undermine not just the profession's economic interests but also its political influence.

The bar sought to remedy this via self-regulation – specifically by drafting rules governing professional standards, bringing order to how lawyers were educated, and formalizing the expectations of lawyerly conduct. According to one account, these were sold internally and to the public as a way to help the profession live up to its higher public calling.[9] Indeed, the 1908 ABA Canons of Ethics were predicated on the belief that lawyers – "as guardians of the law" – were vital to the preservation of a free and democratic society.[10] However, instead of reining in the excesses of elite lawyers, these canons mostly focused on restricting entry into the profession by making it more difficult and more costly to become a lawyer. In turn, restricting the supply of lawyers allowed the

---

[7] Brandeis (1914, p. 321).

[8] For example, in his commencement speech at Harvard University, then-president Theodore Roosevelt criticized members of the bar who worked to undermine the public interest, stating that "many of the most influential and most highly remunerated members of the Bar in every centre of wealth make it their special task to work out bold and ingenious schemes by which their very wealthy clients, individual or corporate, can evade the laws" (Roosevelt 1906, p. 646).

[9] Altman (2002). For example, a 1906 ABA committee report on the practicability of adopting a code of professional ethics exalted the profession as a pillar of the republic noting that "Our profession is necessarily the keystone of the republican arch of government ... [T]he future of the republic depends upon our maintenance of the shrine of justice pure and unsullied" (American Bar Association Committee on Code of Professional Ethics 1907, p. 681).

[10] American Bar Association (1908).

profession to charge more for services, thereby protecting fees and profits while propping up the profession's prestige.

Mechanisms of Self-Regulation

This move toward self-serving self-regulation continued into the twentieth century and has persisted to the present day,[11] even as other white-collar professions (such as medicine) have become increasingly regulated.

How has the legal profession benefited from self-regulation? We isolate three areas: (1) self-policing of industry boundaries, (2) barriers to competition, and (3) self-policing of attorney misconduct. These are in addition to influencing policy arenas in ways that benefit lawyers, which we discussed in depth in Chapter 2. All of these have worked together to increase the profitability and prestige of the profession. In addition, as we note in later discussions, these mechanisms also help explain why and how the legal industry has sought to "capture" the judiciary.[12]

SELF-POLICING OF INDUSTRY BOUNDARIES. Regulating entry into the legal profession has been one of the most important goals and outcomes of a self-regulated bar. As Barton notes "[f]rom its inception the ABA pilloried what it considered to be the undesirable element in the bar and proposed a tightening of bar admission standards because low admission standards had contributed to 'extraordinary numbers' of the 'ignorant' and 'unprincipled' becoming lawyers."[13] However, movements toward tightening standards are also self-serving: Decreasing the numbers of those who could become lawyers (or practice law) not only allowed the bar control over what kinds of people could enter the profession but also reduced the supply of legal professionals, allowing lawyers to charge more for their services.[14]

[11] Some have noted some significant changes starting in the 1970s and 1980s. See, for example, Abel (1986), which notes, among other things, the increasingly variegated nature of the legal profession and its changing professional structure.

[12] See also Wald (2010), Barton (2010), (Barton 2003), Moliterno (2012), and Rhode (2015) for additional details on the regulatory structure of the legal profession.

[13] Barton (2010, p. 114). This has also meant that the bar – by virtue of its professional capture of the judiciary – could also dictate who could become a judge.

[14] Because of this, entry regulation is unsurprisingly a hallmark of regulatory capture. As Stigler (1971, p. 5) argues, "every industry or occupation that has enough political power to utilize the state will seek to control entry."

Oftentimes, the restrictions on bar admission were closely tied to the standardization of educational requirements. In a 1891 report, the ABA made a series of recommendations that still dictate the contours of legal training today.[15] These included rules on entry into law schools, law school curriculum, and even the resources that universities needed to devote to their law programs – rules that are still in place today. Such standards have been justified on the grounds of preventing unqualified individuals from practicing law, but they have also had the benefit of limiting the supply of lawyers. The population-to-lawyer ratio was almost exactly the same in 1950 as it was in 1900, despite a half-century of economic growth.[16] These restrictions on entry into the profession also did little to address concerns about high-paid lawyers working primarily to serve the interests of wealthy individuals and corporations.

The legal profession has found other ways to regulate entry into the profession. Among the most important tactic has been "integrated bars," under which practicing attorneys in a state must belong to that state's bar association. This practice, which was upheld by the US Supreme Court in 1961,[17] means that a state bar membership (including paying dues) is legally required to practice law. As of this writing, slightly more than half of all states have made state bar membership a requirement for practicing law.[18] Such integrated bars bestow two advantages. First, mandatory memberships increase the bar's membership and allow it to collect more dues – which in turn allows the bar to spend more money on lobbying and other organizational activities. Second, having more members makes it easier for bar associations to galvanize support from the "rank and file," creating a ready-made constituency for bar services and lobbying efforts.[19]

BARRIERS TO COMPETITION. A second broad area of self-regulation tactics discouraged lawyers from competing with one another. These operate under the rubric of protecting consumers against predatory and

---

[15] Barton (2010, p. 114).
[16] See Abel (1986, p. 7), who further notes that "[a]s late as 1970, this ratio, which had risen in the early years of the century, still had not fallen back to the level of 1890."
[17] *Lathrop v. Donohue*, 367 U.S. 820 (1961).
[18] Carlton et al. (2015).
[19] We give some examples of how state and national bar associations have galvanized their rank-and-file memberships in Chapter 7, in which we discuss the bar's attempts to oppose judicial reform efforts.

unqualified lawyering but also restrict competition in the legal market, thus protecting existing legal practices and industry profits.

The first of this type of self-regulation has been minimum fee schedules, which establish standardized minimum fees for basic services and drive up prices; many of these rules and codes also ironically specify that lawyers ought to determine their own fees, without being pressured by clients to lower costs.[20] The second of these anticompetitive measures define the practice of "law" broadly, making the practice of law by non-lawyers or out-of-state lawyers illegal. This has had the effect of not only increasing the scope of duties that can ostensibly be performed *only* by lawyers but also artificially limiting the supply of individuals who can provide these services.[21]

The third of these have been regulations on advertising for legal services. Such codes were originally proposed by the ABA as a way to limit frivolous lawsuits and prevent bad actors from tarnishing lawyers' reputations.[22] Since their peak in the 1960s, these restrictions have been relaxed in many states following the US Supreme Court ruling in *Bates v. State Bar of Arizona*,[23] but advertising by lawyers remains subject to state codes of conduct. From the perspective of the bar, however, these ostensibly consumer friendly restrictions have the same effect as the others – to reduce competition in legal services and to maintain higher prices.

POLICING ATTORNEY MISCONDUCT. A third broad area of self-regulation concerns attorney misconduct. Absent any external regulatory body, the ABA and state bar associations often monitor attorney misconduct themselves and without public input.[24] In other instances,

---

[20] See the ABA's current Model Rules of Professional Conduct, which give an overview of the criteria that lawyers should keep in mind when establishing fees (e.g., "the time and labor required," etc.), instructing lawyers to consider "the fee customarily charged in the locality for similar legal services" (American Bar Association 2018, Rule 1.5). Earlier versions of these ethical codes were more explicit that lawyers should consider minimum fees recommended by the bar. For example, the original 1908 Canons called explicitly for lawyers to consider "the customary charges of the Bar for similar services" (American Bar Association, 1908, Canon 12).

[21] With the exception of Washington, DC, moreover, nonlawyers in all fifty states are not permitted to own shares in law firms. These restrictions, as set out in Model Rule 5.4, are justified by the ABA as essential to protect the "core values" of the profession (American Bar Association 2018, Rule 5.4).

[22] These advertising standards were first outlined in the original 1908 Canons (American Bar Association 1908).

[23] 433 U.S. 350 (1977) (upholding the ability of lawyers to advertise for their services because lawyers' advertising was commercial speech).

[24] Maute (2008); Rhode (1981, 2015); Barton (2010).

the oversight is provided by state judges. However, judges – themselves once (or still) members of state or local bars – have proved extremely deferential to the interests of attorneys over those of clients or defendants. This environment has made claiming attorney misconduct extremely challenging for consumers, no matter how badly lawyers have misbehaved.

In making this point, Bruce Shapiro and others have cited one particularly notorious example – instances where attorneys have fallen asleep during criminal trials, including during murder (and death penalty) cases. Defendants challenging convictions on the grounds of "ineffective assistance of counsel" (due to their sleeping attorneys) actually lose these cases at high rates – thus suggesting that attorney misconduct must be so egregious so as to render the concept meaningless. As one judge wrote in rejecting such a claim, "The Constitution says that everyone is entitled to an attorney of their choice. But the Constitution does not say that the lawyer has to be awake."[25] While this represents an extreme example of Barton's "lawyer-judge bias" – and no doubt many judges would not be as forgiving of such misconduct – it does speak to the judiciary's routine deference to attorneys when it comes to issues of unprofessional behavior and misconduct.

Societal Consequences of a Self-Regulated Bar

The ABA and other lawyers' groups have long argued that self-regulation of the legal profession (as opposed to regulation by the government) is in the public's best interest, but there are reasons to think that this may not be an accurate representation, both in terms of societal costs and also in terms of how the public views the bar and the legal profession.

DIVERSITY CONCERNS. First, ample evidence suggests that women and minorities bear some costs associated with this self-regulation. For much of American history, these groups were intentionally barred from entering the legal profession and thus from much of political life (including from the judiciary). Women, for example, could not attend most law schools until the 1950s and 1960s, and most of these early cohorts had extremely few women. Because a law school degree was a necessary prerequisite to practice law (per the ABA), this educational barrier had the effect

[25] Shapiro (1997).

of excluding women from the legal profession. African Americans were barred by *de jure* segregation from attending most flagship law schools throughout the South. In addition, the ABA's move toward accreditation had the effect of closing three historically black law schools – Frelinghuysen in Washington, DC, Virginia Union Law School in Richmond, and Simmons Law School in Kentucky.[26] In sum, as the legal historian Lawrence Friedman has explained, the ABA originated as a "club for white males" with "a rather shameful history of snobbery and bias."[27]

If a legal background is advantageous for pursuing a career in politics – as we discussed in Chapter 2 – then being excluded from the legal profession has put female politicians at a disadvantage. This can be seen in Figure 3.1, which tracks the percentage who are women among (1) law students enrolled in ABA-accredited law schools, (2) federal judges, and (3) members of Congress. We report two separate trend lines for Congress, one for lawyers and another for nonlawyers. Comparing the lag in women as a share of members of Congress among those with law degrees (versus those without) is especially informative. Prior to the 1970s, practically all lawyer-legislators were men. Not until the mid-1990s did the share of members of Congress with law degrees who were women exceed 5 percent, a share that had been reached among members without law degrees in the 1930s. The explanation for this is simple. Prior to the 1970s, as the figure shows, women were largely excluded from the legal profession, resulting in an approximate twenty-year lag between graduating from law school and being elected to Congress. We see a similar lag for federal judges, for whom a law degree is a prerequisite. In other words, the gatekeeping power exercised by the ABA and state bars has had significant negative consequences for the ability of women and minorities to enter into public service.[28]

---

[26] Shepherd (2003); Abel (1986). An infamous example occurred in 1912 when the ABA accidentally admitted three African American lawyers. When the bar leadership became aware, the chair of the ABA membership committee raised the "question of keeping pure the Anglo-Saxon race" (quoted in Auerbach 1977, p. 66). Although the members ultimately voted to allow the three applicants to retain their membership status, all future applicants were required to self-report their racial and ethnic identity, resulting in nonwhite applicants being effectively screened from membership for another half-century.

[27] Friedman (1985, pp. 245–246). Barkan writes that the "massive market control" of ABA helped achieve the goal of ensuring that "its ranks would remain free of the non-elite members of society."

[28] See Robbins and Bannon (2019) for a detailed analysis of diversity in state courts, including a discussion of the importance of career pipelines in diversifying the judiciary.

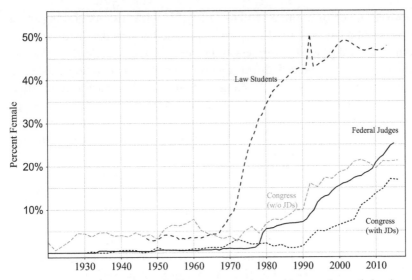

FIGURE 3.1 Historical trends for women as share of law students, federal judges, and lawyer and nonlawyer legislators in Congress.
Sources: American Bar Association; Biographical Directory of the United States Congress; Federal Judiciary Center.

ACCESS TO JUSTICE AND CONSUMER SATISFACTION. The bar's history of self-regulation has also led to criticisms that the bar is too concerned with profiteering and not with serving less advantaged segments of society (a topic we discussed in Chapter 2). The legal scholar Deborah Rhode, for example, has linked self-regulation to the underprovision of legal services for the poor and middle class.[29] Others have argued that the legal market is wracked by market inefficiencies.[30] With costly self-imposed barriers to entry, and with law firms mostly serving wealthy clients, the market for affordable legal services has been neglected.

Perhaps as a downstream consequence, the legal profession has long generated considerable consumer and public dissatisfaction. A study commissioned by the ABA in 2002 found that only 19 percent of consumers surveyed were "very" or "extremely" confident in the legal profession.[31] In addition, a surprising share believed lawyers "contribute

[29] See Rhode (2004). See also Barton (2010); Hadfield (2008).
[30] Crandall, Maheshri, and Winston (2011); Hadfield (2008); Moliterno (2012).
[31] American Bar Association (1999).

not very much or nothing at all to society,"[32] with lawyers ranking at the bottom of a list of trusted professions.[33] The bar has also made enemies out of several powerful business and professional groups.[34] Even lawyers themselves have voiced dissatisfaction with bar associations. A 2012 survey conducted by the Washington State Bar Association found that members rated their satisfaction with the state bar a mediocre average of 3.1 on a 5-point scale,[35] while another survey of California attorneys found that 60 percent of respondents believed the $410 annual attorney licensing fee was too high.[36]

SELF-REGULATION AND CAPTURE OF THE JUDICIARY

All of these patterns raise two key questions. Why does a self-regulated bar persist? And, given the unpopular nature of the self-regulated bar, why has it been tolerated by those in positions of power?

A useful framework for understanding these questions is what the scholarly literature refers to as "regulatory capture." Scholars in this literature have argued that government agencies can be manipulated to serve the interests of those industries that are the targets of oversight.[37] As the economists Laffont and Tirole explain, "[i]nterest groups try to capture government decision-making because it affects the industry and consumers' welfare."[38] Industries, in other words, generally have strong incentives to try to influence the regulatory agencies that exercise oversight over them; and once a government agency is captured by the very industry it is supposed to be regulating, it begins a cycle that becomes very difficult, though not impossible, to break. This behavior taken to its extreme yields a fully self-regulated industry – one that relies on an

---

[32] Pew Research Center (2013).
[33] Gallup (2015).
[34] The American Medical Association is perhaps the most committed adversary of a self-regulated bar, owing to its conflicts over medical malpractice issues. In addition, some prominent critics of the bar's self-regulation come from conservative organizations better known for fighting against excessive government regulations. Through its Institute for Legal Reform, the US Chamber of Commerce has advocated for numerous regulations on the legal profession. See, e.g., www.instituteforlegalreform .com/resource/the-ficala-fix-for-litigation-abuse and www.bna.com/eyes-trump-probiz -n57982084448/.
[35] *The Washington State Bar Association Membership Study 2012* (2012)
[36] *Survey of Members of The State Bar of California, 2011* (n.d.).
[37] Stigler (1971).
[38] Laffont and Tirole (1991, p. 1090).

entity comprised of its own members to set and enforce rules, with no independent or external authority overseeing the regulation.[39]

The legal profession is often seen as a textbook example of a self-regulated industry. However, we believe that the legal profession is different from other industries in several respects, the most important of which is in its total professional capture over a key set of governmental actors: *judges*.[40] To the extent lawyers can be said to be externally regulated, it is only by judges whose authority is constitutionally based and protected by separation-of-powers guarantees. This serves to grant the chief regulators of the legal industry – all of whom, as judges, are themselves members of the legal profession – veto power over legislation passed by state legislatures or ballot measures. In this respect, the bar's relationship with the courts represents a truly exceptional case of *professional capture* – both as a matter of degree and with regards to the entity that has been captured. This is both different and also deeper than other kinds of regulatory capture. Indeed, because lawyers have professionally captured an entire branch of government, we refer to this professional capture as *constitutional capture*.

Contrasting the legal industry with other regulated industries illustrates this key difference. The finance, oil, and airline industries, for example, are regulated by one or more administrative agencies (the Securities Exchange Commission, the Department of the Interior, or the Federal Aviation Administration, respectively). These agencies, however, are not exclusively staffed by members of the regulated industry. Even membership on the Federal Reserve Board of Governors – perhaps the closest analogue to the legal profession's regulatory structure – stipulates that appointees must yield a "fair representation of the financial, agricultural, industrial, and commercial interests and geographical divisions of

---

[39] Kay and Vickers (1988, pp. 310–312). Importantly, one of the most significant rewards of this kind of "regulatory capture" is the power to control *entry* into an industry. As Stigler (1971, p. 5) argues, "every industry or occupation that has enough political power to utilize the state will seek to control entry."

[40] There is an extensive literature in law and economics on the self-regulation of the legal market. For an overview of this literature, see Stephen and Love (2000). For a more detailed overview of self-regulation and its interaction with the judiciary, see Barton (2010). We discuss this in further depth below. Hadfield (2008) has argued that by claiming to pursue both the public good and their economic self-interest, "lawyers use their legitimately unique roles in political and democratic fields to illegitimately protect the production and distribution of a fundamental, fundamentally economic, service." A key point in her argument is that lawyers provide a *unique role in the political and democratic fields* (to use her language), with a particularly strong presence in the courts.

the country."[41] In fact, as of 2017, the bar was better represented than the banks on the Federal Board of Governors.[42]

Table 3.1 illustrates the broader dynamic, with the legal profession juxtaposed against two other comparable white-collar professions: medicine and finance. In contrast to the legal profession, both the medical and the financial industries are either heavily regulated (as is the case with the medical profession) or largely open to entry (banking and finance). Neither of these professions has enjoyed the sort of capture enjoyed by the legal profession and neither can reap the benefits of having the ultimate governmental oversight (to the extent that it exists) provided by a non-reviewable branch of government comprised entirely of its own members. In other words, no other profession or industry enjoys anything comparable to constitutional capture.

As the table shows, the legal profession stands apart from both other industries in terms of favorable regulation and interpretation. Importantly, the regulation of other industries is subject to judicial review; but, for lawyers, the only review happens with members of their own profession – that is, judges.

These advantages are a key reason why bar associations are keen to keep regulation in the hands of state and federal courts – that is, to maintain constitutional capture. In an online statement on the "Independence of the Legal Profession," the ABA reaffirmed its belief that

the primary regulation and oversight of the legal profession should continue to be vested in the court of highest appellate authority of the state in which the attorney is licensed, not federal agencies or Congress, and that the courts are in the best position to fulfill that important function. Therefore, the ABA opposes federal legislation or rules that would undermine traditional state court regulation of lawyers.[43]

Prominent bar leaders have echoed the sentiment that regulation of the legal profession should rest in the courts. For example, in the wake of the Enron scandal (in which lawyers were heavily implicated), a former chairman of the ABA Standing Committee on Ethics and Professional Responsibility wrote, "The very idea of the Senate of the United States enacting or directing others to enact rules of professional responsibility for lawyers should be enough to cause collective professional indigestion

---

[41] 12 U.S. Code § 241.
[42] As of 2017, three out of four members – Janet Yellen, Randall Quarles, and Jerome Powell – have law degrees.
[43] American Bar Association (2016a).

TABLE 3.1 *Regulatory oversight across the legal, medical, and banking and finance industries.*

	Legal Profession	Medical Profession	Banking and Finance
Regulatory entity	State supreme courts, federal courts, bar associations.	Public–private partnership between state medical boards and numerous government agencies (e.g., NIH, CMS, and DHHS).	Board of Governors of the Federal Reserve, FDIC, OCC, CFTC, CFPB, SEC, and other agencies.
Restrictions on who can serve in a regulatory capacity.	Yes. Judges and bar associations claim exclusive power to regulate the legal profession. Professional codes of conduct prevent lawyers from being held accountable to nonlawyers.	Some roles require a medical degree.	Yes. Regulators must meet certain restrictions on conflicts of interest to serve in most agencies.
Source of regulatory authority	Judiciary claims inherent and exclusive power to regulate the legal profession. Judicial authority is constitutionally based.	Statutory and executive.	Statutory and executive.
Civil/Professional Liability and Misconduct			
Discipline	Bar associations.	State medical boards.	SEC and state agencies.
Liability/torts	Yes, but evidentiary standard high and successful malpractice lawsuits rare. Bar associations, judges, and prosecutors shielded from liability by sovereign immunity.	Yes. Physicians frequently sued for malpractice. Evidentiary standards determined by community standards and courts.	Banks have exposure to class action suits and investor lawsuits.

TABLE 3.1 *(continued)*

	Legal Profession	Medical Profession	Banking and Finance
Market Regulation			
Restrictions on entry	Yes.	Yes.	Few restrictions on entry.
Ownership restrictions	Yes, only lawyers can own equity in law firms in most states.[a]	No.	No.
Fee/payment structure	Determined by lawyers and judges.	Yes. Medicare and Medicaid payments are set by government.	No.
Antitrust regulations	State bar associations have an effective monopoly over the practice of law and have exempted the legal industry from antitrust violations.	Medical boards control who can practice law. Profession is subject to outside competition.	Yes.
External Oversight of Regulatory Agencies			
Legislative	No.	Yes.	Yes.
Executive	No.	Yes.	Yes.
Judicial review	Yes, but rare and not performed by individuals outside the profession. Federal courts have developed legal doctrines that discourage review of state regulations.	Yes.	Yes.
Rulemaking Autonomy			
Regulatory entity can veto legislation	Yes.	No.	No.
Open to public comment	No.	Yes.	Yes.

Note: The table briefly details how elements of each industry's regulatory structure compares across several areas. FDIC: Federal Deposit Insurance Corporation; OCC: Office of the Comptroller of the Currency; CTTC: Commodity Futures Trading Commission; CFPB: Consumer Finance Protection Bureau; SEC: Securities and Exchange Commission.
[a] DC is the only exception

and indignation." He further cautioned, "[T]here is no greater threat to lawyer independence than having anyone other than courts establish the lawyer rules for practice."[44] In sum, according to lawyers, to the extent that the legal profession should be regulated, it should be regulated by lawyers themselves *via the courts.*

HOW JUDGES REGULATE LAWYERS

How do judges regulate the legal profession? In what follows, we discuss four interrelated pathways via which judges "regulate" lawyers: (1) judges acting as "rubber stamps" for bar recommendations, (2) evidence of what Barton labels the "lawyer-judge bias" in judges' rulings, (3) judges exempting lawyers from legislative oversight, and (4) judicial shielding of lawyers from antitrust laws. The legal profession gains power and autonomy by exercising professional "capture" of the judiciary.

Judges As the Bar's "Rubber Stamps"

As we noted here and also in Chapter 2, the bar self-regulates extensively through codes of professional conduct, minimum attorney's fees, bar dues, and its jurisdiction over the practice of law. In most states, however, any such changes to professional conduct codes *must be accepted by state supreme courts*, historically considered the appropriate locus of such oversight.[45] Other parties – including state legislatures – are excluded from the process, leaving state bars largely without meaningful oversight from outside the legal profession. This has led, as some have charged, to a regulatory structure that places the legal profession's interests ahead of their own.[46] It has, moreover, led to a structure whereby state courts accept bar association's recommendations mostly "as is."

To give a concrete example, Arkansas is typical in that proposed changes to the state bar must be approved by the state supreme court, which typically adopts such changes with little modification. This includes changes to the code of judicial conduct. For instance, in 2007, the ABA revised its national judicial code of conduct.[47] The Arkansas

---

[44] Fox (2004, p. 864).

[45] See Barton (2010), Chapters 5 and 6, for more on state courts' loose regulation of the legal profession.

[46] Barton (2010, p. 105).

[47] American Bar Association and Center for Professional Responsibility (2007).

Supreme Court called on the Arkansas Bar Association to form a task force to consider the adoption of these modifications; the task force was composed entirely of lawyers and judges.[48] (The chair of the task force was a University of Arkansas law professor who in 2016 was named Chief Justice of Arkansas's Supreme Court as an interim replacement.[49]) Before proceeding, the task force submitted its recommendations to the state bar's House of Delegates for a vote; this was unanimously approved. The Bar Association then filed a petition with the Arkansas Supreme Court to adopt the committee's recommendations, which it did verbatim "with only the deletion of one sentence from a comment."[50] Although public commentary was permitted, the entire process was driven exclusively by lawyers from a small and elite circle.

The protocol followed by the Arkansas Supreme Court is similar to those followed by other state supreme courts, but it is quite at odds with the process used by state and federal regulatory agencies. With most independent agencies, consideration of proposed rules is subject to a period of "notice and comment," whereby members of the public can provide comments and suggestions; regulators are further constrained by statutory laws, administrative procedures, executive orders, legislative oversight, and, ultimately, judicial review. In addition, agency regulators are typically appointed by elected officials or elected by voters and are not exclusively drawn from the industry they are charged with regulating, as judges are. Moreover, regulators can rely on agency staff and resources in performing their regulatory functions. By contrast, state supreme courts have law clerks but do not have a separate pool of experts from which to draw advice. This results in a process largely deferential to state bars.

Pro-Bar Association Bias in the Courts

The second way that judges favor the legal profession is by taking pro-lawyer positions in litigation involving the legal profession. A persuasive explanation behind this is what the legal scholar Benjamin Barton refers to as "lawyer-judge bias."[51] The idea behind this bias is straightforward

---

[48] Brill (2009). See also *In re Arkansas Bar Association Petition to Amend Code of Judicial Conduct*, 374 Ark. Appx. 399 (2008).

[49] This was Howard W. Brill. See Brill (2009).

[50] Brill (2009, p. 3). See also *In re Arkansas Bar Association Petition to Amend Code of Judicial Conduct*, No. 08-924 (2009).

[51] Barton (2010). Barton (2010) also has an excellent overview of the history of this bias and its implications in modern-day litigation and policy.

(and builds on earlier observations): All judges are lawyers by training, and they have practiced and lived their lives as lawyers. It would make sense that they see things from a lawyer's perspective and that this deep-rooted affinity would ultimately influence their rulings, making them inclined to favor the legal profession's position – including positions taken by bar associations.[52] In other words, judges and lawyers "naturally work together to forward joint interests" – and this extends to the courtroom.[53]

How prevalent is this pro-lawyer bias? To investigate, we consider lawsuits against bar associations. If a bias exist, we would expect to see bar associations win more cases than other types of defendants.[54] To examine this, we use the Federal Judicial Center's Integrated Courts Database, which includes detailed information on hundreds of thousands of civil and criminal federal court cases and their outcomes, spanning from 1970 to the present.[55] We identified the set of cases in which a bar association appeared as a named party.[56] We then focused on those instances where a bar association was named as a defendant (as opposed to a plaintiff) and went to trial and received a judgment in federal district court (as opposed to cases that were dismissed or settled out of court),[57] which totaled 420 of the cases.

If a pro-bar association bias does exist, we would expect bar associations to prevail at much higher rates than ordinary defendants. This is exactly what we find: In only 2 of the 420 cases did the district courts rule against a bar association. For those bringing lawsuits against bar associations, this translates into a success rate of 0.5 percent, or about 1 out of every 200 cases. By comparison, the overall success rate for defendants in

---

52 Bias of this sort is consistent with evidence that vocational background can influence the attitudes and choices of legislators. See Carnes (2012) and specifically Matter and Stutzer (2015) on lawyer-legislators.

53 Barton (2010, p. 14).

54 The majority of cases involving bar associations are those where a bar association is being sued. In our federal district data, bar associations were defendants in 420 cases and plaintiffs in 69 cases. We find similar patterns where a bar association is a plaintiff, as opposed to a defendant.

55 These data were downloaded from the Federal Judicial Center's Integrated Courts Database website (www.fjc.gov/research/idb).

56 The names of the litigants become available for district court cases starting in 1985 and for circuit court cases starting in 1998. This accordingly limits our analysis to years where names of litigants are available.

57 We filtered cases using the *disposition* variable in the Federal Judicial Center Integrated Database. Specifically, we exclude cases where the disposition was coded as "motion before trial," "voluntarily," or "settled."

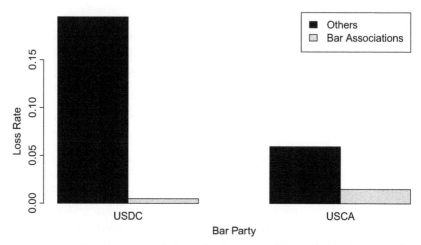

FIGURE 3.2 Losing rates in federal district courts (left) and federal courts of appeals (right) when a bar association is the defendant compared to other kinds of defendants.
Source: Federal Judiciary Center Integrated Courts Database.

federal civil cases is 19.5 percent. This difference means that US district court judges are about forty times more likely to rule against defendants that are not bar associations. For the remaining three cases, the district judge ruled against the bar association's motion to dismiss on legal grounds. In addition, of the 418 cases in which a bar association was a defendant *and won*, the plaintiff in the case appealed to a circuit court in 133 of them. These litigants were no more likely to find relief on appeal. Only 2 of the 133 cases that were appealed resulted in a loss for the bar association.

We note some other considerations that lend themselves to a pro-lawyer bias. For example, litigants have at times requested that judges and clerks recuse themselves on the basis that they are members of the defendant bar association, but these requests have been resoundingly rejected by judges.[58] In addition, while other "captured" agencies remain subject to external judicial review – that is, litigants can sue the captured agency in a court of law – the legal profession's capture keeps it

---

[58] See, for example, the Judicial Conference of the United States, Committee on Codes of Conduct *Advisory Opinion No. 52* (June 2009), which notes, "no impropriety in a judge sitting on a case where an open-membership bar association of which the judge is a member is a party."

largely insulated from external review. When people sue bar associations, in other words, they have nowhere else to appeal but to "captured" courts.[59]

Exempting the Bar from Liability

A particularly important application of Barton's lawyer-judge bias is in courts granting professional bar associations immunity from liability in civil cases, allowing them to avoid opening themselves to legal challenges and costs. This has happened in several ways. First, state bar associations have successfully claimed immunity in federal courts, a protection that shields them from being sued in federal courts in the first place. They have done so on the basis that they are "arms" of the state or of the courts – which are explicitly granted sovereign immunity in federal courts under the Eleventh Amendment to the US Constitution.[60] These claims of immunity have been bolstered by another doctrine, the Rooker-Feldman Doctrine, which prevents federal courts from hearing appeals in cases where bar associations have been challenged exclusively on state-law claims in state courts.[61] Taken together, these legal doctrines put federal courts off limits to those challenging state bar associations, leaving people with no other recourse besides bar-friendly state supreme courts.

Second, state bar associations have used the claim that they are "state actors" for reasons small and large, in contrast to other white-collar professions that cannot claim such status. To give just a few examples, state bar associations have successfully argued that, as state actors, they are exempt from payroll taxes,[62] exempt from property taxes,[63] and exempt from restrictions on lobbying by government agencies.[64] Other cases have found that individual actors working for state bar associations can

---

[59] See Merrill (1996) for a discussion of the court's efforts to correct for regulatory capture.

[60] See, for example, *Kaimowitz v. Florida Bar*, 996 F.2d 1151, 1155 (11th Cir. 1993) (holding that the Florida Bar is an "arm of the Court" and therefore entitled to 11th Amendment immunity); *Hirsh v. Justices of the Supreme Court of California*, 67 F.3d 708 (9th Cir. 1995) (reaching the same conclusion for California); *Thiel v. State Bar of Wisconsin*, 94 F. 3d 399 (7th Cir. 1996) (concluding the same in Wisconsin).

[61] See, for example, *Riley v. Louisiana State Bar Association*, 214 Fed. Appx. 456 (5th Cir. 2007) (refusing to hear an "African-American plaintiff's" claims of discrimination against the Louisiana Bar on the basis of the Rooker-Feldman Doctrine).

[62] E.g., *State Bar of Texas v. United States*, 560 F. Supp. 21 (N.D. Tex. 1983).

[63] E.g., *State Bar of Michigan v. Lansing*, 361 Mich. 185 (Mich. 1960).

[64] *Keller v. State Bar of California*, 496 U.S. 1 (1990).

avail themselves of judicial immunity, which protects people acting in a judicial capacity against civil damages.[65]

Third, state bar associations have also successfully argued that they are so essential to the functioning of the state courts that they are above liability and cannot be regulated by legislatures or the executive. Such arguments have generally been cast as separation-of-powers concerns, the claim being that an independent bar is essential for the maintenance of an independent judiciary. A notable set of cases involving the Washington State Bar Association (WSBA) illustrates this dynamic. In 1991, the state bar's employees tried to organize under the Public Employees' Collective Bargaining Act, which required state agencies to permit collective bargaining. The WSBA refused to recognize the union, and the Washington State Supreme Court agreed with the bar, ruling that it had the discretion to refuse the right of its employees to organize.[66] The following year, the state legislature amended the statute defining "public employers" to include the WSBA specifically, thus removing any discretion. WSBA employees then petitioned the Public Employment Relations Commission regarding their collective bargaining rights. However, the Washington Supreme Court again ruled in favor of the WSBA, noting its core synergy with the state judiciary and that "many of [the bar's] functions are directly related to and in aid of the judicial branch of government" and so "the ultimate power to regulate court-related functions, including the administration of the Bar Association, belongs exclusively to this court."[67] The court ultimately ruled in favor of the WSBA on the grounds that "legislation which directly and unavoidably conflicts with a rule of court governing Bar Association powers and responsibilities is unconstitutional as it violates the separation of powers doctrine."[68] Thus, despite the best efforts of the state legislature, the close relationship between the bar and the courts once again thwarted attempts at regulation.

Lastly, some state codes and regulations explicitly grant state bars immunity from civil lawsuits, particularly those initiated by disgruntled would-be or former lawyers; several of these have been codified and adopted by state high courts in their role as "regulators." An example

---

[65] E.g., *Greene v. Zank*, 158 Cal. App. 3d 497 (1984).
[66] These case details are from *Washington State Bar Association v. State*, 125 Wn.2d 901 (1995).
[67] 125 Wn.2d 901.
[68] 125 Wn.2d 901.

of this comes from Oklahoma, where in 2014 the state supreme court unanimously granted civil liability immunity to the Oklahoma Board of Bar Examiners. This was done to undermine lawsuits concerning "the performance of and within the scope of their official duties relating to the examination, character and fitness qualification, and licensing of persons seeking to be admitted to the practice of law or seeking to be registered as a law student."[69]

Exempting the Bar from Antitrust Laws

Perhaps the most powerful way that the legal profession has maintained its professional and political power is by maintaining its monopoly over the provision of legal services, broadly defined. In doing so, the courts' focus has been on protecting state bars against antitrust claims, including claims of price-fixing or monopolistic behavior.

The issue of whether bar associations should be subject to antitrust laws was taken up by the US Supreme Court in a lawsuit alleging the Virginia State Bar had engaged in price-fixing, *Goldfarb v. Virginia State Bar* (1975).[70] The Court in *Goldfarb* held that bar associations could be subject to the federal Sherman Antitrust Act under certain conditions. Even so, the Court affirmed that a state supreme court's exclusive right to regulate the practice of law could not be infringed and that the "interest of the States in regulating lawyers is especially great since lawyers are essential to the primary governmental function of administering justice, and have historically been 'officers of the courts.' "[71]

The ostensible effect of *Goldfarb* was to establish that lawyers engage in "trade or commerce" and that bar associations are not always immune to antitrust laws, but the practical effect has been to subject bar associations to antitrust laws only in cases where state supreme courts did not approve or condone the bar association's actions or had not been involved in setting the bar's policy, which, given the state courts' official regulatory and oversight functions and close working relationship with the bar, is exceedingly rare. For example, in *Hoover v. Ronwin* (1984),[72] which involved a disgruntled unsuccessful bar applicant, the Supreme

---

[69] See *In Re: Rule Amending Rules Governing Admission to Practice of Law*, No. SCBD-6193 (Ok. 2014).
[70] 421 U.S. 773 (1975). The suit involved a couple challenging the fact that they had to pay minimum fees for basic real estate services, as dictated by the state bar.
[71] 421 U.S. at 792.
[72] 466 U.S. 558 (1984).

Court rejected the antitrust claim and ruled that "[f]ew other professions are as close to the core of the State's power to protect the public. Nor is any trade or other professions as essential to the primary governmental function of administering justice."[73] The ruling in *Hoover* (and others like it) has established the precedent that the bar has wide latitude in behavior, provided that its actions have a sufficiently strong association with the state judiciary and that they can claim status as state actors.[74] This continues to afford bar associations the distinct privilege among private actors (including other industries and professional organizations) of evading basic antitrust regulations.

MECHANISMS OF CAPTURE

We have so far focused on how judicial oversight of the legal profession operates and how the bar has historically benefited from it, which is why the legal profession wants an ideologically aligned judiciary. After all, the judiciary is key to preserving much of the bar association's monopolistic and professional authority; having like-minded judges is important to this purpose.

Yet how has the bar actually *maintained* a captured judiciary? We see at least three ways by which the bar has cultivated, nurtured, and retained substantial control over a third of federal and state governments: (1) formal control over judicial selection mechanisms, including judicial candidate ratings; (2) restrictions on judicial behavior, especially on political activity; and (3) an exclusive monopoly over the pool of judicial candidates. These considerations set the stage for Part II of this book, in which we address how this power over the judiciary bumps up against the interests of political actors, who must respond to the reality that all their judicial candidates necessarily come from the legal profession – an entity that has its own economic, professional, and ideological interests.

---

[73] 466 U.S. at 569.
[74] E.g., *Mothershed v. Justices of Supreme Court*, 410 F.3d 602 (9th Cir. 2005); *Hass v. Oregon State Bar*, 883 F.2d 1453 (9th Cir. 1989); *Scannell v. Washington State Bar Association*, No. 14-35582 (9th Cir. 2016). We also examined how *Goldfarb* has been cited in subsequent cases between 1975, when the case was decided, and 2017; passages from the opinion speaking to the right of the judiciary to regulate the practice of law exclusively have been cited 876 times compared with only 297 citations to passages that establish that the Sherman Act applies to professional organizations – and most of the latter references are made in the context of regulating medical associations.

Selection Mechanisms and Judicial Ratings

One of the most important pathways by which the bar has "captured" the judiciary has been via the bar's explicit involvement in judicial selection. The idea that the legal profession should have a say in the selection of judges – who together comprise one-third of government – has not only deep historical roots (as we discuss in Chapter 7) but also deep support within the profession. According to the Canon 2 of the ABA Canons of Professional Ethics (adopted in 1908), the bar's duty is

to endeavor to prevent political considerations from outweighing judicial fitness in the selection of Judges. It should protect earnestly and actively against the appointment or election of those who are unsuitable for the Bench; and it should strive to have elevated thereto only those willing to forego other employments, whether of a business, political or other character, which may embarrass their free and fair consideration of questions before them for decision.[75]

Thus, a key objective of the legal profession – and of the bar associations that lead it – has always been to shape how judges are chosen.

We discuss how lawyers have historically been involved in judicial selection in Chapter 7. For now, we briefly note several key ways in which the legal profession has formally been involved in the selection of judges. The first has been via "merit commissions," which operate differently across the thirty-four (as of this writing) states that use them but employ the same general principle. These commissions, often comprised explicitly of members of the local bar, recommend a slate of candidates for the bench; the executive (governor of the state) or the legislature will then choose from the slate of candidates.[76] There is no question that merit-oriented commissions explicitly allow local bar associations a very strong, important pull on who becomes a judge, a topic we return to in Chapter 6.

Although different in nature, the involvement of the bar in the selection of judges also extends to appointments-based systems, including the federal judicial system. For example, at the federal level, the ABA's Standing Committee on the Federal Judiciary evaluates candidates to the federal bench according to "qualifications," "temperament," and "integrity,"[77] using these criteria to rate them on a scale from "Not

---

75 American Bar Association Canons of Professional Ethnics, Canon 2 (1908).
76 We discuss merit-oriented commissions in more depth in Chapters 4, 5, and 7. In Chapter 5, we address how merit-oriented selection mechanisms result in a judiciary that is in greater ideological alignment to the bar.
77 American Bar Association (2009).

Qualified" to "Well Qualified." These ratings are then used by executives and legislators in deciding to move the appointment forward; as documented by several studies, lower-ranked candidates are less likely to be confirmed and, if confirmed, take longer to go through the process.[78] Thus, securing favorable approval from the ABA is an important marker for candidates aspiring to judicial office. From the bar's perspective, the use of these ratings conveniently positions the bar as an authority on what it means to be a good judge, an inherently subjective assessment.

However, these ratings – and their use by political actors – are not without controversy, nor without allegations of partisan bias, as we discuss in Chapter 4. Several studies have shown that nominees named by Republican presidents tend to be awarded lower ratings by the ABA as opposed to those named by Democrats.[79] Despite the claims (and the scholarly evidence) that the ABA's qualification ratings appear ideologically skewed against conservative candidates, and despite the evidence that the legal profession itself leans to the left (which we discuss in later chapters), the ABA has consistently maintained that the criteria are nonpolitical and that reliance on any kind of partisan considerations is inappropriate.[80] For our purposes here, we see a straightforward reason why the bar pushes so hard for the use of qualification ratings: They allow the bar an influential say in who does, and who does not, become a federal judge.

Restrictions on Judicial Behavior

Another pathway by which the bar has maintained its capture over the judiciary is by regulating judicial behavior, including political behavior. By making judges adhere to certain nonpartisan codes of conduct, the

---

[78] Allison (1996); Scherer, Bartels, and Steigerwalt (2008); Sen (2014a).

[79] See Smelcer, Steigerwalt, and Vining (2012), which focuses on federal appeals judges. See, however, Sen (2014a), which shows no differences in ratings awarded to Republican- and Democratic-nominated judges at the federal district court level.

[80] For example, the ABA's Coalition for Justice issued a report in 2008 explicitly rejecting political or representational concerns in the selection of judges:

Legislators and other elected officials are meant to be representatives of the views of voters, but in a democratic society that depends upon and respects the rule of law, judges serve the people in a different way. Judges have a responsibility to know and impartially apply the law to the facts of the case at hand ... All judges should be held accountable, but unlike other elected officials they should not be asked to strictly adhere to public opinion. Rather, they are rightly asked to strictly adhere to the law. (American Bar Association 2008, pp. 7–8)

bar ensures that the judiciary is viewed as a fundamentally nonpolitical institution – thus strengthening the perceived importance of merit commissions in the selection of judges and orienting members of the public to emphasize "qualifications" over political considerations.

The regulation of judicial behavior by the bar extends across jurisdictions and applies to federal as well as state judges. For example, the ABA has, since 1924, published a Model Code of Judicial Conduct,[81] which serves as a model for state bar associations throughout the country. The Code is periodically revised but holds firm to several canons, emphasizing perhaps above all else the responsibilities that judges have in promoting the appearance of nonpartisanship.[82] In addition, the ABA provides restrictions on judicial conduct in the course of judicial elections,[83] many of which have been formally adopted by state bar associations. These rules have, for example, prohibited or discouraged judicial candidates from (1) endorsing political candidates, (2) affiliating with political parties or organizations, or (3) soliciting campaign contributions.

These rules have also included restrictions on political activity by judicial candidates. For example, the ABA Model Code of Judicial Conduct dictates that a "judge or candidate for judicial office shall refrain from political activity that is inconsistent with the impartiality, integrity, and independence of the judiciary."[84] In their strictest form, these "announce clauses" forbade judicial candidates from making any statements whatsoever about their personal stances on any issue, political or otherwise, that might end up before the courts. As suggested by some scholarship,[85] members of the public actively look to political or partisan signals as a way to gauge their support for judicial candidates; for that reason, there is good reason to think that such regulations deprive voters of valuable information and thus may serve to suppress electoral competition.

[81] Gallagher (2005).

[82] Rule 2.4c, for example, states that "[a] judge shall not convey or permit others to convey the impression that any person or organization is in a position to influence the judge." Rule 4.2 states that judges shall not "seek, accept, or use endorsements from any person or organization other than a partisan political organization." These sorts of rules are also, of course, somewhat ironic since, of course, the ABA does both.

[83] Many of these are included in Canon 4 of the Model Code of Judicial Conduct.

[84] Canon 5. This requirement once had even broader language that "restricted judges from making political speeches, contributing or soliciting payments for party funds, publicly endorsing candidates for political office, and participating in party conventions" (Gallagher 2005, p. 10).

[85] See, for example, Gibson (2008); Sen (2017b).

These restrictions remained in effect until the US Supreme Court's 2002 ruling in *Republican Party of Minnesota v. White*, which struck down statutes that prohibited judicial candidates from expressing views on political issues.[86] However, even after the ruling in *White*, state bar associations have continued to publish codes and guidelines for ethical conduct for judicial candidates that discourage political behavior. In Ohio, for example, judicial candidates are required to attend a two-hour course on "campaign practices, finance, and ethics" that includes lessons on how to maintain public confidence while running.[87]

We note that, for the most part, bar associations have defended such restrictions on fundraising as a means of promoting impartiality on the courts and have often decried the increased influence of special interests over judicial elections. One consequence of these sorts of rules, however, is that they position bar associations as the sole legitimate source of information on judicial competence and qualifications, while strongly discouraging judicial nominees and candidates from revealing information about their partisan affiliations to voters or politicians.

Monopoly Over the Pool of Judicial Candidates

Finally, the foremost way in which the legal profession has exerted control over the national and state courts is via the custom – codified in many jurisdictions – that judges in courts of law be lawyers first.[88] Currently, all state supreme court justices are former lawyers, and all of the judges in the federal judicial system – including judges all the way from Supreme Court justices to lower magistrate and administrative judges – are former lawyers.[89] This has meant, as several scholars

---

[86] 536 U.S. 765 (2002).

[87] See Rule 4.2(A)(4) of the Ohio Code of Judicial Conduct. The other components of the Codes of Judicial Conduct also call for strong nonpartisanship among candidates. See, e.g., Comments to Rule 4.1 ("Judicial candidates have a special obligation to ensure the judicial system is viewed as fair, impartial, and free from partisanship. To that end, judicial candidates are urged to conduct their campaigns in such a way that will allow them, if elected, to maintain an open mind and uncommitted spirit with respect to cases or controversies coming before them").

[88] The use of nonlawyers in the lower ranks of magistrate judges, traffic judges, and justices of the peace varies from state to state. See Provine (1986), which also documents the bar's persistent efforts to eliminate such "lay" judges.

[89] The last justice to serve on the US Supreme Court without a law degree was Stanley Reed, active from 1938 to 1957. For a biographical overview of the individuals who have served as federal judges, see the Federal Judicial Center's biographical database (www.fjc.gov).

have noted, that judges come to the bench with a traditional law school education and, in most circumstances, years of experience within the traditional practice of law.[90] As such, they tend to see the world as lawyers do and "think like lawyers." This represents an extreme form of *professional* capture; that is, we argue that the regulators (judges) share the educational and professional norms of the regulated industry (lawyers).

Furthermore, professional capture bleeds into other kinds of capture, including capture of policy and ideological preferences; that is, not only are judges former lawyers (thus representing professional capture) but lawyers also want judges who are like-minded in terms of their policy preferences and partisan outlooks (thus representing ideological capture). This observation finds strong support in related literatures on bureaucratic capture. The scholar of bureaucracies James Wilson defined a "professional" as "someone who receives important occupational rewards from a group whose membership is limited to people who have undergone specialized formal education and have accepted a group defined code of proper conduct."[91] In the context of the bureaucracy, professional background, he argues, is important because it exerts an external influence on bureaucrats separate from the organizational incentives of their agencies and can lead bureaucrats to define tasks in a fashion reflecting their training and professional norms and standards. These arguments are no less applicable to judges. In fact, the expectation that judges develop a working relationship with bar associations likely amplifies this effect.[92] As the legal scholar Benjamin Barton observed, "[t]he similarity of thought processes and natural sympathy of judges for lawyers leads inevitably to judicial output favoring lawyers."[93]

All of this represents a dilemma for political elites, many of whom have policy preferences at odds with those of the legal profession and the bar. Indeed, politicians (and voters) are constrained by having to select judges who, at a minimum, have a legal background or, in states with merit selection, have been either hand-picked by nominating commissions or "pre-cleared" by bar associations. This deep tension, in tandem with the bar's own political leanings, is the topic of Chapter 4 and sets

---

[90] See Barton (2010); Bonica and Sen (2017c); Sen (2017a).

[91] Wilson (1989, p. 60).

[92] Supporting this, several studies have found that judges (including Supreme Court Justices) are influenced by their peers and reputational concerns (Choi, Gulati, and Posner 2010; Baum 2009; Baum and Devins 2010).

[93] Barton (2010, p. 15).

the stage for many conflicts between the bar and the political establishment. After all, although the bar's professional capture of the courts is
complete, political actors can still influence the judicial selection process
in ways that undermine its ideological capture.

CONCLUSION

We conclude this chapter by reflecting on its major themes. First, American lawyers have, since the turn of the century, enjoyed oversight
over their own affairs, nurtured by their political influence and also
by the bar's synergy with state and federal judiciaries. This makes the
legal profession something of an outlier: Every other comparable profession – including doctors, accountants, bankers, or architects – is
regulated by state and federal agencies. Some of these (e.g., the oil
industry or the aviation industry) have historically managed to achieve
some degree of regulatory capture. Yet no profession or industry has
enjoyed the autonomy and self-regulation that lawyers have. It is up
to bar associations to decide how lawyers should be educated, who
can engage in the practice of law, and when lawyers should face disci-
plinary measures or be prohibited from practice. It is also up to lawyers
to say who may or may not become a lawyer, an unusual amount
of political power given that lawyers still comprise a disproportion-
ate share of elected politicians and all appointed and elected judges.
Indeed, the overall extent of the legal profession's self-regulation is
truly extraordinary and represents the only instance of constitutional
capture to our knowledge.

The second theme is how the bar and bench have worked together
to insulate the legal profession from regulatory authority from outside
the profession. Although the bar has never been, and continues not to
be, regulated by any government agencies, state courts do have oversight over lawyers' conduct and policy reach. Even so, the professional
boundaries between the bar and the judiciary are blurred: The judiciary
is comprised of former members of the bar, while the bar is overseen by
the judiciary. This close-knit relationship has been mutually beneficial;
judges have given lawyers a significant degree of self-determination over
how the profession is regulated and, in return, lawyers have worked to
safeguard the independence of the judiciary, extend the reach of judicial
review, and empower the courts to set policy. The significance of this is
striking: Just as the courts provide the primary regulatory oversight of

the legal profession, lawyers provide the building blocks and functional oversight of the nation's judiciary.

The third theme is that this regulatory structure gives the bar an interest in pursing not just professional capture of the judiciary but also, to the extent that it can, ideological capture, which is reflected in the bar's interests in judicial selection. As we discussed in this chapter, the bar has secured itself a formal role in the selection of judges in various ways, from mandatory appointments to nominating commissions to issuing formal ratings of judicial candidates via "qualification ratings." In addition, the bar has placed restrictions on judicial behavior and made other recommendations to executives and legislators about the appropriate role of judges. In doing so, the ABA and state bar associations have historically claimed to be motivated not by politics but rather out of concerns of justice and fairness. The end result, however, is that legal professionals have gained considerable control over the kinds of lawyers who become judges and how they behave once on the bench.

As we shall see in the following chapters, the bar's concerns often put it squarely at odds with the interests of political actors, who have their own concerns and priorities in terms of judicial candidates. This tension – between lawyers wanting like-minded judges and politicians wanting friendly courts – marks the fundamental tension behind our framework of the judicial tug of war. We now turn toward explaining this tug of war, continuing with the incentives and priorities of political actors.

PART II

POLITICAL ACTORS AND THE INCENTIVE TO POLITICIZE

4

Politicians, Their Interests, and the Judicial Tug-of-War

"If changing judges changes law, it is not even clear what law is."

Richard Posner[1]

One of the best-known examples of conflict between politicians and the judiciary occurred during the New Deal era with Franklin Roosevelt's infamous "court-packing plan" in 1937.[2] The US Supreme Court – at that time dominated by a group of aging conservatives known as the "the Four Horsemen"[3] – had quickly and systematically struck down key pieces of New Deal legislation. This included legislation to regulate labor relations (the National Industrial Recovery Act), encourage farmers to reduce production and boost commodities prices (the Agricultural Adjustment Act), and regulate labor conditions and the price of coal (the Bituminous Coal Conservation Act).[4] A worry among members of FDR's progressive coalition was that the conservative members of the Court could derail all New Deal legislation, including the Social Security Administration Act and the National Labor Relations Act.

---

[1] Posner (2010, p. 1).

[2] For more on this generally, see, e.g., Burns (2009, chap. 8).

[3] The "Four Horsemen" were Pierce Butler, James Clark McReynolds, George Sutherland, and Willis Van Devanter, who frequently were joined in the Court's right flank by Chief Justice Charles Evans Hughes. The "Four Horsemen" were counterbalanced on the left with "The Three Musketeers" – Louis Brandeis, Harlan Fiske Stone, and Benjamin Cardozo. Another justice, Owen Roberts, frequently joined the Four Horsemen and Chief Justice Hughes to form the Court's conservative majority. See Burns (2009, p. 140).

[4] *Schechter Poultry Corp. v. United States*, 295 U.S. 495 (1935); *United States v. Butler*, 297 U.S. 1 (1936); *Carter v. Carter Coal Company*, 298 U.S. 238 (1936).

However, FDR's landslide win in the 1936 presidential election ensured that he had the political capital to take on the Supreme Court. In the infamous court-packing plan that followed, the president called for a retirement age for the justices of seventy years and, for every justice refusing to retire at seventy, the ability to name a new justice to a new Supreme Court seat – a plan sure to transform the Court decidedly in a more liberal direction. However, the plan was immediately met with hostility from the legal elite and from the American Bar Association (ABA), which thought the proposal was a thinly veiled attempt to limit judicial independence.[5] Many state and local bars responded by passing resolutions condemning the court-packing scheme.[6]

Despite the legal outcry, public support was on FDR's side, making the bill's passage a likely possibility. At this point, in the famous "switch in time that saved nine," Owen Roberts switched his vote on an important case, turning his back on the Four Horsemen and casting his vote instead with the liberal wing in upholding a women's minimum wage law.[7] This switch signaled a new willingness by the Court to consider New Deal legislation. However, the deep fissure between progressive, left-leaning political leaders and an older, much more conservative legal establishment was laid bare for the public to see. In this case, however, the tension was resolved in favor of politicians. The legal establishment, for its part, had saved the Court from the packing scheme but gave up its preferred policy position.

Fissures like this between politicians and the legal establishment are the topic of this chapter. As FDR's court-packing plan demonstrates, politicians have a strategic interest in the nature and composition of the courts. After all – like the US Supreme Court in the New Deal era – courts can not only derail a legislative agenda but also promote certain policy positions. This is especially true when it comes to politically sensitive subjects, such as social issues, civil rights, redistricting, and separation of powers. This makes the courts, at least from the perspective of politicians, important tools for furthering policy goals (or derailing those of

---

[5] McKenna and McKenna (2002, pp. 311–314). The ABA set up a special committee to oppose the bill and conducted a poll of its own members, showing that they opposed the bill 7 to 1 (McKenna and McKenna 2002, pp. 313–314).

[6] See, e.g., McKenna and McKenna (2002, pp. 311–314), which also discusses responses of state and local bars.

[7] *West Coast Hotel Co. v. Parrish*, 300 U.S. 379 (1937).

one's opponents). However, politicians are not unconstrained in choosing judges or in shaping the courts exactly to their liking. FDR, for example, had to contend not only with four life-appointed conservative justices but also with a powerful and influential legal establishment that quickly mobilized and threw its considerable resources against the court-packing scheme.

This fact illustrates the tension that we leverage here. Politicians are fundamentally constrained in shaping the courts by the bar's professional "capture" of the judiciary. This means that they must select judges from members of the legal establishment and, often, have to contend with lawyers through the course of judicial selection and, later, with lawyerly norms. This tension forms the bedrock of what we call the "judicial tug of war." On the one hand, as we explore in this chapter and in Chapter 5, political actors have a strong incentive to shape the judiciary in ways that are amenable to their policy interests. Yet, on the other, the legal establishment has an entrenched interest in maintaining control over the judiciary and protecting its professional and political interests.

This basic intuition allows us to evaluate how "successful" either one (politicians or lawyers) is in the tug of war over the nation's courts. If *lawyers* are more influential (if they have more "pull" in the tug of war), then judges should look more like lawyers in terms of their policy preferences and ideology. If *politicians* are more influential, then the preferences of judges should resemble those of politicians. This gives additional purchase on understanding how courts become "politicized." Specifically, under a selection mechanism that is completely devoid of politics and partisanship, the population of judges should look roughly like the underlying population of elite attorneys – at least ideologically, if not demographically. However, the more that the process becomes "politicized" – and the more that ideology or policy preferences factor into how judges are selected – the less judges will look like attorneys (and the more they will look like politicians). Thus, *ideological selection* becomes a critical pathway for how political actors attempt to wrest control over the judiciary from the legal establishment.

We devote significant attention in this chapter to developing and demonstrating this framework empirically. We do so by introducing two large sources of data, which we then use throughout this book. The first is one of the largest data sets ever collected on the ideology of US lawyers and judges; these data rely on existing work that leverages individual and group political donations to measure ideology.[8] The second is an extensive collection of data on lawyers' and judges' educational and professional backgrounds. We use these data in this chapter to demonstrate several important patterns. For example, our data show that lawyers as a whole tend to be left-leaning; however, our data also show that the judiciary – particularly at the highest and most politically important levels – tends to be more conservative relative to the population of lawyers. This deviation varies from jurisdiction to jurisdiction and hinges on the method used to select judges. For example, we see the strongest deviation at the federal appeals courts, the courts that sit just below the US Supreme Court in the judicial hierarchy and which rely on executive appointment. These findings suggest a subtle push and pull between political actors and the legal establishment, with the "winner" largely dependent on the selection mechanism and the importance of the court. Politicians will, in particular, pull very hard on judicial ideology, but they will orient their efforts toward courts that matter the most, such as the federal courts of appeals. This strategic politicization sets the stage for Chapter 5, in which we explore variation in politicization, starting with the federal court system.

We organize this chapter as follows. We first explore what politicians stand to gain from a like-minded judiciary (and, in tandem, why ideology matters in judicial decision-making); this sets the stage for thinking about political actors as important players in shaping the composition of the nation's courts. We then explain the contours of the judicial tug of war, the incentives of the players, and the ground rules. The framework produces several insights: The more politics and ideology factor into judicial selection (the more politicians "pull"), the less judges will look like lawyers and the more they will resemble politicians; the less this is the case (the more attorneys "pull"), the more judges will resemble attorneys. We then turn to evaluating the tug of war empirically. We show judges are more conservative than lawyers and that this conservative tilt is more pronounced for higher courts. This suggests that politicians are engaging seriously in efforts to influence the ideological composition of the courts but that they do so in a way that prioritizes more politically important courts. The chapter appendix has additional findings that show these are robust, meaningful empirical findings, including a discussion of strategic donations.

---

[8] See, e.g., Bonica (2014).

POLITICAL ACTORS AND THEIR INCENTIVES

As the example of the New Deal–era Supreme Court shows, American courts have had, and continue to have, considerable say over public policy. Recent years have seen the nation's courts rule on freedom of the press, civil rights enforcement, the rights of enemy combatants, criminal procedure and the death penalty, the ability of states to restrict reproductive rights, whether gays and lesbians may marry, and the limits of presidential power. The courts are also often asked to rule on issues of electoral consequence. For example, both state and federal courts handle litigation concerning redistricting, voter ID laws, the rights of voters and access to the polls, and restrictions on campaign contributions and independent expenditures. This makes the courts powerful arbiters in determining whether, and to what extent, state legislatures can draw district boundaries that favor one or the other party, who can access the polls, and how politicians can raise money. Politicians on both the left and the right therefore have strong incentives to use the courts as policy instruments. Who sits on the courts is key to achieving success as a policymaker – especially on issues of high social, political, or electoral consequence.

The Importance of Judicial Ideology

Stepping back a bit, we acknowledge that the idea that ideology does (or should) matter when selecting judges remains controversial. To give a comparison, we of course expect that members of Congress are chosen through a highly partisan and ideological process. After all, Congress is an institution where representatives are elected primarily because of their partisan affiliation and policy preferences. Yet judges are viewed differently. Alexander Hamilton cautioned in the famous *Federalist Papers* about the influence of politics on the courts and on the desire – from an institutional perspective – to keep judges insulated from the vicissitudes of public opinion. Writing in Federalist Number 78, he wrote that lifetime appointments were essential, or else judges "would be [at] too great a disposition to consult popularity."[9] In writing this, Hamilton touched

---

[9] In terms of their relationship to the other branches of government, political independence was key – specifically, "liberty can have nothing to fear from the judiciary alone, but would have every thing to fear from its union with either of the other departments." He further cautioned that "it is in continual jeopardy of being overpowered, awed, or influenced by its co-ordinate branches" (Hamilton, Madison, and Jay 1787, Number 78).

on a broader idea, which is that the character traits and qualifications used to assess preparedness for serving on the bench should be different than those for candidates to political offices and should emphasize professional experience, independence, and impartiality.[10] The nature of a judgeship would "demand long and laborious study to acquire a competent knowledge of them" and "there can be few men in society, who will have sufficient skill in the laws to qualify them for the stations of judges."[11] Among these would be individuals "who unite the requisite integrity with the requisite knowledge."[12]

This view of judges as performing an inherently different and more intellectual role than that of policy-oriented political actors conflicts somewhat with contemporary scholarship. Starting in the early twentieth century, scholars began critiquing existing intellectual frameworks of the interpretation of law as a scientific process – something that could be interpreted mechanically, like an umpire calling "balls and strikes." These "legal realists" believed that a case's context – which included not just the facts of the case but also the social context as well as the identity of the judge – mattered a great deal to how a case was actually decided. As the prominent jurist Jerome Frank noted, "[t]he layman thinks that it would be possible to revise the law books so that they would be something like logarithmic tables, that the lawyers could, if only they would, contrive some kind of legal slider rule for finding exact legal answers … [Yet] the law always has been, is now, and will ever continue to be, largely vague and variable."[13]

The movement toward legal realism dovetailed with a heightened interest in the role of partisanship and ideology in elite decision-making. By the 1940s, scholars began to document the direct influence of politics on judicial decision-making. For example, in an early seminal work the political scientist C. Herman Pritchett looked at the voting of the Roosevelt-era Supreme Court, determining that the identity of the appointing president was highly predictive of voting outcomes and of membership in voting blocs.[14] In another early study, the political

---

[10] There was no active discussion of judicial qualifications at the convention itself (Vile and Perez-Reilly 1990), which, as scholars have noted, is a curious omission given the exhaustive discussion of qualifications of legislative and executive officeholders (Binder and Maltzman 2009, p. 23).

[11] Hamilton, Madison, and Jay (1787, Number 78).

[12] Hamilton, Madison, and Jay (1787, Number 78).

[13] Frank (1930, p. 5).

[14] Pritchett (1948).

scientist Glendon Schubert studied how judges'votes on the Michigan Supreme Court were also predicted by their partisan affiliations.[15] Much of this early work looked at partisanship and its ability to predict voting blocs; even so, the heart of the work cut closer to the strong relationship between ideology and judicial decision-making. In contemporary scholarship, this relationship has been further developed theoretically and tested empirically. For example, Jeff Segal and Howard Spaeth's seminal "Attitudinal Model" documented that partisanship was a strong predictor of justices' voting on important issues[16]; in case after case, these authors showed, justices appointed by Republicans voted in a more conservative direction, while justices appointed by Democrats voted in a more liberal direction. This basic finding has been buttressed by a steady stream of quantitative studies documenting this pattern, not just at the Supreme Court level but also in federal appeals courts, federal district courts, and throughout the state court hierarchy.[17] This burgeoning research arena demonstrated not only that judicial decision-making was heavily influenced by partisanship (or ideology) but that partisanship and policy preferences were an important way in which judges structure their decision-making. Of course, as noted by several scholars, for example, the law and precedent serve as important constraints, as do legal customs and norms.[18] However, partisanship and ideology remain highly predictive of judicial decision-making.

These scholarly findings have resonated with journalistic portrayals of the courts, which have increasingly noted partisan cleavages on important cases. For example, recent coverage of the US Supreme Court has focused on important 5–4 party-line splits in key decisions on same-sex marriage, voting rights, health care legislation, and affirmative action. As the well-known Court reporter Linda Greenhouse observed, "for the first time in the court's modern history, the individual justices are ideologically aligned with the party of the president who appointed them." That, she wrote, "is cause for concern for a chief justice inclined to worry that people will look at Supreme Court justices and see partisans."[19]

[15] Schubert (1974). For more on this early research, see generally Harris and Sen (2019).
[16] Segal and Spaeth (2002).
[17] See, e.g., Sunstein et al. (2006) (on federal courts of appeals judges), Epstein, Landes, and Posner (2013) (on federal judges, including district court judges), and Zorn and Bowie (2010) (all tiers of the federal judiciary).
[18] Epstein and Knight (1998).
[19] Greenhouse (2017).

Courts as Policy Instruments

In this sense, the descriptive empirical literature is quite clear: Ideology predicts and motivates judicial decision-making, perhaps increasingly so in times of polarized politics. In turn, from the perspective of politicians, *this creates incentives to select judges who share their policy views*. To the extent that partisanship – including expressed partisanship or previous behavior suggesting an affinity for one party or another – is predictive of policy views, then it should also be an important consideration for politicians and party elites when assessing potential nominees.

The research on this is ample: Not only do Republicans appoint judges vote in line with conservative positions, but it is possible for the executive (working in tandem with like-minded legislators) to "move the median" on important courts.[20] This holds for Democrats and Republicans alike, although, as we discuss here and in the next few chapters, the pathways that each party will take to achieve these goals will differ. Democrats want to appoint judges friendly to liberal policies, including expanding the size and role of government, civil rights for minorities and women, protections for criminal defendants, and support for regulatory oversight. By contrast, Republicans want to appoint judges who take limited readings of government powers, generally favor law-and-order interests over the rights of criminal defendants, and object to expansive interpretations of statutes and laws pertaining to civil rights and certain personal liberties.[21]

Diverging Incentives for Democrats and Republicans

Both conservatives and liberals (and thus Republican and Democratic party leaders) must grapple with the fact that the legal establishment exercises substantial control over membership in the judiciary. As we have discussed, not only does the bar provide the candidate pool for

---

[20] Numerous papers explore how executives "move the median" to better align important courts with their policy objectives. See, e.g., Krehbiel (2007), Cameron, Cover and, Segal (1990).

[21] To the extent that candidates for judicial office have been active in party politics – whether it be as a candidate for elected office, representative, White House official, donor, or registered member of the party – it provides a strong signal about how they would likely rule on politically charged cases. Both parties rely on these types of heuristics, and candidates for judicial office are well aware of this. This can be seen in the practice, common among conservatives at top law schools, of signaling conservative ideology by way of membership in the Federalist Society.

all eventual members of the judiciary but it takes an active role in policing who can be a judge. Judicial codes of conduct, selection criteria (e.g., "qualifications ratings" that rank candidates on the basis of their qualifications), and the explicit involvement of the bar in judicial selection all add additional leverage in the bar's professional capture of the judiciary.

If the interests and policy preferences of lawyers and politicians are aligned, then the friction resulting from this arrangement should be minimal. During the first half of the twentieth century, for example, lawyers were a staunch Republican constituency.[22] When FDR and the Democrats faced resistance from a conservative judiciary and bar, they adopted the strategy of actively nominating progressive judges, a strategy that came to a head with the Roosevelt administration's court-packing plan. Republicans of this era condemned what they saw as Democratic efforts to politicize the judiciary and called for selecting judges on the basis of merit and professional qualifications.

Today, on the other hand, lawyers are more on the liberal side, and it is now Democrats who accuse Republicans of putting party and ideology over qualifications when selecting judges. Republicans accuse Democrats of appointing activist judges to the bench and backing institutions that shield judges from accountability. These criticisms are rooted in incentives: Both parties want an ideologically friendly judiciary and therefore will actively promote the types of candidates and judicial reforms that best further this goal.

THE JUDICIAL TUG OF WAR

We now turn to developing our framework of the "judicial tug of war" more formally. We take the ideological leanings of the American judiciary as a function of two key factors: (1) the ideology of politicians and (2) the ideology of lawyers. (In subsequent chapters, we also consider a third key component, which is the fact that the way judges are chosen is itself a

---

[22] Historical data on partisanship by occupation is difficult to come by. We make use of historical data on party registration for California from Spahn (2017), which includes data on occupation. Data on party registration from the 1940 California voter file shows lawyers to be among the most Republican-leaning occupations. Nearly 70 percent of the 7,081 attorneys in the voter file registered as Republicans. By comparison, only 43 percent of California voters at the time were registered Republicans. However, as of 2012, only 25 percent of 43,209 California attorneys in our data set who had donated gave more to Republicans than Democrats. This is significantly less Republican than California voters, 37 percent of whom are registered as Republicans.

product of this tug of war; for now, however, we take the formal selection mechanism as a given.) Whether the judiciary tilts to the left or to the right depends on these forces. We describe each one in turn.

Input #1: The Ideology of Political Actors

Despite the bar's total *professional* capture of the judiciary, the legal profession rarely exclusively dictates who does or does not become a judge. Even in states where the bar is given an official role in merit commission nominations, elected politicians must ultimately choose from the slate of nominees identified by the commission. This results in a slippage in capture between absolute *professional* capture and strong (though not absolute) *ideological* capture. The legal profession is interested in both, obviously, but its ability to pursue the latter is hampered by the interests of politicians.

The identity and office of relevant politicians can vary. In some jurisdictions, this includes executives; in others, where "advice and consent" of a legislative chamber is necessary, this also includes legislators. This also must include party players and party elites, who across every jurisdiction have a strong, strategic interest in the ideological composition of the judiciary. For example, courts in many states have the final and often determinative say over important and exclusively political questions – including the legality of redistricting plans, the nature and limits of political speech, and how campaign contributions should be regulated – which all impact political operatives. The close relationship between the ideology of judges and how they decide cases makes these concerns entirely rational.[23]

How does the ideology of politicians map onto the ideology of the courts? Compared to the bar, which tends to be more uniform in terms of professional interests and educational background, there is more ideological variation across the fifty states and the federal system among politicians. Politicians in some states are more conservative than others, reflecting the views of their constituents and party and elite interests; meanwhile, those serving in federal government are reflective of a republican system of government, where more rural and more conservative states have comparably greater representation. All of these factors influence the ideological composition of the nation's elected officials, and we would expect these to be reflected in state and federal judiciaries. It

---

[23] Brace and Hall (1997); Epstein, Landes, and Posner (2013); Sunstein et al. (2006).

would be unsurprising that judges in Alabama or Mississippi were more conservative than judges in California or Massachusetts, reflecting the preferences of politicians in those states.

Input #2: The Ideology of Lawyers

The professional capture of the judiciary by the legal profession presents serious problems for politicians, however. After all, if the legal profession has captured in absolute terms the entire candidate pool of judges, then judges must reflect the preferences and policy beliefs of lawyers to some degree. If lawyers are involved in judicial selection explicitly (e.g., via merit commissions), then we should see an even closer connection. All of this could cause serious problems for political elites, particularly if they are ideologically at odds with the legal profession.

We have evidence that this may be the case in certain jurisdictions. Perhaps the most comprehensive mapping of lawyers' ideologies uses the same data we use here and shows that lawyers are one of the more left-leaning of white-collar professions.[24] Other studies have examined the campaign contributions made by law professors at elite institutions (a pool that is similar educationally to the elite pool from which judges are drawn), finding that they overwhelmingly tend to be made to Democrats; this is a finding consistent with two recent papers using the same data we use here.[25]

If the legal profession exerts a strong pull in the judicial tug of war, then we would expect to see that judges overall are also left-leaning, reflecting both the composition of the bar and its influential role in determining the contours of the judiciary. Of course, we would also expect to see region-by-region fluctuations; lawyers in Alabama are more conservative than lawyers in California (a pattern we document in Chapter 6), which would spill over into the composition of the judiciary; but, even so, conditional on jurisdiction, we would expect lawyers' ideology to correspond closely with the ideology of judges.

How These Competing Forces Shape the Tug-of-War

Our framework posits that the ideology of the judiciary, at its core, is a function of these two inputs, the ideology of politicians and the ideology

---

[24] Bonica, Chilton, and Sen (2016).
[25] See McGinnis, Schwartz, and Tisdell (2004); see also Bonica et al. (2018); Bonica, Chilton, and Sen (2016), which use the same campaigns contribution data that we use here.

of lawyers that form the candidate pool of judges. The extent to which the judiciary resembles either one provides intuition about the relative power of the two. It also gives us an intuition about when political actors will be accepting or even welcoming of the bar's involvement in judicial selection.

We can illustrate the judicial tug of war with some simple examples. For ease of interpretation, we stylize the ideological space on a left-to-right continuum, which we can think of as "liberal" to "conservative" (although this left–right spectrum was not as applicable in earlier points in American history, when a more useful dividing line might have been business elite versus rural interests). For example, in the following we represent the two key "players" in the judicial tug of war as attorneys (*A*) and political actors (*P*):

To assess the relative strength of the legal establishment versus the political establishment in shaping judicial ideology – we must first ask how ideology makes its way into judicial selection. That is, we must assess the extent to which courts have become *politicized*.

IDEOLOGICALLY NEUTRAL JUDICIAL SELECTION. Given this landscape, what would the judiciary look like if judges were indeed chosen *exclusively* on the basis of their qualifications, with no regard for their ideological views and in a nonpoliticized fashion? Alexander Hamilton and others like him advocated for selecting judges not on the basis of partisan or ideological concerns but on the basis of qualifications. Today, institutions such as the ABA promote the selection of judges on the basis of nonideological criteria, such as qualification ratings ostensibly capturing "integrity, professional competence and judicial temperament."[26] This is a theme echoed by numerous legal commentators and political actors.[27] This is also a claim espoused by state and local bar associations, many of which play formal roles in the selection of judges.

If judges were chosen strictly on the basis of qualifications and not on the basis of politics or ideology, then judges would resemble the legal establishment in terms of their political leanings and ideology. It would almost be as if judges were a subset of attorneys, perhaps more elite but

[26] American Bar Association (2009, p. 3).
[27] See, for example, Carter (1994).

no more liberal or no more conservative, because ideology did not factor into their selection. In other words, if judges are chosen from the pool of attorneys without concern for their politics, then comparing the political profiles of lawyers and attorneys should reveal that they look roughly the same (on average). The landscape would look much like the following, in which we denote the judiciary as *J*:

We refer to this possibility as *ideologically neutral (or random)* judicial selection or *nonpoliticized* judicial selection. By this, we mean the selection of judges that does not actively take ideology into account, instead relying on other characteristics (e.g., education or professional experience). We note that this is also different from a selection process that results in an ideologically mixed bench. Consider, for example, several independent agencies within the federal government – for example, the Federal Election Commission (FEC). The laws governing these bodies explicitly mandate that membership must be bipartisan; for that reason, commissions such as the FEC have roughly equal numbers of seats for Democrats and Republicans.[28] Many might describe these selection criteria as "moderate" or "neutral," but, in fact, they are best described as bipartisan: Ideology (in this case partisanship) explicitly factors into the selection process as a means of achieving partisan balance on the commission.

Going back to selection in which ideology plays no role (only qualifications or previous work experience), we make two further observations. The first observation is that lawyers are, as a group, left-leaning in the contemporary American landscape. This was not always the case, but it is empirically true today, as we discuss in depth in our next section.[29] If judges were selected exclusively on the basis of qualifications, and without consideration of ideology, it would result in a similarly left-leaning judiciary.[30]

---

[28] The Federal Election Commission has six commissioners, with "no more than three" being from the same political party (see www.fec.gov/about/leadership-and-structure/).

[29] See also the discussion in Bonica, Chilton, and Sen (2016).

[30] It is possible that judges are not selected on the basis of ideology but, instead, on the basis of things that correlate with ideology – such as race, gender, religion, or educational background. For example, if judges are selected on the basis of distinguished

The second observation directly stems from this: Choosing judges on the basis of professional qualifications (and not on the basis of ideology) is an extremely advantageous strategy for the legal profession. Not only is it seen as normatively attractive and defensible – after all, many would agree that having highly qualified, well-educated judges is in the best interests of the country – but this seemingly high-minded principle about how judges ought to be selected also serves the bar's self-interest. Specifically, choosing judges without taking into account ideology will results not just in a "qualified" pool but also in one that is in step with the profession ideologically.[31] In fact, if the legal profession wanted to increase the likelihood of selecting judges who reflected its views and were likely to further its policies, then selecting judges solely on the basis of qualifications would be an effective strategy. We consider this further in Chapter 7, where we discuss attempts at judicial reform and whether and to what extent the bar has interjected itself in judicial selection.

POLITICIZED SELECTION MECHANISMS This discussion points us to considering the opposing scenario, which is the possibility that judges do not, in fact, end up resembling the legal profession ideologically. The following example represents this kind of scenario, where A, J, and P represent the ideology of attorneys, the judiciary, and politicians, respectively:

This example puts politicians (P) on the ideological right and attorneys (A) on the ideological left, with judges (J) closer to the ideal point of politicians; but the point is broader than this specific configuration: There is an ideological mismatch between attorneys and judges, which points to a different kind of judicial selection. Indeed, the mismatch between attorneys and judges suggests the important role of ideology in judicial selection, one in which ideology is used to craft a judicial bench that

educational accomplishments and people who are highly educated tend to be more liberal, then judges will be more liberal simply because of this relationship. We find at most limited evidence of this. A technical discussion can be found in Bonica and Sen (2017c).

[31] See, for example, Fitzpatrick (2009, p. 676), which notes, "I am skeptical that merit selection *removes* politics from judicial selection. Rather, merit selection may simply *move* the politics of judicial selection into closer alignment with the ideological preferences of the bar."

more closely resembles the preferences of politicians. More broadly, this suggests that politicians are seeking judges who are like-minded and this quest for like-minded judges "pulls" the judiciary closer to the ideological preferences of politicians.

The implications of such a finding are consequential. If the overall ideological distribution of lawyers skews leftward,[32] then conservatives may have to place more effort on the selection and recruitment of (conservative) judges than their liberal counterparts. That is, conservatives will have a greater incentive to look to ideological cues when selecting judges because choosing randomly, or without a sense of ideology, would result in them choosing liberals. This creates incentives for conservatives, and the Republican Party specifically, to push for judicial selection mechanisms that place ideology front-and-center. As we explore in Chapter 7, we should expect Republicans to be more in favor of partisan elections for judges and, if they control the elected branches of government (and appear to continue doing so), executive or legislative appointments. Both of these types of selection mechanisms afford a greater opportunity to introduce ideology into the selection of judges, which on average will favor Republicans.

The implications of this are also normatively important but in ways that challenge partisan priors. "Politicization" has a largely negative connotation and many believe the selection of judges should not be overly political or rely excessively on ideology. However, our judicial tug-of-war framework suggests that, depending on partisan positioning, the use of ideology in judicial selection need not be bad. Using ideology to select judges could, after all, have the potential to result in a more diverse judiciary, one that is more reflective of the concerns of political actors and, by extension, voters. Indeed, if the legal profession is more liberal than the average American, then using ideology ("politicization") in the selection of judges could result in a judiciary that is more representative of ordinary Americans – at least in terms of ideology and partisanship.

Of course, a reliance on ideology and politicization can also be deployed to create a judiciary that is unrepresentative of the American people and, instead, more representative of the preferences of political elites. A politicized judiciary could still be more polarized than the public at large and more reflective of ideological extremes than the ideological center.

---

[32] Bonica and Sen (2017c).

DATA ON THE IDEOLOGY OF POLITICAL ACTORS, LAWYERS, AND JUDGES

At the core of the judicial tug of war is how the interplay between the legal profession and political actors shapes the judicial landscape. Seeing a politicized judiciary would suggest that ideology plays a role in judicial selection. However, to assess this, we need to have actual data on the ideologies and identities of (1) the relevant political actors, (2) lawyers in the United States and its various jurisdictions, and (3) state and federal judges. Only in having this kind of data can we make the inferences suggested by our simple stylized examples.

Obtaining reliable measures of ideology that can be compared across the three groups is challenging. To provide an illustrative example, we know that certain members of Congress are more conservative (or more liberal) because we know their political party (Republican or Democrat) as well as how they vote across hundreds of bills. This is the logic behind well-known measures of ideology for congressional representatives (including the widely used DW-NOMINATE scores), which place members of Congress on a left–right ideological scale based on roll call voting.[33]

For the nation's judges, accurately estimating ideology is more difficult, particularly when we expand beyond the US Supreme Court.[34] First, many judges tend to hear cases by themselves (as trial courts do) or in small groups (as is done in the federal courts of appeals), which makes comparing their voting records to other judges difficult. In addition, judges tend to write nuanced opinions, which represent a stark contrast to the up-or-down votes of legislators. Close readings of judicial opinions afford an excellent viewpoint into the mindset and philosophy of judges, particularly when it comes to legal philosophy and development of legal doctrine. For the comparisons we consider here, however, which involve tens of thousands of judges from across all tiers of state and federal courts, this would be intractable. In addition, the judicial tug of war implies that the ideological composition of the judiciary is influenced

---

[33] Poole and Rosenthal (1985). A comparison between DW-NOMINATE and the measures we use here is provided by Bonica and Sen (2017a).

[34] The Supreme Court has a stable membership, and all nine justices vote on the same cases. This means we can estimate the justices' ideologies using votes (e.g., Martin and Quinn 2002), combinations of votes and text (Lauderdale and Clark 2014), and citations (Clark and Lauderdale 2010). Bridging between similar cases and bills enables scholars to link Supreme Court ideology with congressional ideology (Bailey 2007). The scores we use here map onto several of these existing measures.

by the composition of the bar in varying degrees. Thus, we would need comparable estimates of the ideologies of judges and politicians but also estimates of the ideologies of lawyers across jurisdictions and stages of their careers. This is not feasible using the traditional methods, which focus exclusively on ideological scaling of elites.

For this reason, we look to newer data sources to triangulate the ideologies of lawyers, judges, and political actors, in addition to the more standard measurements (such as identity of the appointing president in the case of federal courts[35] or Party-Adjusted Justice Ideology (PAJID) scores in the case of state courts[36]). Specifically, we leverage a data set that is relatively new to the study of the judiciary, the Database on Ideology, Money in Politics, and Elections (DIME),[37] which we have explored in other work.[38]

The DIME scores leverage a rich database comprised of hundreds of millions of campaign contributions made to state and federal elections between 1979 and 2016 to estimate scores for hundreds of thousands of candidates, tens of thousands of interest groups, and tens of millions of individual donors. DIME's ability to recover scores for donors and candidates along a common dimension makes it possible to compare the ideological preferences of lawyers against judges and politicians. The logic behind donation-based measures is that campaign contributions provide an informative (and necessarily costly) signal about a donor's ideology.[39]

---

[35] A widely used measure of judicial ideology, the Judicial Common Space (JCS) scores, estimates the ideology of lower federal judges by substituting the ideology of the appointing president or some combination of the home-state senators (e.g., Boyd 2011; Epstein et al. 2007; Giles, Hettinger, and Peppers 2001).

[36] At the state level, the Party-Adjusted Justice Ideology (PAJID) scores of Brace, Langer, and Hall (2000) rely on interest group ratings of each state's congressional delegation. More recently, Bonica and Woodruff (2015) use the raw data that we rely on here in constructing state ideology measures from campaign contributions.

[37] See Bonica (2016b). The data are available at https://data.stanford.edu/dime. For the technical details on the DIME scores' construction, see Bonica (2014).

[38] For other work using these DIME scores to study the legal profession, see, e.g., Bonica et al. (2018); Bonica, Chilton, and Sen (2016); Bonica and Sen (2017c); Carnahan and Greenwood (2018); Chilton and Posner (2015). DIME scores have also been used to study a wide range of political actors, including campaign consultants and lobbyists (Martin and Peskowitz 2018), lobbying groups (Hafner-Burton, Kousser, and Victor 2014; Thieme 2017), think tanks (Lerner 2018), corporate elites (Bonica 2016a), federal agencies (Chen and Johnson 2015), and presidential appointees (Bonica, Chen, and Johnson 2015; Feinstein and Hemel 2017; Hollibaugh and Rothenberg 2019).

[39] To illustrate, suppose a person donates $500 to former president Barack Obama and then $500 to 2016 presidential nominee Hillary Clinton. DIME would assign this donor

The DIME scores have been extensively validated in several studies spanning a variety of institutional settings and types of actors.[40] Importantly, we have compared DIME data to other methods of estimating judicial ideology (e.g., Judicial Common-Space scores) and have found a strong correspondence between measures.[41] In addition, the scores have been validated as a measure of individual-level policy preferences and have been shown to be powerful predictors of preferences on a wide range of policy issues (taxes, abortion, guns, health care, etc.), both across and within party.[42]

WHO CONTRIBUTES? What if people do not contribute and, therefore, are not present in the DIME data? Fortunately, the database includes the majority of both elected and appointed judges who tend to be politically active. Regarding state judges, of the seventy state justices first elected to office between 2001 and 2011, sixty-six (or 94 percent) have made campaign contributions. The coverage rate for federal judges is also high. Nearly 65 percent of sitting federal appeals court judges appear in the DIME database as contributors, with the share rising to 72 percent when we limit the sample to those appointed since 2001.[43] In other words, the majority of judges – including both state and federal judges – have made political contributions prior to their service on the court. That 79 percent of the population of interest is captured gives us confidence about using these data to make inferences about the population of judges at large.[44]

an ideological score halfway between Obama (left) and Clinton (center-left). A donor giving $250 to Obama and $550 to Clinton would be assigned a score closer to Clinton than Obama, reflecting that they are likely to be closer to Clinton ideologically.

[40] See, e.g., Bonica (2014, 2019).

[41] Bonica and Sen (2017a,c); Bonica and Woodruff (2015). Additional discussion, including the robustness of the ideological scores to missingness and to strategic giving, can be found in the supplemental appendix of Bonica and Sen (2017c).

[42] See Bonica (2019), which validates DIME scores against a battery of policy items for respondents from the Congressional Campaign Election Study (CCES) for 4,466 respondents who were successfully matched against DIME.

[43] Federal judges who are currently on the bench are barred from making political contributions by the Code of Conduct for United States Judges (Canon 5), which states that a judge should not "solicit funds for, pay an assessment to, or make a contribution to a political organization or candidate." We can, however, estimate DIME scores using political donation activity from earlier in their careers.

[44] For those federal judges in our data set who have not donated, we have imputed scores using the methodology described in Bonica and Sen (2017a). In the multiple imputation model, we include variables capturing the (1) observed DIME and JCS scores, (2) court

For attorneys, the contribution rate is lower than it is for judges. This is not surprising, since they represent a larger share of people who may be less interested in politics. (In addition, the pool of attorneys has greater variation in age and wealth, two factors known to predict political involvement.) However, the percentage of attorneys who have donated is very high – 51 percent – compared to the overall population rate, which the most generous estimates would place at around 5 percent of the adult population. In addition, the contribution-based scores correlate strongly with attorneys' party registration, which we have for at least one state (Florida).[45] These additional checks suggest that our comparisons fairly assess the ideologies of lawyers.

ADDITIONAL DATA ON POLITICIANS, JUDGES, AND LAWYERS. DIME provides a consistent and useful measure of the ideologies of hundreds of thousands of politicians, lawyers, and judges. However, our analyses require additional information, including how judges are selected and where lawyers and judges live. We utilize additional information on state and federal politicians, including legislators and executives, provided by DIME and supplemented it with biographical information from the Biographical Directory of the US Congress. For data on lawyers, we turned to the Martindale-Hubbell legal directory.[46] This directory began as a way for lawyers to advertise their services but has evolved into one of the largest and most comprehensive directories of lawyers.[47] Martindale-Hubbell also includes several attributes important for our analyses, including the universities lawyers attended, graduation years, and states where they were admitted to the bar.[48]

type, (3) law school, (4) birth year, (5) gender, (6) race/ethnicity, (7) employment history, (8) American Bar Association ratings, and (9) clerkships.

[45] Specifically, we examined the correspondence between the DIME data for lawyers and the party registration data for Florida, a key state for which we have lawyers' party registration data. Doing so demonstrated that DIME scores closely predict lawyers' party registration status and vice versa. See also the technical discussion in Bonica and Sen (2017c).

[46] The data used here represent a snapshot of the population of active legal professionals as of 2012. However, we assign scores for any lawyer who has donated at any point between 1979 and 2018.

[47] Whisner (2014).

[48] Some Martindale-Hubbell profiles include additional information, such as the person's place of birth, the name of their current employer, and their stated practice areas. However, not all profiles have this information and so we use it sparingly in the analyses that follow.

For additional data on federal judges, we looked to data provided by the Federal Judicial Center (FJC), which, for every federal judge who has ever served, includes data on education, race, gender, age, identity of the appointing president, ABA rating, and confirmation vote.[49] For state judges, we relied on data collected on state high court judges by Bonica and Woodruff (2015), which we supplemented with data from Martindale-Hubbell for state lower court judges and additional data from Ballotpedia. This website lists the names and background information on judges from all states. (For retired judges, we looked to archived web-based information, both from Ballotpedia and its subsidiary, Judgepedia.) For each judge, we were able to obtain data on educational background, previous judicial experience, and the names and identities of the political actors who made the appointment (if applicable).

Pairing these data with DIME leaves us with scores for 974 judges at the federal level, a figure that included 771 district court judges and 203 circuit court judges, with scores imputed for the remaining judges. At the state level, our data include scores for 12,023 judges at the trial or lower court level and 240 judges at the state supreme court level. For lawyers, we were able to estimate scores for 471,432 attorneys out of the 974,448 listed in the Martindale-Hubbell database, which corresponds to a coverage rate of nearly 50 percent.[50]

WHAT DO THE IDEOLOGIES OF LAWYERS LOOK LIKE?

We now turn to exploring the basic patterns with regard to the overall distribution of lawyers.[51] We present this ideological distribution graphically in Figure 4.1, which also includes the respective DIME scores for prominent national politicians. (Again, as context, negative values indicate liberal, while a more positive score indicates a more conservative ideology.) As the figure shows, the distribution of attorneys skews left. Indeed, the median DIME score for attorneys is −0.52 compared with −0.13 for the entire population of donors; moreover, some 66 percent of lawyers are to the left of the midpoint between the party means for members of Congress.

---

49 www.fjc.gov.
50 Additional technical details on how we paired the data are explained in Bonica and Sen (2017c).
51 See Bonica, Chilton, and Sen (2016) for additional findings.

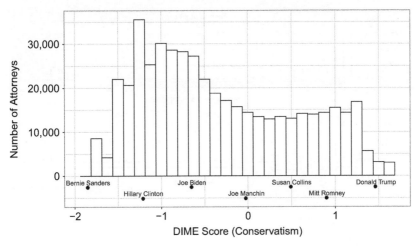

FIGURE 4.1 Ideological distributions of attorneys.
Sources: Martindale-Hubbell; DIME.

Lawyers are even more liberal than other members of highly educated professions, which we show in Figure 4.2. This includes medical
doctors, accountants, and those in banking and finance (bottom three
plots, respectively).[52] Three professions do appear to be more liberal
or, at least, less evenly distributed across the ideological spectrum: academics, technology sector workers, and journalists. Compared to these
professionals, lawyers are comparably more conservative.

The legal profession is also far from monolithic, which is important
to the analyses that follow.[53] Figure 4.3 shows that, for example, older
lawyers tend to be more conservative, as are those who are men or partners in law firms. Two patterns are further worth noting. The first is that
graduates of elite law schools, such as those traditionally in the "Top 14"
of all law schools (a list that includes Harvard and Yale, which produce
many of the nation's judges), are more liberal than others; those attending those schools ranked outside of the top 100 are more conservative.
Given that most judges – particularly at the federal level – tend to come

[52] We confirm the differences in ideologies between these professions using a non-
parametric two-sample Kolmogorov-Smirnov test (KS-test), which uses the maximum
deviation between the two distributions to test the null hypothesis that both groups
were sampled from populations with identical distributions. We obtain similar results
when using difference-in-means t-tests.

[53] See Bonica, Chilton, and Sen (2016) for additional discussion on the ideology of the
legal profession; Bonica et al. (2018) discusses elite law graduates specifically.

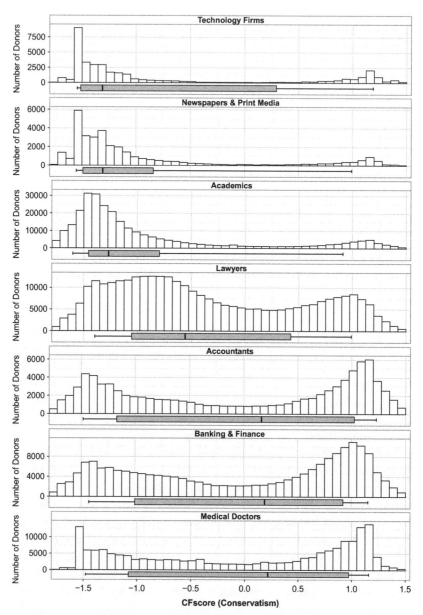

FIGURE 4.2 Ideological distributions for attorneys compared with other professions. Box-and-whisker plots display the median, interquartile range, and the 9th to 91st percentiles for each distribution.
Sources: Martindale-Hubbell; DIME.

OLS regression coefficients, lawyer ideology (DIME score) as outcome variable

FIGURE 4.3 OLS regression coefficients on lawyer ideology for different personal, professional, and educational characteristics. Intervals are 95% confidence intervals.
Sources: Martindale-Hubbell; DIME.

from the more elite law schools, this could push the more elite branches of the judiciary in a more liberal direction.[54]

---

54 For example, all nine justices on the Supreme Court as of 2019 attended either Harvard Law School or Yale Law School. One Justice, Ruth Bader Ginsburg, attended Harvard Law School but then transferred to Columbia Law School, from which she then graduated. In the lower federal courts, approximately 8 percent of judges attended Harvard Law School; approximately one-third attended one of the Top 14 law schools (Sen 2014b).

The second important point is that the ideologies of American lawyers are not homogeneous across state or jurisdiction. This is borne out by Figure 6.2, presented in Chapter 6, which compares the ideological distributions of lawyers across the fifty states. As the figure shows, some states have more liberal attorneys than others, and this correlates roughly with the states's ideological reputation.

Why is this geographic variation important? Judges tend to be drawn exclusively from their home states. Vacancies in California state courts will be filled with lawyers from California, while vacancies in Wyoming will be filled by lawyers from Wyoming. At the federal level, district courts and appeals courts are populated with lawyers and judges from those jurisdictions. To take one example, the fact that lawyers in Wyoming are more conservative matters; in the absence of ideological selection, we would expect judges in Wyoming to be more conservative as well. This also influences how politicians will approach judicial selection. Republicans in Wyoming (where lawyers are more conservative) should be less wary about the bar's involvement in the selection of judges than would Republicans in Massachusetts (where lawyers are very liberal). For this reason, we focus our empirical analyses on specific jurisdictions by comparing judges to politicians and lawyers from within the same state. This allows us to assess politicization more effectively.

ANALYZING THE TUG-OF-WAR EMPIRICALLY

Our analyses show that, as an empirical matter, lawyers lean to the left of center, but how does this correspond to the ideology of the nation's judges? If lawyers gain the upper hand in the tug of war – and ideology is largely kept out of judicial selection – then judges would more closely resemble the ideological leanings of lawyers in a given state. This would be evidence of *ideologically neutral selection*. Yet if political actors want to appoint judges who resemble them (in effect pulling the judiciary closer to them in the tug of war), then judges will more closely resemble the preferences of politicians. Seeing that judges deviate significantly from the underlying population of lawyers, more closely resembling the ideology of politicians, would be evidence of *ideologically based selection* or *politicization*.

Judges Compared to Lawyers

We analyze the tug of war explicitly in Figure 4.4, which shows the distribution of ideologies for judges juxtaposed with those of all lawyers.

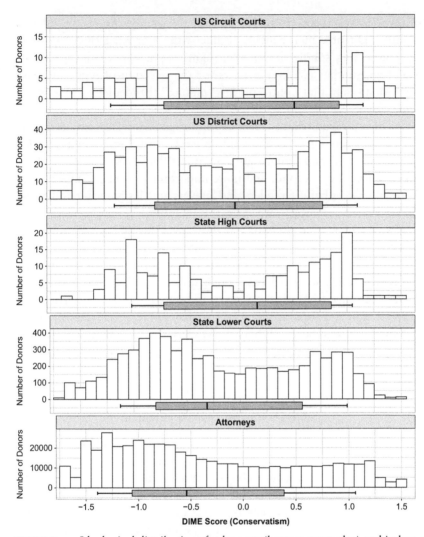

FIGURE 4.4 Ideological distributions for lawyers (bottom-most plot) and judges through various tiers of the US judiciary. Box-and-whisker plots display the median, interquartile range, and the 9th to 91st percentiles for each distribution. *Sources:* Martindale-Hubbell; DIME.

The figure shows that, while lawyers are quite left-leaning, *judges are by far less so*. Indeed, across every tier of the judiciary, judges tend to be significantly more conservative than lawyers, thus showing evidence of ideologically based selection. To provide context, our data show that the average American lawyer is ideologically somewhere in line with Joe Biden and Andrew Cuomo – that is, the center-left part of the ideological spectrum. By contrast, the average American judge is slightly right of center, roughly in line with Peter King (R-NY) – that is, representing solidly the middle, slightly right part of the spectrum. This suggests that ideology matters for the selection of judges at least somewhat – and that politicians are "pulling" the ideology of judges to some extent.

We also highlight some other important patterns. First, we note that both distributions follow a roughly bimodal distribution (with modes in the center-left and center-right), a pattern that characterizes much of American politics. Second, and more important for our argument here, these differences between judges and lawyers are all significant and probably not due to chance.[55] We show this in Table 4.1, which presents the results of a regression showing our measure of ideology as the outcome variable. In the table, a positive coefficient on a variable indicates that the variable is associated with a more conservative ideology. We also include controls that are standard basic predictors of ideology, including gender, age (proxied by graduation year), and state of residence.[56] The table shows that judges are more conservative than lawyers, and this difference is statistically significant (Table 4.1, Models 1 and 2), meaning that we can be fairly confident that this difference is not due to chance alone.

Judges Across the Judicial Hierarchy

To further unpack these differences, we disaggregate the judiciary in various ways. Not only do state courts hear different types of cases than do federal courts but trial courts (both at the federal level and at the state level) tend to hear different cases than do appeals courts. In addition, politicians might have different incentives to politicize certain courts and not others, and these differences might become more salient depending on a politician's ideology.

---

[55] A K-S test gives us a D statistic of 0.12 with a p-value of 0.00. We therefore reject the null hypothesis that the two distributions come from the same underlying distribution.

[56] In all of the models, we include dummy variables for each state in order to account for state-by-state differences in how judges are selected or how they could possibly serve. The use of state fixed effects also serves to account for possible geographic differences in the political context surrounding the selection of judges at the federal level – e.g., by the use of something like senatorial courtesy, the use of which could vary according to state. We unpack these further in Chapters 6 and 7, in which we examine how judicial selection both shapes and is shaped by the tension between lawyers and political actors.

TABLE 4.1 *OLS regression with ideology (DIME scores) as outcome variable. All models include state fixed effects.*

	Model 1	Model 2
Judge	0.133***	
	(0.009)	
Federal Circuit Court		0.354***
		(0.057)
Federal District Court		0.141***
		(0.028)
State High Court		0.222***
		(0.061)
State Lower Court		0.120***
		(0.009)
Federal Magistrate	0.042	0.042
	(0.032)	(0.032)
Federal Administrative Judge	0.180*	0.180*
	(0.082)	(0.082)
State Administrative Judge	−0.061	−0.064
	(0.056)	(0.056)
Female	−0.276***	−0.276***
	(0.003)	(0.003)
Years since Admitted	0.004***	0.004***
	(0.0003)	(0.0003)
Years since Admitted²	0.00002***	0.00002***
	(0.00001)	(0.00001)
Top 14 Law School	−0.126***	−0.126***
	(0.004)	(0.004)
>100 Ranked Law School	0.064***	0.064***
	(0.003)	(0.003)
Constant	−0.573***	−0.573***
	(0.023)	(0.023)
State Fixed Effects	✓	✓
Num. Obs.	472,115	472,115
R-squared	0.167	0.167

***$p < 0.001$; **$p < 0.01$; *$p < 0.05$

We therefore separate state from federal courts as well as trial courts from more politically important appeals courts. These differences in the respective ideologies of these different judges are shown in Figure 4.4, which disaggregates among (1) state lower courts, (2) state higher courts, (3) federal district courts, and (4) federal courts of appeals. The figure reveals several distinct patterns. The first pattern is that each of these groups of judges differs significantly from the overall population of lawyers.[57] For example, the ideological distribution of federal appeals judges (top-most distribution) differs in a more conservative direction from the overall distribution of lawyers (bottom-most plot). The same is true for the distribution of other judges, including those federal district judges and state appeals and lower court judges in the sample. Taken together, overall, judges are more conservative than the underlying pool of attorneys, and these are statistically significant differences. However, these judges also differ from each other, according to where they are in the "judicial hierarchy." The more politically important the court, the less the overall distribution resembles the underlying distribution of attorneys. Put differently, the average judge on a politically more important court (such as a US appeals court) is more conservative than the average court on a less politically important court (such as a state trial court). This is again evidence of ideologically based judicial selection.

CONCLUSION

Our goal in this chapter has been to introduce a second key player in the judicial tug of war, politicians. Like lawyers, elected politicians and party elites have a strong interest in the ideological contours of the judiciary. However, politicians must confront the fact that not only do they have at times limited control over judicial selection but the legal profession has professionally captured the judiciary's membership. This sets up the tension in the judicial tug of war. On the one hand, judges are professionally captured by the legal profession and share their professional interests and ideology; on the other hand, politicians are keen to appoint like-minded judges and work hard to shape the judiciary to best suit their policy interests and political goals. The tension between these two actors influences the ideology of the judiciary at a fundamental level.

How does the judicial tug of war play out in practice? Our results in this chapter show that politicians are effective at "pulling" the courts somewhat closer to their ideal policy points – as evidenced by the fact that we can detect ideological selection at all tiers of state and federal courts. Indeed, our analyses here (and also in subsequent chapters) show that the ideology of the judiciary is not purely reflective of the ideology of

[57] These differences are statistically significant, as shown by a series of pairwise K-S tests.

the legal profession, which suggests that judges are being in part chosen on the basis of their ideology of partisanship. (We rule out alternative explanations in the appendix to this chapter.) Our results also show that the higher the court, the more evidence of politicization. In Chapters 5 and 6, we explore the ways in which this could be impacted by variation in how judges are selected – for example, in comparing the way they are selected in the federal system (with executive appointment) versus in several states (with merit or bipartisan commissions). We also explore why politicians might want to prioritize higher courts, pulling particularly hard in the tug of war for courts that play an outsized role in American politics.

An implication of our empirical analyses is that the political parties face differing incentives in the judicial tug of war. For Republicans, having a more ideologically diverse judiciary is beneficial. For Democrats, ideological diversity is less appealing: The further the judiciary departs from the underlying ideological distribution of attorneys, the more conservative it becomes. These basic facts, we argue, explain the partisan nature of attacks on the courts. In recent years, Republicans have continuously accused Democrats of appointing "activist judges" to the bench and backing institutions that shield judges from accountability. Democrats, on the other hand, have accused Republicans of putting party and ideology over competence and qualifications when selecting judges. Neither party's criticism of the other rings hollow: Both want a politically friendly judiciary and actively work to promote the type of judicial institutions and reforms that best further this goal. For Republicans, this means selecting judges on the basis of ideology in order to cultivate a more policy-friendly bench. For Democrats (and the legal establishment), it means the opposite – trying to keep politics out of judicial selection, instead turning the focus to ideologically neutral criteria, such as qualifications and pedigree.

We note that a broader implication of our framework and certainly of our results is that many judges are indeed being chosen for reasons other than their pure "qualifications." This finding raises questions about judicial selection and vetting. US Supreme Court nominations and confirmation hearings provide a useful example. During each candidate's confirmation hearings, senators tend to ask questions about qualifications – including the candidate's previous professional experience, educational background, previous academic writings, and so on. Explicit discussions of politics, ideology, or how the candidates would rule once on the bench are off limits.[58] Yet our findings call these practices into question: Political actors do not ask nominees questions about politics, ideology, or potential rulings, but the data indicate that these considerations nonetheless seep into the selection of judges.

These results may also be grounds for optimism. As we discussed in our analysis, the nation's pool of attorneys is a left-leaning group – a group that tilts more left-ward than other similarly educated professions (see Figure 4.2). To have a judiciary that simply reflects the ideological preferences of a single profession – a group with fairly idiosyncratic policy preferences (as we discussed in Chapter 2) – seems counterintuitive and perhaps detrimental to the overall health of American democracy. Indeed, to entrust an entire branch of government to a single profession, and then have that profession be out of step with a more ideologically moderate public, runs counter to the spirit of a representative government. To that end, if politicians are actively using ideology to select judges, this could serve to make the judiciary more representative of the American public.

We conclude by noting two open questions, which we take up in the chapters that follow. First, our findings speak to the mechanisms by which judges are selected. The American judiciary is a variegated institution and, at the state level, judges are selected through a mix of executive appointments, merit commission recommendations, nonpartisan elections, partisan elections, and hybrid systems. The analyses we have presented have so far only made crude distinctions between these systems (primarily at the state versus federal level); but this approach overlooks these important differences in how judges are selected. Perhaps the politicization that we see in the American judiciary nationwide is not as obvious – or perhaps is more or less pronounced – in states where judges are elected versus appointed or where merit commissions are dominated by members of the state bar. Chapters 6 and 7 address these key questions.

Second, our findings suggest important differences between more and less politically important courts. Indeed, our results suggest that some of

---

[58] The practice of candidates evading such questions is known as the "Ginsburg Rule," named after Justice Ruth Bader Ginsburg, who notoriously avoided questions having to do with potential rulings, politics, or her ideology during her confirmation hearings. Justice Elena Kagan, who at the time was a law professor at Harvard, noted in a 1995 law review article that the Senate had ceased "to engage nominees in meaningful discussion of legal issues" and that the confirmation process was little more than "a vapid and hollow charade" (Kagan 1995, pp. 920, 941). Kagan herself refused to entertain such questions during her own confirmation hearing fifteen years later.

the strongest cleavages in ideology between the nation's pool of attorneys and the judiciary come at the apex of the national judiciary, at the federal appeals courts and in the state supreme courts. As we explore in the chapters that follow, these are the most politically important courts and, arguably, attract some of the most prestigious and experienced jurists. For these reasons, elected officials and party elites might have special incentives when it comes to these courts. For conservatives, however, the largely liberal landscape of elite legal educational environments could make this challenging. Chapter 5 addresses these questions in the context of the most politically influential courts, the federal judiciary.

CHAPTER APPENDIX

In what follows, we include additional findings pertaining to (1) who makes financial contributions to political candidates and organizations, (2) what predicts ideology among lawyers, and (3) how judges differ from lawyers in terms of what predicts their ideology.

Who Contributes?

As an illustration of who contributes and who does not, Table 4.2 provides a simple analysis of a lawyers' proclivity to donate at all (e.g., whether or not they appear in the DIME data) as the outcome variable. We then regress this variable on gender, age, prosecutor status, law firm partner status, legal academic, status geography, and some simple measures of quality of legal education. Some of the variables do appear to have substantively meaningful and significant relationships to the proclivity to donate. For example, those who are partners in law firms or those who graduated from top ("T14") law schools are more likely to make political contributions than other kinds of attorneys. (Some do not. For example, law professors do not appear to donate more, with the effect essentially disappearing once we include state fixed effects.) As we note above, because this missingness could introduce some bias into our inferences, we present results in the Appendix that impute the missing observations.[59] These results indicate that the overall donor pool is less representative of lawyers with conservative DIME scores. However, the

---

59 We note, however, that law firm partners and top law school graduates might actually be those most likely to become judges, which would have the effect of biasing the donor pool in favor of those most likely to become judges.

TABLE 4.2 *OLS regression, whether individual contributes (is in the DIME database) as outcome variable.*

	Model 1	Model 2
Female	−0.098***	−0.098***
	(0.001)	(0.001)
Years since Admitted	0.023***	0.023***
	(0.0001)	(0.0001)
(Years since Admitted)^2	−0.0003***	−0.0003***
	(0.00000)	(0.00000)
Government Lawyer	−0.195***	−0.207***
	(0.005)	(0.005)
Corporate (in-house counsel)	−0.111***	−0.088***
	(0.002)	(0.002)
Big Law Firm (top 100)	0.096***	0.098***
	(0.002)	(0.002)
Solo Practice	0.008***	0.008***
	(0.001)	(0.001)
Law Professor	−0.020***	−0.015**
	(0.005)	(0.005)
Partner	0.111***	0.117***
	(0.003)	(0.003)
Prosecutor/District Attorney	−0.053***	−0.047***
	(0.004)	(0.004)
Public Defender	−0.070***	−0.056***
	(0.007)	(0.007)
Top 14 Law School	0.086***	0.096***
	(0.002)	(0.002)
>100 Ranked Law School	−0.026***	−0.017***
	(0.001)	(0.001)
Constant	0.159***	0.178***
	(0.002)	(0.010)
State Fixed Effects		✓
Num. Obs.	974,419	974,419
R-squared	0.087	0.105

***$p < 0.001$; **$p < 0.01$; *$p < 0.05$
Source: DIME.

substantive results we obtain are largely consistent with the results we present in the main text.

What Predicts Ideology?

For example, Table 4.3 presents the relationship between DIME scores and several key attributes. Unless otherwise noted, we use the DIME score as the outcome measure. Thus, a negative effect indicates a more

TABLE 4.3 *Predictors of ideology among lawyers. Ideology (DIME scores) are the outcome variables. Larger value indicates more conservative.*

	CFscore	
	Model 1	Model 2
Female	−0.302***	−0.270***
	(0.003)	(0.003)
Years since Admitted	0.006***	0.006***
	(0.0004)	(0.0003)
(Years since Admitted)^2	0.00002**	0.00001
	(0.00001)	(0.00001)
Government Lawyer	−0.352***	−0.175***
	(0.015)	(0.015)
Corporate (in-house counsel)	0.093***	0.120***
	(0.007)	(0.007)
Big Law Firm (top 100)	0.065***	0.078***
	(0.004)	(0.004)
Solo-practice	−0.034***	−0.035***
	(0.003)	(0.003)
Law Professor	−0.347***	−0.373***
	(0.013)	(0.012)
Partner	−0.059***	0.006
	(0.006)	(0.005)
Prosecutor/District Attorney	0.145***	0.181***
	(0.012)	(0.011)
Public Defender	−0.411***	−0.359***
	(0.021)	(0.020)
Top 14 Law School	−0.265***	−0.132***
	(0.004)	(0.004)
>100 Ranked Law School	0.091***	0.070***
	(0.003)	(0.003)
Constant	−0.420***	−0.595***
	(0.005)	(0.023)
State Fixed Effects		✓
Num. Obs.	472115	472115
R-squared	0.056	0.172

***$p < 0.001$; **$p < 0.01$; *$p < 0.05$
Sources: Martindale-Hubbell; DIME.

liberal-leaning ideology (which corresponds to a more negative DIME score); a positive effect indicates a more conservative-leaning ideology.[60]

---

[60] None of these estimates are intended to be causal estimates; rather, these are indicators of what factors predict a more conservative DIME score.

Models 1 and 2 are simple OLS regressions, while Models 3 and 4 are hierarchical linear models with random effects for state, county, and law school attended. For ease of interpretation in Models 2 and 3, we group the law schools into tiers using the 2011 U.S. News and World Report Ranking. The cohorts are (1) schools ranked in the traditional "Top 14," (2) schools ranked 15–25, (3) schools ranked 26–50, (4) schools ranked 51–71, (5) schools ranked 72–100, and (6) schools ranked outside of the top 100.[61]

Table 4.3 demonstrates some very clear patterns that lend support to these data capturing meaningful cleavages. For example, female lawyers are more likely to be liberal-leaning than male lawyers, as are law professors, public defenders, and government lawyers. Also unsurprising is the fact that those who are prosecutors (or district attorneys), corporate in-house counsel, and those who work at "Big Law" firms are more conservative. We also see an increased conservative effect the longer one has been admitted to the bar, a consistent effect throughout the various models, which suggests that older lawyers are more conservative than younger ones.

Recruitment Due to Quality, Age, or Other Characteristics

Our results suggest that ideology plays a strong role in how judges are selected and that the importance varies according to the political importance of the court. These are patterns that we unpack in much greater detail in the chapters that follow, paying particularly close attention to variation according to state and, thus, according to how judges are formally selected. However, it is possible that judges are still selected for reasons unrelated to ideology and that the patterns we are finding are interesting artifacts but not necessarily evidence for ideologically based selection.

RECRUITMENT ON THE BASIS OF AGE We consider the most likely explanation to be that the pool of judges is simply older than the rest of the population. As we also see in Table 4.3, those who are older tend to be more conservative. This is largely borne out by other studies in American politics: Voters who are older tend to be more conservative on

---

[61] The rank changes somewhat over time; however, the composition of the Top 14 law schools (the "T14") has rarely changed.

many policy issues (e.g., crime, redistribution, and education spending) and more likely to identify as Republicans. If judges are simply older than the rest of the lawyerly population, then this could plausibly explain why judges as a whole tend to be more conservative. Indeed, on this point, the average age of a federal judge in the United States is around fifty, while the average age of an attorney in the United States is lower.

We note, however, that the effect of age does not diminish the separate effect of the judge variable (Table 4.3). In addition, even if the average judge was twenty years older than the average lawyer, the cumulative effects of the age gap would not account for the entire difference in comparing judges to other individuals. Although this strikes us as a possible explanation for some of the differences we see, it does not explain the entirety of the gap between judges and lawyers in terms of ideology.

RECRUITMENT OF RACE OR GENDER We can also rule out other explanations regarding characteristics that do vary according to ideology – that is, that judges are recruited or selected for reasons that are superficially unrelated to political beliefs but that, inevitably (and perhaps unintentionally), vary according to political belief. The most obvious such characteristic would be demographic. Ever since the Carter administration started aggressively recruiting women and ethnic minorities, presidents and other governing executives have tried to make the judiciary more reflective of the population as a whole. This extends, too, to the state level, although the impact has been moderated by the selection process for judges. Nonetheless, attempts at making the judiciary more reflective could have the effect of inadvertently selecting also on ideology, thus making the judiciary less reflective of the pool of attorneys. Although this clearly could be the case, we see no evidence that this mechanism is driving our results: If selection on the basis of race/gender was increasing – for example, if more women and minorities than are represented in the pool of attorneys were selected into the judiciary – then the judiciary should lean more to the *left* than the overall pool of attorneys.

RECRUITMENT OF QUALIFICATIONS Another explanation that is easy to rule out is whether judges are selected on the basis of superior credentials. If judges are selected purely on the basis of superior credentials, then we should see that the ideology of judges lean more toward the ideology of those who graduated from top law schools. This, again, is something we do not see. If lawyers from top law schools were over-represented among judges, then we would expect judges to more closely resemble those graduates – for example, to be even more left-leaning than the rest of the lawyerly population.

5

Political Incentives and Politicization in the Federal Courts

"Look at my more recent colleagues, all extremely well qualified for the court, and the votes were, I think, strictly on party lines for the last three of them, or close to it, and that doesn't make any sense. That suggests to me that the process is being used for something other than ensuring the qualifications of the nominees."

Chief Justice John Roberts[1]

In March of 2001, the administration of George W. Bush announced that the White House would no longer submit the names of potential nominees to the federal courts for vetting by the American Bar Association (ABA).[2] The move was controversial. Since the 1950s, US presidents from both parties had allowed the ABA the courtesy of confidentially vetting and rating federal judicial candidates before their names became public. However, more recent years have seen serious concerns arise in conservative circles about the ABA's influence over the federal courts and the possibility that it was biased – and biased strongly – against conservative candidates. Fed up with this perceived bias, Bush's attorney general, Alberto Gonzalez, pulled the plug. "[T]he question," he wrote in a strongly worded open letter to the ABA's leadership, "is whether the ABA should play a unique, quasi-official role and thereby have its voice heard before and above all others." Ultimately, the White House – echoing the voices of many conservatives in various branches of

[1] Roberts (2016).
[2] See Gonzales (2001).

state and federal governments – did "not think that kind of preferential arrangement is either appropriate or fair."[3]

The Bush administration's decision to eliminate the ABA's private vetting of judicial candidates generated a barrage of criticism from Democrats. Senator Chuck Schumer (D-NY) called it a "sad day for American justice" and complained, "For the last 50 years, the ABA was an essential part of the process, making sure that there was quality rather than ideology. Now all of that has changed."[4] Senator Patrick Leahy (D-VT) warned that denying the bar the ability to vet candidates would lead to "embarrassment" if unqualified candidates were to be named to the federal bench.[5] The ABA's president panned the move, maintaining that its evaluation process "provides a buffer from partisanship and a buffer from political patronage" and expressing the ABA's "concern[]" that politics may be taking the place of competence in the review."[6]

However, the move heartened many on the right, tapping into a long-held grievance against the ABA. Members of the Federalist Society, an organization of conservative law professors and lawyers, were "delighted" at the announcement, with many of them having "yearned for such a move."[7] One conservative lawyer, cheered, "It's high time that the White House sent the ABA packing."[8] This conservative resentment toward the bar has persisted moving forward. In 2017, Republican Senator Ben Sasse (R-NE) took to the House floor to declare that "The American Bar Association is not neutral. The ABA is a liberal organization that has publicly and consistently advocated for left-of-center positions for more than two decades now."[9] Republican Senator Ted Cruz (R-TX), in applauding the Trump administration's continuation of the Bush policy forbidding the ABA's confidential vetting, complained that "the notion of a non-ideological organization has been belied by the

---

[3] See Gonzales (2001).
[4] ABC News (2001).
[5] ABC News (2001). Leahy's comments foresaw the nomination of Harriet Miers to the US Supreme Court. Miers, a long-standing confidante of George W. Bush, was immediately excoriated as being unqualified to sit on the Court (Fletcher and Babington 2005), and she was eventually replaced with the more experienced John Roberts.
[6] Quoted in Goldstein (2001).
[7] Lewis (2001), which also notes that the Federalist Society "had taken on the bar association as a target in its publications, an outgrowth of the resentment conservatives have felt about the lawyers' organization since 1987 when it gave a mixed evaluation to Judge Robert H. Bork's candidacy for the Supreme Court."
[8] Goldstein (2001).
[9] Lewis (2001).

conduct of the ABA over the years. The ABA today is an openly liberal advocacy group."[10]

The partisan and ideological conflict surrounding the ABA's role in the vetting of federal judicial candidates – and the resulting uproar when the Bush White House refused to maintain the ABA's privileged role – highlights how federal courts have become a flashpoint in the judicial tug of war. These courts – and especially the US Supreme Court – make final policy determinations on issues such as civil rights, religious freedoms, the death penalty, reproductive rights, political redistricting, and the separation of powers among state and federal branches of government. This makes the people who sit on the federal courts – and their selection – a priority for both party leaders and the legal elite. Indeed, both federal politicians (including critics of the ABA) and members of the legal establishment have preferences over what federal courts look like: Republican senators would like more conservative federal judges, while Democratic senators would like more liberal ones. The legal establishment, which leans in a more liberal direction, has long agitated for political considerations to stay out of federal judicial selection.

In this chapter, we explore what our framework of the judicial tug of war predicts and explains about the federal courts system, the pinnacle of the US judiciary. Importantly, for the federal courts, political actors – such as presidents and senators (especially those sitting on the important Senate Judiciary Committee) – have the power to make judicial appointments, with the legal establishment having relatively little power. What this means, and what we show here, is that federal politicians have wide discretion to demand and select the kinds of federal judges they want – and this, in turn, means that they use ideology (and partisanship) to pull these judges closer to their own policy preferences. In other words, the judicial selection mechanism tips the tug of war's hand in favor of political elites.

Given their weak formal role in judicial selection at the federal level, is the legal profession irrelevant? Hardly. As we discuss in this chapter, federal judges are unsurprisingly the cream of the crop in terms of pedigree, professional experience, and legal education. Attending an elite, high-caliber law school (e.g., Harvard, Yale, Stanford, or the University of Chicago) makes it far more likely that a lawyer will be elevated to the federal bench. However, most of these elite schools, as we show, have

---

[10] Shortell (2017).

earned their reputations as liberal bastions, producing graduates who are, on average, well to the left of the profession at large.[11]

We argue that this fact constrains conservative politicians (usually Republicans) looking for a suitable supply of conservative candidates for promotion onto the federal courts. Given the relative scarcity of elite, conservative lawyers, Republicans will have a harder time staffing all openings and finding candidates that meet the bare minimum criteria. However, this is good news for the supply of young conservative lawyers; for them, the relative scarcity means less competition and more opportunities for federal judgeships. As evidence of this, we show that, conditional on graduating from a top law school, conservatives have a better chance of being selected as a judge. In addition, we examine evidence documenting the growing importance of signaling conservative ideology – for example, via candidates' involvement in ideologically oriented professional organizations, such as the Federalist Society. All of these suggest that politicians must operate within the constraints established by the tug of war: Even though they have wide latitude when it comes to the federal courts, the legal profession still plays a powerful gatekeeping power.

This chapter proceeds as follows. We first provide an overview of the federal courts and a brief discussion of how judges are selected onto the courts. We then present systematic evidence of ideologically based selection – which suggests that federal politicians have pulled the federal judiciary quite close to their preference point in the course of playing the judicial tug of war. We then evaluate how these patterns map onto legal pedigree – specifically, law school attended. We show that, conditional on graduating from a top law school, conservatives have an easier time securing federal judgeships. We next tie this into a framework of the labor market by considering both supply- and demand-side concerns. Specifically, we consider the strategic choices made by candidates interested in pursuing a judicial career (the "supply"). We next consider the strategic incentives faced by both presidents and senators in deciding which candidates to nominate and confirm (the "demand"). We conclude by exploring the implications of this analysis for future ideological battles over the nation's judiciary.

---

[11] For more on the development of the ambient liberal environment within the law more generally, see Teles (2012, chap. 2), who refers to this as "the Liberal Legal Network." The liberal ideological pattern within law schools has been quantitatively explored in other papers. See, for example, Bonica et al. (2018) and Chilton and Posner (2015).

THE POLITICAL AND LEGAL IMPORTANCE OF THE FEDERAL COURTS

Early American history had a decentralized judiciary, with the courts of the various states meeting the country's early legal needs. However, over time, it became clear to the framers of the US Constitution that this was insufficient: Interstate commerce, as well as the business being conducted by the federal government, required a federal judiciary – one that would be relatively limited in jurisdiction but one that was powerful enough to handle the centralized government's business needs as well as the feuds between the federal government and the various states. For this, the framers looked both to Anglo-American tradition as well as the existing state court system. Following English tradition, where judges were commissioned by the crown, it was natural that appointment of these judges would be handled by the American head of government, the US president.

Even so, with the exception of the establishment of the US Supreme Court, the federal constitution is silent on the size and structure of the federal courts. The only mention of the court system of the United States is that "[t]he judicial Power of the United States, shall be vested in one supreme Court, and in such inferior Courts as the Congress may from time to time ordain and establish".[12] In terms of how judges for this "Supreme Court" would be selected, the Constitution gives the power to the president, who "shall nominate, and by and with the Advice and Consent of the Senate, shall appoint ... Judges of the supreme Court, and all other Officers of the United States."[13] However, the Constitution says nothing about the number of justices who should be on the Supreme Court or about the number and nature of lower courts.

Subsequent implementation of the federal courts system was therefore left to the majority-lawyer First Congress, which we discussed briefly in Chapter 2.[14] This Congress enacted the Judiciary Act of 1789, establishing the federal court system as we would recognize it today. Specifically, the act established lower federal courts, including trial courts in each of the thirteen states (and two in Virginia and Massachusetts) as well as several intermediate appeals courts. In lieu of calling for the appointment

---

[12] US Constitution Article III, Section 1.

[13] US Constitution, Article II, Section 2.

[14] As we noted in Chapter 2, seventeen out of the twenty-eight senators in this First Congress were lawyers (or 60 percent) and thirty-one out of the sixty-four representatives (or 48 percent) were lawyers.

TABLE 5.1 *Authorized judgeships in the US federal courts, as of 2018.*

Court	Authorized Judgeships	2017 Caseload
US District Courts	577	367,937
US Courts of Appeals	179	58,951
US Supreme Court	9	71
US Court of Federal Claims	16	1,922
US Court of International Trade	9	313
Total	890	

Note: Column 2 corresponds to 2017 caseloads and, for the Supreme Court, cases heard.
Source: Administrative Office of the US Courts.

of appeals court judges, the original Judiciary Act had Supreme Court justices "riding circuit" to hear appeals; this practice served to unite the interests of judges and local lawyers' organizations, bringing them together socially as well as professionally.

Over time, subsequent congressional statutes grew the size and scope of the federal courts to include appointed federal appeals judges and federal trial judges. Today, the federal system is organized with the US Supreme Court at the apex of the hierarchy, with the intermediate US courts of appeals below it. As of our writing, thirteen such appeals courts exist, eleven corresponding to different geographic areas, one separately for the District of Columbia, and one designated to hear cases involving patents (the US Court of Appeals for the Federal Circuit). Below these are the ninety-four district courts; several states have multiple district courts (e.g., New York and California), while other states only have one (e.g., Massachusetts and Wyoming). Table 5.1 displays the number of authorized judgeships, as of 2018, by court.

Why are appointments to the federal courts so important to elected officials and party leaders? First, the federal courts – and the US Supreme Court in particular – are tasked with being the final interpreters of the US Constitution. As Chief Justice John Marshall wrote in his infamous ruling of *Marbury v. Madison*, "It is emphatically the province and duty of the judicial department to say what the law is."[15] That is, the Supreme Court – not Congress and not the executive – is the final interpreter of the US Constitution, and the Constitution itself supersedes any statute enacted by Congress. This was further affirmed by subsequent rulings, such as 1958's *Cooper v. Aaron*, in which the Court unanimously

[15] *Marbury v. Madison*, 5 U.S. 137, 177 (1803).

affirmed that "the federal judiciary is supreme in the exposition of the Constitution."[16] These cases have clarified that the judges on the federal courts – not individual state executives or governments – were the final interpreters of the US Constitution.

Second, and relatedly, the federal courts have the authority to review congressional statutes – a power embedded in the separation-of-powers framework of the US Constitution. This means that the federal courts – and the federal courts alone – can declare acts of Congress unconstitutional. (In addition, judicial supremacy means that such rulings cannot be changed or altered by subsequent acts of Congress.) As Marshall continued in his famous *Marbury* ruling, "If, then, the Courts are to regard the Constitution, and the Constitution is superior to any ordinary act of the Legislature, the Constitution, and not such ordinary act, must govern the case to which they both apply."[17] This also means that federal courts can declare state laws unlawful if they conflict with the federal constitution. Recent years have seen federal courts exercise this power with regard to unlawful searches and seizures, declarations of marriage, environmental regulations, and the rights of criminal defendants.

The power to interpret the law also extends to interpretations of congressional statutes, and, although Congress can obviously rewrite its statutes in a way that circumvents a federal court's interpretation, as a matter of fact it does so rarely. An example of this concerns voting rights and the Supreme Court's decision in *Shelby County v. Holder*,[18] a 2013 ruling that struck down portions of the Voting Rights Act of 1965 (VRA). As of our writing, these portions of the VRA – which could have been rewritten and updated in a straightforward fashion – remain untouched, leaving the law's ability to protect minority voters substantially compromised. This has had tremendous ramifications, and, as of the 2013 ruling, a number of states have instituted tough voting identification laws that might be disenfranchising some US citizens. This is just one example where the Supreme Court's role in the interpretation of statues became vitally politically important.

Third, the federal courts have the unique power to adjudicate disputes between the various states, as well as any cases involving the US government. This is again stated in the US Constitution (and also implicit in the American federal system of government, where the power of government

---

[16] *Cooper v. Aaron*, 358 U.S. 1, 18 (1958).
[17] *Marbury v. Madison*, 5 U.S. 137, 178 (1803).
[18] 570 U.S. 2 (2013).

is divided between the federal government and the governments of the various states).[19] The federal courts are also statutorily authorized to hear cases in which the parties are citizens of different states.[20] Thus, by default, issues that pertain to highly charged topics – such as states suing one another, or litigation across state lines – will be handled by federal not state courts. These tend to be the most expensive cases, ones involving multistate operations and businesses. These also tend to be the ones with the largest potential political impact.

Lastly, the federal courts handle all cases involving the workings of the federal government or legal violations by federal officials, making federal courts the default venue for important separation of powers cases involving the relationship between Congress and the executive. The federal courts are also default venues for considerations of presidential powers, including the power of the president to imprison enemy combatants, to deploy troops, to initiate border activity, and to negotiate on behalf of the United States. Federal courts also handle a large number of civil rights lawsuits involving allegations of misconduct by federal officials, including immigration officials and federal law enforcement officers.

These issues speak to the federal courts' *importance for politicians*, but what about the federal courts' *importance for the legal establishment*? While much of the regulation of state and local bars is handled by state courts,[21] federal courts still occupy a special place within the broader legal community, serving the most prestigious appointments to which a young lawyer can aspire. So important are the federal courts that entire legal organizations have come into existence to motivate and train students to pursue careers on the federal bench. (We discuss these later in the chapter, when we consider the influence exerted by organizations such as the Federalist Society.) In addition, young graduates of top law schools are encouraged to pursue clerkships with federal judges as a way of building their résumés and fostering professional networks. Clerking for a federal judge is, for many, the first step toward a lucrative and prestigious legal career.

Despite this influence, the federal courts are not necessarily the most productive or expansive in their reach. To give some context on this

[19] US Constitution, Article III, Section 2.
[20] US Constitution, Article III, Section 2.
[21] See our discussion in Chapter 3 for more on the regulation of state bar associations by state courts; we discuss the relationship between the bar's composition and the composition of state courts in Chapter 6.

point, as Table 5.1 shows, there are nearly 900 authorized federal judgeships. As a point of comparison, these 900 judges work alongside roughly 1,800 clerks. This pales in comparison to the roughly 20,000 staffers working in Congress or the roughly 2 million people employed by the executive branch.[22]

The federal courts are also much leaner than their state counterparts, which we discuss in much more depth in Chapter 6. While the federal district courts hear roughly 400,000 cases, the court of appeals adjudicate roughly 60,000 cases. Meanwhile, the Supreme Court, the apex of the federal courts system, hears roughly 70 or 80 cases per year – about 0.002 percent of the total number of cases filed in the federal system. These cases are, however, the most politically and legally important cases in the entire country – suggesting that each individual case is outsized in terms of importance and potential political impact.

THE SELECTION OF FEDERAL JUDGES

The political importance of the federal courts – as well as the nature of lifetime appointments – raises the stakes when deciding who sits on these courts. In this section, we explicitly consider the incentives from the perspectives of the two actors in our tug of war: (1) politicians and (2) the legal establishment.

Politicians' Roles and Incentives in the Selection of Federal Judges

Put simply, politicians have an incentive to appoint individuals to the federal courts who share their policy preferences and partisan interests. The policy importance of choosing like-minded, ideological allies has been amply noted by the academic scholarship. For example, in his seminal look at the history and patterns behind federal judicial selection, the political scientist Sheldon Goldman noted that appointing presidents face a "constant tension between patronage, merit, and policy-ideology considerations in the appointments process."[23] Importantly, Goldman was careful to note the role of political patronage in guiding presidential appointments – particularly so for the Truman and Eisenhower administrations. However, for more modern presidencies – including the Reagan presidency, which in many ways forged a new approach for

---

[22] Ornstein et al. (2017).
[23] Goldman (1997, p. 359).

judicial appointments – the guiding standard was furthering policy. Of Ronald Reagan, Goldman notes a "presidential policy agenda achieved prominence" with "well over half their appeals court appointments of the policy-agenda type."[24] Ultimately, for Goldman, "presidential agendas and judicial selection are intimately tied" and "policy agendas tend to predominate in times of political realignment."[25] More recently, the alignment between presidential ideology and that of their nominees has come into striking focus. As the Supreme Court news reporter Linda Greenhouse observed in 2017,

[for] the first time in the court's modern history, the individual justices are ideologically aligned with the party of the president who appointed them. There are no crossovers, no William Brennan or Harry Blackmun or John Paul Stevens, Republican-appointed justices who ended their careers as liberals, and no Byron White, appointed by President John F. Kennedy and a dissenter from the court's liberal rulings on abortion and criminal procedure.[26]

Mechanics of Selection

How effective are political actors in pursuing their partisan objectives as they relate to the courts? Our tug-of-war framework from Chapter 4 helps address this by highlighting the relative importance of politicians within the federal system. Other selection systems in the United States – at the state level, at least – prioritize the legal establishment (in the case of merit commissions) or voters (in the case of judicial elections). On the other hand, the federal system puts nearly all power in the hands of the US president and his aides, working in conjunction with Senate majority leaders.[27] If the US Senate and the White House are controlled by the same party, then this is straightforward: The president will nominate

---

[24] Goldman (1997, p. 360). Goldman writes, "For Roosevelt, the partisan, personal, and policy agendas were typically interwoven," while Reagan "clearly trumpeted his presidential motivation, that of furthering his policy agenda" (Goldman 1997, p. 360).
[25] Goldman (1997, p. 361). More generally, "We will see over the years, for example, the gradual waning of the influence of the national party organizations on the selection process and the lessening to some extent of the dispensing of judges as political patronage" in favor of policy considerations (Goldman 1997, p. 14). We return to these themes in Chapter 7, in which we discuss attempts at judicial reform, and Chapter 8, in which we consider the downstream consequences of the judicial tug of war – in particular when we consider the externalities of polarization within the courts.
[26] Greenhouse (2017).
[27] For a step-by-step walk through on the "mechanics" of federal selection, see Goldman (1997, pp. 9–12).

an ideological ally, someone who – like Trump's nomination of Neil Gorsuch – solidifies the party's preferred ideological positioning on the court and accurately and closely represents the ideological interests of the politicians who named them.[28] If the Senate and the White House are controlled by different parties, then the situation becomes more nuanced but not entirely different: The president will in this case nominate someone who satisfies their own preferences but also those of the median Senate Judiciary Committee member, sacrificing ideological proximity to the extent necessary to secure confirmation. The resulting candidate may be someone who is slightly more moderate but nonetheless still ideologically aligned with the president.[29]

This process underscores that the federal system consolidates nearly all the power over judicial selection to (1) the president (and by extension his aides) and (2) the US Senate. As a formal matter, members of the public are kept entirely out of the process. To the extent that the public is involved, it is through lobbying on the Senate and via public complaints and criticisms; and, although research has shown that the public's lobbying of US senators about Supreme Court candidates is effective,[30] the effect of this contact is limited. There is no popular vote, no public notice and comment period, a stark contrast to state-level systems in which elections play a key role.

The limited public involvement and the direct influence and discretion of political actors were by design. Writing in *The Federalist Papers* No. 76 on the nature of the president's appointment power, Alexander Hamilton wrote that the president was particularly well suited to appoint judges because he will "feel himself under stronger obligations, and more interested to investigate with care the qualities requisite to the stations to be filled, and to prefer with impartiality the persons who may have the fairest pretensions to them."[31] As for the public, Hamilton wrote in *Federalist* No. 78 that the judiciary should be kept insulated from the

---

[28] This is, of course, subject to other interests of the executive, including geographic diversity, demographic diversity, and political patronage. More of this is discussed in Goldman (1997), in particular his discussion of the Carter administration's push to select more female and minority judges in the 1970s.

[29] For more on the impact of home-state senators on judicial appointments, see Songer (1982), which documents that judges adopt policy positions more in line with those of their home-state senator.

[30] See, for example, Kastellec, Lax, and Phillips (2010), which finds that positive home-state support positively influences the probability that a senator will vote in favor of the candidate.

[31] Hamilton, Madison, and Jay (1787).

vicissitudes of public opinion; otherwise "there would be too great a disposition to consult popularity."[32] For our purposes, this relative power means that political actors have strong leeway to name and confirm those whose ideologies are compatible with their own. At the federal level, we would therefore expect federal politicians – including senators but especially the president – to exert a very strong "pull" in the judicial tug of war.

THE BAR'S ROLE IN THE SELECTION OF FEDERAL JUDGES

Even though politicians exercise a large role in the selection of federal judges, the bar also plays an important role, which we consider in light of our broader framework. We consider two pathways through which this influence operates: (1) providing the candidate pool, particularly when it comes to extremely elite lawyers, and (2) formal involvement by bar associations, specifically the ABA. Regarding the importance of the former, we consider the legal establishment's professional capture of the federal judiciary to be driven almost entirely by elite legal circles.

Providing an Elite Candidate Pool

First, the legal establishment has pushed political actors to only consider extremely elite, extremely qualified lawyers for the federal courts – all of whom have formidable and well-established professional roots. This practice is not particularly long-standing. As we note in Chapters 2 and 3, the legal profession writ large – and therefore judges – was not was not focused on educational requirements and pedigree. Starting in the mid-twentieth century, however, legal organizations began to push toward a professionalized judiciary, which included the federal courts. In summarizing some historical trends, Goldman notes that "the American Bar Association's entry into the selection process strengthened the forces within each administration favoring the professionalization of the judiciary, particularly at the district court level."[33]

---

[32] Hamilton, Madison, and Jay (1787).

[33] Goldman (1997, p. 358). In looking at the federal appeals courts, Goldman further notes that, "as with the district courts, we can see the professionalization of the judiciary, except that this professionalization spanned the entire fifty-six-year period. The proportion with neither judicial nor prosecutorial experience fluctuated, and the spread was more than 17 percentage points. The lowest proportion was for the

The bar's push toward increased professionalization of the judiciary has operated in tandem with the increasing oversight by bar associations over legal education, including the institutionalization of formal requirements and bar accreditation. The result has been a narrowing in the educational and professional path that young lawyers must follow to become a federal judge. At the US Supreme Court, all justices at the time of our writing are graduates of just three law schools, Harvard, Yale, and Columbia.[34] For the lower courts, according to statistics from the Federal Judicial Center, out of 276 active federal appeals judges at the time of our writing, 44 list Harvard Law School in their educational profiles (approximately 16 percent), while another 28 judges list attending Yale Law School (approximately 10 percent). In other words, about a quarter of all judges in the federal appeals courts attended just two law schools, Harvard and Yale.[35] For district courts, too, graduates of elite law schools – including Harvard, Yale, Chicago, Stanford, and Columbia – are heavily overrepresented. The strong connection between elite educational environments and the federal bench has created an unusual situation: Fully a third of the federal government is reliant primarily on graduates of just a handful of extremely elite legal programs.

The strong reliance on elite legal training has also created an unusual ideological problem. This is evident in Figure 5.1 in which we plot the average ideology scores for graduates of elite versus non-elite law schools. (We define "elite" here and elsewhere as including the historical "Top 14" law schools, a group whose composition has not changed in decades.)[36] As before, the ideology is based on DIME scores, which roughly range from liberal (−2.0) to conservative (+2.0). Thus, what Figure 5.1 shows is that graduates of the top law schools are much more liberal than are graduates of other law schools.[37]

Roosevelt and Eisenhower appointees and the highest for Carter's and Reagan's" (Goldman 1997, p. 353). To be clear, however, the trend corresponded with increased ABA involvement, but it is not clear that the ABA's involvement caused it.

34 The figure is so striking that, at the 2017 Harvard Law School reunion, Chief Justice John Roberts joked, "Harvard does not need numbers to make her influence felt. Now I am sure that remains true today. But why take a chance?" (Barnes 2017).

35 We conducted this search on August 3, 2018, using the Federal Judicial Center's online database, www.fjc.gov. The numbers are slightly lower for US District Court judges. Of currently 1,010 active sitting judges (as of August 3, 2018), 78 list Harvard Law School in their professional profiles and 45 list Yale Law School.

36 The Top 14 (or "T14") law schools include Yale, Harvard, Stanford, Columbia, Chicago, New York University, UC-Berkeley, University of Pennsylvania, Michigan, University of Virginia, Duke, Northwestern, Cornell, and Georgetown.

37 The differences between these distributions are significant, as confirmed by a Kolmogorov–Smirnov test.

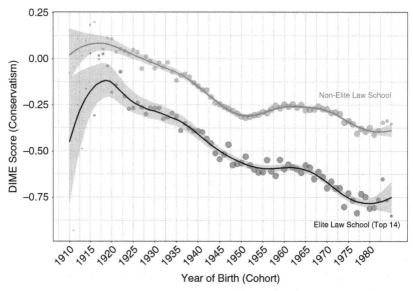

FIGURE 5.1 Average ideology for graduates of non-elite versus elite (T14) law
schools over time. Elite graduates are much more liberal.
Source: Martindale-Hubbell; DIME.

The strong left-leaning tendency among elite law school graduates
creates different challenges and incentives for conservative and liberal
politicians. Indeed, the liberal landscape at elite institutions means that
conservatives have to look further and more deeply to find suitable
talent. For this reason, as we discuss later in this chapter, conservatives in elite legal circles have set up conservative networks aimed
at nurturing, cultivating, and identifying elite conservative talent. The
best and most obvious example of this is the Federalist Society, the
conservative-leaning intellectual organization that was founded to chal-
lenge a "form of orthodox liberal ideology which advocates a centralized
and uniform society."[38] As one commentator described it, the early
Federalist Society members were "ideological outliers who struggled
to gain credibility in class and acceptance on campus."[39] Another

[38] www.fed-soc.org/aboutus/. See also Teles (2012, p. 136), which argues that the Federalist Society is a "provider of public goods" in that it engages in recruitment of law
students, invests in human capital of members, nurtures conservative legal ideas, and
encourages social networks. For more on the intellectual foundations and goals of the
Federalist Society, see Hollis-Brusky (2015).

[39] Hicks (2005, p. 628).

noted that, "As the Federalists see it, the society's founders were scrappy outsiders who were waging a lonely struggle against the pervasive liberalism of America's law schools."[40] No longer: Today, the Society boasts nearly 200 chapters across the country, and claims 4 current Supreme Court Justices among its members. As the political scientists Lawrence Baum and Neal Devins noted, "the role of the Federalist Society is the natural culmination of a decadeslong evolution of judicial selection by Republican presidents, one that has made ideological credentials more central to the nomination process."[41]

The importance of the Federalist Society in terms of signaling and identifying potential conservative candidates to Republican Party operatives should not be understated. From conferences to law school chapters to the support of faculty research, the Federalist Society has played a key role not just in developing conservative jurisprudence but also in terms of providing a signaling mechanism for conservative candidates. For example, the scholar Steven Teles notes in his history of the conservative legal movement that "[n]o conviction about the Federalist Society is as tenacious as the belief that it plays a key role in Republican administrations' selection of federal judges, especially since the Bush Administration limited the role of the ABA."[42]

A good example of the strong reliance on the Federalist Society by Republican administrations has been the Trump administration. As Devins and Baum noted in the months before Trump's nomination of Neil Gorsuch,

Whoever Trump chooses will not simply be vetted by the Federalist Society; that nominee will be a Federalist Society loyalist – as he explicitly said, a Federalist "pick." Nine of the 21 names on the short list that was released in September and formed the pool of potential selections spoke at the 2016 Federalist Society annual convention a week after the election – prompting USA Today to call the convention an "audition" for "Supreme Court wannabes." Whether or not they are members, nearly all the 21 are listed as "experts" on the society's website. Three appeals court judges who are considered top contenders – Thomas Hardiman, William Pryor, and Neil Gorsuch – are Federalist Society members who regularly speak at society events. Pryor, for example, has spoken at every annual convention since 2006.[43]

---

[40] Toobin (2017).
[41] Baum and Devins (2017).
[42] Teles (2012, p. 157).
[43] Baum and Devins (2017).

The depth of the conservative pipeline operates in tandem with close connections between the Federalist Society and executive officials. One commentator even noted that the Federalist Society's president effectively served as President Trump's "subcontractor" in the nomination of Neil Gorsuch, the conservative federal court of appeals judge.[44] More broadly, Federalist Society membership is an important signal for young conservative lawyers interested in federal judicial clerkships, an important pathway for a prestigious career in law. As Teles presciently noted, "[c]onservatives had to create a web of intellectual, political, and network entrepreneurs who could generate new legal ideas, dedicated activists, litigation centers, and connections between individuals across the country that could certify individuals across the country as ideologically suitable for positions as clerks and judges."[45]

The overwhelming liberal tilt of the elite legal academy has perhaps undermined a liberal response to conservative organizations such as the Federalist Society. The best sense of a liberal counterpart has come from the American Constitution Society (ACS), which was founded in 2001 (some sixteen years after the founding of the Federalist Society) after the events of *Bush v. Gore* and the 2000 presidential election. Somewhat similarly to the Federalist Society, the ACS aims to "nurtur[e] the next generation of progressive lawyers, judges, policy experts, legislators and academics."[46] However, although the ACS has been welcomed in Democratic circles, the influence pales to that enjoyed by the Federalist Society among Republicans, to the consternation of some liberal legal observers.[47]

---

44 See Toobin (2017), which further notes that "[Federalist Society President Leonard's] role in the nomination capped a period of extraordinary influence for him and for the Federalist Society. During the Administration of George W. Bush, Leo also played a crucial part in the nominations of John Roberts and Samuel Alito. Now that Gorsuch has been confirmed, Leo is responsible, to a considerable extent, for a third of the Supreme Court."

45 Teles (2012, p. 179).

46 www.acslaw.org/about.

47 More recent efforts by left-of-center organizations have attempted to structure liberal conversations about potential candidates; so far, these have remained limited in impact. See Kim (2019). Teles argues that the Federalist Society itself was a direct conservative response to the ABA, which many deemed to be overwhelmingly liberal. See Teles (2012, chap. 5). The ABA, of course, is ostensibly non-ideological and aims to serve as "the national representative of the legal profession" (see www.americanbar.org/about_the_aba).

Qualification Ratings

In addition to the background milieu and the involvement of the legal establishment in the nurturing and identifying of legal talent, there is one way in which the mainstream legal establishment does involve itself explicitly in the selection of federal judges: qualification ratings of potential candidates to the federal courts.

As we noted in our introduction to this chapter, the ABA has historically assisted in "rating" judicial candidates. Specifically, the president – aided by the Department of Justice and other advisors – develops a list of potential candidates for a judicial vacancy. This private list is then forwarded to the ABA, which, through its Standing Committee on the Federal Judiciary, evaluates the candidate's record, reads their written work, and speaks with former law clerks and coworkers. Candidates are also required to fill out a detailed questionnaire that "seeks wide-ranging information related to a prospective nominee's fitness for judicial service."[48] The committee then votes to rate the candidate on a scale from "Not Qualified" to "Qualified" to "Well Qualified" according to three nonpartisan criteria: "integrity, professional competence and judicial temperament."[49] Traditionally, presidents at this stage can then move the nominations forward or, as is sometimes done, quietly drop them.

ABA ratings are consequential: Research has shown that, even among otherwise comparable candidates, candidates who are more poorly rated struggle in the confirmation process and their confirmations fail at higher rates.[50] Several studies have also found that candidates nominated to federal appeals courts who are conservative are more likely to get poorer ratings from the ABA than are candidates who are liberal.[51] Another study looking at district court judges found no ideological differences in ratings but did find that female and minority candidates were awarded lower ratings, which then hurt their eventual chances of confirmation.[52]

Because of this perceived anti-conservative bias, the ABA has lost influence with Republican administrations. As we noted in our introduction to this chapter, the George W. Bush administration broke with decades

---

[48] American Bar Association (2009, p. 4).
[49] See American Bar Association (2009, p. 3). A fourth rating, "Exceptionally Well Qualified," was eliminated in 1989.
[50] See, for example, Sen (2014a), which shows that confirmation ratings predict confirmation failure (but do not predict judges' reversal rates once they are confirmed). See also Lott (2005), which shows that poor ratings prolong the confirmation process; but see Nixon and Goss (2001) for different conclusions.
[51] See Smelcer, Steigerwalt, and Vining (2012), Lott (2005).
[52] Sen (2014a).

of custom and refused the ABA the "courtesy" of pre-vetting nominees. The practice was resumed under the Obama administration, but was again suspended immediately on Donald Trump's inauguration in 2017. This Republican reticence – and even outright hostility – to a courtesy extended to the ABA is no surprise given our framework, since it affords a left-leaning legal establishment a role to play in judicial selection at the highest level.

THE JUDICIAL TUG-OF-WAR AT THE FEDERAL LEVEL

We now turn to applying our framework to the federal courts. Recall that the judicial tug of war posits that the ideology of the judiciary will be a function of two "inputs": (1) the ideology of pertinent political actors and (2) the legal establishment.

On the first point, a reasonable assumption is that the president will, first and foremost, attempt to fashion a bench that is most favorable to their policy views and policy priorities.[53]

On the second point, the legal establishment can be a counterpoint. Given the overall leaning of the bar as well, we would expect that the bar would prefer (perhaps implicitly) judges more in line not only with bar leadership but also with the more elite membership from which federal judges are drawn. In addition, given the importance of the federal courts in terms of national-level policy, and given the strong interests of the legal establishment in issues such as federalism and the authority of the courts compared to the other branches of government, we would expect that the legal establishment would want to invest judges who are reflective of the bar's priorities and interested in protecting its legitimacy. In other words, we would expect bar elites to prefer judges who look like them – that is, judges who are more left-leaning.

However, when it comes to the federal appointments process, political actors can exercise more influence than the legal establishment. We

---

[53] Of course, as suggested by the historical record, politicians can use the federal courts as political patronage, using specific appointments to curry favor with political factions or demographic groups. See the excellent discussion of this in Goldman (1997), who documents the use of federal court nominations as political patronage for several presidential administrations. The Carter administration, for example, nominated many women and minority judges in part to shore up support among these groups in the broader electorate. Nonetheless, we believe, a safe assumption is that political actors will generally turn to political patronage concerns only after being satisfied about the ideological tenor of the courts.

would therefore anticipate that they have a stronger pull in the tug of war to shape the judiciary via the use of ideology in judicial selection. As we discussed in Chapter 4, we can check this by assessing whether judicial selection at the federal level is "politicized" versus "ideologically neutral." Under politicized (or ideologically based) judicial selection, we would expect the ideological composition of the federal bench to be different from the elite pool from which such candidates are drawn. On the other hand, under ideologically neutral selection, we would expect ideology not to factor into the selection of judges; judges instead are chosen on the basis of objective criteria, such as previous experience, qualifications, and perhaps demographics (e.g., geographic dispersion, race, or gender).[54] We would expect to see no discernible difference between federal judges and elite lawyers in terms of ideology. Of course, given what we know of the federal courts, of federal judicial selection, and of their political importance, we anticipate seeing evidence of the former as opposed to the latter.

EVIDENCE OF IDEOLOGICAL SELECTION ONTO FEDERAL COURTS

We now turn to investigating what the data have to say on this question. To do so, we conduct several comparisons: (1) we compare the relative ideologies of lawyers to national level politicians, (2) the ideologies of lawyers to federal judges, and (3) the ideologies of federal elected officials (specifically the Senate and the president) to the ideologies of federal judges. If our tug-of-war framework is predictive, the fact that the president and the Senate appoint federal judges should mean that judges are more likely to resemble the preferences of elected officials (and less likely to resemble the preferences of lawyers). This would be evidence of *ideologically based selection.*

As our data, we use the campaign contribution scores as we did before. These DIME scores, to briefly summarize, place actors on a unidimensional scale from conservative to liberal. The scores have the benefit of relying on campaign contributions, which are made by and to elected officials, lawyers, and federal judges; this enables easy comparisons among

---

54 A strong possibility is that some of these characteristics could correlate with ideology, but, overall, we would expect that ideologically neutral selection would not actively incorporate ideology or partisanship into the selection of judges.

the three groups.[55] To give some context of coverage, our data cover 100 percent of federal elected officials and 73 percent of federal judges.[56] For federal judges who have not donated, we are able to impute ideological scores for them based on available characteristics.[57] Thus, we are fairly confident that our data capture a good amount of ideological activity from federal politicians, federal judges, and likely federal judicial candidates.

Comparisons Between Tiers of the Federal Judiciary

The DIME scores for the various tiers of the federal judiciary (federal district judges and federal appeals court judges) are presented in Figure 5.2, along with the ideological distribution of attorneys. Our interest is in comparing how the overall distribution of federal judges compares to the ideological distribution of lawyers. If there is a large, detectable difference, then this would suggest ideologically based selection – in turn implying that presidents and politicians in Congress are "pulling" in the tug of war. If there is no difference, then this would suggest evidence of ideologically neutral selection or that lawyers and the legal elite are "pulling" federal judges closer to their preferred position.

The figure demonstrates evidence of the former, not the latter: Specifically, each group of federal judges differs meaningfully from the overall distribution of lawyers, with all of the judicial distributions being more conservative overall.[58] This, we believe, is evidence of ideological selection and implies that politicians are leaning on ideological criteria in naming and confirming federal judges and that they are doing so in a fashion that makes this pattern statistically noticeable.

Several other facts are worth noting. First, the overall distribution of judges varies meaningfully across courts. Indeed, the higher and more

---

[55] As we noted in Chapter 4, federal judges are prohibited by the Code of Conduct for United States Judges from making campaign contributions (see Canon 5). However, most federal judges donated to campaigns before they were invested onto the federal courts, meaning that they are in our data. More on the technical details and tests showing robustness to missingness can be found in Bonica and Sen (2017c) and Bonica and Sen (2017a).

[56] The 73 percent figure is for federal judges appointed between 2000 and 2018.

[57] The baseline coverage is high compared to the overall coverage for lawyers (around 48 percent) and for the population at large (5 percent). See Bonica and Sen (2017c). For details on the imputation procedure, see Bonica and Sen (2017a).

[58] These differences are all statistically significant, as evidenced by a series of Kolmogorov–Smirnov test and differfences-in-means tests.

politically important the court, the less the overall distribution resembles the distribution of attorneys. The most conservative courts (and thus the least representative of the overall distribution of lawyers) are the US Supreme Court, followed by the US courts of appeals, followed by the US district courts.[59] Thus, our analyses suggest that *the higher or more politically important the court, the stronger the evidence for ideologically based judicial selection.*

Second, we can also situate these results within a broader political context, which highlights the importance of the analysis. Indeed, we know quite a bit about ideology on the Supreme Court – primarily because there are only nine justices but also because journalists have covered the partisan and ideological landscape of the Court extensively. However, we know significantly less about the ideological landscape of the other tiers of the federal judiciary, which are now crisply illustrated by Figure 5.2. For example, consider the distribution of attorneys. The median DIME score for attorneys is −0.47 for attorneys who attended non-elite law schools and −0.84 for those who attended elite law schools. By contrast, the median DIME scores is −0.03 for federal district court judges and 0.51 for federal circuit court judges. Federal judges are considerably more conservative than the attorney population, especially when compared to the population of graduates of elite law schools from which federal judges are disproportionately drawn.

STRATEGIC SELECTION AND CONSERVATIVE SCARCITY

These findings raise two important puzzles that our framework is equipped to address. The first is why we would see these patterns at all – why are federal courts and, especially, higher federal courts more representative of the preferences of political actors? The second is how we can reconcile the relatively more conservative nature of the higher courts with the liberal nature of more prestigious law schools. Why is it that federal appeals judges are so conservative given that Harvard, Yale, Stanford, and Columbia produce fairly liberal graduates on average? The

---

[59] All pairwise comparisons result in statistically significant differences. Specifically, a K-S test between the ideologies of US Supreme Court justices and the federal appeals judges is significant, suggesting that these judges come from different ideological distributions; a K-S test of the ideologies of federal appeals judges and federal district judges also results in a significant test statistic, suggesting a meaningful difference there as well.

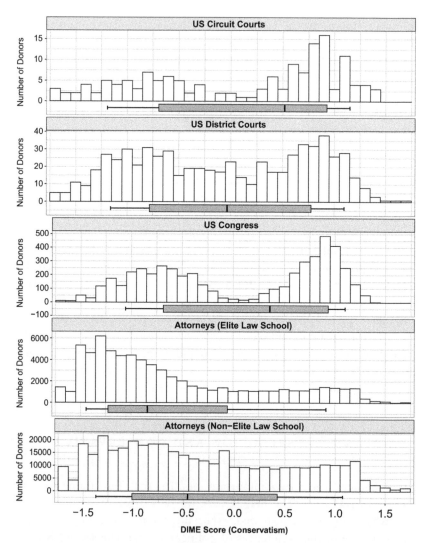

FIGURE 5.2 Comparison of ideological distributions for graduates of non-elite and elite (top 14) law schools, law clerks, and judges.
Note: Box-and-whisker plots display the median, interquartile range, and the 9th to 91st percentiles for each distribution.

former question speaks to demand-side concerns from the perspective of political actors. The latter, on the other hand, speaks to supply-side concerns, at least from the perspective of the legal establishment and the law school elite. We consider both in turn.

DEMAND-SIDE CONCERNS: WHY DO WE SEE PROPORTIONALLY MORE CONSERVATIVES IN HIGHER COURTS? Our results show that political actors are having more success at politicizing – or introducing ideology into judicial selection – at the higher court level. This explains why the Supreme Court, followed by the federal appeals courts, is the most aligned with the preferences of politicians. In addition, we note that this "success" comes from a conservative direction; that is, the introduction of ideology is making the higher courts more conservative, in turn implying that conservative politicians are the ones introducing ideology into judicial selection. However, they are doing so more at the higher court level, starting with the Supreme Court and then moving downward through the federal judicial hierarchy.

We think that a likely explanation behind these patterns is the relative scarcity of conservative law graduates (and the relative surplus of liberal law graduates) at the very elite levels, which we saw in Figure 5.1. Given their relatively fewer numbers, conservative judicial candidates are underrepresented among the elite ranks compared to their liberal counterparts. This means that conservative politicians must make a choice: They do not have enough pedigreed candidates to comfortably staff all tiers of the federal judiciary with experienced conservative graduates of elite law schools. Instead, they must orient the candidates that they do have to those judicial seats that are the most valuable – naturally, these are seats on the US Supreme Court and the federal courts of appeals. These courts inevitably hear the most important cases filed in federal courts; for the Supreme Court and the courts of appeals, these are the cases that are likely to have the most significant political ramifications. For conservatives trying to optimize the impact of their appointments given a limited pool of conservative candidates, orienting these resources toward the higher courts makes sense.

We see the implications of this argument play out most strongly in times when conservatives are making great efforts to rearrange the federal courts, often exacerbating the relative scarcity of conservative candidates. For example, the Republican-controlled Senate in the 114th US Congress under the last two years of the Obama administration (2015–2017) kept many federal judicial seats open purposefully by denying Obama nominees hearings. (The case of Merrick Garland was just the most prominent of these.) In doing so, Republican leaders weighed the political costs of such a maneuver against the probability of having a Republican winner in the 2016 presidential contest. This bet paid off, leaving incoming Republican Donald Trump with the largest number of empty judicial vacancies of any modern president – 88 vacancies on the federal district courts, 17 on the courts of appeals, and 1 (and eventually 2) on the Supreme Court.

Given our empirical finding that conservatives are relatively underrepresented among pedigreed lawyers, this would actually present something of a problem – how could so many seats be filled? Our framework predicts two outcomes. The first is for conservatives to prioritize higher courts, orienting the better conservative candidates toward service on the Supreme Court and federal courts of appeals. The second would be for conservatives to relax qualification standards for other lower-court judges, looking outside of the top law schools and top credentials in order to satisfy ideological priorities.

These predictions have been largely borne out. Trump quickly appointed two highly pedigreed men – Neil Gorsuch and Brett Kavanaugh – to the US Supreme Court. Both were viewed very favorably by peers within legal elite circles, including by the ABA, which unanimously rated them both "Well Qualified";[60] However, Trump also put forward a record number of candidates to the lower federal courts who were ultimately rated "Not Qualified" – the lowest possible rating – by the ABA. As of May 2020, 9 of Trump's 234 nominees have been rated "Not Qualified" as opposed to none of Obama's nominees.[61] In addition, Trump's nominees have been less likely to be awarded the top category, "Well Qualified": 60 percent compared to Obama's approximately 70 percent.[62] These figures are even unfavorable to earlier Republican administrations, suggesting that these poor ratings are not a result of ABA bias against conservatives, as suggested by several papers.[63] Instead, they suggest that the sheer number of vacancies at the start of the Trump term had taxed the relatively thin pool of conservative legal talent, thus forcing White House officials to look deeper into the pool – and therefore at less polished candidates – for consideration.

THE SUPPLY SIDE: WHAT DOES THIS MEAN FOR YOUNG CONSERVATIVES? Our analysis here also has implications about the incentives on

---

[60] See www.americanbar.org/groups/committees/federal_judiciary/resources/supreme -court-nominations/.

[61] https://ballotpedia.org/ABA_ratings_during_the_Trump_administration

[62] These statistics come from Bump (2017).

[63] Papers such as Smelcer, Steigerwalt, and Vining (2012) have suggested some anti-conservative trends in ABA ratings. See, however, Sen (2014a) for findings to the contrary at the federal district court level.

the supply side – specifically the professional incentives of potential judicial candidates. This includes elite law students starting to think about possible career paths, one of which could include a prestigious career in the federal judiciary.

From the perspective of young law students at prominent law schools, the prospects for a career on the federal courts change according to their ideology – after all, these law schools are among the most liberal in terms of the ideology of their faculty and their graduates.[64] A liberal law graduate, for example, would be one of many, and would actually have a fairly remote chance of being plucked to serve on the federal courts; by contrast, a conservative law graduate, being one of extremely few, would have a much better chance. Specifically, we would predict that, holding demand constant, conservatives would have, on average, a better chance of becoming federal judges than would liberals. These improved odds get even better in times of Republican presidential administrations (and even better in times when Republicans control both the White House and the Senate). At these times, Republican politicians are actively seeking out qualified, conservative candidates; given the relative scarcity of such candidates, the odds for a conservative law graduate trying to make their way onto the federal courts would be significantly higher than if the same candidate were liberal.

We can check this intuition using our data. Specifically, we subset our data to only look at graduates of the Top 14 law schools – traditionally the elite law schools that produce the lion's share of federal judges. We then examine, among this subset, whether a lawyer's ideology (as measured by their DIME score) predicts if they will become a judge. Seeing a positive correlation means that conservatives are indeed more likely than are liberals to be "plucked" into careers in the judiciary.

The results in Table 5.2 reveal that graduates of elite law schools that went on to become judges are far more conservative than their peers, as evidenced by the positive and significant coefficients on the judge variables. This provides strong evidence of these supply-side considerations: Given Republican demand for judicial candidates, and given the relative scarcity of qualified conservatives, graduates of these programs who

---

[64] For more on the ideology of elite law schools' faculties, see Bonica, Chilton, and Sen (2016). The data presented in that paper make clear that the ideologies of law faculty are even more liberal than those of law school alumni; because law faculty are extremely central in networking and promoting their students as law clerks (including writing important recommendation letters and making informal phone calls), this might further bias these elite legal networks in a liberal direction.

TABLE 5.2 Ideology and career outcomes for graduates of Top 14 law schools with at least fifteen years of experience (as measured by the time since first being admitted to the bar).

	Model 1	Model 2	Model 3
Federal Circuit Courts	0.459***	0.437***	0.432***
	(0.104)	(0.104)	(0.101)
Federal District Courts	0.237***	0.215***	0.211***
	(0.070)	(0.069)	(0.068)
State High Courts	0.371***	0.349**	0.373***
	(0.139)	(0.138)	(0.135)
State Lower Courts	0.117***	0.095***	0.061**
	(0.026)	(0.026)	(0.025)
Public Defender		−0.663***	−0.561***
		(0.091)	(0.088)
Prosecutor/District Attorney		−0.125**	−0.042
		(0.053)	(0.051)
Law Professor		−0.396***	−0.354***
		(0.019)	(0.019)
Government Lawyer		−0.429***	−0.319***
		(0.028)	(0.027)
Female			−0.355***
			(0.009)
Years since Admitted			−0.002
			(0.001)
Years since Admitted^2			0.0001***
			(0.00002)
Constant	−0.503***	−0.481***	−0.514***
	(0.004)	(0.004)	(0.026)
N	52983	52983	52769
Adj. R-squared	0.001	0.014	0.062

***$p < 0.01$; **$p < 0.05$; *$p < 0.1$
The reference category is lawyers in private practice.
Sources: DIME, Federal Judicial Center.

are conservative are more likely to end up on the federal courts. As an intuition check, we further restrict the sample on graduates who are at least fifteen years into their careers (as measured by the time since first being admitted to the bar). These are people who are nearing their forties, the age at which lawyers begin to think more seriously about a career in the judiciary as a possible option.[65] We see similar effects for these

[65] The average age of Article III judges on appointment is around fifty. See Federal Judicial Center, Demography of Article III Judges, 1789-2017 (www.fjc.gov/history/exhibits/graphs-and-maps/age-and-experience-judges).

individuals: Elite law school graduates who are ideologically conservative have a better chance of becoming federal judges than those who are liberal.

An intuitive representation of this is provided by Figure 5.3, which presents the predicted probabilities associated with becoming a federal judge according to ideology, conditional on a lawyer having graduated from a Top 14 law school. By no means is becoming a federal judge a high-likelihood event; the chance of an elite lawyer becoming a federal judge is extremely low, regardless of ideology. Yet as ideology becomes more conservative, the likelihood of an elite lawyer becoming a judge increases. For example, looking at the federal appeals courts, a candidate moving rightward about one unit in DIME score terms (about a shift of about half the distance between the parties in Congress) results in a twofold increase in the likelihood that that person will become a federal judge. The increased probabilities are about the same for federal district courts.

For young lawyers, the implications of this are significant: The relative scarcity of conservatives at the elite level means that signaling one's conservative ideology could be important to becoming a federal judge. Of course, the baseline probability of a lawyer, even an elite one, becoming a judge is low; however, being a conservative comes with a sizable improvement. We also believe that this empirical reality, evident in Figure 5.3, is a key reason behind the rise of conservative legal organizations such as the Federalist Society. The Federalist Society was founded in part to isolate and nurture conservative talent, with an eye toward populating the courts (and especially the federal courts) with conservative intellect. Not only does an organization such as this help conservative politicians identify conservative talent but membership in the organization helps young conservatives signal their conservative ideology – thus allowing them to distance themselves on paper from their liberal colleagues.[66] By furthering networks between younger and older conservatives as well, the Federalist Society also shapes young lawyers' intellectual and jurisprudential developments – also important given the relative scarcity

---

[66] Teles (2012, chap. 5), which notes of the early Federalist Society members that "clear ideological positioning, not cautiousness, was now an affirmative qualification for appointed office. In its early years Federalist Society membership carried a stigma within legal academia, but it was precisely the willingness to bear this stigma that made Society membership a valuable signal of true-believership for conservatives in government" (p. 142).

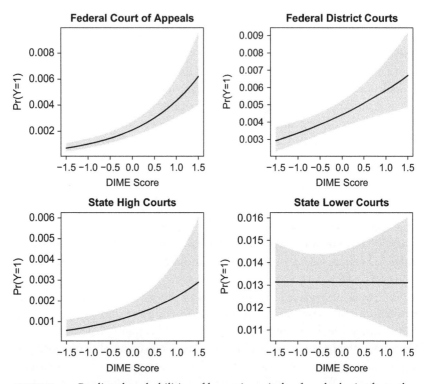

FIGURE 5.3 Predicted probabilities of becoming a judge for, clockwise from the top left, (1) federal appeals courts, (2) federal district courts, (3) state high courts, and (4) state lower courts for graduates of Top 14 law schools. In each plot, the *x*-axis represents ideology, while the *y*-axis represents the probability of becoming a judge. For all judge types, as ideology becomes more conservative, the probability of a lawyer going on to become a judge increases.
Sources: DIME, Federal Judicial Center.

of conservatives in legal academia, as documented by several empirical studies.[67]

We believe that these basic patterns also help explain the opposite phenomenon, which is the lack of a left-leaning organization rising to the level of insider influence enjoyed by the Federalist Society. Because conservatives are relatively more scarce, the Federalist Society serves an important function for both politicians and judicial candidates in terms

[67] For more on the intellectual environment of the Federalist Society, see Hollis-Brusky (2015). For more on the ideology of law professors, see Bonica et al. (2018), which documents the left-leaning tendencies of law professors across nearly every area of the law school curriculum.

of connecting political demand with the limited legal supply. Yet, for liberals, who are by far more numerous among the professoriate and among students, the same concerns are not present. Liberal elected officials and party leaders need less formal assistance in identifying elite, liberal talent; after all, the modal Harvard Law School graduate is left of center, as are the elite professors writing recommendation letters and making phone calls. Simply hiring a random subset of Harvard or Yale law review editors would satisfy the ideological concerns of liberals, leaving them with a federal bench amenable to liberal interests. Indeed, to put it bluntly, the data show that liberals do not have to work as hard as conservatives to attract qualified candidates.

CONCLUSION

We conclude by noting the key takeaways for our judicial tug-of-war framework, as applied to the federal courts. First, the federal courts handle some of the most important cases in the United States. These include important questions involving the interpretation of the US Constitution, as well as the interpretation of federal statutes. The US Supreme Court also oversees the lower federal courts, which handle cases involving redistricting, unlawful conduct by federal officials (including immigration and federal law enforcement officers), conflicts between citizens of different states, and the conduct of the president and of US congressional representatives. All of these make the federal courts the most politically important courts in the entire country. In turn, this makes the composition of federal courts a highly contentious, politically charged topic.

These political stakes mean that federal politicians and party leaders care deeply about the composition of these courts. Liberals will want judges who will uphold government programs, who support expansive government reach, who support women's reproductive rights, and who strike down racially discriminatory laws. By contrast, conservatives will seek judges who are skeptical of the federal government's power, who are more lenient with states trying to legislate social issues, and who are more racially conservative. Depending on the party in the White House, Republicans and Democrats may be more or less likely to support judicial candidates who take expansive (or limited) views of executive power. These concerns will be reflected in the kinds of people that each party attempts to put on the courts.

Second, the judicial tug of war is a compelling way to predict the composition of the federal courts. The fact that federal judges are appointed by the president (with the advice and consent of the Senate) privileges the input of elected officials and party leaders. For that reason, we should not be surprised that federal judges reflect the preferences of politicians. However, the legal establishment has a strong role to play, specifically in shaping the elite candidate pool from which judges are drawn. The graduates of the prestigious law schools from which members of the federal courts are drawn tend to be overwhelmingly liberal, as is the national-level legal establishment. For ideological liberals, this is an attractive reason to focus on "qualifications" and "pedigree," as opposed to policy views: Doing so will lead to a mostly left-leaning, ideologically aligned federal judiciary. For ideological conservatives, this is more problematic: They must look deeper or further afield for conservative talent, being unable to rely exclusively on pedigree or qualifications.

In terms of drawing conclusions about ideology, this basic fact – that the candidate pool for federal judges tends to be liberal – means we can estimate the degree to which ideology matters in selection by looking at the degree of politicization, or ideologically based judicial selection. Our data clearly show evidence of this politicization – federal judges are more conservative than are elite lawyers, suggesting that ideology plays a massive role in the selection of these judges.[68] In terms of the judicial tug of war, this means that politicians are "pulling" judges closer to their preferred policy positions. In addition, we have evidence that politicians do this in a strategic fashion: How conservative judges are (and how much they deviate from the legal establishment) fluctuates with the court level, with higher appeals courts being more reflective of the preferences of politicians. This has broad implications not just for how conservative politicians go about recruiting conservative candidates but, from the perspective of young conservative lawyers, about the importance of networking and aggressively signaling one's conservative views.

We conclude this discussion by noting an important normative takeaway. We have drawn out the observable implication that seeing significant deviations between lawyers and judges suggests that ideology is an important factor in judicial selection, meaning that politicians are selecting judges precisely to shape the ideological contours of the courts.

---

[68] We can rule out that judges are being chosen on the basis of characteristics that correlate with ideology, including gender, race, age, or professional background. Many of these analyses can be found in the appendix to Chapter 4.

Our findings and conclusions might sit poorly with those who believe that judges should be selected on the basis of their intellect, reasoning, and qualifications and not on the basis of some sort of ideological "litmus test." However, this is not without implications: Selecting on these attributes to the exclusion of ideological considerations would result in a left-leaning judiciary – palatable to some but seriously objectionable for many others. On the other hand, the increased reliance on ideology in the selection of judges might have some advantages. Legal elites tend to be liberal; in the absence of ideological selection, judges would be more liberal as well – and likely more liberal than the average American. Put differently, if we wished judges to look more like the general public, then some degree of ideological selection would introduce more ideological diversity than the judiciary would otherwise enjoy.

Our analysis also suggests a role of the courts in the judicial tug of war that is akin to a political prize – a tool for furthering politics and policy by two elements that are frequently in ideological and strategic opposition. This makes the courts an inherently political institution, a label that we do not shy away from but one that stands in contrast with courts' public persona. Our viewpoint is also one not often shared publicly by political elites. For example, in a 2019 letter addressed to the clerk of the Supreme Court, a group of Republicans wrote that "[t]here is no greater example of the genius of our Constitution than its creation of an independent judiciary," one that operates "without regard to the identity of the parties or the politics of the moment."[69] Judges, too, publicly tout their images as nonpartisan. John Roberts once said, "I've been elected by nobody" and that "[w]e do not have Obama judges or Trump judges, Bush judges or Clinton judges."[70] We do not take issue with judges holding themselves out to be nonpartisan or apolitical. However, the data are clear: Judges are most certainly chosen for their ideology. The talk of nonpartisanship may be important for the courts' legitimacy, and holding out the courts as apolitical may be important for political operatives keen to keep partisan consideration out of public view. However, we believe that such talk often hides true motives.

All of these implications build on an important point, which concerns the role played by judicial selection. The federal system is one that prioritizes political actors over either the legal establishment or the public at large – resulting in a judiciary that largely reflects political interests

[69] McConnell et al. (2019).
[70] Quoted in Dwyer (2019).

(whether judges admit this or not); however, this is not the case for many courts systems within the fifty states, many of which formally involve local and state bar associations by way of merit nominating commissions. We might expect that, under such systems, the judicial tug of war serves to help the legal establishment promote and further its own interests. We turn to these questions in Chapter 6.

6

Politicization in the States and Across Judicial Selection Mechanisms

"Judicial independence is vital and necessary for fair and just rulings from our courts. But judicial independence must rest firmly on the consent of the people."

Kansas Governor Sam Brownback[1]

The federal courts hear matters of great national and political importance, but they only preside over around 400,000 cases per year.[2] On the other hand, state courts might hear upward of 100 million cases per year – nearly 300 times as many as the federal courts in an average year.[3] Not only are state courts more likely to handle cases that influence the lives of ordinary Americans (such as family law and criminal proceedings), but they are tasked with interpreting state constitutions; this means that state courts are often at the forefront of deciding issues of great political controversy – including the administration of elections, redistricting, controversies over public funding, and civil rights issues involving state-law claims.[4]

---

[1] Quoted in (Severino 2013).

[2] See Table 5.1 in Chapter 5.

[3] The statistics on case-level statistics come from the Court Statistics Project, a division of the National Center for State Courts.

[4] A prominent example of a state court that served to alter the direction of national-level discourse is the Supreme Judicial Court of Massachusetts, which in 2003 ruled that the state's denial of marriage licenses to same-sex couples was unconstitutional under the state (not federal) constitution. See *Goodridge v. Dept. of Public Health*, 798 N.E.2d 941 (Ma. 2003). This ruling set the marriage equality movement on a rapid path toward national-level acceptance, culminating in a US Supreme Court ruling declaring marriage

For these reasons, partisan infighting about the selection of judges can be even more vitriolic at the state level. Kansas is one example. The state is unusual in selecting judges through a complicated patchwork of systems.[5] At the state supreme court level, Kansas's seven judges are chosen by the governor but from a list created by a judicial nominating commission comprised partly of lawyers. (We discuss these nominating commissions at greater depth in our discussion of selection mechanisms and also in Chapter 7.) At the state appeals court level – just below the state supreme court – judges are nominated by the governor but subject to approval by the legislature; and, the lower court trial level, trial judges are selected by a variety of systems. Some districts elect their judges; others select their judges via gubernatorial appointment, based off of names provided by a commission.

This patchwork system has been controversial, not just for variation in case outcomes[6] but also because of the ideological and partisan consequences. The Kansas Supreme Court, selected in part by the Kansas bar, provides a good example of this. The court was viewed for many years as a moderate court,[7] but a series of rulings in the early 2010s infuriated conservatives.[8] The supreme court's liberal rulings stood in contrast with the rightward shift among Kansas politicians and its Tea Party-backed governor, Sam Brownback, a conservative Republican elected in 2010 with a mission to slash taxes and government services. These shifts put conservative Kansas politicians squarely at odds not just with the courts but also with what they perceived to be the overly powerful and liberal-leaning bar.[9]

---

a fundamental right for all same-sex couples across the country (*Obergefell v. Hodges*, 576 U.S.).

[5] For more on how Kansas selects judges, see Ballotpedia, https://ballotpedia.org/Judicial_selection_in_Kansas.

[6] See Canes-Wrone, Clark, and Kelly (2014), Lim (2013), and Huber and Gordon (2004) for evidence showing that variation in Kansas's judicial selection leads to differences in court outcomes.

[7] According to one account, "[t]he court is largely viewed as moderate, reasonable, and business-friendly" (Caplan 2016).

[8] This included a 2014 ruling regarding the method by which the state of Kansas funded its public schools – which upended conservative plans about how to redistribute funds. We discuss the Kansas Supreme Court in more depth in Chapter 7.

[9] On the campaign trail in 2014, Brownback used attacks on judges to animate his conservative base. For example, in an October 2014 church rally, Brownback decried the state of same-sex marriage rights and cautioned that "[w]e need to push forward our candidates that stand for this country, that stand for faith, that stand for family, that stand for freedom" (quoted in Siebenmark 2014).

In this chapter, we explore the puzzle of states like Kansas, in which state courts appear out of step with state politicians and state-level political trends. In explaining this, our argument first looks to the states' lawyers – which remain an important players in the judicial tug of war at the state level. Not only have the states formed a patchwork of idiosyncratic judicial selection mechanisms, but they also vary in terms of their legal culture and local lawyer ideology. Kansas politicians are among the most conservative of any state – and this was particularly true in the early 2010s – but lawyers practicing in Kansas are on average left of center. This created tension between Tea Party politicians like Sam Brownback and the lawyers staffing Kansas's judicial nominating commissions.[10] Regional variation in attorney ideology across states is pronounced. The Texas bar – which has many members specializing in oil and gas – is, on average, more conservative than the New York bar – many of whose members tend to focus on business transactions and general litigation. Both of them are more conservative than the Washington, DC bar, which has many members working for the federal government or in the nonprofit sector. As we show in this chapter, the ideology of local bars – and the rich variation across states – directly influences the ideological composition of different state courts through the state bars' professional capture of the judiciary.

In addition, unlike the federal system, where politicians from the party in power have wide latitude in appointing their preferred judges, states vary in both the extent and manner by which politicians influence judicial selection. Many states, like Kansas, use a mix of systems in choosing judges. Others – for example, Arkansas and Oregon – select judges via direct, nonpartisan elections, meaning that voters are not explicitly informed of the partisan allegiances of the candidates when casting their ballots. Others – for example, Alabama and Texas – select judges via partisan judicial elections, with judges advertising their party affiliations on television, radio, in print, and on the ballot. Others – for example, Colorado and Iowa – have institutionalized lawyers' involvement in the process by using nominating commissions to identify a set of candidates from which the governor can then choose a final slate. Others still – for example, Massachusetts and New Jersey – rely on gubernatorial

---

[10] Bonica and Sen (2017b). Of course, many of the Kansas politicians are themselves lawyers. Sam Brownback, for example, received his law degree from the University of Kansas and worked as a lawyer for a few years before entering politics. See www.nga.org/cms/sam-brownback.

appointment, similar to the federal system. As we show in this chapter, these differences constrain the two main players in the judicial tug of war – the state bars and state politicians – in different ways. The general incentive structure of the judicial tug of war is the same, but the rules by which the game is played, and the strategies employed, differ.

In linking these forces, we expand our theory of the judicial tug of war. We continue to highlight how the courts' leanings will be a product of both the preferences of the state's bar (i.e., the pool of potential judicial candidates) and the preferences of political actors. However, unlike our previous analyses, this chapter engages how the mechanism by which judges are selected – via partisan elections, nonpartisan elections, executive appointments, or merit commissions – substantially impacts the power dynamics. In particular, the more sensitive the selection mechanism to political influence, the more political actors will be able to introduce ideology into the selection of judges. Thus, as we discussed in Chapter 5, the federal system – which gives much power to political actors – will result in judges more likely to share the preferences of politicians. However, the less sensitive the style of judicial selection is to political considerations, the less likely political actors will be able to do the same. For example, in Kansas, where lawyers' organizations have much more formal input, judges will be more likely to share the policy preferences of attorneys and less so those of politicians.

In explaining these forces, our framework of the judicial tug of war provides a useful synthesis for how to understand state-by-state variation in the nature and composition of state courts. We also take the opportunity to generalize more broadly about what kinds of selection systems result in a more or less politicized judiciary. This discussion sets the stage for the important issue of judicial reform – and the idea that selection mechanisms are fundamentally a product of the tension between the legal establishment and politicians – in Chapter 7.

This chapter proceeds as follows. First, we explore how the bar varies in terms of ideology from state to state. We then systematically compare the contemporary ideologies of lawyers in each state to political actors, showing how the ideological tension – the "tug of war" – between the legal profession and political actors varies across states. This motivates our inquiry into the impact of the four main types of judicial selection used across the states: (1) executive (gubernatorial) appointments, (2) partisan elections, (3) nonpartisan elections, and (4) merit commissions systems. We show how the underlying ideological composition of candidate pools interacts with the various selection mechanisms to produce more conservative or more liberal state courts. As we show, some selection mechanisms afford the bar more political power, while others afford political actors more power. Lastly, we examine several notable examples, including Kansas, Virginia, Connecticut, Montana, and North Carolina. These examples illustrate the fact that the selection of judges is itself a political process – one that can be altered if political actors are consistently stymied in creating the judicial body that they desire. This sets the stage for our discussion of partisan attempts at judicial reform, which we address in Chapter 7.

THE IDEOLOGY OF LAWYERS, STATE BY STATE

Our judicial tug-of-war framework posits that the ideological composition of the courts is a function of two factors: (1) the ideology of political actors and (2) the ideology of lawyers, from which judges are drawn. (As we discuss shortly, the relative importance of each is significantly influenced by another factor, (3) the judicial selection mechanism currently in place.) Both of these factors vary from state to state. Some states' politicians are more conservative, while in other states they are more liberal; some states have liberal bars while other states have more conservative bars. This variation directly impacts the composition of the judiciary.

In this section, we unpack in more detail the second component, the ideology of lawyers. Because state judges, with rare exceptions, are exclusively drawn from lawyers practicing within the state, the ideological leanings of a state's attorneys tend to be reflected in the state's judges.[11] Here, we consider two contemporary sources of variation in state-by-state legal culture: legal education and overall legal ideology.[12]

Legal Education

While most federal judges tend to attend very elite law schools such as Harvard, Columbia, or Yale, the education of *state* judges is more

[11] Federal judges also tend to come from within the jurisdiction, but the relationship usually is not so tightly coupled. As we noted in Chapter 5, federal judges attended just a handful of the top law schools, such as Harvard or Yale (Sen 2014b), and there are no real geographic constraints for certain federal courts, including the US Supreme Court and the influential US Court of Appeals for the DC Circuit.

[12] For more on state-by-state variation in the legal profession, see Bonica, Chilton, and Sen (2016). For more on state-by-state variation in the legal academy, with a particular emphasis on law professors, see Bonica et al. (2018).

varied. Some attend these same elite schools, particularly if they serve in states that are home to these institutions (such as Massachusetts, New York, or Connecticut, in the cases of Harvard, Columbia, and Yale). However, many judges tend to attend flagship state universities in their home state and then remain in-state after graduating. To give an example, as of 2019, all seven justices on the Kansas Supreme Court were educated at law schools within the state.[13] In Massachusetts, also as of 2019, only one justice out of the seven members of the Massachusetts Supreme Judicial Court attended law school out of state (at the University of Chicago).[14] In the nine-member Texas Supreme Court, as of 2018, all but three justices attended law schools in Texas.[15] This home-state bias is fairly typical of the composition of state courts, a pattern suggesting that in-state legal education is likely to be a powerful predictor of the mindset of a state's judges: If the educational environment within a state is overwhelmingly liberal (or conservative) this will likely have an impact on the ideology of the state's judiciary.

To investigate the ideological variation in the educational environment, we examined the contemporary ideological distributions of graduates of law schools. We did so by looking at the same campaign donations–based ideological scores that informed our previous analyses; however, for these analyses, we disaggregate lawyers according to which law schools they said they attended, using the self-reported information from Martindale-Hubbell.[16]

Figure 6.1 presents these analyses. It shows the ideology of graduates from the set of law schools that have produced the largest number of judges. This list includes not just the traditional "Top 14" law schools, which tend to be overrepresented in the federal courts, but also many important state flagship or leading state law schools – attended by many

[13] As of 2019, four of the seven justices on the Kansas Supreme Court attended Washburn University School of Law in Topeka, while the remaining three justices attended the University of Kansas Law School in Lawrence. See www.kscourts.org/kansas-courts/supreme-court/justice-bios.

[14] As of 2018, three members of the Massachusetts Supreme Judicial Council attended Harvard Law School, two attended Suffolk Law School in downtown Boston, and one attended Boston University Law School. See www.mass.gov/service-details/supreme-judicial-court-justices.

[15] See www.txcourts.gov/supreme/about-the-court.

[16] For the technical background on the DIME scores and how they are constructed, see Chapter 3. Additional technical explanations and more results are found in Bonica and Sen (2017c), Bonica and Sen (2017a), and Bonica (2014). Note that these analyses include all graduates that we have in our data; this could include people who were not contemporaries of the judges in our analyses of judicial ideology.

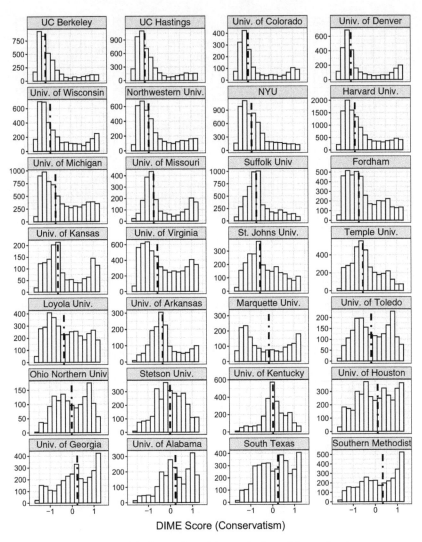

DIME Score (Conservatism)

FIGURE 6.1 Ideology of graduates of selected law schools.
Note: Law schools shown are those with the largest number of graduates going on to serve as judges according to our data. Law schools are ordered from the most liberal to the most conservative. Dotted lines indicate the median ideal point of each law school's alumni.
Sources: DIME, Martindale-Hubbell.

current and former state judges. For ease of interpretation, organize the figure from most liberal (the University of California, Berkeley) to most conservative (the University of Mississippi).

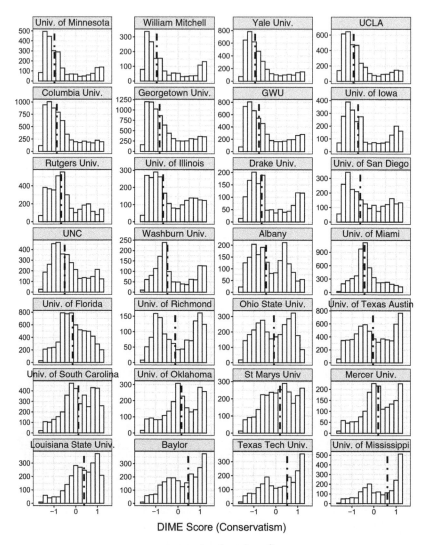

DIME Score (Conservatism)

FIGURE 6.1 *(continued)*

The figure makes it clear that the state flagship or leading law schools vary substantially in terms of their ideology.[17] For example, California's

---

[17] We make no inferences regarding the causal effect that different law schools might have in *influencing* or *changing* the ideology of young law students. Indeed, our patterns could be explained exclusively by the sorting of young people into different educational environments. For example, a young person who leans to the left politically may be drawn to the law school at the University of California, Berkeley, which is known for

state flagship law schools – the University of California, Berkeley and the University of California, Hastings College of Law – are the two most liberal in Figure 6.1 (in the top left). The law schools at UCLA and Stanford rank among the most liberal law schools. This has implications for California judges, who are largely educated in-state and whose connections to the bar and to the professional climate in California are close. Given these liberal-leaning tendencies, we might expect that California state judges are quite liberal as well. We also note many elite law schools – which tend to produce federal judges and also a high share of certain states' judges – tend to be among the most liberal in terms of the ideologies of their graduates.

We see the opposite for schools in other states. In Texas, for example, the flagship University of Texas Law School, located in Austin, is one of the more conservative-leaning law schools on our scale. Other almae *matres* of Texas Supreme Court justices – Southern Methodist University, the University of Houston, Texas Tech University, and South Texas University – are all relatively conservative. Although we have fewer comparisons with regards to states like Mississippi (which only has two law schools), Kansas (two law schools), and Alabama (three law schools), we see similar patterns there – these states' flagship law schools are among the most conservative in our sample. We would expect that, in line with other graduates from these law schools, state judges tend to reflect these more conservative leanings.

Legal Culture

We also consider the contemporary ambient legal climate and how this might vary from state to state. As we discussed in Chapter 3, state bars are politically powerful: Not only do lawyers constitute the core group from which judges are drawn but bars are influential in dictating judicial codes of conduct, selecting judges, and shaping the norms and customs under which judges operate. Judges, after all, come from this

---

its robust public interest program. By contrast, a student who leans to the right might be more drawn to the University of Texas, which is located in a Republican-leaning state and leans in a more conservative direction. These patterns could hold for those interested in becoming judges. For example, exceptional candidates who are interested in signaling their conservative leanings and judicial aspirations, might choose to attend the University of Chicago, which is known for its law and economics focus and for its many distinguished conservative alumni. Bonica et al. (2018) has additional information on some of these patterns. For more on the ambient liberal environment in American law schools, and on conservative responses, see Teles (2012).

ideological environment: More conservative bars tilt the scale toward more conservative judicial candidates and, vice versa, more liberal bars tilt the scale toward more liberal judicial candidates.

Two factors are worth noting. The first is geographic clustering. Like other industries, lawyers tend to cluster in certain areas. For example, lawyers working in large corporate law firms tend to cluster in large, business-oriented metro areas, such as New York City, Los Angeles, Houston, and Atlanta. Government attorneys tend to cluster in Washington, DC or in state capitals such as Atlanta or Boston. However, metropolitan areas tend to be more liberal than other places in their states, meaning that it is no surprise that lawyers in these areas are more liberal than people elsewhere.[18]

Second, the geographic divides also mask professional divides. Although New York, Houston, and Washington, DC are all hubs for large law firms that employ thousands of lawyers, their practice areas differ. New York firms are well known for business and financial services, such as mergers and acquisitions and antitrust litigation. Washington, DC firms have specialty practices in administrative law, regulation, and appellate litigation. Houston firms have historically focused on oil and natural resource law. We might expect these sorts of regional differences to influence the legal culture within the various states, with lawyers in practice areas such as oil and gas being more conservative and lawyers in government litigation being more liberal.

As evidence of these regional patterns, Figure 6.2 disaggregates our ideology data on lawyers' ideologies by state. The data are presented with states ordered from most liberal to most conservative. Echoing our analyses of law schools, states with more liberal law schools also tend to be those with the most liberal lawyers. These include California, New York, Massachusetts, Connecticut, and Pennsylvania, which are clustered in the top left of the figure. Among those states that have the most conservative lawyers (relatively) are Wyoming, Texas, Mississippi, and Alabama, also unsurprising given the more conservative nature of those states' law schools. To some extent, these patterns reflect the relative reputation of these states in terms of their politics, with the Texas, Mississippi,

---

[18] In fact, our data show that, conditional on *city* (not state) location, lawyers are actually more conservative than the average resident of their city. That is, a lawyer residing in Los Angeles is, on average, more conservative than the average Angelino but more liberal than the average Californian. This could mean that the patterns we observe in Chapter 3 are due to political sorting and that lawyers are, conditional on where they live, actually more conservative. Even so, it remains the case that the profession as a whole is more liberal than other similarly educated professions.

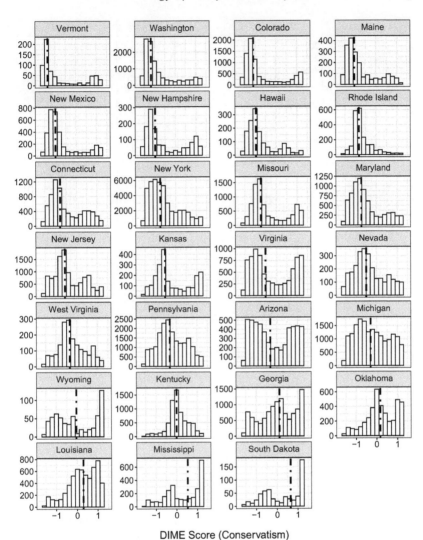

DIME Score (Conservatism)

FIGURE 6.2 Ideology of lawyers by state. *Note:* States are ordered from the most liberal to the most conservative. Dotted lines indicate the median ideal point of attorneys in each state.
Sources: DIME, Martindale-Hubbell.

and Alabama bars being comparably more conservative than the New York, Massachusetts, and California bars. Also in line with their politics, states like Ohio display bimodal patterns, echoing their reputation as "bellwether" states in national politics.

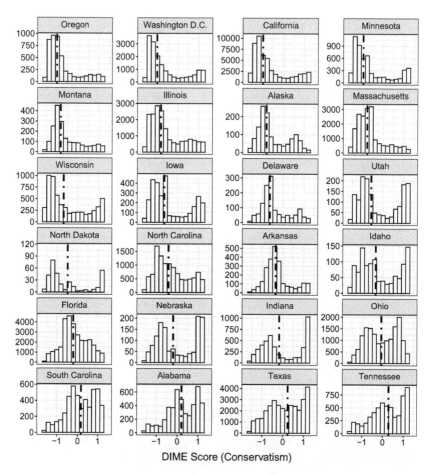

DIME Score (Conservatism)

FIGURE 6.2 *(continued)*

However, some states' bars differ quite markedly from what we would expect given their political reputations. For example, our data for Alaska, Arkansas, Missouri, Montana, and West Virginia – otherwise fairly conservative states – show lawyers in these states to be more liberal-leaning. A different example of a bar somewhat out of step with its state's political reputation is Virginia, which, due to the rapid encroachment of the DC suburbs, currently leans in a more liberal direction.[19] At the same time, however, our data show the ideologies of Virginia attorneys are

---

[19] In the 2008, 2012, and 2016 elections, Virginia went to the Democratic presidential candidate; in addition, as of 2019, four out of the five last governors have been Democrats.

solidly bimodal. This, we think, is reflective of the more conservative character of the University of Virginia Law School (certainly compared to other Top 14 law schools, which we can see in Figure 6.1) and the more conservative parts of the state.

VARIATION IN POLITICAL ACTORS' IDEOLOGY

In this section, we describe variation in the ideology of political actors across states. For this analysis, we identified the set of politicians elected to nonjudicial state-level office for each state between 2006 and 2016. This provides a measure of the ideological leanings of political actors across states, which, due to the common contribution-based measurement strategy of DIME, allows for direct comparisons between attorneys, judges, and politicians within and across states. It also provides a general measure of state policy leanings based on the revealed preferences of voters signaled by the candidates they elect to express political positions within state government. That is, the distribution of elected politicians in a state provides a baseline for what we should expect judges to look like if they too were selected on a purely politicized basis.

Figure 6.3 presents these analyses. Again, we observe substantial ideological variation across states. Here, the differences observed across states more closely tracks partisan leanings revealed by two-party vote shares in presidential elections and other measures of state-level ideology, with Vermont as the most liberal state and Idaho as the most conservative.[20] Combining the measures of ideology for lawyers, judges, and politicians in each state lays the groundwork for the empirical analyses that follow.

VARIATION IN JUDICIAL IDEOLOGY BY STATE

How does the judicial tug of war between politicians and attorneys shape judicial composition across the various states? According to our framework, we can look at specific empirical patterns to reason inductively on how the tug of war is working. For example, if judges resemble politicians (and not attorneys) in terms of their own ideological leanings, this would be indicative of politicized selection, or that politicians are

---

[20] See the supplemental appendix of Bonica and Sen (2017b) for an analysis that compares our state-level averages based on the DIME scores of politicians elected to state office with alternative measures of state ideology, including state-level presidential two-party vote shares and the Berry et al. (2013) measures of citizen and government ideology.

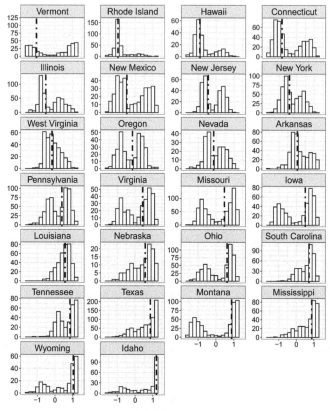

DIME Score (Conservatism)

FIGURE 6.3 Ideology of elected politicians by state.

Note: The histograms cover ideal points of all elected politicians serving in legislatures and statewide office who served between 2006 and 2016. States are ordered from the most liberal to the most conservative. Dotted lines indicate the median ideal point of politicians in the state.

Source: DIME.

"winning" the tug of war by pulling the ideology of courts closer to their preference point. If judges and lawyers are similarly minded (i.e., we cannot rule out differences between the two), then we would say there is ideologically neutral selection (or no evidence of politicization) and that attorneys are "winning" the tug of war via their professional capture of the courts.

States provide more interesting variation with which to study these dynamics than is the case at the federal level. For example, there are

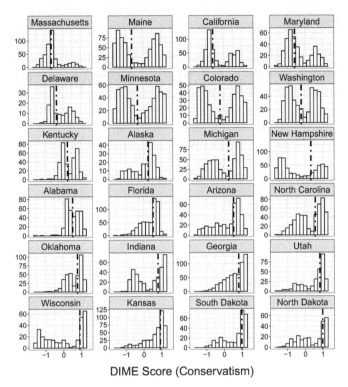

DIME Score (Conservatism)

FIGURE 6.3 *(continued)*

states where lawyers and politicians share similar ideological views, and so there may not be much interest by politicians to politicize. One example of this is Massachusetts, a state where both lawyers and politicians are both left-leaning (Figure 6.2). Applied to Massachusetts, our framework would predict that tensions between elected officials and the bar over the judiciary will be fairly minimal – both prefer a left-leaning judiciary that reflects their shared liberal interests. In other states, however, politicians and judges might be in ideological opposition. This is certainly the case in Kansas, where, in the early 2010s, politicians veered sharply to the right while the Kansas bar remained center-left (Figure 6.2).

To get a sense of how the data speak to the state-by-state tension between state bar associations and state political elites, we turn to our measures of ideology. Looking at the campaign finance scores is again useful here, because we can place all individual actors – not just political actors but also lawyers across the fifty states – on the same scale.

Figure 6.4 presents these data for each state. For each state on the vertical axis, we denote the relative ideological positions of the state's attorneys (A), judges (J), and political actors (P).[21] For purposes of interpretability, we center each state on the position of the average attorney and plot the average ideology of politicians and judges in the state relative to this baseline. This helps capture the relationship of interest, the extent to which judges differ ideologically from lawyers in their state.

Figure 6.4 conveys several patterns of interest. First, lawyers are consistently to the left of politicians. In only one state (Rhode Island) is the average politician to the left of the average attorney. Second, there is substantial variation in how judges are positioned relative to lawyers and politicians. In some states – notably Virginia and Texas, which rely on legislative appointment and partisan elections, respectively – judges more closely resemble the politicians than they do the lawyers in their state. In most other states, the average judge is situated somewhere in between the average attorney and the average politician, evidence of the judicial tug of war playing out. In the remaining states, the average judge is to the left of the average lawyer, of which nearly all (eight out of ten) of these states use merit commissions to select judges. Third, the figure is noteworthy because it shows that there are very few instances in which political actors are successful in *completely* politicizing the courts, or in shifting the courts to be in total alignment with their preferences. We can see this because there are very few instances where P and J completely overlap with one another, although some states (Virginia and North Dakota) come close.

All of this highlights the central tension in the tug of war over the judiciary. Again, Kansas provides a useful example. In recent years, Kansas politicians have moved to the right ideologically (e.g., when pushed rightward by the state's Tea Party in the 2010s), while the bar has been comparatively more liberal. This increasing divide has meant that Kansas politicians are ideologically distant both from attorneys and, perhaps more importantly, from judges. As we discuss in Chapter 7, we believe that, in the absence of politicians moving more to the center, such a large gap is untenable: With enough time, politicians will eventually change judicial selection to move away from nominating commissions comprised of lawyers and consolidate more power over the composition of the

---

[21] All of these ideological estimates were done using campaign finance data as before. The sample includes 471,432 lawyers and 12,263 state court judges active as of 2012 and 20,668 politicians elected to state office between 2006 and 2016.

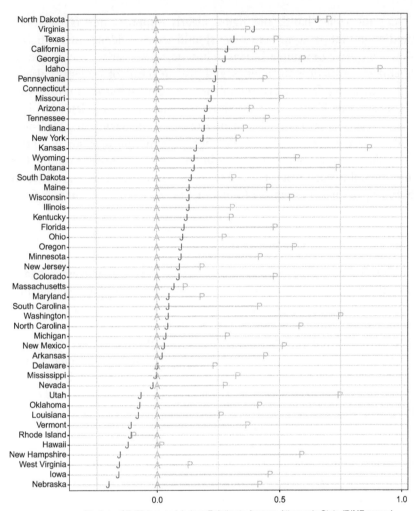

Ideology of Politicians and Judges Relative to Average Attorney in State (DIME scores)

FIGURE 6.4 Comparison of average ideology of judges and politicians relative to attorneys. The *x*-axis is centered on the average ideology of attorneys in each state. States are ordered (from top to bottom) by the signed distance between judges and attorneys. The symbols are interpreted as follows: *A* = Attorneys, *J* = Judges, and *P* = Politicians.

judiciary in the hands of politicians. That is, as we explore in Chapter 7, political actors will try to "tug" the judiciary closer and closer to their preferred position and they will do so, if they must, by changing the very way in which judges are selected.

On the other hand, the figure clearly supports our framework's prediction that, in some states, we should see no evidence of politicization. One telling example is Massachusetts, which, as we mentioned, is liberal in terms of state politics and also in terms of its legal culture. Given this, our framework would predict that politicians and lawyers want the same kind of judges – those who are also to the left of center. This is exactly what the data demonstrate: In Massachusetts, attorneys and political actors are all in close alignment and, unsurprisingly, so too are judges. Substantively, this is a win-win arrangement for both the bar and for politicians, resulting in state court rulings that are agreeable to both. We discuss these sorts of outcomes in more depth in Chapter 7.

SELECTION MECHANISMS

The results presented in Figure 6.4 hint at but do not deeply engage with the important role played by existing judicial selection mechanisms. However, how judges are selected – and the formal institutions that constrain or enable politicians or bar association leaders – play a significant role in shaping the contours of the courts. As Table 6.1 shows, some state courts are staffed exclusively via executive appointments, similar to the federal courts, which allow the legal establishment at most only advisory input into the judicial selection process. Other states incorporate organized bar membership into the judicial selection process via nominating commissions. This allows the legal profession to exercise a strong influence over which judges are eventually selected, limiting in some respects the extent to which political actors can rely on ideology in selecting judicial candidates. Still others select judges through legislative appointment. Virginia is one such unusual example.

In this section, we provide context of how state judges in the United States are selected. Consistent with the coding scheme in place by organizations such as Ballotpedia, we group judicial selection mechanisms into four broad categories: (1) political (executive) appointments, (2) partisan elections, (3) nonpartisan elections, and (4) merit commission selections.[22] Many states employ more than one of these. For example, as we discussed in our introduction to this chapter, Kansas employs

---

[22] These summaries were accurate at time of our writing. Ballotpedia (http://ballotpedia .org) has up-to-date summaries of each state's judicial selection system, some of which we summarize in Table 6.1. Additional information is maintained by the National Center for State Courts (www.judicialselection.com).

TABLE 6.1 *Judicial selection mechanisms for state supreme and state appeals courts, as of 2019.*

	State Supreme Court	State Appeals Court
Alabama	Partisan Election	Partisan Election
Alaska	Assisted Appointment	Assisted Appointment
Arizona	Assisted Appointment	Assisted Appointment
Arkansas	Nonpartisan Election	Nonpartisan Election
California	Executive Appointment	Executive Appointment
Colorado	Assisted Appointment	Assisted Appointment
Connecticut	Assisted Appointment	Assisted Appointment
Delaware	Assisted Appointment	
Florida	Assisted Appointment	
Georgia	Nonpartisan Election	Nonpartisan Election
Hawaii	Assisted Appointment	
Idaho	Nonpartisan Election	Nonpartisan Election
Illinois	Partisan Election	
Indiana	Assisted Appointment	Assisted Appointment
Iowa	Assisted Appointment	Assisted Appointment
Kansas	Assisted Appointment	Executive Appointment
Kentucky	Nonpartisan Election	Nonpartisan Election
Louisiana	Partisan Election	Partisan Election
Maine	Executive Appointment	
Maryland		Assisted Appointment
Massachusetts	Executive Appointment	Assisted Appointment
Michigan	Nonpartisan Election	Nonpartisan Election
Minnesota	Nonpartisan Election	Nonpartisan Election
Mississippi	Nonpartisan Election	Nonpartisan Election
Missouri	Assisted Appointment	Assisted Appointment
Montana	Nonpartisan Election	
Nebraska	Assisted Appointment	Assisted Appointment
Nevada	Nonpartisan Election	
New Hampshire	Assisted Appointment	
New Jersey	Executive Appointment	
New Mexico	Partisan Election	Partisan Election
New York	Partisan Election	Assisted Appointment
North Carolina	Partisan Election	Partisan Election
North Dakota	Nonpartisan Election	Other
Ohio	Nonpartisan Election	Nonpartisan Election
Oklahoma	Assisted Appointment	Assisted Appointment
Oregon	Nonpartisan Election	Nonpartisan Election
Pennsylvania	Partisan Election	
Rhode Island	Assisted Appointment	
South Carolina	Legislative Election	Legislative Election
South Dakota	Assisted Appointment	

TABLE 6.1 *(continued)*

	State Supreme Court	State Appeals Court
Tennessee	Executive Appointment	Executive Appointment
Texas	Partisan Election	Partisan Election
Utah	Assisted Appointment	Assisted Appointment
Vermont	Assisted Appointment	
Virginia	Legislative Election	Legislative Election
Washington	Nonpartisan Election	Nonpartisan Election
West Virginia	Nonpartisan Election	
Wisconsin	Nonpartisan Election	Nonpartisan Election
Wyoming	Assisted Appointment	

Note: "Assisted Appointment" refers to any kind of nominating commission.
Source: Ballotpedia.

nominating commissions as well as elections. Other states tend to use only one kind of selection mechanism. Texas, for example, uses partisan elections for all its state judges. This variation results in different outcomes: Some selection mechanisms (such as executive appointments) benefit state politicians when it comes to the composition of the judiciary, while others (such as nominating commissions) better serve state bars and the legal profession.

Political Appointments

The most straightforward appointments system is one in which the state executive appoints judges, usually with the advice and consent of the upper legislative chamber. (This is also the judicial selection mechanism advocated by the constitutional framers and the one used by the federal government.) An example of this is New Jersey, in which the governor names all of the judges in the state, after which they must be confirmed by the New Jersey Senate.[23] Overall, this makes New Jersey's judicial selection among the most similar to the federal judicial system. Other gubernatorial appointments states tend to cluster in New England and in the Northeast; this includes New Hampshire, Massachusetts, Maryland, and Connecticut.

---

[23] The exception here are appointments to New Jersey municipal courts, who are appointed by city mayors, with the approval of the corresponding city council. More details are available at https://ballotpedia.org/Courts_in_New_Jersey.

Most states employing executive appointments, however, do not use such appointments in all instances or for all judicial vacancies. For example, for New York appellate division courts, the governor can appoint any judge who has first won a seat onto the state supreme courts (which in New York are the highest trial courts). The system is thus one that mixes gubernatorial appointments with elections.[24] Other states feature appointments for only some tiers of the judiciary. In Maine, for example, the governor appoints justices on the Maine Supreme Court, the state appeals courts, and the state trial courts. However, judges must be elected (in partisan elections) onto state probate courts, which handle and administer trusts and estates.[25]

Most states that rely on executive or gubernatorial appointments offer state bar associations very limited roles in the judicial selection process. Bar associations may, however, still weigh in with advisory recommendations or qualification ratings. For example, in New Jersey, the state bar association's Judicial and Prosecutorial Appointments Committee "[c]onducts a confidential review of prospective judicial and county prosecutor candidates and advises the Governor whether the prospective candidates are qualified for appointment for those offices. These duties are performed under a compact established with the Governor."[26] Just like in the federal system, however, these sorts of recommendations are entirely advisory, meaning that elected officials in states with executive appointments resoundingly have the upper hand in the judicial tug of war.

Partisan Elections

Several other states rely primarily on partisan elections for the selection of their judges. As their name implies, judicial candidates in these states run in elections with their party identifications (Republican, Democrat, or some other party) displayed directly on the ballots, shown in advertising, or otherwise conveyed to voters. Many of

---

[24] https://ballotpedia.org/Judicial_selection_in_New_York.

[25] https://ballotpedia.org/Maine_judicial_elections.

[26] https://tcms.njsba.com/personifyebusiness/Leadership/StandingCommittees/Judicialand ProsecutorialAppointmentsCommittee.aspx. New Jersey's protocol is similar to the federal courts, in which the American Bar Association (ABA) has traditionally vetted nominees for the White House before their names are forwarded to the Senate. Of course, as we noted in our introduction to Chapter 5, Republican administrations have rejected the ABA's involvement in the private evaluation of potential nominees.

these candidates can also obtain financial backing and other electoral support (e.g., endorsements) directly from the parties and from party elite.[27]

How partisan elections are administered varies from state to state in ways that could influence the ultimate pool of judges selected. For example, in Texas all judges are elected through partisan elections (including partisan primaries), all the way from judges at the trial court level to the state supreme court level. In addition, judges must run again in a partisan election at the conclusion of their terms (where the terms are of varying length).[28] Similarly, in North Carolina, which we discuss again in Chapter 7, all judges must run in partisan elections, a practice that was instituted in 2016.[29] In other states, judges may be elected initially via partisan elections, but then must run in uncontested or nonpartisan elections thereafter. Judges in Illinois, for example, are initially elected to ten-year (or six-year) terms via partisan elections, but, once on the bench, subsequent races for reelection are nonpartisan.[30]

Many scholars believe that the election of judges provides benefits both to the judiciary and to the general public. For example, Chris Bonneau and Melinda Gann Hall have argued in their influential work on state courts that electing judges forces them to be accountable to ordinary Americans, particularly on issues people care about the most. "Justices who are elected (especially from unsafe seats) and who must face voters regularly to retain their seats (particularly where terms of office are short)," they write, "have a strong incentive to consider constituency preferences on those few issues that are publicly salient and politically visible."[31] It is, they argue, "far better for justices to draw upon public perceptions and the prevailing state political climate when resolving difficult disputes than to engage in the unfettered pursuit of their own personal preferences."[32]

Other scholars have further pointed out that judicial elections contribute to judicial independence (at least from political actors) and

[27] Around 30 percent of all contributions made to judicial candidates come from the parties themselves. See Bannon, Lisk, and Hardin (2017, p. 11).
[28] https://ballotpedia.org/Judicial_selection_in_Texas.
[29] Specifically, all of the seven justices on the state supreme court are elected to eight-year terms via partisan elections; in addition, as of December 2016 and March 2017 respectively, all state appeals judges and all state superior court judges are chosen by partisan election as well. See https://ballotpedia.org/Judicial_selection_in_North_Carolina.
[30] https://ballotpedia.org/Judicial_selection_in_Illinois.
[31] Bonneau and Hall (2009, p. 14).
[32] Bonneau and Hall (2009, p. 15).

thus serve to enhance the legitimacy and influence of the judiciary. For example, the legal historian Kermit Hall noted that the rise of partisan elections of state appeals judges was a result of moderate lawmakers "want[ing] the appellate judiciary to command more, rather than less, power and prestige. Far from being hostile to judicial power, they intended to enhance it."[33] In agreement, Bonneau and Hall note that "the process of elections is the only one that can make judges completely independent from the legislature and the governor."[34] Indeed, the fact that judicial elections allow judges to draw the source of their power directly from the people, as opposed to from political actors, broadens their base of power and makes them more coequal to elected branches of government.

On the other hand, partisan elections have engendered significant opposition from legal elites, including many former judges.[35] The first critique is that elections force judges to engage in political campaigning, thereby inviting the unseemly possibility that campaign money could influence the decision-making process.[36] Former judges have been vocal on these points. For example, former US Supreme Court Justice Sandra Day O'Connor said in a well-publicized speech that "[j]udicial elections powered by money and special interests create the impression, rightly or wrongly, that judges are accountable to money and special interests, not the law."[37] Another former federal judge likewise complained, "I cringe at the constant contention that judges should be held 'accountable.' They are accountable to the laws and the Constitution. They should not be subject to the whim of those who find certain past rulings objectionable or seek to influence future ones by buying elections."[38]

---

[33] Hall (1984, p. 348).

[34] Bonneau and Hall (2009, p. 7).

[35] Many of these critiques also apply to nonpartisan elections as well, although the criticisms have been the most strident in the context of partisan elections.

[36] According to the Brennan Center for Justice, this influx became most pervasive around the year 2000, with approximately 45 million dollars being raised by candidates on state judicial races – a "62% increase over 1998" (Sample et al. 2010). In addition, the Brennan Center also reports that "from 2000–09, independent groups and political parties spent at least $39.3 million on television time, about 42 percent of total ad costs" (Sample et al. 2010, p. 8). Interestingly, the top donors to judicial campaigns are not individuals but rather organizations – including plaintiffs' lawyers, unions, corporations, and organized action committees (Bannon, Lisk, and Hardin 2017).

[37] Rankin (quoted in 2013). O'Connor has in the past supported the use of other selection mechanisms besides partisan elections. See http://iaals.du.edu/quality-judges/projects/oconnor-judicial-selection-plan.

[38] Sarokin (2014).

The second, and related, critique is that judicial elections undermine judicial independence – thus negatively influencing the tenor and quality of judicial decision-making. For example, Justice O'Connor wrote in an opinion piece that "voters generally don't express much interest in the election of judges" and that the same voters "are less likely to devote themselves to the core value of judicial independence, because when judges apply the law fairly and impartially they cannot guarantee the outcome any particular voter might want. But fair and impartial judging is an essential part of our government, and must be preserved."[39] These criticisms have led to broader concerns that the political parties and special interests have exercised undue influence over the courts, in turn leading to an erosion in public trust in the court system.[40]

In terms of its impact on decision-making, several studies have documented that elected judges decide some cases differently than those appointed by executives or via nominating commissions. However, these studies have mostly looked at specific issues, as opposed to overall judicial ideology. For example, Canes-Wrone, Clark, and Kelly find that nonpartisan elections lead justices to pander to the public on high-profile cases such as those involving the death penalty, while Huber and Gordon find that judges reelected via partisan elections are more punitive on sentences than those facing retention via merit commissions.[41] Another set of papers has found that larger damages are awarded in states with elections versus appointments.[42] In a fascinating long-term analysis,

[39] O'Connor (2007). The same former judge wrote,

> Bad enough that judges receive contributions from lawyers or potential clients, that corporations can now pick their judicial candidates, that the public is usually unaware of the qualifications of the candidates and that the campaigns are frequently degrading. But then add to that – possible influence over the decision making process – that judges are deciding cases (and worse – imposing the death penalty) in order to win votes. (Sarokin 2014)

[40] The evidence on this is somewhat mixed. Gibson suggests that, when "judges express their policy views during campaigns for elected judgeships, no harm is done to the institutional legitimacy of courts" (Gibson 2009, p. 1298). However, the same research finds that judges *receiving campaign contributions* does damage the courts' institutional legitimacy. See also Gibson et al. (2011), which finds some negative effects from "politicized campaign ads" on court support but that there is no difference between traditional ads and negative attack ads.

[41] Canes-Wrone, Clark, and Kelly (2014) and Huber and Gordon (2004).

[42] Helland and Tabarrok (2002), Tabarrok and Helland (1999). However, see Hanssen (1999), which finds that there is less litigation in states with elections versus appointments.

Berkowitz and Clay show that states settled initially by civil law countries are more likely to have partisan elections, which they argue result in lower-quality judges.[43] Perhaps most broadly, Choi, Gulati, and Posner do not find any clear differences in terms of overall performance or independence between elected versus appointed judges, but they do find that elected judges focus their efforts on productivity, whereas appointed judges issue fewer but higher-quality opinions. The authors interpret this as evidence that elected judges behave more like politicians, while appointed judges behave more like legal professionals seeking to enhance their legal reputations.[44] Taken together, these papers suggest that different formal selection processes not only create different incentives for judicial behavior but could also result in judges with different policy (or ideological) preferences and professional interests.

In terms of our framework, this research also suggests that partisan elections refine judges' political sensitivity, making them more in sync with the broader political preferences of the electorate and of political elites. This is not surprising: For many partisan elections, party elite are hugely influential in determining which candidates are on the ballots, which candidates are endorsed (or not) by party elites, and which candidates receive party funding. Another consequence is that statewide shifts can have a significant impact on down-ballot voting, including in the votes for judicial candidates. A good example of this is Texas, which has had partisan elections for all of its judges since 1876, making it a long-standing adherent to partisan judicial elections.[45] As one former Republican Texas Supreme Court judge explained:

we have the ability to straight-ticket vote here and so, in 2008, when I was on the ballot, it was McCain versus Obama, and Republicans in Texas by a large margin voted for McCain but they voted straight-ticket. So they voted McCain and every single Republican down the ballot. And in Harris County that year, Obama was extraordinarily popular so they voted for Obama and every Democrat down the ballot. I won [my] election easily, [but] in Houston there was almost a complete

---

43 Berkowitz and Clay (2006). See also Hanssen (1999).
44 Choi, Gulati, and Posner (2010). This is consistent with the arguments of Sandra Day O'Connor and other former judges who have argued that elections result in judges with questionable motives. For example, citing sexist comments made by an elected judge that she encountered earlier in her career, O'Connor noted, "he was a disaster and that we shouldn't be electing people of that caliber – they shouldn't be elected. If they were appointed, we would never have had that man on the bench. And he's not the only one" (excerpted from Feerick, O'Connor, and Kaye 2012, p. 1152).
45 www.judicialselection.us/judicial_selection/index.cfm?state=TX.

sweep of Republican judges—they were replaced by Democrats. That makes no sense. These votes are not based upon the merits of the judge but on partisan affiliation and if its not party affiliation it's the sound of your name.[46]

Thus, partisan elections, as the example of Texas illustrates, are more likely than other selection mechanisms to result in judges whose preferences will align with overall partisan tendencies and with the political proclivities of the electorate at any given moment.

Although partisan elections leave room for political influence via party leaders, they tend to afford the legal profession only a very limited say in judicial elections, limited mostly to endorsements or published recommendations.[47] We believe that the lack of meaningful influence is a plausible reason why the ABA and other state bars have opposed the use of judicial elections more broadly. In 2003, for example, the ABA commissioned an exhaustive overview of the judicial selection process. In the resulting report, they wrote, "The preferred system of state court judicial selection is a commission-based appointive system" and, "For states that cannot abandon the judicial reselection process altogether, judges should be subject to reappointment by a credible, neutral, non-partisan, diverse deliberative body."[48] Partisan elections have also been roundly criticized by former judges, including those who served under such systems.[49]

Nonpartisan Elections

By contrast, a number of states elect their judges in a nonpartisan manner. For the most part, this means that ballots must leave off explicit

---

[46] Cohen (2013).

[47] Some local bar associations publish guides oriented to helping voters assess who are – and who are not – qualified judicial candidates. For example, the Texas Bar Association conducts a poll of its members on the various candidates and publishes the results. The association is careful, however, to explain that the guide is "in no way an endorsement of any candidate by the State Bar of Texas, its officers, directors, or staff." See www.texasbar.com/Content/NavigationMenu/AboutUs/ResearchandAnalysis/Ju dicialPoll/default.htm.

[48] American Bar Association (2003).

[49] In Texas, for example, numerous former judges have spoken out against the state's partisan elections system. According to one judge, "We shouldn't have partisan elections. I do not like the concept of a Republican or Democratic judge. I think fundraising undermines the confidence in a fair and impartial judicial system" (Cohen 2013). Another former judge pointed out the vicissitudes associated with running in tandem with the political cycle: "In November, many good judges lost solely because voters in their districts preferred a presidential candidate in the other party" (quoted in Ramsey 2017).

partisan information. In some cases, all such information must be kept away from voters, and judicial candidates also cannot be endorsed by party leaders or party organizations.[50] A key question in thinking about our framework is how truly "nonpartisan" these sorts of elections actually are. The answer largely depends on locality, norms, and rules. One example is North Carolina, which in 2016 relied on nonpartisan competitive elections to elect justices onto its state supreme court.[51] Despite the nonpartisan nature of the election, many people knew full well that the incumbent, Robert Edmonds, was a Republican and his challenger, Mike Morgan, was a Democrat. Edmunds, for example, was endorsed by organizations associated with "law & order" causes, including state sheriff's associations, while Morgan was endorsed by civil rights groups, environmental groups, labor unions, and then-president Barack Obama.[52] The endorsements, combined with the partisan backgrounds of the two candidates, left little question about their partisanship, even though information about partisanship was not provided on the ballot. As one observer commented, "Though state-level judicial elections do not come with partisan labels, that does not mean that the candidates themselves are not partisan."[53]

Studies back up the idea that partisanship appears to be among the more important traits that voters look for in evaluating judicial candidates, therefore questioning whether nonpartisan elections simply have the effect of withholding information that voters actually want.[54] Other studies have found strong effects of partisanship on outcomes in nonpartisan elections, suggesting that voters are nonetheless still using partisan cues even in nonpartisan elections.[55] Finally, other studies have gone further and noted, via experimental data and voter survey data, that nonpartisan ballots are ineffective in

---

[50] See Salokar (2007, p. 345), who notes, "In states that hold nonpartisan elections, judicial candidates are generally not permitted to identify or announce endorsements from political parties or associations identified with political parties, whether or not those endorsements are solicited, and candidates may not declare their own party affiliation."

[51] As we discuss in Chapter 7, North Carolina has since moved to partisan elections, a move initiated by conservatives frustrated with the liberal nature of the state courts.

[52] For a list of Edmund's endorsements, see www.justiceedmunds.com/endorsers1#sh eriffs (accessed May 2, 2018). For a list of Mike Morgan's endorsements, see www .judgemikemorgan.com/election/ (accessed May 2, 2018).

[53] Caulder (2016).

[54] See, for example, Burnett and Tiede (2015), Sen (2017b).

[55] Baum and Klein (2007) and Rock and Baum (2010).

keeping partisan concerns out of voters' minds when evaluating judicial candidates.[56]

That said, many believe that nonpartisan elections offer distinct advantages over partisan elections. Although scholarly evidence suggests that partisanship is highly predictive of decision-making,[57] the concern is that an emphasis on partisanship distracts voters away from a reasoned evaluation of competence and quality. This, many have argued, undermines judicial independence. For example, in her editorial, Justice O'Connor criticized partisan elections, arguing that "the first step that a state like Pennsylvania can take to reverse this trend is replace the partisan election of its judges with a merit-selection system, or at least with a nonpartisan system in which the candidates do not affiliate with political parties."[58] This concern about independence has been echoed by several scholars.[59]

Merit Commissions (the Missouri Plan)

The last type of selection mechanism that we consider involves the use of nonpartisan or bipartisan advisory commissions. This type of plan was first adopted by Missouri in 1940 and is thus also referred to as "the Missouri Plan."

Although how they work varies from state to state, the general framework is that a nonpartisan commission evaluates possible candidates for a judicial vacancy and then recommends either an individual or a list (known as a panel or a slate) to the state's governor. The governor then chooses one or some subset to fill the vacancy or vacancies. In some states, the judges selected via the process of nominating commissions are awarded life tenure (e.g., in Rhode Island);[60] however, in most states, the appointment is for some fixed term. In some states (e.g., South Dakota), judges who are named through a nominating commission must

---

[56] Bonneau and Cann (2015).

[57] See our earlier discussion in Chapters 1 and 4. Scholarly studies documenting the important role of ideology and partisanship in judicial decision-making include Segal and Spaeth (2002), Sunstein et al. (2006), and Epstein, Landes, and Posner (2013), among many others. See Harris and Sen (2019) for an overview.

[58] O'Connor (2007).

[59] See, e.g., Berkowitz and Clay (2006, p. 419). See, however, Canes-Wrone and Clark (2009) for a rebuttal of these points.

[60] www.judicialselection.us/judicial_selection/methods/selection_of_judges.cfm?state=RI.

then run in a nonpartisan election at the conclusion of their term.[61] In other states (e.g., Hawaii), the nominating commission reevaluates judges to determine whether they should be retained.[62] Other states reverse the process. In California, the governor can nominate anyone who has been admitted to practice law in the state for at least ten years; only once the candidate is named by the governor are they evaluated by the Commission on Judicial Appointments.[63]

States also vary in terms of the composition of judicial nominating commissions. Some states rely on nomination commissions with mixed memberships comprised of lawyers named by the state's bar association and individuals (often nonlawyers) named by the state's governor. For example, Missouri's Appellate Judicial Commission is comprised of three lawyers elected by the members of the state bar, three nonlawyers chosen by the governor, and then the chief justice of the Missouri Supreme Court.[64] Utah's bipartisan appellate court nominating commission consists of seven commissioners, all appointed by the governor. The Utah Bar names six nominees to serve as commissioners; from this list the governor must choose two. In addition, no more than four commissioners may be from the same political party and no more than four may be members of the Utah State Bar.[65]

The use of nominating commissions is thought to yield three advantages. First, having a merit commission involved in the selection of judges was thought to relieve partisan infighting over judicial positions and to lessen the influence of politics on the judges themselves. As the famed Harvard Law School dean Roscoe Pound declared, "[P]utting courts into politics and compelling judges to become politicians, in many jurisdictions has almost destroyed the traditional respect for the bench."[66] Second, these merit plans had the benefit (to many) of doing away with judicial elections, in which judges spent time away from the bench to campaign and fundraise. Lastly, and related to these other factors, merit commissions were believed to increase judicial independence and to

---

[61] www.judicialselection.us/judicial_selection/methods/selection_of_judges.cfm?state=SD.
[62] www.judicialselection.us/judicial_selection/methods/selection_of_judges.cfm?state=HI.
[63] Trevor et al. (2017).
[64] https://ballotpedia.org/Missouri_Appellate_Judicial_Commission.
[65] See Utah Code 78A-10-202.
[66] Pound (1964, p. 748).

shield judges from obviously partisan and political forces.[67] We discuss the transition in many states from elections to merit commissions in greater depth in Chapter 7 when we consider how selection mechanisms are themselves a product of the tension between the bar and political actors.

Though merit-oriented systems have proved popular with legal elites, they have proved less popular with politicians.[68,69] As we discuss in Chapter 7, this has included many conservatives who believe that these plans place too much power in the hands of left-leaning lawyers' groups and, in particular, extremely litigation-focused trial attorneys. For example, a white paper published by the conservative Federalist Society cautioned against the spread of merit commissions and noted that,

Where a particular interest group controls the organized bar, we can expect to see judicial selections reflecting the interests of that particular group. In Missouri itself, it has recently been argued with great force, the plaintiff's bar has succeeded in dominating the state at all levels of government, and this has made Missouri, in at least one year, Americas No. 1 plaintiff's venue.[70]

The same report warned that there must be "some skepticism with regard to the purported benefits of having unaccountable lawyer-activists meeting in secret to develop 'approved' lists of judicial candidates."[71] There is scholarly evidence on this point (also cited in the Federalist Society report).[72] For example, one important law review article found evidence that merit commissions favor the selection of more Democratic judges in Missouri and Tennessee.[73]

Others have criticized the systems for putting too much power in the hands of legal elites, a population subset that has historically

---

[67] The reasoning was also echoed by Albert M. Kales, the president of the American Judicature Society and one of the earliest proponents of merit selection, who wrote that "[p]utting courts into politics, and compelling judges to become politicians ... has almost destroyed the traditional respect for the Bench" (Kales 1927).

[68] The ABA's 2003 report on judicial selection named merit commissions as the preferred method for judicial selection, by far more preferable than selection by election.

[69] Alfred P. Carlton Jr. and others (2003). Former judges also agree. For example, retired US Supreme Court Justice Sandra Day O'Connor developed an "O'Connor Selection Plan," which calls for a judicial nominating commission, followed by gubernatorial appointments, and then retention elections.

[70] Presser et al. (2003).

[71] Presser et al. (2003).

[72] Presser et al. (2003).

[73] Fitzpatrick (2009).

excluded women and minorities from its ranks. For example, the same Federalist Society report criticized merit commissions as "hav[ing] a built-in bias toward whatever group of lawyers control local bar associations," and that these lawyers tend to lean in a white, male, and older direction.[74] The actual evidence is somewhat mixed across states.[75]

JUDICIAL SELECTION IN THE TUG-OF-WAR

For our purposes, these various selection mechanisms fundamentally shape the rules governing the judicial tug of war between the legal profession and party leaders, helping one side versus the other. To be more precise, the more that the selection mechanism allows ideology (or partisanship) to be used in the selection of judges, the more that political actors will "win" at the tug of war – that is, the more the resulting judicial composition will ideologically resemble that of political actors. The less that selection mechanisms permit ideology to be used, on the other hand, the more the bar will win – that is, the more the judiciary will resemble the pool of lawyers from which it draws. Put differently, allowing politics or partisan information to enter into the selection of judges gives politicians a lot of power; by contrast, keeping politics out, and sticking to "merit" and "qualifications," hands more power to the state bar, permitting it to mold the judiciary according to its ideological profile.

For these reasons, gubernatorial selection systems and partisan elections will most benefit politicians out of step with the legal establishment. For partisan elections, the logic is straightforward: These are elections that specifically put parties, party platforms, and ideology front and center. Although many have argued that this also results in candidates who are equally qualified (or "legitimate" in the public's eyes) or who are more responsive, these are not our outcomes of interest; our concerns are to evaluate the kind of ideology (and by extension, rulings) that partisan judicial elections produce; and, because they explicitly incorporate concerns about ideology, partisan election systems will produce a judiciary

---

74 Presser et al. (2003).
75 For example, Hurwitz and Lanier (2003) find no differences in diversity across different selection mechanisms. Bratton and Spill (2002) find that nominating commissions can increase gender diversity when all-male judicial panels form the starting baseline but that political appointments (particularly by Democrats) tend to be more diverse.

that deviates more from the underlying pool of attorneys. That is, parties and voters will, working together in partisan election systems, *produce a judiciary that is more reflective of partisan concerns* – including those of party leaders and of dominant voting coalitions.[76]

The second judicial system that will afford a greater role for ideology and for partisanship are political appointments, including gubernatorial and legislative appointments. These are selection systems that explicitly hand the power of judicial appointment to elected politicians. Indeed, for most of these, the executive is front and center and, to the extent that they must compromise, it is with another body comprised of elected officials. This allows political elites wide discretion in appointing judicial candidates that are ideologically like-minded. Political appointments also, again by design, offer state bar associations a very limited role. At most, these organizations issue advisory opinions (such as qualifications ratings), but these are often ignored. Ultimately, *because political appointments freely allow for partisanship and ideology to be taken into account in judicial selection, and permit professional bar associations a very limited role, they will produce a judiciary that represents the interest of political actors, not attorneys.*

By contrast, two other systems – selection based on some version of the Missouri Plan and nonpartisan elections – should be more likely to limit the role of ideology in judicial selection. Under these two systems, we should see a judiciary that more closely resembles the underlying pool of attorneys, reflecting the professional capture of the judiciary by the bar and the limited nature of political involvement. This would suggest, substantively, a more limited role of ideology in judicial selection – that is, judicial selection that is less politicized.

Before turning to an empirical investigation of these claims, we make one important normative point, which is that more politicization need not be bad in terms of rulings and judicial ideology. As we noted before, one possible advantage of the increased reliance of ideology in the selection of judges is that it may (though not necessarily always does) result in a judiciary that is more diverse and more reflective of the interests of voters (expressed via politicians). On the other hand, a lessened role of

---

[76] Importantly, such systems need not produce a judiciary reflective of all citizens or even of all voting adults. Straight-ticket voting often trumps individual scrutiny of judicial candidates; furthermore, as we discuss in Chapter 7, party leaders often play outsized roles in deciding which candidates to put up for election, leading judicial candidates to reflect partisan interests first and foremost.

ideology in judicial selection – furthered by selection systems that limit political actors' involvement – need not be good, from our perspective. Indeed, as argued by some scholars,[77] the use of merit commissions could result in a judiciary that is ideologically out of step with the average voter.

Empirical Tests

We now turn to an empirical investigation of how different judicial selection systems across the states could impact judicial ideology. To begin, we categorize the states' judicial selection methods into four general categories: (1) gubernatorial/legislative appointment (which we refer to as *Executive Appointment*), (2) merit selection systems that combine appointment with some sort of nonpartisan or bipartisan nominating commissions (*Nominating Commissions*), (3) elections with party affiliation of judicial candidates listed on the ballot (*Partisan Elections*), and (4) elections without party affiliation listed the ballot (*Nonpartisan Elections*). We next determine the selection mechanism used by states for each of their courts.[78] Categorizing judicial selection into these four categories is complicated by two factors. First, many states operate with either hybrid judicial selection systems, or have different selection systems for different tiers of their judiciary. (For example, Kansas uses different selection mechanisms for different trial courts throughout the state.) The data we use allow us to identify which judges were selected under which selection mechanism, making it more straightforward to group individuals together according to selection mechanism. The second factor is interim vacancies. Most states – including those with judicial elections – rely on gubernatorial appointments to fill interim vacancies. This is a pervasive practice, with upward of 30 percent of judges in elected seats having originally been appointed to fill some sort of interim vacancy. Because our data allow us to identify a judge's initial method of selection, we can see whether this earlier appointment fits into the ideological mapping of the judiciary.

---

[77] See, e.g., Fitzpatrick (2009), who argues that the use of nonpartisan nominating commissions results in a more Democratic-leaning judiciary.

[78] To identify the selection mechanism for individual judges, we rely on data compiled by Ballotpedia on judicial selection methods used at the state-court level. We supplement this with individual-level data on judicial selection methods scraped from the profile pages for judges, which allows us to identify judges who were initially selected as interim appointments.

We can use this analysis to expand the judicial tug-of-war framework to incorporate selection mechanisms. Specifically, we check how the ideological composition of the judiciary is, or is not, a function of (1) average attorney ideology, (2) average ideology of the political actor in the state, and, now, (3) the selection mechanism. We expect that all three will have a role to play in shaping the judiciary, with the influence of the attorney ideology and the ideology of the political actor in the state being conditioned by the selection mechanism.[79]

Results

An overview of these results is presented in Table 6.2, which flexibly tests how different selection mechanisms do, or do not, impact the ideology of the resulting judicial composition. By interacting several variables as well, the table also checks whether, under each selection mechanism, lawyers or politicians are better off (i.e., have more of an impact on judicial ideology).[80] To provide additional information, Model 1 of the table codes judges according to their *present* method of selection, while Model 2 records judges by their *initial* method of selection (which, as we noted tends to be gubernatorial appointments). The outcome for both is the DIME score of the average judge, with a larger number (more positive) indicating a more conservative judiciary.

Both columns bear out the intuition of the judicial tug-of-war framework. Consider the average lawyer effects in Model 2, which examines how judges were initially appointed. These show a positive interaction between average lawyer ideology and (1) nonpartisan elections and (2) nominating commissions. Substantively, this means that, as lawyers become more conservative in places that have these judicial selection systems, so do judges. This suggests that these selection mechanisms are

---

[79] Technically, the model we estimate is as follows:

$$J_{si} \sim (P_s + A_s) * (Appointed_{si} + Merit_{si} + Partisan\ Election_{si}$$
$$+ Nonpartisan\ Election_{si}) + X_{si} \qquad (6.1)$$

where J_{si} is the ideal point of judge i in state s, P_s and A_s are the average ideal points for politicians and attorneys in that state, and X_{si} is a vector of individual-level controls for gender, age, and law school attended. Interacting selection methods with A_s and P_s captures how responsive judicial ideology is to attorneys and politicians in the state.

[80] Table 6.2 also includes basic controls for the legal environment, including the average number of lawyers attending an elite (Top 14) law school, the average number of years of practice experience, the percentage in the jurisdiction that are female, and the average age.

TABLE 6.2 *Analysis of how different selection mechanisms impact judicial ideology.*

	Model 1	Model 2
Exec. Appointment	0.114	0.202
	(0.130)	(0.107)
Nominating Commission	0.348***	0.417***
	(0.092)	(0.089)
Partisan Election	−0.089	−0.086
	(0.093)	(0.094)
Nonpartisan Election	0.323***	0.305***
	(0.078)	(0.080)
Avg. Lawyer×Partisan Election	−0.439*	−0.425*
	(0.177)	(0.180)
Avg. Lawyer×Nonpartisan Election	1.011***	0.987***
	(0.106)	(0.111)
Avg. Lawyer×Nominating Commission	1.334***	1.488***
	(0.180)	(0.171)
Avg. Lawyer×Exec. Appointment	0.079	0.295
	(0.363)	(0.247)
Avg. Politician×Partisan Election	1.171***	1.131***
	(0.120)	(0.121)
Avg. Politician×Nonpartisan Election	−0.059	−0.049
	(0.097)	(0.104)
Avg. Politician×Nominating Commission	−0.267*	−0.283**
	(0.111)	(0.108)
Avg. Politician×Exec. Appointment	0.666**	0.749***
	(0.253)	(0.183)
Years since Admitted	−0.008*	−0.008*
	(0.003)	(0.003)
Years since Admitted^2	0.0001*	0.0001*
	(0.00004)	(0.00004)
Female	−0.258***	−0.256***
	(0.018)	(0.018)
Top 14 Law School	−0.123***	−0.124***
	(0.028)	(0.028)
> 100 Ranked Law School	0.027	0.025
	(0.016)	(0.016)
In-State Law School	0.039*	0.036*
	(0.016)	(0.016)
R-squared	0.196	0.196
N	11,294	11,294

***$p < 0.001$; **$p < 0.01$; *$p < 0.05$

Note: In each model, judge DIME scores are the outcome variable. Model 2 includes interim replacements recoded by their initial method of selection.

Sources: Martindale-Hubbell, DIME, Ballotpedia.

sensitive to the preferences of the average lawyer in the jurisdiction. We see similar patterns for the average politician effects with the two other selection mechanisms, (1) executive appointments and (2) partisan elections. The positive interaction between average politician ideology and each selection system indicates that, as politicians become more conservative, so do judges. This is strong evidence that judicial ideology reflects politicians' ideology in these circumstances.

From the perspective of politicians, the key question is which of these four selection mechanisms is best given the conditions in their state. Figure 6.5, which analyzes each of the four selection mechanisms separately, provides an answer. For each plot, the *x*-axes represents the average ideology of elected politicians in a state. The *y*-axes represents average judicial ideology, also from left to right (bottom to top). Seeing vertical movement in the observations as politicians become more conservative suggests that judicial ideology responds to changes in politicians' ideology.

Looking at Figure 6.5, we see that two selection systems stand out as being highly sensitive to the preferences of politicians: executive appointments and partisan elections. For each of these, as political actors become more conservative, so do judges. This suggests that these two judicial selection systems facilitate the influence of ideology in judicial selection. By contrast, two selection systems are *in*sensitive to the preferences of politicians: nominating commissions and nonpartisan elections. Under these systems, the ideology of politicians in a state has little to no influence on the ideological composition of the state courts. Thus, under these systems, political actors would likely be thwarted even if they did try to move judicial ideology.

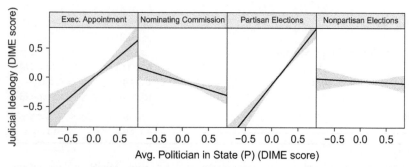

FIGURE 6.5 Judicial ideology as a function of changes in politicians' ideology, disaggregated by judicial selection mechanism.

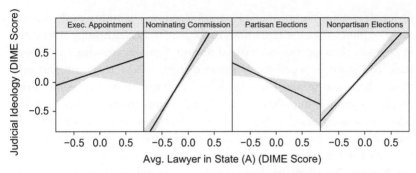

FIGURE 6.6 Judicial ideology as a function of changes in lawyers' ideology, disaggregated by judicial selection mechanism.

We can also use a similar strategy to investigate the impact that lawyers' ideologies will have – that is, whether certain selection systems will be more or less sensitive to changes in lawyers' ideology. This analysis is presented in Figure 6.6. The *x*-axes represents here represent the average ideology of lawyers in the state from left-leaning to right-leaning. The *y*-axes again represents average judicial ideology. As before, seeing vertical movement as lawyers become more conservative would suggest that judicial ideology is responsive to changes in lawyers' preferences. That is, as state lawyers are more conservative, so too are judges.

Two judicial selection systems are particularly sensitive to the preferences of lawyers: nominating commissions and nonpartisan elections. Under both, as lawyers become more (or less) conservative, judges follow suit, which we can see from the upward slope in judicial ideology. This suggests that both of these systems prioritize the input and influence of the legal establishment. By contrast, two other systems are fairly *in*sensitive to the preferences of lawyers: gubernatorial appointments and partisan elections. Under these systems, the preferences of lawyers do not change much what judges look like: As lawyers get more conservative (or liberal), what judges look like ideologically stays mostly constant. These systems, as we have discussed throughout, keep lawyers fairly distant from the process of judicial selection, instead prioritizing the interests of party leaders and elected officials.

Both of these figures highlight just how central judicial selection mechanisms are to understanding ideologically based judicial selection and, by extension, the judicial tug of war. Selection systems that rely on merit commissions and nonpartisan elections exhibit far lower levels of ideologically based judicial selection, under our definition, than gubernatorial or legislative appointments or partisan elections. In addition, the importance of judicial selection methods in shaping judicial ideology is reflected in partisan rhetoric around judicial reform. Conservative-leaning groups have routinely opposed merit commissions, which they contend give undue influence to the bar. On the other hand, state bar associations and left-leaning groups have generally advocated in favor of merit-based selection and opposed judicial reform efforts aimed at weakening judicial nomination commissions. However, this raises the point that support for merit selection is, given the distribution of attorney ideology, a much easier position for those on the left to take. We return to these themes in Chapter 7, in which we address partisan attempts at judicial reform.

CONCLUSION

We conclude by noting the key conceptual and empirical takeaways of this chapter. The first is that the fifty states (plus the federal system) vary substantially in terms of their legal culture. Some states – for example, California – have extremely liberal law schools that produce very liberal law graduates. Other states – for example, Virginia – have more conservative ones. In addition, states differ in terms of their practice areas. Some states focus more on conservative-leaning practice areas, such as oil and natural gas law (e.g., Texas), others on more liberal-leaning areas, such as regulatory litigation and government work (e.g., Washington, DC). Taken together, this variation means that the legal profession in some states will be more conservative (or liberal) than in others.

Second, this variation results in a different dynamic for the judicial tug of war. In some states (e.g., Massachusetts), lawyers will be in strong alignment with political actors – this will result in a happy coexistence, where factions are content with choosing like-minded judges; but, in other states (e.g., Kansas), conservative politicians will clash with a liberal-leaning bar. At the center of this tug of war will be the judiciary, at once shaped by the bar's professional capture but also serving in tension with the preferences of a conflicted elected class. In these states, we expect to see conflict regarding how judges are selected – much as Kansas saw in the mid-2000s. We discuss this more in Chapter 7.

Third, the formal way in which judges are selected changes how the judicial tug of war is played. Some states hew to appointments systems that look very similar to the federal system of executive appointments, while others have looked to nonpartisan or bipartisan merit commissions. Still others have established nonpartisan and partisan judicial elections.

As we showed in this chapter, these systems impact the types of judges selected and their potential ideological affinity with state politicians and with the state legal establishment. Selection mechanisms that rely more on the involvement of political actors or the provision of partisan information will be the ones where, perhaps unsurprisingly, partisanship and ideology will matter more. This is important because it will mean that the resulting judges will be more likely to reflect the preferences and ideologies of the pertinent political actors (and less so the preferences of attorneys). These set up political actors to "win" at the judicial tug of war. On the other hand, the more insulated from partisanship the selection mechanism is – that is, the more reliant it is on ostensibly nonideological criteria such as merit or qualifications – the less partisanship and ideology permeate judicial selection.

We reiterate that our findings in this chapter do not mean that some selection mechanisms are necessarily better or worse than others, despite the fact that some allow for easy politicization. On this point, other scholars have compared the qualifications of elected versus appointed judges or whether elected or appointed judges are more or less independent.[81] Our focus is instead on what courts selected under different systems *look like ideologically* and, by extension, how they will rule. Liberal voters and politicians should prefer selection systems that promote the bar's interests as an active player in judicial selection; these will, given a left-leaning bar, result in an ideologically left-leaning judiciary. Conservatives, on the other hand, should prefer selection systems that introduce ideology more explicitly, since these allow the political establishment more of a role in shifting the ideology of the judiciary away from the liberal establishment. Both approaches are means to an ideological end. We also note that, to the extent that lawyers are politically or ideologically out of step with the state population, ideologically oriented selection can be an attractive way to introduce ideological diversity in the courts.

Lastly, we note a key question unaddressed by these findings. These analyses took judicial selection mechanisms as fixed. How judges are selected is, however, hardly fixed but instead deeply impacted by the

---

[81] A good overview of the many of the major issues is provided by Choi, Gulati, and Posner (2010) and Bonneau and Hall (2009).

political forces that shape both the legal culture and the political climate. Indeed, that selection mechanisms so prominently play a role in shaping what states' judiciaries look like makes them a ripe target for ambitious politicians at ideological loggerheads with lawyers and judges. We consider attempts at judicial reform in Chapter 7, in which we extend our tug-of-war framework to predict instances where such reform attempts may be initiated.

PART III

RAMIFICATIONS OF THE JUDICIAL TUG OF WAR

7

The Politics of Judicial Reform

"Some would argue that we do have some activist judges, and the thought would be if you're going to act like a legislator, perhaps you should run like one."

Republican congressman from North Carolina[1]

In 2016, Republican Donald Trump won the White House by putting together a winning coalition of states across the South and industrial Midwest. One of the states crucial to Trump's winning coalition was North Carolina, which had voted Democratic in the 2008 presidential elections. However, although Trump won the state and Republicans held on to control of both houses of the North Carolina General Assembly, Democrats had a strong showing in a number of races at the state level. This included a race involving the North Carolina Supreme Court, in which Mike Morgan, a Democrat, defeated incumbent Bob Edmunds, a Republican. Morgan's win was significant.[2] Like many state high courts, the North Carolina Supreme Court hears a wide variety of important cases, including cases involving redistricting within the state. Prior to Morgan's victory, Republicans controlled the court, with a slim 5–4 majority. Morgan's victory, however, changed that calculus: Democrats now held the majority, 5–4, and the balance of power to decide cases that could affect the political futures of Republicans across the state. A

---

[1] Quoted in Corriher (2018).
[2] One commentator noted that "Republicans became convinced that [Mike Morgan] only triumphed because his name was listed first, and included no partisan affiliation. They speculated that many voters assumed he was a Republican, since Republicans were listed first in other races" (Stern 2018).

few days after the election, one North Carolina newspaper called Mike Morgan "the most powerful Democrat in North Carolina."[3]

Republican outrage and anxiety simmered, and, in response, they acted to change how North Carolina's Supreme Court justices were elected. Previously, and up to the 2016 election, North Carolina justices were selected via nonpartisan elections; after the election, and just before the swearing in of a Democratic governor, the outgoing Republican governor Pat McCrory signed into law a shift in the election of North Carolina Supreme Court justices, from nonpartisan elections to *partisan* elections.[4] As a Republican sponsor argued, "People are not any more or less partisan because they have to list their party affiliation on the ballot. What we're trying to do is just be open, transparent and honest about it."[5] North Carolina has now moved the election of all its judges – not just supreme court justices – from nonpartisan to partisan elections, with subsequent legislation enacted over the veto of the Democratic governor.[6]

Why did North Carolina Republicans act so quickly in shifting the state's elections from nonpartisan to partisan? Building off our judicial tug-of-war framework, we use this chapter to generalize a broader theory that both explains and predicts attempts at judicial reform such as the one that took place in North Carolina. As we explained, our judicial tug of war posits that the more liberal the bar, the more of an incentive conservative politicians will have to introduce ideology into judicial selection (and, vice versa, the more conservative the bar, the greater the incentives liberal politicians will have to introduce ideology into judicial selection). However, in this chapter we explore a natural consequence: What happens when the existing judicial tug of war results in politicians losing too frequently? What will elected officials do if they are repeatedly unable to pull the judiciary sufficiently close to their preferred ideal point?

In these circumstances, we argue in this chapter, elected officials will seek to change the rules of the game. With enough sufficiently hostile judicial rulings, they will seek to rewrite the rules of judicial selection entirely, usually by making it easier for judges to be selected on their ideology or their politics. Thus, in cases like North Carolina, we will expect to see political actors move the judicial selection process

[3] Batten (2016).
[4] Blythe (2016).
[5] Under the Dome Blog (2015).
[6] Jarvis and Blythe (2017).

toward mechanisms that allow ideology a more prominent role, including partisan elections and gubernatorial appointments. At the very least, we would expect states to move toward restricting merit commissions and the role played by lawyers – for example, by changing the composition of merit commissions to be bipartisan or comprised of nonlawyers.

Importantly, the nature of judicial reform attempts will depend on the ideological configurations of the two political parties in tandem with the ideology of the legal establishment. North Carolina illustrates nicely the many reform attempts that we see throughout the various states: Conservative politicians are changing judicial selection to make it more partisan. Yet, importantly, at other points in US history, the ideological configurations were reversed – lawyers were seen as more conservative, meaning that conservative politicians had an incentive to push for greater bar involvement. Indeed, as we discuss, this dynamic – which characterized much of the mid-twentieth century – led to the spread of the use of merit commissions, starting with Missouri in 1940 and moving through other states in the Midwest and West. Today, many states have merit commissions, but, as the ideological valance of the legal profession has changed, the pendulum has shifted among conservative politicians away from these more merit-oriented selection mechanisms and toward politicized ones.

We organize this chapter as follows. First, we provide a walk-through of how the judicial tug of war explains how the alignment of politicians and lawyers will predict attempts at judicial reform – that is, at changing the rules of the game. Next, we apply this framework to the history of judicial reform US, taking a broad look at the political conflict between these two key players and how that conflict has precipitated key waves of reform. This exploration is at the national level, but we next turn to the state level by looking at three in-depth case studies: (1) Florida in 2001, (2) Kansas in the early 2010s, and (3) North Carolina in 2016. Each example shows that attempts at judicial reform are a product of tensions between the bar and the political class, amplified by a perceived hostile judiciary. We then conclude this chapter by discussing what our framework implies for partisan attempts at judicial reform in the future.

WHAT PREDICTS JUDICIAL REFORMS?

Our theory of the judicial tug of war argues that judicial ideology is a function of the ideology of political actors and of the legal establishment, their relative power being decided by judicial selection methods. If the two are in alignment, then conflicts are limited: Both agree what the judiciary should look like, and politicians will be fairly content in allowing the legal establishment a fair amount of discretion in the selection of judges. If the two are in tension, however, then political actors will have an incentive to introduce ideology into the selection of judges and to wrest control away from the legal elite.

This basic framework illustrates the incentives behind judicial reform once we mix in another key ingredient: controversial judicial rulings. Political actors will be tolerant of an ideologically unfriendly judiciary so long as judicial rulings are favorable; but once judicial rulings become (or threaten to become) unfavorable – particularly on politically important or publicly salient issues – then elected officials and party leaders will push more strongly to reform judicial selection to draw in more favorable judicial candidates.

STYLIZED EXAMPLES. We illustrate some of the scenarios that lead to judicial reform attempts with several hypothetical examples. As in Chapter 4, we stylize the ideological space on a left-to-right continuum, which we can think of as "liberal" to "conservative" (although this left-right spectrum was not as applicable in earlier points in American history, when a more useful dividing line might have been business elite versus rural interests).

For example, the following represents the two key players in the judicial tug of war, attorneys (*A*) and political actors (*P*):

This representation puts the two in direct tension, with *A* on the ideological left and *P* on the ideological right. (This is a relative positioning that is similar to the national-level ideological positioning in the modern-day period.) In this case, partisan politicians would – if designing a judicial selection mechanism from scratch – favor a selection process that puts much of the power in the hands of party and political elite – such as partisan elections or executive appointments. Anything else would risk giving attorneys influence over the system, moving judges closer to the legal establishment's preferred position via their professional capture over the judiciary.

We can also consider another simple configuration:

$$A \quad P$$

In this situation, *A* and *P* are both on the ideological right-hand side of the spectrum. This puts their interests in alignment, meaning that they want similar things from judges and courts (as it would if they were both left-leaning). Practically speaking, if politicians here were designing a judicial selection process from scratch, they would be comfortable with a process allowing attorneys wide latitude in the selection of judges – for example, via nonpartisan elections in which bar associations recommend candidates or via merit commissions. Indeed, such a process could be triply beneficial: Not only do politicians get a judiciary that is ideologically favorable but they also curry favor with the legal establishment and are able to proclaim to members of the public that ideology has nothing to do with judicial selection, a solidly defendable public position.

We can also consider situations in which the already existing judicial structure presents a conflict, exacerbating preexisting tensions between politicians and the legal establishment. Specifically, we consider instances where judges issue rulings that prime the ideological conflict between politicians and the lawyerly establishment. For example, consider the following, in which we denote the judiciary as *J*:

$$A \quad J \qquad\qquad P$$

Here, the average judge is ideologically distant from the average politician but closer to the average attorney.[7] Historically, this captures much of what we see in American politics, with the ideology of the average politician fluctuating much more rapidly and widely than the ideology of the average lawyer.[8]

What would our theory suggest here? We would expect that such a configuration would be unstable and create pressure among politicians to politicize the judicial selection process. After all, political actors

---

[7] Deductively, we posit that this is an ideologically neutral selection mechanism (such as nonpartisan elections or merit commissions), since the pool of judges actually comes close to representing the ideological interests of attorneys.

[8] In these stylized examples, *P* is a purposely generalized conception of the balance of political power in a state. It might be reflective of the median legislator or the median member of the ruling party's leadership.

would come to be frustrated with a judiciary out of ideological alignment with themselves (and possibly also with voters). Over time, pressure for judicial reform would mount, and we would move toward a selection mechanism that allows greater influence for ideology and partisanship. Thus, if this state was one in which judges were selected via a merit-oriented commission or a nonpartisan election, we would expect the majority party to attempt to reform the judiciary by introducing a stronger role for the executive or a stronger role for partisanship in the selection process. As we discuss in the next section, we have historically seen many instances of this type of ideological alignment.

Historically, we might also see the following arrangement:

This suggests an instance where the judiciary is out of step ideologically with both players in the tug of war – a rare occurrence but one that has happened historically and also in a handful of states. What does our theory of the tug of war predict in these cases? We predict that these are cases where political elites have a strong incentive to influence the positioning of judicial ideology, since judicial ideology is at this point quite distant from their own. However, judicial ideology is also distant from the ideologies of attorneys – which are, in this case at least, quite close to that of political actors. In such scenarios, we predict an easy, noncontroversial path for judicial reform; for political actors, they have a reason to involve the professional bar in these attempts, since the bar would also have a valid reason for altering judicial ideology. We would therefore not be surprised if judicial reform attempts in these instances would move toward merit-oriented commissions – which would have the effect of moving judicial ideology not just closer to that of the professional bar but also toward the ideology of political actors.

APPLYING THE PREDICTIVE TUG-OF-WAR TO THE HISTORY OF JUDICIAL REFORM

These are simple stylized examples but they help illustrate how attempts at reforming judicial selection originate. We now turn to applying this basic predictive version of the judicial tug of war to the history of judicial reform movements. To do so, we look broadly at both national-level movements and then state-specific examples. Our purpose here is not only to understand the dynamic of power but, more importantly, to understand how this dynamic of power can shape, and has shaped, the processes by which judges are selected.

We note that a large literature has addressed the subject of judicial reform, specifically from the vantage point of historical causes of reform attempts and their impact on the independence (or not) of the judiciary.[9] However, our focus here is slightly different. We focus on a generalizable framework that helps predict both elite behavior and judicial outcomes – that is, we develop a framework that explains the behaviors of politicians and of lawyers and, in so doing, predicts whether and how they will try to reform the courts. The history of judicial reform helps us illustrate the applicability of this theory, but we certainly do not attempt to convey all of its nuances.

EXECUTIVE APPOINTMENTS IN EARLY AMERICAN HISTORY. At the time of the country's founding, Anglo-American judges were generally appointed by the Crown. This tradition was passed onto the colonies, whose early judges were also Crown appointments and thus representatives of the monarch. Following American independence, this logically transitioned into a system whereby judges were appointed by the executive – in the federal case, by the president. As a check on this executive power, the US Constitution established a judicial selection system that ensured lifetime appointments for judges given the "advice and consent" of the Senate.

We discussed in Chapter 5 how this system places enormous discretion about the composition and nature of the judiciary in the hands of the political class; but why did the legal establishment play along? As we discussed in Chapter 2, the bar formed the American aristocratic class, meaning that the bar and elected politicians were intimately bound, not just by shared composition but also by class and business interests. As Alexis de Tocqueville noted, "The government of democracy is favorable to the political power of lawyers, for when the wealthy, the noble, and the prince are excluded from the government, the lawyers take possession of it in their own right."[10] These factors made appointment by the executive

---

[9] An in-depth treatment is provided by Shugerman (2012), an excellent exploration of the relationship between political factions and the interests of the bar. See also Kritzer (2015) and Winters (1965).

[10] Tocqueville (1835, p. 250).

acceptable to both legal and political elites: Under our theory of the tug of war, the legal class had no reason to object to this traditional system, since its interests were strongly and intimately intertwined with those of elected officials.

This synergy between the interests of the bar and those of elected officials is another reason why executive appointment was used by the first states joining the union – namely, states in New England and the Eastern Seaboard.[11] Several of these states – including Massachusetts, New Hampshire, and New Jersey – continue to have a judicial selection system that relies on some sort of executive appointment.[12] As we noted in Chapter 6, today these are states where the political and legal elite continue to be in ideological alignment, a dynamic that creates little incentive to change how judges are selected.

MOVEMENT TOWARD JUDICIAL ELECTIONS. The early nineteenth century saw not only territorial expansion and the admission of several new states into the union but also a rising interest in local rule, anti-elitism, and populism. For many Americans, the idea of an elite judiciary, appointed by the executive for lifetime appointments, was contrary to this and smacked of aristocratic privilege; these sentiments were no doubt stoked by the fact that many lawyers were educated in faraway cities such as Boston, New York, and New Haven.[13] As early as the 1810s, the first local judges were being elected in Georgia and Indiana.

In terms of the judicial tug of war, this movement among politicians toward populism meant that the interests of elected officials and the bar (and those who were already judges) were drifting. Populist President Andrew Jackson himself "called for judicial elections and seven-year terms for federal judges."[14] However, as some have noted, the initial rise of populist politicians such as Jackson was by itself

---

[11] "Of these original states, seven provided for the selection of judges by the legislature, five by governor and council, and one, Delaware, by governor and legislature" (Winters 1965, p. 1082).

[12] An exception to this pattern is Connecticut, which has elected judges and which gave elected legislators some judicial powers (Shugerman 2012, p. 14). Shugerman (2012, p. 14) notes how Connecticut later served as an early model for those calling for judicial elections, a group that included Thomas Jefferson.

[13] As we noted in Chapter 2, this anti-elitist sentiment intertwined with the structure of local bars, leading for more local training and regulation.

[14] Shugerman (2009, p. 1073).

not the exclusive driver behind the push toward judicial elections.[15] Rather, the critical disruption came in the form of a political crisis, in which a court decision (or likely forthcoming decision) exacerbated ideological differences between populist or rural politicians and the more conservative older guard of political actors, whose interests were more closely intertwined with the bar and thus with the existing judicial bench.

Mississippi in the 1830s is an illustrative early case of these various forces.[16] Prior to this point, Mississippi state politics (including seats on the most important courts) had been controlled by conservative interests, particularly from Natchez, the old state capital that was also "a mecca for lawyers."[17] Highlighting the close relationship between the lawyerly class and the political and judicial elite, the legal scholar Ariela Gross notes that, in Natchez, the "transition from lawyer to planter, and sometimes to planter-judge, was an important one among the lawyers who made their business representing parties to civil disputes owning slaves."[18] However, the state's legal and political elite came under challenges from more rural, populists interests, a political tension worsened by unpopular state court rulings on slavery and debtors' rights, as well as concern about the US Supreme Court's ruling in favor of Cherokee Native Americans in *Worcester v. Georgia* (1832).[19] These were viewed as representative of the interests of establishment politicians and lawyers and as hostile toward rural interests.

---

[15] According to Shugerman (2012, p. 66), a characterization of this period was that

> judicial elections were rare, unless there was a unique political conflict that made the appointments process seem unfair or unrepresentative. Many other states strongly supported Andrew Jackson and switched many offices over to direct elections, but they still rejected judicial elections in the 1830s. Alabama, North Carolina, and Pennsylvania help illustrate the strong and enduring commitment to appointing judges in this era, and they help demonstrate that the revolution of judicial democracy required a game-changing series of events to shatter the tradition of judicial appointment. In terms of judicial elections, not much changed during the 1830s. But the turmoil in American politics and economic life during the 1930s set the stage for the revolution in judicial democracy.

[16] Jed Shugerman has an extensive discussion of Mississippi judicial reform attempts in this time period. See Shugerman (2012, pp. 66–83).

[17] Gross (2000, p. 97).

[18] Gross (2001, p. 97).

[19] 31 U.S. (6 Pet.) 515 (1832).

Wary of courts' involvement, rural politicians and voters pushed for the election of judges, which was formalized in a constitutional convention in 1832. This made Mississippi the first state to have an entirely elected judiciary.[20] After 1832, the tenor of Mississippi courts shifted, as intended by populist politicians, away from the business and legal elite in Natchez and toward more rural interests. According to one critic, the election of judges had meant "life and property are less secure than in any other [state], and its public credit is lost beyond redemption. The *repudiation* [of debt] is openly avowed, and crime and murder stalk about in open day."[21]

The populist political energy of the first part of the nineteenth century, in tandem with controversial court rulings, paved the way for a broader movement toward partisan elections in the 1850s.[22] After Mississippi came New York, with a constitutional convention in 1846. This was followed by Illinois (1848), Kentucky (1850), Michigan (1850), Pennsylvania (1850), Texas (1850), Indiana (1851), Maryland (1851), Missouri (1851), Ohio (1851), Virginia (1851), Louisiana (1852), and Tennessee (1853). States using judicial elections also included several newly admitted states, such as California (1849), Kansas (1859), Minnesota (1857), Oregon (1857), and Wisconsin (1848). Other states adopted judicial elections only for lower courts. These included Alabama (1850), Arkansas (1848), Connecticut (1850), Iowa (1846), and Vermont (1850).[23]

Generally speaking, concerns in these states paralleled the discussions in Mississippi. According to the legal historian Kermit Hall, advocates of judicial reform "believed that election would diminish the power of judges to frustrate the will of popularly elected legislators by making the judges accountable to the same electorate."[24] By contrast, conservative politicians – whose interests were tied together more closely with the legal

---

[20] Winters (1965, p. 1082). The debate in Mississippi over judicial elections echoed modern-day themes. For example, Shugerman writes that the rural proponents of judicial elections "framed their argument for judicial elections in terms of relative judicial independence" while their conservative opponents "focused on general judicial independence, to enable the courts to protect individual rights – specifically, property rights. Their rhetoric was lofty, but they also knew that their economic interests depended upon the protection of the judges from populist pressures" (Shugerman 2012, p. 73).

[21] Quoted in Shugerman (2012, p. 76, emphasis in original).

[22] As the legal historian Kermit Hall notes, "Of twenty-one constitutional conventions held during these years, nineteen approved constitutions that allowed the people to elect their judges." (Hall 1983, p. 337).

[23] These facts and dates come from Hall (1983, Fn. 1); see also Shugerman (2012, appendix A).

[24] Hall (1983, p. 341).

establishment – believed that "[p]opular democracy in the selection of judges ... threatened to subject judges to the whim of the people and the manipulation of party leaders, to breed contempt for the judicial process, and to hasten the day when nonlawyers would preside on the bench."[25] As for the legal profession itself, law professor Jed Shugerman notes in his study of judicial reform that most members of the legal profession – particularly in terms of organized bar leadership – tended to oppose judicial elections and that support for judicial elections came mostly from internal "'radicals' or populists, not leaders of the profession."[26] Bar leaders also opposed other attempts at reforms – for example, by opposing proposed constitutional reforms that "gave lay people more access to the courts and opened up the legal profession to the broader public. Such inclusiveness was not part of the bar's agenda."[27]

Thus, in terms of our framework, the middle of the nineteenth century saw political actors drifting ideologically from lawyers, predictably creating tension with regard to the courts. Note that, unlike later time periods, lawyers were hardly liberal; in fact, the legal establishment's interests centered mostly on business and property interests (and, in the South, on protecting and expanding slaveholder interests). This dovetailed with the preferences of conservative politicians but clashed with the increasingly powerful rural and populist interests. Although this ideological alignment does not conform clearly with modern-day left-right spacing, we can roughly think of this component of judicial reform as being captured by the following

where P^P are populist politicians, P^C are conservative politicians, and J and A are judges and attorneys, respectively. As the example shows,

---

[25] Hall (1983, p. 341).

[26] See the discussion in Shugerman (2012, pp. 115–116).

[27] See, however, Hall (1983), which argues that members of the legal profession were influential in moving toward the election of judges in large part because lawyers comprised many of the attendees at key constitutional conventions, representing a strategic and politically moderate voice. Specifically, lawyers, Hall argues, wanted a more powerful, coequal judiciary – one that was more independent of politicians' control. As one delegate to a constitutional convention argued, "Elect your judges ... and you will energize them, and make them independent, and put them on par with other branches of government" Hall (1983, p. 350). Shugerman, however, takes issue with this interpretation by noting that elite bar leaders were nearly uniform in opposition to judicial elections and that nonlawyers were much more likely to be supportive of such measures than lawyers.

populist-leaning politicians who came into power around this time period had every incentive to shift the ideology of the judiciary. As the conservatives' power subsided, via a series of constitutional conventions, they were able to do so.

PUSH TOWARD NONPARTISANSHIP. Put into practice, the political ramifications of direct party involvement in judicial elections began to become more obvious as the nineteenth century progressed and the South moved through Reconstruction and northern cities industrialized. Specifically, as party machines grew in influence, and consolidated power in local and city governments. judicial elections began to be perceived by the public (and criticized by detractors) as overly partisan and corrupt. In this time, as Shugerman notes,

[a] new perspective on partisanship developed: Partisan elections created a judiciary that was more easily captured by ideology and special interests. Candidates had to rely heavily on party connections to be nominated and elected. The elected judges were perceived as being beholden to their party, and their independence and integrity were questioned once they were on the bench.[28]

The situation was particularly contested in large metropolitan areas, in which party machine politics dictated which candidates would run and, in so doing, dictated the fates of judicial elections. For example, New York City's notorious Tammany Hall network of Democratic Party operatives "aroused public indignation by ousting able judges and putting in incompetent ones."[29] At the same time, "similar conditions in other states led to a revulsion against the elective system soon after it was established."[30]

This "revulsion" led to pushes against the use of partisan elections and a new interest in other forms of judicial selection. New York voters rejected moving the state courts back toward an appointments-based system in 1873, but some states did – these included Vermont (1870) and, interestingly, Mississippi (1868).[31] Other states – persuaded by arguments from progressives – experimented with nonpartisan judicial elections, particularly so around the turn of the twentieth century. This included states in the upper and industrialized Midwest, such as Ohio,

[28] Shugerman (2012, p. 167).
[29] Winters (1965, p. 1083).
[30] Winters (1965, p. 1083).
[31] On New York's failed referendum, see Shugerman (2012, p. 152). See also Winters (1965, p. 1083).

Minnesota, Wisconsin, Wyoming, and also in the Sun Belt, such as Arizona.[32] The movement toward nonpartisan elections saw limited success, however: "the absence of party identification on the general ballot was only cosmetic, and merely removed a piece of information from the voter in the voting booth."[33] In addition, some scholars have noted that this historical trend toward nonpartisan elections resulted in voters losing interest and therefore being less likely to show up to vote.[34]

The legal elite – never backers of judicial elections to begin with – not only publicly shared in concerns about corruption and lack of independence but also worried about the damage to the broader legal establishment. For them, judicial elections resulted in the worst that the bar could offer – judges who were less visibly intellectual and more sensitive to the crass partisanship of electoral politics. This seeming corruption and seediness of political machine judges brought disrepute to the legal profession and, in their view, undermined the goals of all lawyers. For some, it was a question of expertise and ability. One writer from the Yakima (Washington) Bar, wrote, "The voters are helpless when asked to determine by their ballot those qualities of character, learning, courage, and judicial temperament that go on to make up a good judge, especially when there are numerous competing candidates."[35] Another commentator, the early twentieth-century legal philosopher Jerome Frank wrote, "The lay attitude toward lawyers is a compound of contradictions, a mingling of respect and derision. Although lawyers occupy leading positions in government and industry, although the public looks to them for guidance in meeting its most vital problems, yet concurrently it sneers at them as tricksters and quibblers."[36]

Several prominent legal leaders – including lawyer-legislators and lawyer-judges – spoke on this idea of judicial corruption delegitimizing the entire profession. In an influential address before the American Bar Association in 1913, former president and future Chief Justice of the United States William H. Taft decried the populist nature of electing

---

[32] "[B]y the end of the twentieth century, about twice as many states had nonpartisan judicial elections than had partisan elections" (Shugerman 2012, p. 170).

[33] Shugerman (2012, p. 170). This echoes contemporary research on public attitudes toward judicial nominees, for example Sen (2017b), which finds that withholding partisan information about judicial candidates from members of the public simply leads them to rely on other cues that might be correlated with partisanship (such as race or gender).

[34] Shugerman (2012, p. 170).

[35] Hutcheson (1937, p. 931).

[36] Frank (1930).

judges, excoriating what he believed to be the debasement of the judicial calling. "Men are to be made judges not because they are impartial, but because they are advocates," he wrote, "not because they are judicial, but because they are partisan."[37] A similar theme was echoed in a widely discussed 1906 address by Roscoe Pound, future dean of Harvard Law School and then-president of the American Bar Association, who cautioned that Americans were growing frustrated with the administration of justice and this frustration was due to "[p]utting courts into politics and compelling judges to become politicians in many jurisdictions has almost destroyed the traditional respect for the Bench."[38]

However, this was also a matter of simple business interests: Popularly elected courts were less likely to favor business interests. Several business organizations spoke out forcefully about the danger that elected judges presented to business interests. Writing to the *American Bar Association Journal* in 1937, a representative of the New York State Chamber of Commerce complained, "It is unfair to the judge who is able and honest that, to secure and retain his position, he must subordinate him self to and become a cog in this system. The system must be changed. The bench should have the complete respect and confidence of the public. The facts stated show why that has been impaired."[39]

MERIT COMMISSIONS. The solution to the problem, however, was not straightforward. Progressives favored a stronger connection to American voters; by contrast, members of the legal elite wished to have the bar – and therefore their own interests – play a stronger role in the selection of judges. Accordingly, they argued in favor of orienting selection toward greater "professionalization" of the judiciary, which they believed not only would "create a more efficient, expert bench," but also "would help business interests."[40]

Perhaps the strongest advocate for reconsidering judicial selection systems that relied on partisan and nonpartisan elections was Albert M. Kales, a law professor and one of the founders of the American Judicature Society (and its director from its founding in 1913 until his death in

---

[37] Taft (1913, p. 423). He further added that candidates for judgeships were "supplicants before the people" and that "nothing could more impair the quality of lawyers available as candidates or depreciate the standards of the judiciary" than judicial elections (p. 422).
[38] Pound (1906, p. 450).
[39] Chamber of Commerce of the State of New York (1937, p. 531).
[40] Shugerman (2012, p. 174).

1922).[41] Kales took a hard stance against the political machinery behind judicial elections. In a 1914 speech before the Minnesota State Bar, for example, he noted that

our judges, while they go through the form of election, are not selected by the people at all. They are appointed. The appointing power is lodged with the leaders of the party machines. These men appoint the nominees . . ..The voter only selections which of two or three appointing powers he prefers. Whichever way he votes he merely approves an appointment by party organization leaders.[42]

As a response, Kale and others encouraged something different – a system of choosing candidates that he believed was both more transparent and also more engaging with the bar and its expertise. Bar elites were motivated by an already developing pattern, in which local bar leaders were informally advising parties about potential nominees and bar associations in various cities were holding "bar primaries" in which incumbent judges were evaluated and then eventually endorsed in subsequent elections.[43]

These were the intellectual beginnings of the merit plan system, strongly endorsed by the legal establishment and by business groups.[44] Missouri, being the first to enact such a plan in 1940, is instructive.[45] In Missouri, frustration with elected judges – who comprised the supreme court and three appeals courts – built up through the first part of the twentieth century, worsened by a series of political scandals and the involvement of political machines. The perception of corruption was so bad that *The St. Louis Post-Dispatch* called Missouri judges "a humiliation to the law and to the city."[46] Recognizing the danger that this

---

[41] The aim of the American Judicature Society was to promote the integrity and the administration of justice in the US courts. The organization was disbanded in 2014 and much of its work on tracking judicial reform efforts and judicial ethics was folded into the National Center for State Courts.

[42] Kales (1927, pp. 133–134).

[43] See Shugerman (2012, p. 174), which notes that merit-style systems were also becoming more commonplace in civil service hiring. In terms of elected judges, see also Taft (1913, p. 421), which acknowledged that "able judges have been nominated often through the influence of leading members of the Bar upon the politicians who controlled the nominations."

[44] See Shugerman (2012, pp. 173–176). These were also known as AJS-style plan, after the American Judicature Society.

[45] For more on Missouri's adoption of the plan, see Hunter (1991).

[46] See Shugerman (2012, pp. 197–207). See also Hunter (1991, pp. 70–71), which notes: "Political machines and party bosses in St. Louis and Kansas City largely controlled the election of judges, including the selection of party nominees for judicial positions. Court dockets became congested as judges were forced to spend their time keeping their

perception of corruption and cronyism posed to the legal profession writ large, the Missouri Bar Association began considering merit-style reform in 1937 through its Missouri Institute for the Administration of Justice, spearheaded by a group of Republicans.[47] The plan was strongly supported by the Chamber of Commerce, along with other business-friendly groups[48] and was eventually enacted into law after a popular referendum bypassed the Missouri legislature.

The Missouri example showcases the close collaboration between conservative business interests and the legal establishment – an important component across several early merit plan states, including California and parts of the South. Indeed, for most of the states outside the South – and in contrast to the present day – it was the Republican Party that agitated for judicial reform oriented toward merit commissions, supported in their efforts by state bar associations and chambers of commerce. Within the South, the picture was more complex in terms of partisanship, if not necessarily in terms of ideology. There, racial anxiety over the possibility that newly enfranchised black voters could elect black judges pushed political, legal, and business elites toward merit commissions.

Importantly, all of these strategic unions highlight a key component of our judicial tug-of-war framework: the importance of political and legal players in having a judicial selection mechanism that selects ideologically favorable judges. In terms of applying our framework, our theory predicts reform as a result of these quarter-century ideological dynamics, as synthesized in the following example attorneys, respectively.

where *P* are politicians, *J* are judges, and *A* attorneys, respectively. Here, the incentives for change are evident: Both politicians and attorneys were, in the mid-to-late twentieth century, in the conservative position, putting them somewhat at odds with a popularly elected and more liberal judiciary. Both would have an incentive to move to a system that would push the judiciary to the right.

political fences mended and campaigning for re-election. In addition, the judges were beset with problems and outside influences."

[47] Shugerman (2012) also notes that the merit plan was opposed by city bar associations in Missouri because these were part of Democratic Party machinery.

[48] Shugerman (2012, p. 203).

Merit systems, which have the added benefit of appearing apolitical and more rooted in objective qualifications, were an ideal, bridge-building path forward. Thus, it is no surprise that, in the twenty-five years that followed Missouri's adoption in 1940, nearly a dozen states switched away from elections to merit commission. These include Alabama (1950), Kansas (1958), Iowa (1962), Nebraska (1962), Illinois (1962), Florida (1964), Colorado (1964), Utah (1965), and North Dakota (1965). By 1990, a plurality of states had moved to a merit-oriented commission system.

JUDICIAL REFORM IN THE MODERN DAY

Moving to the turn of the twenty-first century, however, the pendulum swung back – with merit-oriented commissions increasingly under attack. Indeed, in today's context, "judicial reform" efforts generally refer to attempts at dismantling the merit-oriented commissions systems implemented in the 1950s and 1960s. For the most part, the push has been toward either elections (nonpartisan and partisan) or gubernatorial appointments. In some states, reform attempts include revising the structure of the state courts so as to allow more judges to be selected or to minimize their influence through other mechanisms.

How does our framework help predict or explain the present-day push against judicial selection-based merit commission? First, the lawyers have ideologically moved leftward since the mid-twentieth century, a fact documented by several studies of the legal profession.[49] This has been the case at most of all of the top law schools (including the T14, which traditionally have sent the largest numbers of graduates on to judicial careers).[50] For example, our analysis in Figure 5.1 in Chapter 5 showed how the graduates of these top programs have become more left-leaning essentially in the last quarter of the twentieth century.

---

[49] See our discussion in Chapters 2, 4, and 6. Teles (2012, chap. 2) refers to this liberal professional environment as the liberal legal network, summarizing that "[t]he rise of legal aid, along with the maturation of an earlier generation of lawyers raised under the New Deal, led to a dramatic shift in the character of the organized bar, from being a staunchly conservative force to one that actively assisted the [liberal legal network]. In this same period, law schools began to change as the elite legal professoriate grew steadily more liberal." See Teles (2012, pp. 22–23).

[50] See our discussion in Chapters 2, 4, and 6. See also previous work in Bonica, Chilton, and Sen (2016) and, in the context of legal academia specifically, Bonica et al. (2018). For a qualitative explanation behind this liberal shift, see Teles (2012, pp. 35–46).

Given that the vast numbers of judges come from these ranks, the increasingly left-leaning tendency of the legal establishment changes the dynamics of the tug of war substantially. Specifically, merit commissions, which maintain power in the hands of the legal profession, would lead to judges who more closely reflect the preferences of the bar – in this case, left-leaning preferences. We should not be surprised to see the charge against merit commissions being driven by conservative politicians in response to what they believe are "activist" judges promoting liberal agendas. At the core of these critiques is a belief that merit commissions fundamentally shift the ideology of the resulting judiciary to be more liberal than what these politicians would prefer.[51]

Recent evidence of systematic conservative attacks on merit commissions is abundant.[52] One Republican lobbyist in Missouri complained that merit commissions are just a "different kind of politics, and it's behind closed doors."[53] Another complained about a Pennsylvania merit commission proposal: "Where is it written in Pennsylvania's Constitution that lawyers should have more power to choose judges than teachers, firefighters, police officers, plumbers, or anyone else for that matter?"[54] Most transparently, a former judge writing for the conservative-leaning Heritage Foundation, admitted that "I believe the sophisticated folks who argue for merit selection really know that merit is just an attractive ruse, and what is really going on is that merit selection gives them the best chance to get judges on the bench who share their political and policy views."[55] Many of these criticisms have been echoed by business-friendly allies. For example, the *Wall Street Journal* complained in an editorial, "Though the Missouri Plan is supposed to keep politics out of the process, it has instead transferred power from voters to state bar associations and legal groups that control the judicial commission. The

---

[51] See Fitzpatrick (2009) for evidence that the use of merit commissions results in more liberal judiciaries.

[52] According to one account, "There's a pattern: First, a local Federalist Society chapter publishes a paper questioning merit selection ... Then a poll of state voters appears from the Polling Company, run by GOP pundit Kellyanne Conway. The questions are carefully crafted to elicit hostility to merit selection (in Tennessee, questioners helpfully pointed out that the commission could include 'criminal defense lawyers')" (Brandenburg 2008).

[53] Quoted in Messenger (2010).

[54] Pero (2013). This particular author was not from Pennsylvania but rather affiliated with the Michigan-based American Justice Partnership, a conservative-leaning lobbying organization.

[55] Taylor (2010).

result is a system that's contentious and opaque – and has tipped the state courts steadily to the left."[56]

CASE STUDIES OF JUDICIAL REFORM: FLORIDA, KANSAS, AND NORTH CAROLINA

We illustrate these contemporary judicial reform efforts – and the overall ideological dynamic seen across much of the United States – with three concrete examples: (1) the Florida courts shortly after the 2001 presidential election, (2) the Kansas courts in the early 2010s, and (3) the North Carolina courts shortly after the 2016 presidential election. For each case, we identify the existing judicial selection mechanism, the ideological configuration of political actors and the bar, and the judicial crisis exacerbating the ideological cleavages and, finally, provide an overview of the proposed reforms and intended outcomes.[57] Each of these case studies illustrates how the judicial tug of war predicts attempts at judicial reform.

An "Activist" Court Goes Too Far: Florida in 2001

In the days immediately following the 2000 presidential contest between Republican George W. Bush and Democrat Al Gore, it became clear that the eventual victor would be decided by the state of Florida, where votes were too close to call. In response, several Florida counties – including Democratic-leaning Palm Beach and Broward counties – began recounting ballots. However, a few days after the election, on November 15, the Florida Secretary of State, a Republican, filed paperwork in the Florida courts to try to stop these recounts. These challenges ultimately made their way toward the Florida Supreme Court, which, on December 8, issued a 4–3 ruling that ordered statewide recounts to continue.[58]

The politics surrounding the Florida Supreme Court are precisely what concern us here. The court had, at the time, tended to reach mostly unanimous rulings, making the narrow 4–3 ruling a bit of an anomaly.[59] Partisan responses were further flamed by the fact that all seven of the judges on the Florida Supreme Court at the time had been appointed

---

[56] Wall Street Journal Editorial Board (2008).
[57] We adapt these cases studies from our earlier work, Bonica and Sen (2017b).
[58] *Gore v. Harris*, 772 So. 2d 1243 (Fla. 2000).
[59] Firestone (2000).

by a Democratic governor,[60] a fact that led to charges that the ruling was politically motivated.[61] For many Republicans and conservatives, the actions of the Florida Supreme Court were tantamount to outrageous interference by a liberal court in a fair election. Eventually, the US Supreme Court intervened and, in its own controversial (and party-line) 5–4 ruling, stopped the Florida recounts. Gore conceded to Bush shortly after.[62]

JUDICIAL SELECTION AT THE TIME OF REFORM. At the time of the 2000 presidential election, the selection of Florida Supreme Court judges relied on a merit commission system, followed later by retention elections. According to a study of Florida's judicial selection processes, "Under this system, a judicial nominating commission composes a list of potential nominees, which is then given to the governor, who then selects from among the listed individuals. After serving one year, the incumbent stands in a retention election and, if successful, serves for a term of six years."[63] (At the time, Florida used nonpartisan elections for circuit and county judges.)[64] The Florida bar had an important role to play in these commissions: Of the nine members on the state's Judicial Nominating Commission, three were chosen by the governor, three by the Florida Bar Association, and three jointly by the governor and the bar. This meant that "the political views of the Bar influence[d] the types of individuals recommended for selection and, thus, are material to understanding the political dynamics affecting judicial selection."[65]

IDEOLOGY OF THE BAR AND OF POLITICAL ACTORS. At the time of the proposed 2001 reforms, the pertinent political actors leaned to the right ideologically. Republicans held the governorship (with Governor

---

[60] Toobin (2008, p. 174).

[61] Many commentators have argued a liberal, all-Democratic bench involving itself on behalf of a Democratic candidate was a key reason why the US Supreme Court became involved. Toobin (2008, p. 180), for example, notes that "[t]he conservatives, especially Scalia, were outraged that the Florida Supreme Court seemed to be rewriting the state election code. He wanted to slap that court down, at least rhetorically. O'Connor, too, didn't like the way the Florida justices appeared to be freelancing – and helping Gore." Such an ideological understanding of Supreme Court review comports with scholarly accounts documenting that the Court decides to hear appeals based in part on lower courts' ideology. See, for example, Songer, Segal, and Cameron (1994).

[62] *Bush v. Gore*, 531 U.S. 98 (2000).

[63] Lanier and Handberg (2001, fn. 12).

[64] Barnett (2000, p. 413).

[65] Lanier and Handberg (2001, p. 1044).

Jeb Bush, brother of Republican presidential candidate George W. Bush) and lieutenant governorship (Frank Brogan) and also had majorities in both the Florida House and Senate.[66]

The Florida bar, on the other hand, has had (and did have at the time) a reputation for being liberal-leaning and more friendly to the Democratic Party. In endorsing the proposed reform measures, one Republican wrote that the Florida Bar "has an agenda. Like the [American Bar Association], the Florida Bar claims to be non-partisan, yet the Florida Bar has appointed more than twice as many Democrats as Republicans to the present Circuit Court [Judicial Nominating Commission]. That's 60% to 25% – hardly a balanced number."[67] The same representative complained,

the sadly unfortunate truth is that the [Judicial Nominating Commission] process has gained a reputation for nominating judges based on politics, rather than the qualifications of the applicants. The fact is, in other professions such as medicine, nursing, and real estate, it is the Governor who determines who will serve on their professional boards. The Florida Bar, when selecting nominees, has a vested interest. They will be trying their cases in front of these judges.[68]

We find evidence for this reputation by examining the Martindale-Hubbell legal directory for lawyers who were active around the time of the 2000 presidential election: Of the 36,352 lawyers active in Florida around this time, approximately 60 percent who had donated gave primarily to Democrats.

According to our theory, Florida in 2000 represents the right catalyst of ideological and partisan tensions that would lead to judicial reform. Three factors lead to this conclusion. First, the state had a merit-oriented system for selecting its supreme court justices that gave wide latitude to the state's bar association. Second, the ideology of the bar was significantly different (in this case to the left) from that of the state's lawmakers.[69] Lastly, the Florida state supreme court's controversial ruling ordering recounts to continue provided the perfect "activist court" foil for Republicans to begin to push for judicial reform. Given the ideologies of the various actors involved, we think that judicial reform was a

---

[66] See https://ballotpedia.org/Florida_State_Legislature#Partisan_balance_1992-2013.
[67] Byrd (2001).
[68] Byrd (2001).
[69] The directionality of attorneys and politicians makes no difference; we would have seen the same attempts at reform if the ideology of the bar was significantly to the *right* of state lawmakers, so long as the two were far apart.

question of *when* rather than *if*; for example, by many accounts, murmurs of attempting judicial reform were heard as early as Jeb Bush's gubernatorial election in 1998.[70]

To use a stylized representation, the following captures Florida around this time period:

This situation, we believe, would point to reform attempts to lessen the influence of the bar, thereby allowing politicians (*P*) to move judicial ideology (*J*) in a more conservative direction.

PROPOSED JUDICIAL REFORMS. These predictions are supported by two judicial reform attempts that immediately followed the 2000 election. One of these, House Bill 367, sought to change how Florida's judicial nominating commission was staffed by "allowing all nine commissioners to be selected by the governor and eliminated the staggered terms of the commissioners by tying their tenure directly to the governor's term in office."[71] According to the Republican house speaker, "By designating responsibility to the Governor in appointing the nine member Judicial Nominating Commission, the people of Florida are able to become active participants in the system through their elected Governor, rather than having one profession monopolize the entire nominating process."[72] The bill easily passed, largely along party lines; it was signed into law by Governor Bush in June 2001.[73]

---

[70] Hendricks (2001); Shaw (2001). One report from shortly after the election noted: "[Governor] Bush and Republican lawmakers have been engaged in a rhetorical and political battle with the [Florida supreme] court for the past year and a half. The court struck down the Legislature's effort to speed up executions in April. More recently, the court struck down a pro-death penalty constitutional amendment approved by voters because it said the ballot language was confusing. The court has also frustrated lawmakers' attempts to restrict abortion" (Becker 2000). However, the Florida Supreme Court's involvement in the 2000 presidential election hastened these attempts (Salokar and Shaw 2002).

[71] Salokar and Shaw (2002, p. 61).

[72] See www.leg.state.fl.us/data/Legislators/house/033/press/week2.pdf. As one scholarly review noted, this reform had the effect of "giving [Governor Bush] all but total control of the selection [of] Florida's appellate judges and a heightened degree of influence over the state's trial courts when there is an interim appointment" (Lanier and Handberg 2001, pp. 1049–1050).

[73] Salokar and Shaw (2002, p. 61).

The state legislature also considered a series of bills designed to strip power away from the judicial nominating commissions and move it toward the governor. These were ultimately unsuccessful but showcase the frustration of legislators with the state bar. For example, House Joint Resolution 627 was a proposed amendment to the state constitution that would have eliminated judicial nominating commissions and moved nominating power to the governor. Another proposed amendment, Senate Bill 1794, would have required state appeals and trial court judges running for reelection to win a two-thirds majority of votes in order to stay in their seats – a significant hurdle. (If a judge lost, then the governor would fill the seat.) The same bill also called for the elimination of Florida's judicial nominating commissions and – in a move that would have likely gutted the bar's professional standing – would have removed the requirement that state attorneys must join the Florida State Bar. Other failed amendments were more specific in stripping the bar's power over judicial nominating commissions.[74]

Unsurprisingly, the state bar association condemned these proposals. In a letter urging bar members to take political action, Florida's bar association president warned that the amendments would "increase the influence of politics in the court system." He further wrote that the bar's outside counsel had cautioned that the proposals "would remove all checks on the politicization of judicial selection, place incumbent judges at the whim of the legislature or any groups dissatisfied with a particular decision, and significantly reduce the independence of the judiciary, a critical element in the maintenance of a just and democratic society."[75]

Rightward Shift in Politics: Kansas in the 2010s

We now turn to another example that illustrates the predictive power of the judicial tug-of-war framework: Kansas. As we discussed in our introduction to Chapter 6, the state is similar to other states in the early 2010s in that the effective mobilization of the Tea Party pushed elected officials sharply to the right. This rightward shift among state politicians set the stage for significant fights over the influence and composition of

---

[74] For a discussion of these additional unsuccessful reform measures, see Salokar and Shaw (2002, p. 61).

[75] Russomanno (2001). Furthermore, in response to House Bill 327, "the Florida Association of Criminal Defense Attorneys rose in opposition" and "[t]he Florida Bar also voiced opposition, citing the damage it would do to judicial independence and the state judiciary" (Salokar and Shaw 2002, p. 62).

courts and of judicial nominating commissions that nicely illustrate the implications of the judicial tug-of-war framework.

JUDICIAL SELECTION AT THE TIME OF ATTEMPTED REFORM. Like many other states in the 1950s and 1960s, Kansas moved away from judicial elections and to the Missouri Plan for its state supreme court. Under its plan, a nominating commission composed of four lawyers (chosen by the state's bar) and four nonlawyers (chosen by the governor) would recommend a slate of candidates; the governor would then choose appointments from the slate.[76] Judges would then be subject to periodic retention elections. The use of a nominating commission was used not only for the Kansas state supreme court but also (until 2013) for judges on the courts of appeals. (As we noted in Chapter 6, the state uses a variety of selection mechanisms to choose its trial judges.)[77] According to one scholarly account, "No other state in the union gives its bar majority control over its supreme court nominating commission. Kansas stands alone at one extreme on the continuum from more to less bar control of supreme court selection."[78]

As of the early 2010s, the Kansas Supreme Court had a reputation as "moderate, reasonable, and business-friendly."[79] However, a series of unfavorable rulings on important conservative issues galvanized opposition on the more extreme right. The first of these was the Kansas Supreme Court's 2014 reversal of a death sentence handed out to two perpetrators of a series of gruesome murders known as the "Wichita Massacre." The second of these was a 2014 ruling that struck down public school funding provisions as being unequal and directed the state legislature to provide more funding to poorer districts.[80] Both generated significant public and political backlash. The families of the victims of the Wichita Massacre organized a well-publicized (but ultimately unsuccessful) movement to defeat several of the justices in their retention elections.[81] Political

---

[76] Specifically, Kansas's plan "provides for a statewide supreme court nominating commission, composed of a member of the bar from each of the four congressional districts as well as a non-lawyer member from each district. The lawyer members are selected by a vote of the members of the bar in each congressional district, while the non-lawyer members are appointed by the governor" (Jackson 2000, p. 34).

[77] For more on how courts of appeals judges and district judges are selected in Kansas, see https://ballotpedia.org/Judicial_selection_in_Kansas.

[78] Ware (2007, p. 387).

[79] Caplan (2016).

[80] *Gannon v. State*, 319 P.3d 1196, 1251–53 (Kan. 2014).

[81] Mann (2014).

actors also joined the criticism. In response to the school funding ruling, the Republican leader of the Senate complained that the supreme court was engaged in a "political bullying tactic" and "an assault on Kansas families, taxpayers and elected appropriators."[82]

IDEOLOGY OF THE BAR AND OF POLITICAL ACTORS. While the Kansas Supreme Court was moving left, Kansas politicians were rapidly moving to the right. The 2010, 2012, and 2014 state elections saw the Tea Party movement bring in more conservative Republicans into state office across the country, with particular success in the Midwest. In Kansas, this had the effect of pushing more centrist Republicans toward a practical alignment with Democrats and strongly undermining the power of Republican moderates.[83] In addition, former US senator Sam Brownback, a Tea Party – backed extreme conservative, won the 2010 and 2014 Kansas gubernatorial races.

The power of the new conservative faction in Kansas politics translated into strong and consistent attacks on the state judiciary, especially ideological ones. One member of the Kansas House complained that the selection process via merit commission made it "virtually impossible" for conservatives to be appointed to the federal courts and that the process "tends to exclude others who are equally qualified because they don't fit the preferred political profile."[84] According to several accounts, many of these complaints were made privately by the conservative governor, Sam Brownback. As one member of the House Judiciary Committee noted, "The complaint isn't that the court is unqualified. The complaint is the courts are not ruling the way that the governor wants."[85]

By contrast, the data show that the Kansas bar was (and continues to be) liberal-leaning. For example, from the Martindale-Hubbell legal directory, we were able to identify 5,812 attorneys practicing in the state. As of 2011, 2,211 of these lawyers appear in our campaigns contribution data as having donated to a political campaign. Of these, 63 percent

---

[82] Eckholm (2016). As *The Kansas City Star* noted, "Conservatives have a list of grievances, including rulings on abortion laws and capital punishment, but it is the high court's mandate that the Legislature fund schools equitably that has really lit the fires" (Rose 2016). According to Simon (2013), the "leftward tilt of the judiciary has been evident in Kansas, where the nominating commission passed over two prominent conservative candidates for the Court of Appeals, snubbing Governor Brownback in the process."

[83] Simon (2012).

[84] Quoted in Simon (2012).

[85] Carpenter (2015).

(1,400) donated primarily to Democrats. (By this, we mean that more than half of the money they contributed went to Democratic candidates.) By contrast, most Kansans are rightward leaning: In the 2012 presidential election, Republican presidential candidate Mitt Romney won 61 percent of the vote and Republicans won or held 92 out of 125 seats (74 percent) in the state house and 31 out of 40 (78 percent) seats in the state senate.

Applying our framework to this ideological landscape gives us the following stylized representation:

Given this landscape, our theory predicts that politicians will be unhappy with the state of the judiciary and with judicial selection. This is exactly the scenario under which we would expect to see attempts at judicial reform. However, for the legal elite, this would be a quite satisfactory scenario. For example, one former judge commented that "[t]he merit-based system has served Kansas well and is held in high regard across the country, as evidenced by the fact it is utilized in nearly three-fourths of all states for appointments to some or all of those states' courts. I am not persuaded Kansans should compromise and accept the second-best system."[86]

PROPOSED JUDICIAL REFORMS. As predicted by our theory, these tensions led to a number of proposed judicial reforms, all instigated by Republicans and with strong support from the Republican governor. However, although these reform measures had strong support among the more conservative wing of the Republican Party, some of them have been ultimately unsuccessful. The reform attempts can be grouped into three substantive areas.

The first attempts sought to consolidate judicial selection for the Kansas courts (the supreme court and appeals courts) under gubernatorial control as opposed to via merit commission. Under these proposals, the governor would appoint judges directly (with no nominating commission), with the advice and consent of the Senate. For the appeals courts, the legislation (House Bill 2019) was successful and signed into law by Governor Brownback in March 2013 despite popular opposition.[87] For

---

[86] Quoted in Bonica and Sen (2017b).

[87] See Karmasek (2013), which notes that "According to the survey, 61 percent of state voters oppose making any changes to the current system."

the state supreme court, however, the proposal cleared the House of Representatives, but stalled in the Senate Judiciary Committee, generating tension between the governor and state senators. One Republican member of the judiciary committee claimed that the governor argued in private conversations that the "method of judicial selection in Kansas had to be transformed to place on the bench judges who vote the 'way we want them to' on cases" and that the governor at one point "pointed his finger at me and said, 'Tim, why can't you go along with us on this judicial selection issue and let us change the way we select judges so we can get judges who will vote the way we want them to?' "[88]

The second set of attempts sought to undermine the authority of the Kansas courts in response to the supreme court's 2014 school funding ruling. In response to that ruling, the Kansas legislature passed House Bill 2338, which stripped the state supreme court's authority to appoint the chief justices of the state's judicial districts. In addition, the legislature passed another bill, House Bill 2005, which would have defunded the entirety of the Kansas judiciary if it struck down any portion of House Bill 2338. However, the Kansas Supreme Court declared House Bill 2338 unconstitutional.[89] Moderates then pushed the Kansas legislature away from a constitutional showdown with the courts, and subsequent attempts to defund the judiciary were abandoned with the passage of House Bill 2449, which made portions of House Bill 2005 invalid.[90]

The third set of attempts have involved senators trying to impeach members of the Kansas Supreme Court. For example, in 2016, the Kansas Senate passed Senate Bill 439, which detailed "a list of impeachable offenses for Kansas justices and other elected officials, including 'attempting to subvert fundamental laws and introduce arbitrary power' and 'attempting to usurp the power of the legislative or executive branch of government.' "[91] As of our writing, the bill had yet to be addressed by the House of Representatives.

An open question is why so many of these attempts were unsuccessful. (The governor did sign into law the 2013 bill that moved appeals court selection from merit commissions to gubernatorial appointment.) One answer is the unstable and rapidly shifting political environment. Despite

---

[88] Carpenter (2015).
[89] See *Solomon v. State*, 364 P.3d 536 (Kan. 2015), which held that portions of House Bill 2338 violated the separations-of-powers clause of the state constitution.
[90] Shorman (2016).
[91] Lefler (2016).

the power enjoyed by Tea Party – backed politicians in the early 2010s, their hold was both controversial and short-lived: By 2016, more moderate Republicans had replaced several conservative Tea Party – backed representatives, weakening the party's right flank.[92] This led to a swift move away from right-wing conservative policy positions and undermined the aggressive push for judicial reform. In 2017, for example, the Republican-controlled legislature overrode Brownback's veto to reverse his signature tax cuts.

Under our framework, this ideological shift moved the political power in the state closer to the ideological middle, easing tensions with the legal establishment and with the judiciary. Kansas remains interesting, however: Given the ideological landscape, any future rightward movement in the political balance of power in the state legislature or in governor's mansion might lead to rejuvenated judicial reform attempts; and, per our framework, we anticipate that these would be moves to replace judicial nominating commissions for the state supreme court with gubernatorial appointments or with partisan elections.

When Elections Are Not Enough: North Carolina in 2016

Both Florida and Kansas involved conservative political actors pushing against merit-oriented commissions and the perceived influence of the state bar association. However, what happens when ideological tensions flare in the context of judicial elections? We now turn to examine North Carolina, the example from our introduction to this chapter, around the time of the 2016 presidential election. The state illustrates that, given the right ideological context, reform attempts can also target unwelcome judicial elections results.

JUDICIAL SELECTION AT THE TIME OF ATTEMPTED REFORM. Similar to several other states, North Carolina moved from partisan judicial elections to nonpartisan elections through the 1990s and early 2000s.[93] As of 2016, the seven justices on the North Carolina Supreme Court were

---

[92] See Berman (2016), which notes: "The electoral blowback left even supporters of the governor acknowledging that he and his allies in the legislature had simply gone too far, too fast for the majority of voters in one of the nation's most heavily Republican states."

[93] For superior court judges, this happened in 1996, and for district court judges in 2001. In 2002, the North Carolina General Assembly passed the Judicial Campaign Reform Act of 2002, which also extended nonpartisan elections to appeals courts and, in what concerns us most here, to the North Carolina Supreme Court.

elected for eight-year terms, at the conclusion of which they would stand for reelection.[94]

Right before the 2016 general election, the time period that concerns us here, four of the North Carolina Supreme Court justices were Republicans and three were Democrats, giving Republicans a razor-thin majority. This slim majority made a key difference: The state supreme court has historically handled several key redistricting cases, including most recently the legality of the congressional district map based on the 2010 US Census. Opponents of various proposed maps had claimed that the General Assembly racially gerrymandered oddly shaped districts containing the majority of the state's African-American voters, but the state supreme court rejected many of these challenges in 2014 on narrow party-line grounds,[95] leading the US Supreme Court to reorder a consideration of the issue in 2015.[96] The state supreme court again rejected the challenges, allowing Republicans to claim another victory.[97]

However, this decision was a narrow 4–3 ruling along party lines, which showcased just how precarious the Republicans' majority was. Compounding this was the fact, as we noted in our introduction to this chapter, that one of the four Republicans, Bob Edmunds, was up for reelection in 2016. Edmunds initially ran for his seat in 2000 as a Republican and was a registered Republican. In addition, although his endorsements did not list Republican Party elites, he was endorsed by several law-and-order organizations. By contrast, Edmunds's opponent, Mike Morgan, was endorsed by several civil rights organizations and by then-president Barack Obama. Thus, despite the ostensibly nonpartisan nature of the election, both men would have been easily identified by knowledgeable voters as partisans.[98]

IDEOLOGY OF THE BAR AND OF POLITICAL ACTORS. At a national level, the election of Donald Trump and the maintenance of Republican majorities in the US House and the US Senate saw the nation move

---

[94] See North Carolina State Constitution, Article IV.

[95] *Dickson v. Rucho*, and *NAACP v. State of North Carolina*, No. 201PA12-2.

[96] The Court remanded the case for further consideration in light of *Alabama Legislative Black Caucus v. Alabama*, 575 U.S. (2015).

[97] *Dickson v. Rucho*, 781 SE 2d 404. Litigation then resumed in the federal courts, culminating in the Supreme Court ruling of *Cooper v. Harris*, 581 U.S. (2017), which struck down various components of the 2011 North Carolina plan.

[98] This fact was not lost among partisan critics. See, e.g., Binker (2017), which reports that critics of nonpartisan elections "also point out that political parties have always distributed slate cards at the polls playing up judges who share their political affiliation."

to the right. However, although Trump won the state of North Carolina, the state's Republican incumbent governor, Pat McCrory, lost an extremely narrow, drawn-out contest to his Democratic challenger, Roy Cooper. In the General Assembly, little changed. In the State House of Representatives, Republicans lost one seat but held on to their significant majority, 74–46 (out of 120 representatives). In the state senate, Republicans gained one seat to hold on to their secure majority, 35–15 (out of 50 senators).[99] Of course, as we discussed in the introduction to this chapter, Mike Morgan (the Democrat) defeated Bob Edmunds (the Republican) in the supreme court race: The final tally, 54.5 percent to 45.5 percent was decisive.

In terms of the ideology of the bar, North Carolina follows many other states in having a left-leaning legal profession. We find evidence of this in the attorneys listed in the Martindale-Hubbell directory practicing in North Carolina. Of these 9,211 lawyers, 72 percent donated primarily to Democrats and other liberal groups.

Thinking about our judicial tug-of-war framework, the events of the 2016 election shifted the critical median member of the North Carolina state supreme court leftward, while the bar and politicians remained to the left and right, respectively. The following example captures the ideological distribution of the relevant players *before the election,*

where *J* in this case denotes the median member of the state supreme court. *After the 2016 election,* however, the median of the North Carolina Supreme Court shifted to the left, changing the ideological landscape and the incentives for party leaders:

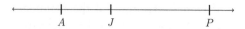

What would the judicial tug-of-war framework predict in this postelection landscape? Given the ideological distance between the supreme court (*J*) and the median political actor (*P*), this postelection configuration is untenable: Our framework would anticipate not only judicial reform but the kind of reform aimed at introducing more ideology (or partisanship) into judicial selection. In addition, our framework would

---

[99] https://ballotpedia.org/North_Carolina_elections,_2016.

predict that any reforms would further aim to lessen or limit any role for the North Carolina bar or the state legal establishment, whose perceived preferences would do political actors no favors and would instead push judges further to the left.

PROPOSED JUDICIAL REFORMS. The subsequent repeated attempts to curtail, pack, or make more partisan the North Carolina courts bear out this intuition. The first push for judicial reform came immediately after the 2016 election but before the Democratic governor was inaugurated; it was thus at the behest of a Republican-controlled legislature and with the support of a lame-duck Republican governor.[100]

This lame-duck General Assembly enacted two bills oriented toward shifting the balance of power on the state's courts.[101] The first significant change was to make elections to the state supreme court and appeals courts explicitly partisan (as opposed to nonpartisan), allowing the judges' party affiliations to appear next to their names on the ballot. This is squarely in line with our framework predictions: Introducing partisanship into judicial elections would (hopefully, from the perspective of conservatives) bring the judiciary closer in line with the partisan breakdown of political actors. Legislation one year later (House Bill 100) also made elections for superior and district court positions partisan; this legislation overrode a veto by the Democratic governor.[102]

The second key change was more specific to the North Carolina judicial hierarchy and aimed at adding a possible extra step before cases could be appealed to the North Carolina Supreme Court.[103] Previously, parties appealing cases to the North Carolina Supreme Court could proceed immediately after having their cases heard by a three-judge court of appeals panel – an intermediate court with fifteen total members, eleven of whom were Republican at the time. After the reform, the court of appeals had greater authority to rehear any appeal by sitting *en banc*, with all fifteen members sitting together at once. In addition, the reform measures stripped the ability of parties appealing certain kinds of cases (e.g., cases alleging state constitutional or federal law violations) from

---

[100] Given Republican supermajorities in both houses of the North Carolina General Assembly, it is likely that these judicial reform bills could have also overcome a Democratic veto.

[101] These were Senate Bill 4 and House Bill 17, signed by Republican Governor Pat McCrory on December 16 and 19, 2016, respectively.

[102] Jarvis and Blythe (2017).

[103] These measures were part of Senate Bill 4.

appealing from the trial court directly to the state supreme court. For Republicans, these measures provided the additional protective hurdle of having more cases – particularly important cases involving redistricting challenges – be processed by a very Republican intermediate court. For progressives, the rule changes were negative. One advocacy organization leader complained, "It also means that every case will be ruled on first by a majority of Republican judges. This further encourages more partisanship instead of fostering an impartial judiciary."[104]

Two other types of reform have been floated, but (as of this writing) have not yet come to pass. The first considered allowing the outgoing Republican governor to make new appointments to the court, expanding its size while adding some Republican seats. However, the idea of a quickly enacted "court packing" by a lame-duck governor was met with immediate criticism, including strongly worded critiques from influential newspapers in Raleigh, Charlotte, and Winston-Salem and threats of litigation from leading civil rights groups.[105] The second involved abolishing judicial elections altogether and moving toward legislative appointment by the state assembly. Given that Republicans controlled both houses in the North Carolina General Assembly, and given that redistricting has made continued Republican control a strong possibility, these appeared to be safe ways to introduce more ideology into judicial selection. As of our writing, this has yet to be put forward but has been cited as a possibility by Republican lawmakers.[106]

Our theory would predict opposition from the legal establishment and from judges themselves. Unsurprisingly, then, reaction to the proposed reforms by the legal establishment has largely been negative. One former judge wrote, "Voters freely admit they don't know much about those who run for the bench and evidently lawmakers didn't think the voters were selecting enough Republican judges, so now we will politicize judicial elections."[107] Another commented her concern that Republicans had

---

[104] Quoted in Way (2016). Republicans also eliminated at least one primary cycle (in the 2018 election) for a number of judicial vacancies, giving them time "to consider changes to election districts in the trial courts" (Blythe 2018). These changes were instituted as part of Senate Bill 656, which – like some of the other legislation we discuss here – overcame a veto from the Democratic governor.

[105] Abadi (2016).

[106] See Blythe (2018), which notes, consistent with our theory, that Republicans "also have said that lawmakers also wanted to consider abandoning the election of judges for a selection system that would give the legislature a prominent role in who rules in the courtrooms."

[107] Campbell (2018).

"firebombed the courthouse across the state, creating chaos, and I think it's all to gain a partisan advantage. They have not liked case decisions, and they need to get friendly judges in there."[108] As for the North Carolina Bar Association, its statement simply was that "the Bar Association in general opposes the election of judges."[109]

The situation in North Carolina also highlights the interesting role of voters. Recall that our argument is one in which the bar provides the candidates for the judiciary, and the degree to which the bar and political actors are aligned explains the extent to which the political parties will be incentivized to politicize (and also to reform). Throughout we have examined this tension by looking at the ideology of *political actors*, and not members of the public. We do so for two reasons. The first is that the ideology of political actors tends to correspond roughly with the ideology of voters – when voters lean conservative, so do political actors. The second is that we believe that, from a pragmatic perspective, the preferences of voters actually matter less than the preferences of political actors.

This may be a controversial position, but the case of North Carolina illustrates this second point. In the 2016 election in North Carolina, a comfortable majority of voters (approximately 54 percent) voted for supreme court candidate Mike Morgan, the Democrat. (A case could be made that perhaps North Carolinians did not know the ideological profiles of the two men running for office, but the men's partisan background – and the prominent endorsements by the likes of politicians like Barack Obama – makes this unlikely, especially given the statewide victories of the Democratic candidate for governor.) Despite voters' fairly clear preferences, Republicans nonetheless pushed for judicial reform. This points to the notion that, in assessing the respective importance of political actors' preferences or voters' preferences, it is the former that dominates, not necessarily the latter. Indeed, if North Carolina suggests anything, it is that voters' preferences, as expressed by either partisan or nonpartisan elections, are an additional mechanism that can be manipulated by the parties to accommodate their interests.

CONCLUSION

We conclude this chapter by noting the key predictive implications of the judicial tug-of-war framework for attempts at judicial reform. The way

---

[108] Yeoman (2017).
[109] Boughton (2017).

judges are selected is far from fixed. To the contrary, judicial selection is, at a fundamental level, a highly strategic political calculation, and it has been this way dating back to the Constitutional Convention. Politicians must be careful in choosing a procedure that leads to judges who reflect their own interests. On the other hand, legal elites also have a strong interest in maintaining as much control as possible over the composition of the judiciary; for them, lobbying for a judicial selection process that protects their own professional and business success is an important pathway to a friendly judiciary. As the interests and preferences of party politicians and the bar have shifted – and aligned or moved further apart – so too have each party's incentives for certain kinds of judicial selection mechanisms.

Underlying this is the fact that how judges are selected has significant political and ideological consequences in terms of judicial composition. The more that politicians are content to allow judges to resemble the bar's leanings overall – for example, in cases where the political and legal elite are in ideological alignment – the more that politicians will back and endorse judicial selection mechanisms that limit the role of ideology and focus on ostensibly "ideologically neutral" criteria, such as qualifications and experience. This will include judicial selection procedures such as merit-oriented commissions (the Missouri Plan, for example) or even nonpartisan elections. The less that politicians want judges to resemble the bar – that is, the further apart politicians and the legal elite are in terms of their ideological leanings and policy preferences – the more they will back judicial selection mechanisms that strongly limit the role that bar leaders play. This will include processes such as gubernatorial (or legislative) appointments or partisan elections. This basic intuition strongly predicts past and ongoing attempts at changing how judges are selected.

Our framework also contributes to existing debates about judicial reform. As we noted in this chapter and in Chapter 6, much discussion about the benefits and drawbacks of different selection processes concerns two broader normative points. The first is *independence* – that is, which selection mechanism results in judges who are more independent from politicians or from voters. The literature suggests that appointed judges might be more independent, but the concept is elusive and other papers have questioned its utility. (In addition, the concept of independence is squarely in tension with another normative concern, which is whether judges are or should be held accountable.) The second is *quality* – and whether judges who are elected are somehow less qualified than judges who are appointed or selected via merit commissions.

Some papers have found that they might be, while others have challenged these conclusions.[110]

However, although these are obviously important considerations, our discussion in this chapter engages and brings to the forefront what we believe is the most important consideration: the *ideological consequences* of selection mechanisms. For politicians, we believe, the pertinent motivating question has never been (and will never be) whether judges are really qualified or independent – so long as judges are qualified "enough," the concern has always been whether judges will vote in the way that politicians want. The same is true for the legal elite; although their concerns speak more broadly to public trust in the legal establishment (and thus speak instrumentally to perhaps deeper worries about "qualified judges"), the bottom line has always been more important: Will judges' votes reflect the professional interests and policy preferences of the bar?

In fact, focusing on "qualified judges" or "judicial independence" – as per the public discourse – may allow politicians and the legal establishment to further their interests. Lawyers can extol selection on the basis of objective, elite qualifications, or political actors can hammer points about accountability and voters' preferences – both will be more palatable to voters wary of creeping partisanship and party polarization. However, we believe that these points are primarily smokescreens that shield more straightforward and strategic concerns about judges' preferences and how they will vote. We pick up these themes in Chapter 8, where we discuss the downstream consequences of the judicial tug of war on polarization and judicial decision-making.

[110] See our discussion in Chapter 6 on partisan elections.

8

The Tug of War, Polarization, and Judicial Conflict

"We do not have Obama judges or Trump judges, Bush judges or Clinton judges. What we have is an extraordinary group of dedicated judges doing their level best to do equal right to those appearing before them."

John Roberts[1]

"Instead of a 6-3 liberal Supreme Court under Hillary Clinton, we now have a 5-4 conservative Supreme Court under President [Trump]."[2]

White House Press Secretary Sarah Sanders

In 2018, on the last day of the US Supreme Court's term, Justice Anthony Kennedy, a Reagan appointee, announced his intention to retire. His retirement – though perhaps unsurprising in hindsight – nonetheless took observers by surprise. Kennedy had for years served as the important median justice on the Supreme Court, operating as the key fifth vote for both conservative and liberal majority coalitions. Kennedy's vote had thus been crucial in a number of cases, including cases establishing the rights of same-sex couples to marry and decisions regarding the use of affirmative action in schools and universities. Given the unusual nature of the Trump presidency – and especially given Trump's streak of populist appointments – many would have expected Kennedy to attempt to stay on for a bit longer.

---

[1] Quoted in Sherman (2018).
[2] https://twitter.com/presssec/status/1048687047400218624.

However, Kennedy's gamble paid off: Just a few weeks after his announcement, Trump named a former Kennedy law clerk, federal appeals judge Brett Kavanaugh, to replace the median justice. For Republicans, the initial pick was an ideological dream: Kavanaugh was a reliable conservative with strong ties to the Republican Party. Kavanaugh was also a strong choice for the conservative legal elite: As a graduate of both Yale College and Yale Law School, he had served as a clerk on the Supreme Court and then subsequently occupied several prestigious appointments. Kavanaugh also had the seal of approval from the conservative-leaning Federalist Society. As one observer commented at the time, "the story here is that President Trump went with a known and reliable insider whose nomination will thrill the conservative legal community."³ Over time, Kavanaugh's confirmation was derailed by accusations of sexual misconduct. Nonetheless, his supporters within conservative elite ranks, including Republican senators and leaders of the Federalist Society, held firm, and he was confirmed with a near party-line vote, 50–48, in October 2018.⁴

Kavanaugh's nomination illustrates several consequences of the judicial tug of war and the captured judiciary that we have explored throughout. First and foremost, the appointment illustrates the raw political power of the legal establishment, which initially promoted and vetted Kavanaugh. Indeed, Kavanaugh – a graduate of Yale Law, former Supreme Court clerk, and federal judge – was the ultimate legal insider, particularly within elite conservative circles with close ties to the Republican Party. The second is the power of the politicians involved. With Kennedy occupying a swing position, the onus was on Trump and Senate Republicans to choose a conservative that would shift the Court's median rightward. By choosing an individual known to be more conservative than Kennedy and with deep connections to the Republican Party, Republicans ensured that the balance of power on the Court would shift rightward, better representing the interests of the conservatives wielding appointment and confirmation power.

However, Kavanaugh's appointment crystallizes a further theme that we explore in this chapter – just how important the courts are to politicians. Indeed, replacing Kennedy, one of the few justices known to cross

---

³ Kerr (2018).
⁴ One Democratic senator, Joe Manchin (D-WV), voted in favor of Kavanaugh, and one Republican senator, Lisa Murkowski (R-AK) voted against him. One Republican abstained to attend his daughter's wedding.

ideological lines, would ensure that the Court would be divided down a 5–4 ideological split for some time to come. According to legal scholars Lee Epstein and Eric Posner, this would have stark consequences for bipartisan rulings. Few of the justices, they argued, "ever voted against the ideology of the president who appointed them. Only Justice Kennedy, named to the court by Ronald Reagan, did so with any regularity. That is why with his replacement on the court with an ideologically committed Republican justice, it will become impossible to regard the court as anything but a partisan institution."[5] Thus, Kavanaugh's appointment – and the Court's move to the right – would have the effect of enabling further, and perhaps deeper, polarization on the Court.

In this chapter, we focus on these implications stemming from the judicial tug of war. How does the judicial tug of war worsen polarization and conflict on the courts? As we argue in this chapter, the ideological movement of courts in one direction or another – via the tug of war – increases polarization as older judges are replaced (albeit slowly) with newer, more ideological ones. We can see this polarization unfurl as the judicial tug of war plays out. In addition, this polarization has implications for concrete outcomes. Not only do litigants face greater uncertainty in times of increased judicial polarization but they are also more likely to face judicial conflict. Specifically, we show that greater polarization is linked with more cases being heard (and fewer cases being dismissed) and more dissents. Thus, the tug of war – in which judges are pushed and pulled in different directions – can lead to negative externalities throughout the judicial hierarchy.

Although the trend of increased politicization and polarization in the courts appears to be widely acknowledged, very few studies have examined these issues among tiers of the judiciary. That said, many studies have explored polarization among political actors, members of the public, and the media[6].[7] This gap is surprising. As we have discussed throughout, America's courts address questions of significant public importance, which could be affected by ideological divisiveness on the courts. In turn, as many believed happened with *Bush v. Gore*, this

---

[5] Epstein and Posner (2018).
[6] For an analysis of polarization among political actors, see McCarty, Poole, and Rosenthal (2016). For scholarship on polarization among members of the public, see Fiorina and Abrams (2008); Hetherington (2001); Layman and Carsey (2002). For scholarship on polarization in the media, see Prior (2013).
[7] For some studies exploring polarization in the courts, see Devins and Baum (2016); Clark (2009).

could negatively impact perceptions of the courts. Public support for judicial institutions (such as the Supreme Court) appears to be declining[8] – an important implication for an institution that relies on the public's goodwill to legitimize its rulings. This makes understanding the implications of the judicial tug of war for polarization and conflict particularly important.

We organize this chapter as follows. We first discuss, at a more conceptual level, how the tug of war could lead to greater levels of ideological polarization on the courts, giving several stylized examples. We next document the existence of judicial polarization by focusing specifically on the federal courts. Here, we show that more politicized courts (such as the federal appeals courts) are also the more polarized ones; we also show how these patterns are dynamic, with courts becoming more polarized with each successive presidential administration. This provides evidence that the ongoing push and pull of the judicial tug of war can lead to polarization in the courts. Next, we turn to documenting the downstream consequences of polarization on judicial conflict. We show that polarization increases instances of dissent, a reliable marker of judicial conflict. As we note in our conclusion to the chapter, these are important consequences of the forces that we describe in this book, suggesting that the judicial tug of war has the potential to create externalities more broadly within the courts.

THE RELATIONSHIP BETWEEN THE TUG-OF-WAR AND POLARIZATION

Our discussion in Chapter 7 explored the conditions under which politicians (or, in rarer occasions, the legal establishment) will agitate for judicial reform. For example, given sufficiently left-leaning judges and a liberal bar, conservatives will push for reforms that give more power to political actors and afford a greater role to ideology and partisan signals. By contrast, given the same liberal bar, liberals will push toward selection mechanisms that give control to merit commissions or to other mechanisms that prioritize qualifications over political or ideological views. Importantly, the opposites can occur as well: Liberal politicians will chafe against giving too much control to a conservative bar, as was the case during the New Deal era in the mid-twentieth century. These incentives

---

[8] McCarthy (2014).

related to the ideological distribution of judges, lawyers, and politicians will predict when judicial reform attempts are likely to occur.

One consideration that we left unexplored is the polarizing consequences of these ideologically driven reform attempts – that is, how the judicial tug of war can heighten partisan tensions and push judges toward ideological extremes. The logic behind such a process is simple. Suppose that the political value of judgeships increases – for example, if judges are ruling on important issues that are of increasing political salience to at least one of the political parties. We can make a compelling argument that this has been the case throughout the last twenty to thirty years, particularly as the Supreme Court has taken on challenging issues especially crucial to Republican campaign strategies, such as reproductive rights, same-sex marriage, and civil rights. Indeed, as political scientists such as Sheldon Goldman have noted, appointments to the courts have departed from patronage considerations to concerns involving policy; more and more, presidents see federal appointments as a way to further their policy agendas.[9]

Given such politically important judgeships, the incentives increase for political actors to install more and more ideologically proximate judges – resulting in the push for judicial reform (as we discussed in Chapter 7). As this process plays out, an older generation of judges – chosen at a time when judges were chosen under less politicized selection mechanisms – is replaced by more ideologically extreme individuals. This replacement effect then stretches and pulls the judiciary toward the ideological extremes, leaving the population of moderate judges to dwindle. The process is further exacerbated as politicians themselves polarize – as has been the case in recent times.[10]

Stylized Examples

We can see this a bit more clearly as we consider some stylized examples. Suppose we have the standard ideological profile seen across many states, in which the legal establishment leans left and the political class leans right:

9 Goldman (1997).
10 McCarty, Poole, and Rosenthal (2016).

As before, A denotes attorneys, P denotes political actors, and J denotes the judiciary. Illustrative of many American jurisdictions, this arrangement suggests a situation where political actors will be unsatisfied with the status quo; after all, J is much closer to the preferences of attorneys than to the preferences of politicians.

POLARIZATION AND JUDICIAL REFORM. How will political actors (P) in most jurisdictions respond? As our discussion in Chapter 7 showed, political actors will have strong incentives to interject more ideology into the selection of judges. If the selection mechanism that yielded this configuration involves merit commissions – as is currently the case across many states – then politicians will attempt to make these more political or to shift power to elected branches. If the existing judicial selection mechanism involves elections, then politicians will attempt to make these partisan. In sum, the history of judicial reform that we discussed in Chapter 7 suggests that politicians will attempt to change judicial selection to result in judges more of their liking.

What does this mean for judges, J? Given judicial reform and changes to judicial selection, this means that the ideological distribution of J will shift, most likely closer to P; but this simply cannot happen overnight. In courts with lifetime appointments, this can only occur with deaths or retirements; in places that have periodic elections, a judge's term must expire before they can be replaced. This means that, even with a successful pass at judicial reform, it would take some time – years possibly – in order to see the full fruits of reform in terms of the ideological distribution of judges.

A logical implication of this is that newer judges will deviate somewhat from older judges, as newer judges reflect the fruits of judicial reform while older judges adhere to the ideological outcomes yielded by the older selection mechanisms. In other words, the new judges will look more like political actors in terms of their ideology, while older judges will look more like the legal establishment. The following illustrates this gradual shift from old (J_{old}) to new (J_{new}):

As this example shows, ideological differences will emerge between older and newer judges. This process, whereby older judges are gradually replaced with newer judges, illustrates how the tug of war can result in polarization over time within judicial ranks.

Of course, the state of polarization is not permanent; with enough time, sufficient numbers of older judges will be replaced and the variation around judicial ideology will decline. (That is, more and more judges look like politicians in terms of their ideology and policy preferences.) However, the tug and pull of the judicial tug of war will undoubtedly create polarization and conflict within the courts.

POLARIZATION IN APPOINTMENTS SYSTEMS. Polarization can still occur under appointments systems, an important point since the federal courts – arguably the most important of the judicial tiers – employ executive appointments (by the president with the advice and consent of the Senate).

Specifically, if the selection turns on ideology, then the candidates named will closely reflect the ideologies of the elected officials who named them. After all, as our analysis in Chapter 6 showed, out of all possible judicial selection mechanisms, political appointments systems are the most sensitive to politicians' preferences. Accordingly, if politicians polarize, then judicial candidates should too. This undermines the position of the legal establishment in the judicial tug of war, making the ideology of lawyers (which would ordinarily have a moderating effect in times of high polarization) even less relevant. In addition, the movement back and forth between Democrats and Republicans will naturally result in polarization: As each president attempts to bring the judiciary closer to their ideal ideological point, they will nominate candidates more to the left (or right) to facilitate the move. This is a straightforward implication of our judicial tug-of-war framework.

In addition, the judicial tug of war predicts that, given ideological opposition between the bar and elected officials, elected officials will choose to limit the involvement of bar associations and legal elites in judicial selection and the appointment of federal judges. That is, appointments will become even more partisan in nature, reflecting the increased ideological stakes; this could include rejecting the opinions of the legal establishment, depending on the ideological concerns involved. (Our discussion in the introduction to Chapter 5 of the George W. Bush administration rejecting the involvement of the American Bar Association in the evaluation of judicial candidates is one example.) The end result of both processes is the same: Judges appointed by the party in opposition to the legal establishment will become more extreme.

In terms of downstream consequences, both of these factors – polarization in the elected official ranks and removal of the legal establishment in the vetting of judicial candidates – will polarize the judiciary. Indeed, just as in instances of judicial reform, the process of older judges being gradually replaced with newer, more ideologically extreme judges will result in polarization over time within judicial ranks.

EMPIRICAL EVIDENCE OF POLARIZATION IN THE FEDERAL COURTS

We can use various techniques to measure polarization among judges across time. To make the analysis more straightforward, we focus first on the federal courts. We do so for several reasons. First, although we would expect polarization within state courts to increase following instances of judicial reform, such instances are rare, raising difficulties in making quantitative assessments. Second, the variation in politicians' ideologies across the fifty states makes it difficult to map politicians' and judges' ideologies over time. Focusing on the federal courts – although perhaps less insightful because of the nature of the judicial selection mechanism – allows us to sidestep these issues.

To measure polarization, we take a cue from the scholarship on legislative polarization.[11] We first group judges by the party of the appointing president and calculate the average ideology of judges in each group, Republicans or Democrats. (We do so using the same contribution-based DIME scores we have used throughout.) We then calculate the distance in average ideology between the two over time. We do note, however, that the interpretation of the polarization trend for federal judges differs somewhat from a legislative context. In Congress, members have official party affiliations. In the federal courts, where judges are appointed by partisan presidents but have no official affiliations of their own, presidents can nominate judges from the opposing party. Thus, the polarization trend can reflect a combination of presidents appointing fewer judges from the opposing party and a tendency to appoint more ideologically extreme judges from their own parties.[12]

---

[11] See, e.g., McCarty, Poole, and Rosenthal (2016).
[12] In Table 8.1, we report polarization measures based on a metric developed by Esteban and Ray (1994) that does not rely on partisan affiliation.

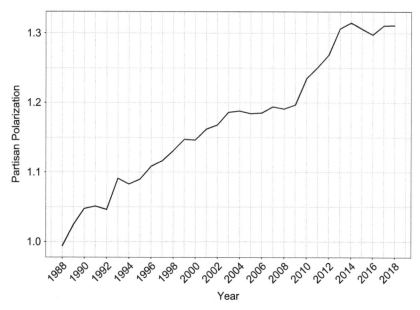

FIGURE 8.1 Ideological distance between federal judges appointed by
Democratic and Republican presidents.
Sources: Federal Judicial Center Biographical Directory; DIME.

Polarization Over Time

Figure 8.1 plots the increase in polarization starting in 1988, as measured
by the distance in average ideology of Republican- and Democratic-
appointed judges. (The party trends are calculated based on the set of
all judges actively serving in a specified year, including those appointed
by earlier administrations; thus, for the year 2018, this incorporates
all judges in active status as of that year.) As the figure makes clear,
polarization under this measure has increased steadily over this period,
commensurate with the rise in polarization observed in Congress and
elsewhere in American politics.

To provide some concrete numbers, our data show that the distance
between judicial appointees from each party increased from 0.99 in 1988
to 1.33 in 2018. For comparison, the distance between the parties in
Congress, based on the same DIME scores, increased from 1.26 to 2.21
during the same period. By this measure, the federal courts were about as
polarized in 2018 as Congress was in the mid-1990s. The rise in polarization has been steeper in the politically more important federal courts
of appeals than in the federal district courts, increasing from 1.04 to
1.56 compared with an increase from 0.98 to 1.27 in district courts. The

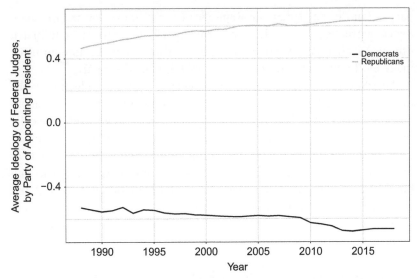

FIGURE 8.2 Ideological trends for federal judges by party of appointing
president.
Sources: Federal Judicial Center Biographical Directory; DIME.

federal courts of appeals were about as polarized in 2018 as Congress
was in the mid-2000s.

Figure 8.2 plots the average ideology for judicial appointees by party
for the same period. Judges appointed by both parties have polarized,
although the shift is slightly stronger among Republicans – roughly
around an average 0.20 shift in DIME scores in a more conservative
direction as opposed to around an average 0.10 shift in a more liberal direction for Democrats. This comports with scholarly findings that
Republicans in Congress have moved further to the right than their
Democratic counterparts have to the left.[13] It is also consistent with
findings based on contribution-based measures of ideology that show
both parties have moved toward ideological extremes at roughly similar
rates.[14]

What is driving this trend toward greater polarization? As predicted
by our analysis and by the fact that appointments systems yield a
judiciary largely reflective of the concerns of political elites, judges
appointed by Republicans largely match the more conservative nature of
Republicans in federal office and judges appointed by Democrats largely
match the center-left leaning of Democrats in federal office. As both

---

[13] McCarty, Poole, and Rosenthal (2016).
[14] See, e.g., Bonica (2014) and Bonica, McCarty, Poole and Rosenthal (2015).

parties (and in particular the Republican Party) move toward the ideo-logical extremes, the judicial appointments will therefore move to match this new reality. A natural consequence of this is that the appointments made by Republicans and Democrats will drift further apart.

An additional vantage point is provided by Figure 8.3, which plots the ideological distribution of federal judges appointed during past presiden-tial administrations. We can see the overall trend toward ideologically motivated selection when comparing the ideological distributions of appointees from earlier administrations with more recent ones. A near majority of Ford administration appointees were moderates, reflecting both Gerald Ford's moderate views (particularly on domestic issues) and the less politicized climate of judicial selection. Clearer divisions begin to emerge starting with the Carter and Reagan administrations, with both seating judges more ideologically aligned with their respective par-ties.[15] As the presidents appoint judges at more ideological extremes, the distance between appointments made by the two parties widens.

We see similar trends when we examine the average ideology of judges by birth year. Figure 8.4 plots the absolute value of average judicial DIME scores, which provides a general measure of ideological extrem-ity, by year of birth. (In other words, ideologically extreme conservatives and ideologically extreme liberals would be assigned the same absolute score.) The trend shows that judges from more recent generations are, on average, significantly more ideologically extreme than those from earlier generations. As these younger judges replace those from earlier gener-ations, polarization has increased in turn. This trend shows no sign of slowing in the near term, with both parties appearing to double down on the strategy of appointing ideological allies. Our example of the conser-vative Brett Kavanaugh replacing the more moderate Anthony Kennedy, which we discussed in our introduction to the chapter, is a valuable illustration of this tendency.

Polarization at the Circuit Level

We also consider variation across various courts, focusing first on fed-eral circuit courts. Through a process commonly referred to as "venue shopping," litigants entering the federal courts sometimes have a mod-icum of discretion over which of the federal appellate jurisdictions (or "circuits") in which to file their case. If a case is appealed to the circuit courts, it will be assigned to a panel of three judges randomly drawn from

[15] For more on how various presidents approached judicial nominees, see Goldman (1997).

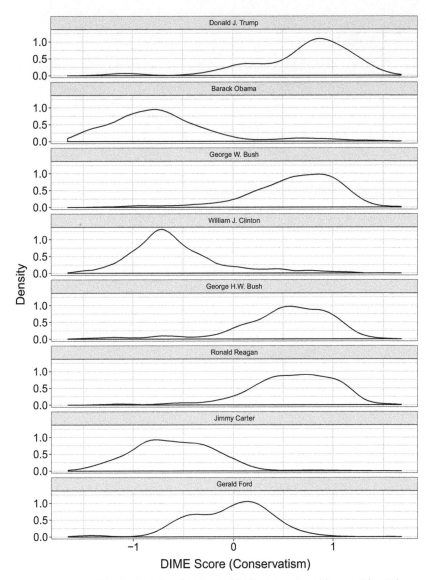

FIGURE 8.3 Ideological distributions of judges appointed by presidential administrations.
Sources: Federal Judicial Center Biographical Directory; DIME.

within the circuit. This makes the ideological leaning of the circuit an important consideration, especially for politically charged cases. Certain circuits have developed reputations as liberal or conservative venues. For

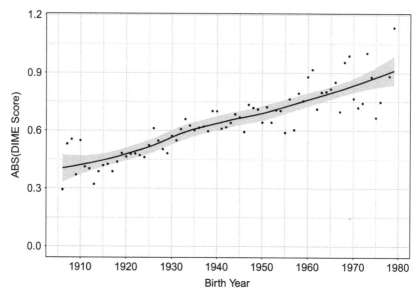

FIGURE 8.4 Average absolute value of judicial DIME scores by birth year
cohorts. Larger values indicate more ideologically extreme judges.
Sources: Martindale-Hubbell; DIME.

example, the California-based US Court of Appeals for the Ninth Circuit
has a reputation as a liberal bastion within the federal judiciary, while
the Louisiana-based US Court of Appeals for the Fifth Circuit is considered more conservative. Litigants better served in one circuit might
be poorly served in another; for example, larger corporations fighting
employment discrimination challenges might be better served in the Fifth
Circuit, while environmental groups or civil liberties groups might be
better served in the Ninth Circuit or the First Circuit.

The dynamics of the tug of war, driven by changes in partisan control
in Washington, influence the composition of the courts. A change in partisan control of the White House corresponds with a sudden shift in the
ideological composition of judicial appointees. The effects on the courts
are not felt immediately but rather more gradually as seats on the federal bench open up due to deaths or retirements. To show this gradual
ebb and flow, we calculated the ideological median of each of the circuits
by year from 1988 through 2018. Figure 8.5 displays the trend lines by
circuit. The horizontal axes represent the year, while the vertical axes
are the circuit medians, with a more positive (larger) value indicating a
more conservative score. The figure also plots the average ideology for
Democratic and Republican appointees serving on each circuit.

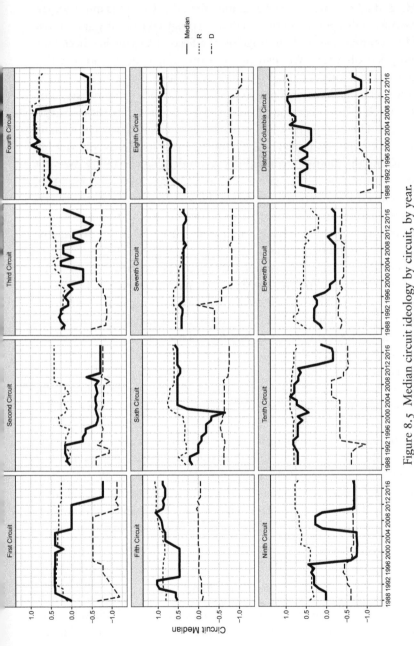

Figure 8.5 Median circuit ideology by circuit, by year.

Note: Solid lines indicate court medians. Dotted and dashed lines indicate the average ideology of judges appointed by Republican and Democratic administrations, respectively.

Sources: Federal Judicial Center Biographical Directory; DIME.

The figure reveals considerable variation in median circuit ideology within and across circuits. For example, the Fifth Circuit is quite conservative during this period, with a median ideology consistently at or above 0.5. By contrast, the median judge on the Second Circuit has been consistently left-of-center. We also observe substantial fluctuations within some circuits. Consider the Virginia-based Fourth Circuit. The Fourth Circuit is known for being a moderate-conservative court; however, soon after Barack Obama became president in 2009, the court shifts sharply to the left. The same is true for other circuits, including the DC Circuit, the Ninth Circuit, and the Third Circuit. Despite its reputation as a liberal bastion, the Ninth Circuit exhibits considerable variability over this period, with the median judge on the circuit being right-of-center, albeit only slightly, for roughly half the years shown. This speaks to the closely contested nature of many circuit courts. Similar to the Supreme Court, many circuits are a partisan appointment or two away from swinging dramatically to the right or left.

In terms of polarization, as judicial appointees have tracked the ideology of appointing politicians, the size of the partisan swings have become increasingly large. The back-and-forth swing on the politically influential Court of Appeals for the District of Columbia is a striking example. To give some context, this court of appeals – based in DC – is one of the more prestigious federal courts. Not only does it hear larger numbers of administrative cases (because it hears cases originating in the district) but, because the nation's capital has no "home-state" senators, it is also the most sensitive to the preferences of the executive. (That is, the president does not need to consider the preferences of any moderate senators.) In 2012, the DC Circuit median was the most conservative of any circuit. By 2014, Barack Obama made four consecutive appointments and had transformed it into one of the more liberal courts. Although not shown in Figure 8.5, more recent conservative Trump appointments will leave this court with a large ideological gap between the Obama appointments (such as Sri Srinivasan) and Trump appointments (such as Neomi Rao).

Polarization at the Panel Level

We can also assess the extent to which panels are polarized. When litigants file cases in federal courts, they expect cases to be handled fairly – and that one litigant should not have a greater chance of winning their case simply because of the identity of the judges hearing their case, or whether they filed their case during a Republican administration (with more Republican-appointed judges) or during a Democratic administration (with more Democratic-appointed judges). Even so, this is not the case. Studies have shown that the composition of the three-judge panel assigned to hear a case has a large effect on the ruling. For example, several studies have shown that federal appeals panels (which are comprised of three judges) that have more Republican appointees are more likely to issue conservative-leaning rulings than are panels that have more Democratic appointees.[16] Even intermediary compositions are important; scholarship has shown that a panel where Republican appointees outnumber Democratic appointees 2–1 will rule differently (on average) than a panel where Republican appointees occupy all three seats.[17]

In order to assess whether polarization at the federal courts is observable at the panel level (a topic of perhaps greater importance to litigants than cross-court polarization), we constructed a new data set containing all federal appeals cases decided between 2003 and 2016.[18] This allowed us to obtain the names of each of the judges who sat on the panel that heard the case.[19] Combining this with our ideological scores from the campaign contribution data allows us to calculate for each panel a median ideology, which we can then compare to the overall circuit median. Seeing more fluctuation associated with the panel medians would indicate more variation within the panels – variation that is perhaps more often overlooked by commentators but nonetheless introduces great uncertainty for litigants in terms of court outcomes.

Figure 8.6 presents the distribution of panel medians. To give some additional context, we also include a dashed vertical line, which represents the overall circuit median (e.g., the median for the Court of Appeals for the First Circuit, the median for the Court of Appeals for the Second

---

[16] Sunstein et al. (2006).

[17] See Sunstein et al. (2006), which shows the more general pattern that randomly assigned panels can be used to assess the causal effects of different panel composition. Sunstein et al. (2006) also shows evidence of panel effects, or that individual judges can influence the votes of their colleagues. For example, having just one Democrat on a panel can push their Republican colleagues in a more liberal direction, despite the Democrat being in the minority.

[18] These came collected from the Federal Judicial Center's Integrated Database, which provides detailed data on the case characteristics and outcomes. We combined these data with the text of the opinions themselves, which came from CourtListener (http://courtlistener.org).

[19] This ranged from three judges for three-judge panels to sixteen for certain cases heard by all of the judges in the circuit sitting *en banc*.

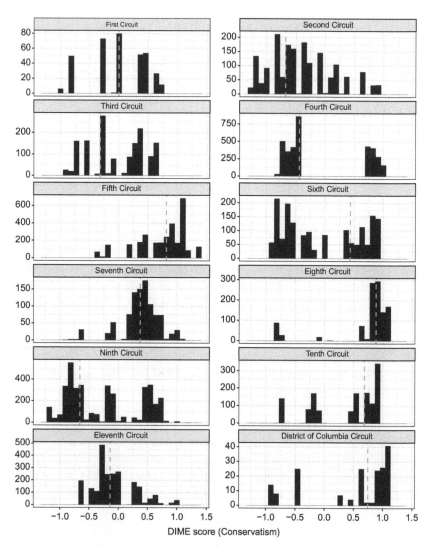

FIGURE 8.6 Variation in circuit panel ideology (median ideology of panel),
within circuit.
Sources: DIME; Federal Judicial Center Integrated Database; CourtListener.

Circuit, and so on). Even in circuits where the median is reliably to the
right or left of center, a sizable percentage of cases are heard by circuit panels where the median judge is out of step ideologically with the
overall court's leaning. (In fact, regressing panel medians on circuit medians explains just 28 percent of the overall ideological variation in panel

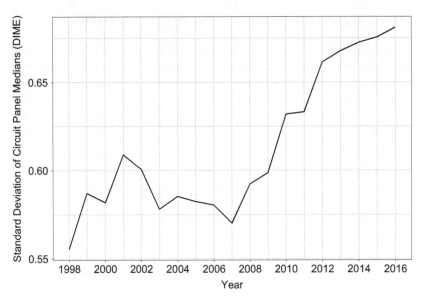

FIGURE 8.7 Standard deviation of circuit panel medians by year.

ideology.) All of this suggests a perhaps surprising amount of ideological variation present within circuits – a factor that creates considerable uncertainty for litigants entering into the federal appeals system.

How do these patterns reflect polarization over time? Figure 8.7 sheds light on this question. This figure plots the standard deviation of the ideological distribution of all federal appeals panels (vertical axis), from the mid-1990s moving forward (horizontal axis). This provides a general metric of polarization. For example, a low standard deviation would suggest very little variation – or that panels are mostly uniform in their ideology. However, a larger standard deviation is indicative of a polarized setting in which panels are either very conservative or very liberal. A larger standard deviation would thus suggest greater polarization across the federal appeals system and thus greater uncertainty for litigants. As Figure 8.7 shows, there have been increases in polarization across time, indicating clear evidence of the tug of war. Specifically, we note an increase in polarization around the start of George W. Bush's administration (2001) and also again at the start of Barack Obama's administration (2009). From the perspective of litigants, the back and forth in ideology of judicial appointments creates a deeply polarized judicial landscape.

POLARIZATION ACROSS THE JUDICIAL HIERARCHY

One implication that we explored in earlier discussions – for example, in our discussion of the federal courts in Chapter 5 – is that, given limited resources, politicians will prefer to orient their resources toward more politically important courts. After all, if there are not enough conservative (or liberal) judicial candidates to go around, it makes sense to orient these individuals toward the courts best positioned to make a substantial political difference. These would include federal appeals courts and also state high courts, which exhibit the greatest degree of politicization, or departure in ideology from the underlying pool of attorneys that make up potential candidates.[20]

We can look downstream to examine the consequences of this kind of strategic selection. Specifically, as more ideologically extreme individuals are appointed (by ideologically extreme politicians) to higher courts, we would expect greater polarization in these courts to follow. In addition, federal judges serve lifetime appointments; this means that older judges will take longer to retire, thereby creating a longer lag between older judges and newer ones, also exacerbating polarization at these higher courts. The implication of this is that polarization should be the most extreme at politically important courts, in particular federal courts (specifically federal courts of appeals) and state high courts.

Fortunately, we can use our ideological measures to calculate how polarized – that is, how distant – different tiers of the judiciary are. However, in order to calculate polarization for federal and state courts jointly, we are unable to rely on the party of the appointing elected official (which does not apply widely at the state level and which is less relevant in states that rely on other kinds of judicial selection systems). Instead, we follow existing literature in using a well-known polarization measure used in political science scholarship on the courts.[21] This measure operates by calculating the ideological distance between all individuals, weighted by the number (or mass) of individuals at each single

---

[20] As we discussed in Chapter 5, the staffing resource constraint is particularly challenging for conservative politicians because conservatives are underrepresented among the legal elite, particularly when we examine only graduates of elite law schools whose alumni disproportionally populate elite state and federal courts. Thus, conservative political actors will direct their scarce resources (qualified conservative judicial candidates) to the most politically important courts. At the state level, these are state high courts. At the federal level, these are federal appeals courts and, obviously, the U.S. Supreme Court.

[21] Here, we are motivated by Clark (2009), whose work on the U.S. Supreme Court used a measure developed by Esteban and Ray (1994).

TABLE 8.1 *Polarization across levels of the judiciary and, for comparison, also within the US Congress and among attorneys.*

	Polarization
US Congress	0.246
US Circuit Courts	0.224
US District Courts	0.220
Attorneys	0.207
State High Courts	0.205
State Lower Courts	0.197
US Magistrate	0.196
US Administrative	0.195
State Administrative	0.192

Note: Coefficients calculated following Esteban and Ray (1994) (higher levels indicate increased polarization).

ideological point. Thus, if two judges share the same ideology, they have "low" polarization; but, if another judge is ideologically distant, then the distance between her and her two colleagues would be amplified by the fact that she is far apart from two colleagues instead of just one. This generalized measurement strategy allows us to compare polarization in the courts not just with Congress but also with attorneys overall.

Table 8.1 reports the polarization statistic for different groups of judges; substantively, a higher statistic means that the group is more polarized. We also report the polarization measure for US congresspersons and for lawyers in the United States overall, both as comparisons. Table 8.1 reveals that polarization varies across levels of the judicial hierarchy, with higher courts being more likely to be polarized. Indeed, our data show that federal appeals courts are the most polarized, followed by the federal district courts and then state high courts. The courts that are least polarized under this measure are state lower courts and federal magistrate and administrative courts. As we discuss in the introduction to Chapter 9, administrative courts are currently among the least politicized courts in operation in the United States. At the federal level, administrative law judges are shielded from the interjection of politics by the fact that they are not "Article III judges" and thus currently considered nonpolitical appointments whose confirmation requires no input from the Senate.

IMPLICATIONS OF THE TUG-OF-WAR AND POLARIZATION

We have so far demonstrated that the tug of war between the various players could result in greater polarization in the nation's courts; but beyond greater uncertainty for litigants, why should this matter? In this section, we examine the potential spillover effects of greater polarization on the workings of American courts. Our suspicion is that greater polarization will lead to greater conflict within the courts.

To explore this, we focus the analysis on dissent rates within the federal appeals courts – which our previous analyses showed to be among the most polarized courts in the United States. Dissents tend to be a marker of conflict among the courts, suggesting underlying, strongly felt disagreement about a particular case. Indeed, although Supreme Court rulings frequently feature dissents – including instances of multiple dissents and partial dissents – federal appeals cases tend to have far fewer dissents. There are several reasons for this. First, many cases are straightforward, presenting little issue over which to conflict. Second, dissents divert judges' resources (including the valuable time of their law clerks) away from processing other cases. Lastly, because dissents are by definition written by judges in the minority position, they do little to change the actual case outcome.[22] Thus, dissents are costly and their presence could suggest underlying conflict about a case's outcome.

We investigate whether polarization within a panel – which we define here as the ideological distance between the most liberal and the most conservative judge on the same three-judge panel – is positively related to the presence of at least one dissenting opinion. This regression analysis is presented in Table 8.2. (The presence of a dissenting opinion is the outcome variable.) The top row of the table shows a clear positive relationship between polarization and a dissent. Specifically, an ideological gap of a one-unit shift on the DIME score scale (or about half the distance between the parties in Congress) is associated with a 2 percentage point increase in the probability that one of the judges will issue a dissenting opinion. In addition, we check that these results are not being driven by idiosyncratic features of the various circuits or the diverse nature of cases across time. We do so by controlling for these in the second column of the

---

[22] Of course, there are other reasons to dissent. For example, dissents could be a useful signal for judges keen to signal interest in a Supreme Court appointment, a kind of "strategic" dissent (e.g., Black and Owens 2016).

TABLE 8.2 *Logistic regression with dissenting opinions on three-judge panels as the outcome variable.*

	DV: Dissenting Opinion by Panel Judge	
	(1)	(2)
$|DIME_{max} - DIME_{min}|$	0.603***	0.451***
	(0.025)	(0.025)
Constant	−4.432***	−3.477***
	(0.036)	(0.120)
Circuit Fixed Effects	No	Yes
Year Fixed Effects	No	Yes
N	228,146	228,146
Log Likelihood	−26,122.940	−24,346.520
Akaike Inf. Crit.	52,249.880	48,743.040

***p < 0.01; **p < 0.05; *p < 0.1
Note: The sample covers cases decided in US circuit courts between 2003 and 2015. Dissents in part are coded as dissenting opinions.
Sources: DIME; Federal Judicial Center Integrated Database; CourtListener.

table, which includes fixed effects capturing the circuit as well as the year. The positive relationship between panel ideological variation and more dissents holds, suggesting that this is not something that is explained by variation across circuits or years. This effect is also sizable, which can be seen in Figure 8.8. The most polarized panels are about three times as likely to produce a dissenting opinion as the least polarized panels.

In sum, greater variation in ideology within a panel will translate into more dissents. Why might this matter? As increased judicial resources are taken up by dissents, we would expect the processing of cases to slow down – resulting in delays for litigants across judicial tiers. In addition, from a substantive perspective, increased dissents tend to sow confusion within and across circuits. Indeed, as has been shown by some scholarship, the presence of a dissent is an important predictor for when a court will hear a case *en banc* and, ultimately, whether the Supreme Court will intervene.[23]

[23] For more on the determinants on the decision by a court of appeals to hear a case *en banc*, see George (1999). For more on the role of dissents in the Supreme Court's decision to hear a case, see Caldeira, Wright and Zorn (1999).

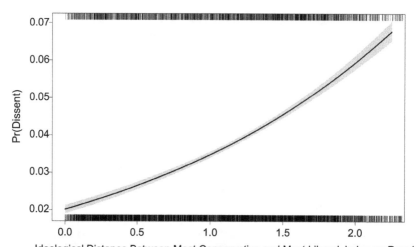

FIGURE 8.8 Change in predicted probability of panel dissents by within-panel polarization.
Sources: DIME; Federal Judicial Center Integrated Database; CourtListener.

CONCLUSION

We conclude with some broader takeaways from this discussion. We have previously cast the judicial tug of war as one in which politicians and the legal establishment wrestle over an important political prize – the courts. From the perspective of the players of the tug of war, the importance of the courts is obvious. Politicians want like-minded judges because they value policy implementation: Republicans want judges who advance socially conservative policies, while Democrats want judges who protect personal liberties and civil rights. For lawyers, courts serve as the only entity that exercises any oversight over the legal profession; moreover, they value judges who tend to prefer the same policies that they do.

In this chapter, we take the next step to show that, aside from these outcomes, the judicial tug of war is not without additional costs or externalities. Indeed, changing the ideological makeup of judges rapidly or over time can have negative effects that spill over into the workings of the judiciary, affecting and influencing not just case outcomes (what politicians and lawyers care about) but also the procedural posture of a case as well as judicial conflict. In addition, the tug of war serves to create polarization, which, as we have discussed here, can serve to increase uncertainty for lower-court judges and for litigants. All of these factors add costs to an already strained judicial system.

This is an important point to consider. In our previous chapters, the overarching focus has been that the players in the tug of war care ultimately about one goal: To influence (and possibly to change) the ideological composition of the courts and thus court rulings. Yet the pursuit of these goals by shifting the ideological balance of power is not frictionless or costless. Shifting the ideology of courts takes time and, with time, we would expect to see polarization within the courts. In other words, the judicial tug of war has important externalities that have so far been unexplored and further add complexity to the American judicial system.

We conclude with some thoughts about polarization moving forward. Specifically, we consider two broader patterns – which we discuss in more depth in the concluding chapter that follows. The first is a general rightward shift within Republican Party membership – a pattern that emerged during the 1980s and accelerated with the rise of the Tea Party in the early 2010s. This trend has greatly changed the tenor and composition of Republican representation in state and national legislatures. The second is a more subtle, but no less important, leftward shift among lawyers. This trend started earlier, in the 1960s and 1970s, but has maintained momentum, and it means that elite candidates for the judiciary are overall more left-leaning than ever before. This divergence suggests to us that the patterns that we documented in this chapter will perhaps be felt with even greater force as the American political landscape becomes more and more polarized.

9

Conclusion: American Courts in Times of Increasing Polarization

"[T]here is no such thing as a Republican judge or a Democratic judge. We just have judges in this country."

Neil Gorsuch[1]

"Where do these judges come from? You know a judge is a very special person. How do you hire thousands of people to be a judge? So, it's ridiculous. We're going to change the system, we have no choice for the good of our country."

Donald Trump[2]

In July 2018, the administration of Donald J. Trump made a very important move regarding the appointment of federal judges. This was not the nomination of Neil Gorsuch to replace Antonin Scalia, who had died months before under the administration of the previous president. Neither was it the momentous announcement of the conservative federal appellate judge Brett Kavanaugh to replace moderate swing justice Anthony Kennedy. Instead, the bombshell – mostly glossed over by the mainstream press and drowned out by a rapid news cycle – was an executive order on how the thousands of lower-tier judges adjudicating minor issues in the federal bureaucracies could be selected. Specifically, the executive order called for their selection not on the basis of a centralized,

---

[1] Nomination of Neil M. Gorsuch (2007, p. 70).
[2] Trump (2018).

competitive selection process (historically overseen by the Office of Personnel Management) but instead at the discretion of individual agency heads.[3]

Although fairly modest in its language, the executive order was nonetheless important: By removing a standard, nonpartisan, and centralized hiring process, the White House explicitly moved toward treating administrative law judges not as ordinary civil servants but as political appointments. Giving individual federal agency heads the authority to choose their own administrative law judges could, as observers pointed out, lead them to purposefully select judges on the basis of their views on deregulation, immigration, and government redistribution – all with an eye toward aligning them with party policy and interests. As one law professor observed, the Trump administration's move turned "administrative law judges within the executive branch from somewhat independent civil servants into politically appointed and politically removable bureaucrats who basically will have no one to answer to other than the administration officials who are responsible for their appointment."[4]

Liberals immediately (and unsurprisingly, given the expectations of our judicial tug-of-war framework) accused the administration of interjecting politics into the selection of judges. The ranking Democrat on the House Ways and Means Committee complained, "[a]llowing the appointment of judges who are big campaign donors, beholden to industry, or otherwise unqualified will result in unfair, biased rulings that harm ordinary Americans."[5] Another wrote on social media that this "dangerous move by the Trump Administration applies a 'loyalty oath' favoring the political agenda of the President."[6] The legal establishment reacted, per our framework, predictably. A veteran administrative judge, speaking to the press anonymously, noted that "[Trump] didn't have to do any of this. This is all bogus, and it's to take control over the judiciary. This

---

[3] Executive Order 13843: Excepting Administrative Law Judges from the Competitive Service (signed July 10, 2018) ("[C]onditions of good administration make necessary an exception to the competitive hiring rules and examinations for the position of [Administrative Law Judge]"). The federal government employed some 2,000 administrative law judges, with the majority of these (around 1,500) working within the Social Security Administration.

[4] Quoted in Khalid (2018).

[5] Quoted in Yoder (2018).

[6] https://twitter.com/repdinatitus/status/1017063624181993472. In response to the executive order, a bipartisan group of moderate senators have sponsored an amendment to reverse Trump's executive order, but this has not been taken up by Congress (Wagner 2019).

is a total assault on due process for the American people."[7] Meanwhile, the American Bar Association (ABA) ominously cautioned that the order "has the potential to politicize the appointment process and interfere with the decisional independence of [Administrative Law Judges]."[8]

The example of Trump's politicization of the selection of administrative law judges illustrates many of the themes we have explored in this book, providing a useful synthesis of the implications of our judicial tug-of-war framework. First, the switch aptly illustrates the extant political power of the American legal establishment and its ability to capture certain governmental entities that in other countries would be within the purview of regulatory agencies. As of the time of Trump's executive order, for example, nearly 2,000 civil-servant judges – all trained lawyers – served in the federal bureaucracy, making tens of thousands of decisions regarding social security payments, environmental permitting, and immigration asylum claims. This kind of capture exactly illustrates the broad power of the legal establishment through all rungs of American politics, from sweeping legislation in Congress to asylum claims involving individuals. Indeed, the power of the legal profession has extended not just toward shaping state and federal courts but also toward shaping American institutions and policy – as the example of administrative judges clearly shows. The result, we believe, is a legal and political system that puts lawyers at the heart of governmental decision-making – which in some cases may privilege lawyers' interests over the public good.

Second, the relationship between the legal establishment and political actors creates a tug of war, one in which judges are often caught in the middle. The harder politicians pull, the more courts will resemble political elites and their preferences. The more that the legal establishment pulls, the more the courts will reflect the interests of lawyers (and particularly of elite lawyers). Throughout this tug of war, we think, courts are basically a political prize to be fought over. Trump's actions with regard to administrative judges, and liberals' outrage at his move, also illustrate this. Indeed, a key point in the controversy over administrative law judges is the fact that these judges rule on key points of policy, making partisan players highly interested in their composition. In other words, judges are policy tools that can be used by politicians on both the left and the right.

Third, this tug of war informs how the different participants view attempts at judicial reform. Given that legal elites lean to the left,

---

[7] Quoted in Feinberg (2018).
[8] Quoted in Weiss (2018).

conservatives will agitate toward selection mechanisms that afford the maximum opportunity to select judges on the basis of policy positions, ideology, and partisanship; by contrast, liberal politicians will focus on selection mechanisms that rely more on "merit" or "qualifications," a position echoed by the legal establishment. Trump's executive order, which moved the selection of administrative judges away from a centralized, nonpartisan (and merit-oriented) system and toward selection by political appointments is not only entirely predicted by our tug-of-war framework but will, as we have shown throughout the book, likely result in administrative judges being much more amenable to the interests of those making the appointments. In other words, from the perspective of the Trump administration and other Republican party elites, politicizing the selection of administrative law judges is a wise and strategic move. We therefore expect that attempts to reverse the move to politicize administrative law judges will fail, blocked in the Senate by those in the Republican Party's right flank.

In this conclusion, we provide a broader discussion of each of these three takeaways, and how our tug-of-war framework helps to explain the consequences of these forces. We conclude by taking note of two broader trends in American politics that have implications for the judiciary specifically. The first, illustrated by the Trump administration, is the increasingly rightward trend among Republican politicians, not just in the White House and in Congress but throughout the level of the states. The second is the increasingly leftward trend among younger lawyers, particularly at the most elite levels. Although a causal exploration of these trends is beyond our scope in this book, our tug-of-war framework provides a lens through which we can understand the potential consequences of these forces. The United States has never been as polarized as it is today, and this, we believe, has significant ramifications for American institutions – including the judiciary – that have yet to be fully explored.

TAKEAWAY #1: AMERICAN LAWYERS ARE POLITICALLY POWERFUL

Our first main takeaway is that the bar – the legal profession writ large – is a surprisingly politically powerful entity within American politics. As we discussed in this book, lawyers played crucial roles in the development of American law and government. The First Congress, key in establishing both the contours of the federal government and also the federal judiciary, was comprised primarily of lawyers, and twelve of the first sixteen presidents were lawyers. It is therefore no surprise that American institutions have been crafted in a way that prioritize the legal profession as the nation's "political class," creating protections for lawyers and for the practice of law.

This privileged position within the political hierarchy persisted over the course of the nineteenth and twentieth centuries, although not without some shifts and turns. As of 2020, twenty-seven of the forty-five men (60 percent) who have served as president have been lawyers. In addition, roughly between 40 percent and 60 percent of representatives and senators (both at the federal and state level) are lawyers, a figure that represents the continued importance of American lawyer-legislators. On top of this, the legal establishment's capture of the judiciary means that *100 percent of all judges* – at both the state and the federal level – are lawyers. We think there are several important consequences associated with this outsized political power.

The first is that lawyers have come to enjoy a large amount of autonomy over their own affairs. Specifically, the close connection between the political and legal class meant that their interests often convened: A prosperous bar was a prosperous political and commercial class, and vice versa. Given this close, intimate connection, the legal establishment has been allowed the rare ability to regulate its own behavior and police its own members. In defense of a self-regulated bar, supporters have argued that bar associations serve the public interest by ensuring access to high-quality legal services; they have also argued that an independent legal profession is fundamental to the workings of democracy. However, the truth is murkier; as we have discussed throughout, the self-regulated nature of the American bar has allowed it to grow into the largest legal industry on the planet. Compared to their peers, American lawyers are more numerous, wealthier, and more politically powerful; even so, there is little evidence that the American system of justice is more efficient, better able to serve the poor, or more equitable. Rather, the evidence presented in Chapters 2 and 3 indicates the opposite.

This leads us to consider a second and related point, which is that the legal profession has been able to use its political clout and control over the judiciary to shift policy in ways that privilege the legal industry, serving to make it more profitable and prestigious. These policies may yield more profits per lawyer, but, as our analyses show, they have costs as well. Indeed, our comparison of the United States and other developed democracies shows that the United States lags behind in terms of important justice metrics. These include relatively lower access to legal services, particularly for poorer people, and higher incarceration rates. These factors suggest that a self-regulated legal profession is not particularly essential to the preservation of democracy (as the legal profession would argue) per se but, instead, has thrived as a result of the profession's ability to marshal political and judicial power in pursuit of its own interests.

Comparisons with other countries crystallize these patterns and suggest possible avenues of reform. One instructive example is the Netherlands. The Netherlands ranks first in access to justice and incarcerates a tenth as many of its citizens as the United States does. At the same time, however, the Dutch legal services sector is far less lucrative and its liability costs are among the lowest in the world. One reason for this stark contrast, we believe, is that the Netherlands does not require any formal training to provide legal services, meaning that it has effectively eliminated the legal profession's monopoly on the practice of law. This has given rise to legal clinics around the country that provide legal aid to low- and middle-income families. By contrast, the United States graduates thousands of law students each year who potentially could provide these services but are channeled into high-end corporate law practices or otherwise fail to pass the bar.[9]

The third point is that the legal profession has come to enjoy a substantial sway over the nature and professional composition of the courts – what we refer to as judicial capture. As the courts slowly became the only government entity that exercised control over the legal profession, a symbiotic relationship developed. Lawyers would populate courts, staff them, provide judicial rules of conduct, and, in some cases, exercise a formal role in judicial selection; and, for their part, courts helped to further the interests of the legal profession and serve as the only government oversight over the legal profession. The end result of this arrangement has been a regulatory landscape that uses the legal profession and courts as a pathway for significant chunks of regulatory policymaking, as opposed to administrative and regulatory agencies. The example that we used at the beginning of this chapter – that of federal administrative law judges – highlights the legal profession's entrenchment within policymaking administrative units. In addition, the legal profession has come to exercise professional capture over an entire third of government – a unique case of what we term constitutional capture.

---

[9] See, e.g., Rhode (2015).

These factors are all deeply influenced and shaped by the fact that the legal establishment is a well-defined group with its own preferences and ideological leanings. We have empirically documented that these ideological leanings are currently on the left side of the ideological spectrum, making lawyers as a whole more liberal than the US public and even more liberal than other similarly well-educated professional classes. This has not been the case historically, as we discussed in Chapters 2 and 3.

TAKEAWAY #2: COURTS ARE BOOTY IN THE TUG-OF-WAR BETWEEN LAWYERS AND POLITICIANS

The preferences and power of the legal establishment often put it at odds with the political establishment and elected officials. Sometimes – as we discussed in Chapters 6 and 7 – the interests of the legal establishment and political actors will be in close alignment. This harmony was evidenced earlier in US history and is also clear from present-day examples, such as Massachusetts.

However, at the national level and across several states, the interests and policy preferences of the bar and of the political establishment can be at odds. This, we have argued, will result in the judicial tug of war. On the one hand, political actors will want the courts to rule favorably on policies and legislation that they care about; for that reason, they will try as much as possible to select candidates who share their ideology. However, lawyers and the legal establishment also have policy preferences and goals; given the enormous power they wield via the professional capture of the judiciary, they will also be able to influence which judges are appointed and elected, tipping the balance toward those who share their ideology and preferences.

This tension undergirds the tug of war. To the extent that political actors and the legal establishment are aligned, the tension will be lessened: Both are on the "same side" in what they wish to see in the courts. (That is, they are both "pulling" in the same direction.) We would expect, under this scenario, that courts will echo the preferences of these two groups and that political actors will be content with a judicial selection mechanism that facilitates input (both formal and informal) from the legal community. A politically feasible and straightforward system would be one that relies primarily on "merit" and "qualifications" – characteristics that appear ideologically neutral, yet would allow the political and legal establishment to end up with ideologically compatible judges.[10]

The more interesting scenario is what happens when the interests of political elites and those of the legal establishment diverge. In these cases, politicians and lawyers may be on opposing sides of the tug of war, fighting over the courts that are trapped in the middle. Here, how judges are selected plays a key role. If political actors are given more power – for example, as they are in systems that prioritize executive appointments or elections through partisan systems – then politicians will be able to "pull" harder on the rope, moving the judiciary closer to their preferred ideological position. We see this in many states in which executive appointments have resulted in judiciaries whose preferences and ideology closely align with those of political actors. The federal system, which has no formal role for the legal establishment, most clearly illustrates this intuition: As our analysis shows, the ideological leanings of federal judges closely reflect the ideological leanings of the pertinent political players.

All of this serves to highlight an important point underlying our framework and analyses: Under our argument of the judicial tug of war, the courts are first and foremost political booty – a prize to be fought over by different sides of the tug of war. Readers might think this is a cynical way to view what is essentially a highly important, coequal branch of government – one that is tasked with the interpretation of state and federal constitutions and also with judicial review. Moreover, judicial decision-making is viewed by many as being among the most nonpartisan, most intellectual forms of decision-making. Indeed, many people, not just academics but also members of the public, believe that judges are "umpires calling balls and strikes," not strategic actors interested in achieving policy or ideological outcomes.

Nonetheless, we believe that it accurately reflects how the courts actually fit within the American framework of government and its constantly changing ideological landscape. As some of the constitutional framers themselves argued in *Federalist Number 78*, the judiciary "has no influence over either the sword or the purse; no direction either of the strength or of the wealth of the society; and can take no active resolution whatever."[11] This, in theory, makes the courts inherently less powerful than

---

[10] This is an observation made by Fitzpatrick (2009), who notes that such merit-oriented selection systems prioritize judges with certain ideological profiles (on average).

[11] Hamilton, Madison, and Jay (1787).

the other branches of government, unable to enforce their own rulings, extract rents, or coerce behavior. Judges are also limited in which cases they can hear, stymied by the federal constitution's requirement that they hear only "cases and controversies," a prohibition that means that judges cannot issue advisory opinions. Although the legal profession in the United States is strong and much of regulatory policy is handled through the legal system, the courts are less powerful agents compared to the legal establishment and to political actors.

All of this means that the courts are a valuable political prize for the legal and political establishment. Favorable courts are a significant asset for elected officials and party leaders, particularly for those whose political agendas map onto issues routinely addressed for the courts. For conservatives, this includes traditional social issues such as abortion and civil rights; more recently, it also includes free speech (including corporate and political speech) and immigration. For liberals, important topics handled by the courts include personal freedoms, oversight over administrative agencies, and civil rights. And, for lawyers, the rewards are obvious: Having like-minded judges furthers the bar's own professional interests, including not just rulings on individual cases but also rulings that serve to buttress a more powerful legal establishment. As a bonus, having a like-minded, well-qualified, and highly pedigreed judiciary by extension lends reputational benefits to the entire legal profession.

TAKEAWAY #3: IDEOLOGICAL CONFIGURATIONS DETERMINE JUDICIAL REFORM AND ITS CONSEQUENCES

We can understand these competing, conflicting incentives via our framework of the judicial tug of war, which provides a blueprint to assess who has "won" or "lost" this fight, as well as the important consequences of liberals and conservatives trying to outmaneuver each other and change the rules of the game.

Indeed, a natural consequence of the tug of war is that, depending on their underlying ideological interests, politicians (and, to a lesser extent, members of the legal establishment) will try to modify how judges are selected to suit their interests. For conservative politicians, the rules of the tug of war can often be frustrating, especially if legal elites lean to the left, as they do now. Merit commissions and nonpartisan elections frustrate conservatives' interests by making it harder to select judges on the basis of ideology or partisanship, thus leading to the selection of more liberal-leaning judges. In these states, we expect to see conservatives agitate over and over again for a greater role of ideology, politics, and partisanship in the selection of judges. For these politicians, executive appointments and partisan elections are extremely attractive – they facilitate the introduction of ideology directly, leading to judges who are more ideologically compatible.

This is exactly what we have seen in the last few decades and what the contemporary examples of Florida, Kansas, and North Carolina illustrate. In states such as these, conservatives have pushed – and pushed hard – for partisan elections and executive appointments, denouncing what they have labeled as "activist judges." Some of the attempts at judicial reform have been controversial, and not all have been successful. However, these have been largely popular with the conservative base. Moving forward, we expect continued efforts to introduce ideology and partisanship into the selection of judges in places such as these, where conservative politicians have dominated the political landscape and where, historically, merit commissions or other merit-oriented systems have been the norm.

For their part, if lawyers (and, in particular, elite lawyers) lean to the left, liberal politicians will advocate for more ideologically neutral judicial selection systems – such as merit commissions and nonpartisan appointments. The reasons why are straightforward. These selection mechanisms allow liberal politicians to select judicial candidates on the basis of ostensibly nonideological criteria (among them qualifications or pedigree) yet still yield an ideologically compatible judiciary. Indeed, for liberals, pushing towards "qualified judges" is a win-win proposition: Doing so allows them to appear above the political fray in supporting the nonpartisan selection of judges, while still allowing them to enjoy the benefits of ideologically friendly and like-minded judges. In this sense, the judicial tug-of-war framework provides compelling predictions about where attempts at judicial reform will develop and what those reforms might look like.

We note one important caveat: This discussion – and, indeed, much of what we have discussed in this book – highlights *contemporary* ideological dynamics. These roles could, however, easily be switched: With a conservative legal profession, conservative politicians would be the ones to support qualifications-based criteria, while liberal politicians would agitate for more politicized selection processes. As we discussed in Chapters 6 and 7, this was the case for much of the nineteenth and twentieth centuries. Although we see no immediate reason why the current dynamics could change, our framework is certainly flexible enough to incorporate that possibility.

LOOKING TO THE POLARIZED FUTURE

We conclude by noting some important developments that will no doubt influence the ideological landscape we have discussed. In so doing, these forces will shape the tug of war and determine the contours of the nation's judiciary in the decades to come.

RIGHTWARD SHIFTS AMONG ELECTED OFFICIALS. The first development – decades in the making – is a rightward shift in the ideology of national- and state-level elected officials. Part of this has been associated with the ongoing rise and effectiveness of right-leaning movements, such as the Tea Party, which gained strength through the 2000s and 2010s and facilitated the rise of national-level candidates such as Sarah Palin and Donald Trump. (We documented some of their effects in our discussion of Kansas' judicial reform in Chapter 7.) The overall impact of these has been to shift the ideology of Republican Party representation to the right, also pushing the average ideology of representatives rightward and weakening the center-right position held by more moderate Republicans.[12] At the national level, the 2016 election is a good example of the rightward shift. Although the forces at play were complicated – ranging from a backlash against outgoing President Barack Obama, white working-class ambivalence toward Democratic candidate Hillary Rodham Clinton, and the possibility of election interference by foreign agents – the end result was not: National politics and dialogue sharply shifted to the right. With a new populist-leaning conservative in the White House (Donald Trump) and strong and conservative Republican majorities in Congress, conservatives were well positioned to move forward with a conservative policy agenda and in making hundreds of federal court appointments.[13]

---

[12] The rightward shift among Republicans (paired with relative stability in ideology among Democrats) has been well documented using DW-NOMINATE scores as well as the donation-based measures used here. Documentation of this, as well as a discussion of possible explanations and consequences, is provided in Barber and McCarty (2015).

[13] As we discussed in Chapter 5, the initial consequences of this shift have been seen in the record numbers of federal judges appointed, many of whom have received rare "Not Qualified" ratings from the ABA. This illustrates the challenges for conservatives in

In addition, at the state level, the election of 2016 yielded twenty-six states in which Republicans controlled all elected branches of government, compared to only eight in which Democrats held the same relative power.[14] From our perspective, given current rightward political shifts at the national and state levels, our theory predicts that attempts at interjecting more ideology into judicial selection will become more numerous and more urgent. The pressure will be particularly strong as Republicans push policy changes on social issues – the cornerstone of many Republicans' platforms and an arena in which the courts are particularly decried as obstacles. In addition, as Republican-controlled legislatures increasingly move to solidify partisan control over Congress and state legislatures, they will take an even stronger interest in redistricting. As we have discussed in the context of the North Carolina Supreme Court, state courts are often the key battleground over the constitutionality of redistricting plans. As Republicans become more aggressive in enacting and defending partisan gerrymandering, the battle over who sits on state courts will become more aggressive as well.

LEFTWARD SHIFTS AMONG YOUNGER (PARTICULARLY ELITE) LAWYERS. The other point of tension that will exacerbate the tug of war is that younger lawyers are becoming more liberal over time, a trend that started in the 1970s and has accelerated through the present day.[15] We show some of this in Figure 9.1, which documents this pattern using DIME scores. The figure shows changes in average lawyer ideology, smoothed over time, for lawyers who graduated from law school between 1935 and 2011. The figure clearly shows a steady and substantial drift to the left, shown graphically by the downward movement in average lawyer ideology by year of law degree. We note that this trend generally follows the cohort effects among the general population[16] and trends observed in other professions, notably physicians.[17]

After the 1970s and 1980s, the leftward trend is clear among lawyers. A very likely partial explanation is the increasing diversity of law schools

---

appointing large numbers of conservatives, given conservative scarcity among top law graduates.

[14] Information about partisan composition of state legislators comes from Wikipedia (https://en.wikipedia.org/wiki/List_of_United_States_state_legislatures).

[15] For more on the earlier, liberal shifts in law school ideology, see Teles (2012, chap. 2).

[16] Ghitza and Gelman (2014).

[17] Bonica et al. (forthcoming).

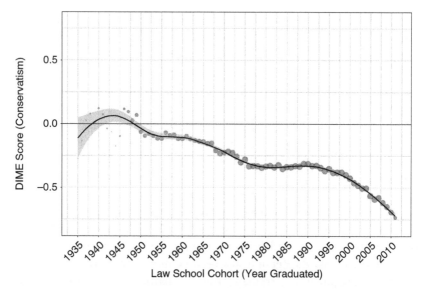

FIGURE 9.1 Average lawyer ideology by law school graduate cohorts.
Note: Point sizes are log-weighted by the number of graduates in each cohort.
Sources: DIME; Martindale-Hubbell.

and of the legal profession. Long a profession composed mostly of white Protestant men, the legal profession rapidly diversified to include more left-leaning women, African Americans, Jews, and Latino/as through the 1970s and 1980s, to the point where women now account for a majority of all law students. Moreover, by one account, "[w]omen and ethnic minorities, whose representation in law schools shot up in this period, reported even greater aversion to traditional corporate law careers and had ideological preferences further to the left."[18] However, another possible partial explanation is an increasing correspondence between higher education and Democratic affiliation, a recent pattern that has become only stronger since the 2016 election.[19] This correlation between education (particularly at the elite level), we believe, is likely to continue in the

[18] Teles (2012, p. 40). For accounts of the proportion of female law students, see Olson (2016).
[19] While income – and not education – used to be a stronger predictor of partisanship, education is now a stronger predictor, with whites without a college degree being more likely to identify as Republicans and those with a college degree (or higher, such as a law degree) being more likely to identify as Democrats. For a popular look at this phenomenon, see, e.g., Harris (2018).

near future and to further tensions between highly educated legal elites and conservative elected officials.

Another possible explanation is that more and more young people are sorting – perhaps on the basis of ideology – into different career paths. Although this is an open research question, we suspect – and have good anecdotal reasons to believe – that highly educated left-leaning students are more and more likely to pursue careers in law, service work, academia, and journalism, while similarly educated right-leaning students are pursuing more remunerative careers in business, banking, finance, and consulting, as well as in law enforcement and in the military. The question of ideological sorting is beyond the scope of this book, but we do see evidence consistent with this explanation in our data. We also see evidence of this in qualitative accounts of the liberal trends in law schools due in large part to their greater focus on public interest law, clinics, and direct legal services.[20]

IMPLICATIONS FOR THE JUDICIAL TUG OF WAR. These two components – politicians (in particular Republicans) moving to the right and lawyers (particularly at the elite level) moving to the left – have significant implications for the judicial tug of war. First, as the elite ranks of lawyers become more liberal and as politicians become more conservative, tensions between politicians and the bar will grow. The growing ideological gap between these groups will increase the likelihood of reform attempts oriented toward stripping the bar of involvement in judicial selection. This will include a shift across a variety of states away from merit commissions, bipartisan commissions, and nonpartisan elections and toward explicitly political processes. North Carolina is an excellent example of this trend. With its conservative-leaning General Assembly, and with politicians dissatisfied with the more liberal-leaning state supreme court, North Carolina has made radical shifts in moving away from nonpartisan to partisan elections, stripping the governor (then a Democrat) of court-related powers and reorganizing the way cases are appealed through the judicial hierarchy.

Second, the rift between the bar and Republicans will only deepen as the more liberal law student cohorts replace the comparably more conservative retiring cohorts. This is perhaps a key, fundamental problem faced by conservatives; after all, conservatives can move control away from the bar with judicial reform attempts, but there is less they

[20] Teles (2012).

can do about young people's ideological sorting and the dearth of conservative graduates of elite programs. A possible indication of what is to come is the administration of Donald Trump, which faced many judicial vacancies in tandem with a dearth of conservative candidates. Unsurprisingly given our data about top law graduates, a record number of Trump's candidates have been rated "Not Qualified" by the ABA, suggesting a willingness by conservatives to look beyond standard pedigree and experience in finding ideologically suitable (i.e., conservative) young candidates. In other words, rather than compromising on ideology, conservatives may have to compromise on qualifications and pedigree – perhaps raising public criticism but prioritizing an ideologically compatible judiciary. In addition, and also unsurprisingly, the Trump administration has outsourced much of its vetting to the Federalist Society and its network of conservative scholars.[21] As conservative law graduates become more scarce at the elite level, we would expect that the importance of these structured talent-finding networks will increase in importance.

CONCLUSION

In this book, we attempted to address the underlying puzzle raised by political conflicts over the nation's judiciary. Why is it that conservatives have constantly raised the battle cry of "activist judges," and why have they spent much of the past decades spearheading and initiating attempts at judicial reform? Why have liberals countered by emphasizing qualifications and experience over ideology, and why have they decried the ongoing "politicization" of the courts? These questions not only speak to the way that political elites and partisans approach judicial appointments but also speak directly to the role of the judiciary itself.

Our answer to these questions relies on a different way of thinking about the broader American political landscape. As we have argued in this book and shown through new data and empirical evidence, the American judiciary is intimately shaped not just by the political proclivities of partisan leaders but also by the political contours and ideological preferences of the legal establishment. The American bar is a key political player whose ability to leverage an elite status has profoundly shaped American politics and policy for centuries. This power has allowed the

---

[21] Baum and Devins (2017).

bar not only to grow its influence but also to extract powerful political rents – including, most importantly, the power to regulate itself and its members. In other words, that just a small fraction of people with law degrees – just o.4 percent of the current US population – has near majority control over two branches of government and complete control over a third is significant, and its full political ramifications have yet to be fully explored.

The legal establishment's power extends with particular force to the judiciary. Not only do lawyers have a strong sway over judicial codes of conduct but they also play a formal or informal role in the selection of judges. At an even more fundamental level, the legal establishment exercises complete control over the environment in which judges are trained, provides the pool of candidates from which judges are drawn, and intellectually channels elite candidates of various ideological stripes toward the judiciary. All of these components lead us to conclude that the legal establishment has exercised professional capture over the judiciary. Because of the role and stature of the judiciary within the broader framework of American government, we refer to this as "constitutional capture" – to our knowledge, the only such instance.

This idea of capture informs our broader theory of the judicial tug of war, which we can use to understand patterns of politicization in judicial selection through state and federal courts. Put simply, the more that judges resemble the pool of candidate attorneys, the more that the judiciary has been "captured" by the legal establishment (i.e., the more that lawyers are "winning" the tug of war). On the other hand, if judges do not resemble the legal establishment but instead resemble the preferences of politicians, then we have good reason to think that political elites have been able to "pull" further (making them winners in the tug of war). Thinking about judicial selection this way puts the courts squarely in the middle, making them a significant political prize.

In addition, this simple framework helps us develop predictions about where attempts at judicial reform will develop. Specifically, a greater ideological rift between the bar and political officials will create tension, thereby leading politicians to adopt measures to limit the bar's influence. This would mean more frequent attempts at shifting judicial selection toward partisan systems, including partisan elections, appointments by elected officials (e.g., by governors), and other kinds of systems that allow explicit consideration of ideology and partisanship. On the other hand, a synergy between the bar and elected officials will lead to the opposite; in these cases, political leaders will be inclined to pursue judicial selection mechanisms that allow the bar a large amount of influence and input into the selection of judges. This could include the reliance on merit-oriented commissions, prenomination vetting of candidates by professional legal organizations, and nonpartisan elections.

The judicial tug-of-war framework not only helps explain the current environment surrounding the nation's courts but also provides a powerful way to think about the composition of the courts moving forward. In the current political dynamic, Republicans are understandably frustrated with the legal establishment, whose interests tend to conflict with theirs. For this reason, they agitate against "activist" judges and decry their rulings on conservatives' favorite issues. They push for the introduction of partisanship as much as possible and tussle to "reform" the courts in ways that allow them to pick and choose candidates on the basis of ideology. Democrats, on the other hand, understandably have every reason to oppose the use of partisanship or ideology in judicial selection; for them, involving ideology in judicial selection has mostly downsides, while keeping judicial selection focused on qualifications and pedigree has mostly upsides. This is why we see Democrats decry the "politicization" of the courts or the "partisan maneuvering" of Republicans.

Throughout, we think of courts as a political prize and of the politicization of courts as a consequence of the tug of war. Although this may be unsettling, there are reasons to consider the politicization of the courts a part of the healthy process of American democracy. Indeed, the bigger political anomaly is perhaps not so much that American politicians want judges and courts to share their policy preferences; in our view, what is somewhat unusual about the US context is the political power of the legal establishment and its professional capture over the judiciary. Thinking about politicization as a way for political actors to push back on this professional capture and to introduce more ideological diversity in the courts is encouraging. However, the ideological consequences of such actions will, as we have noted throughout, always depend on the partisan and ideological landscape of politicians, parties, and the legal establishment: The political push against the legal establishment might be cause for optimism for some (particularly on the right, currently) but perhaps cause for anxiety for others (particularly on the left).

We conclude by highlighting a perhaps obvious implication of our argument: Recent years have seen US courts rule on some of the most significant policy controversies of the day, including redistricting, campaign finance, affirmative action, health care reform, and civil rights. In addition, the last few years have seen increased battles over judicial vacancies and appointments and increased attacks from both the right and the left over the possibility of "activist" or "politicized" judges. Across the fifty states, moreover, Republicans and Democrats have pushed (or opposed) attempts at judicial reform, including limiting judicial terms, threatening to impeach sitting judges, reducing the influence of the professional bar, and calling for partisanship to play a role in judicial elections. Recent elections – which have seen increased polarization among the political parties – have only served to fan these flames further and, we believe, to make the issue of judicial selection even more salient. In the years to come, we expect that talk of judicial reform will become even more partisan and controversial.

Bibliography

Abadi, Mark. 2016. "People in North Carolina Are Freaking Out Over Rumors of a Republican 'Power Grab' to Pack its Supreme Court." Business Insider, December 7. *www.businessinsider.com/north-carolina-supreme-court-packing-pat-mccrory-2016-12*

ABC News. 2001. "Bush Dumps Bar Ratings of Judges." ABC News, January 7. *https://abcnews.go.com/amp/US/story?id=93753&page=1*

ABC News. 2016. "'This Week' Transcript: Ted Cruz, John Kasich, Marco Rubio, Bernie Sanders, and Donald Trump." ABC News, February 14. *http://abcn.ws/1TjimcC*

Abel, Richard L. 1986. "The Transformation of the American Legal Profession." *Law and Society Review* 20(1):7–18.

Abel, Richard L. and Philip Lewis. 1989. *Lawyers in Society: Comparative Theories*. Washington, DC: Beard Books.

Allison, Garland W. 1996. "Delay in Senate Confirmation of Federal Judicial Nominees." *Judicature* 80(1):8–15.

Altman, James M. 2002. "Considering the ABA's 1908 Canons of Ethics." *Fordham Law Review* 71(6):2395–2508.

American Bar Association. 1908. "Canons of Professional Ethics." American Bar Association.

American Bar Association. 1999. "Perceptions of the U.S. Justice System." *www.americanbar.org/content/dam/aba/migrated/marketresearch/Public Documents/perceptions_of_justice_system_1999_1st_half.authcheckdam.pdf*.

American Bar Association. 2008. "Judicial Selection: The Process of Choosing Judges." Chicago: American Bar Association Coalition for Justice.

American Bar Association. 2009. "Standing Committee on the Federal Judiciary: What It Is and How It Works." American Bar Association.

American Bar Association. 2003. "Justice in Jeopardy: Report of the American Bar Association on the 21st Century Judiciary." American Bar Association.

American Bar Association. 2016a "American Bar Association Fights to Preserve the Independence of the Legal Profession." *www.americanbar.org*

American Bar Association. 2016b. "Legislative Policies of the American Bar Association." www.americanbar.org/content/dam/aba/uncate gorized/GAO/legislativeissueslist.authcheckdam.pdf

American Bar Association. 2017. "ABA National Lawyer Population Survey Historical Trend in Total National Lawyer Population 1878–2017." www.americanbar.org/content/dam/aba/administrative/mark et_research/Total National Lawyer Population 1878-2017.authcheckdam.pdf

American Bar Association. 2018. Model Rules of Professional Conduct. www.americanbar.org/groups/professional_responsibility/ publications/model_rules_of_professional_conduct/model_ rules_of_professional_conduct_table_of_contents/

American Bar Association and Center for Professional Responsibility. 2007. Model Code of Judicial Conduct. American Bar Association.

American Bar Association Committee on Code of Professional Ethics. 1907. "In re the Advisability and Practicability of the Adoption of Canons of Ethics by the American Bar Association." *Annual Report of the American Bar Association* 31:681–685.

Andrias, Kate, Dmitry Bam, Joseph Blocher et al. 2016. "Statement of Constitutional Law Scholars on the Supreme Court Vacancy." American Constitution Society.

Auerbach, Jerold S. 1977. *Unequal Justice: Lawyers and Social Change in Modern America*. Oxford: Oxford University Press.

Bailey, Michael A. 2007. "Comparable Preference Estimates Across Time and Institutions for the Court, Congress, and Presidency." *American Journal of Political Science* 51(3):433–448.

Baldwin, Simon E. 1917. "The Founding of the American Bar Association." *American Bar Association Journal* 3:658–695.

Bannon, Alicia, Cathleen Lisk, and Peter Hardin. 2017. "Who Pays for Judicial Races?" The Brennan Center. *www.brennancenter.org/our-work/research-re ports/who-pays-judicial-races-politics-judicial-elections-2015-16*

Barber, Michael J. and Nolan McCarty. 2015. Causes and Consequences of Polarization. In *Solutions to Political Polarization in America*, ed. Nathaniel Persily. Cambridge: Cambridge University Press, pp. 15–58.

Barkan, Steven. 2015. *Law and Society: An Introduction*. Abingdon: Routledge.

Barnes, Robert. 2017. "How Many Harvard Law School Grads Does It Take to Make a Supreme Court?" *The Washington Post*, October 26. *www.washingtonpost.com/politics/courts_law/how-many-harvard-law-school-grads-does-it-take-to-make-a-supreme-court/2017/10/26/970e5460-baa2-11e7-be94-fabbof1e9ffb_story.html*

Barnett, Martha W. 2000. "The 1997–98 Florida Constitution Revision Commission: Judicial Election or Merit Selection." *Florida Law Review* 52(2):411–423.

Barton, Benjamin H. 2003. "An Institutional Analysis of Lawyer Regulation: Who Should Control Lawyer Regulation-Courts, Legislatures, or the Market." *Georgia Law Review* 37(4):1167–1250.

Barton, Benjamin H. 2010. *The Lawyer-Judge Bias in the American Legal System*. New York: Cambridge University Press.

Batten, Taylor. 2016. "GOP Gets Wonderful, Awful Idea on Supreme Court." *The Charlotte Observer*, November 11. *www.charlotteobserver.com/opinion/opn-columns-blogs/taylor-batten/article114252053.html*

Baum, Lawrence. 2009. *Judges and Their Audiences: A Perspective on Judicial Behavior*. Princeton: Princeton University Press.

Baum, Lawrence and David Klein. 2007. Voter Responses to High-Visibility Judicial Campaigns. In *Running for Judge: The Rising Political, Financial, and Legal Stakes of Judicial Elections*, ed. Matthew J. Streb. New York: New York University Press, pp. 140–164.

Baum, Lawrence and Neal Devins. 2010. "Why the Supreme Court Cares About Elites, Not the American People." *Georgetown Law Journal* 98:1515–1581.

Baum, Lawrence and Neal Devins. 2017. "Federalist Court: How the Federalist Society Became the De Facto Selector of Republican Supreme Court Justices." *Slate*, January 31. *https://slate.com/news-and-politics/2017/01/how-the-federalist-society-became-the-de-facto-selector-of-republican-supreme-court-justices.html*

Baumgartner, Samuel P. 2007. "Class Actions and Group Litigation in Switzerland." *Northwestern Journal of International Law and Business* 27(2):301–350.

Becker, Jo. 2000. "Florida's Supreme Court: Partisan or Impartial?" *The Washington Post*, November 18. *www.washingtonpost.com/archive/politics/2000/11/18/floridas-supreme-court-partisan-or-impartial/a1fd278f-5524-4c51-94c6-9af865431354/*

Berkowitz, Daniel and Karen Clay. 2006. "The Effect of Judicial Independence on Courts: Evidence from the American States." *The Journal of Legal Studies* 35(2):399–440.

Berman, Russell. 2016. "Kansas Republicans Rebuke Their Conservative Governor." *The Atlantic*, August 4. *www.theatlantic.com/politics/archive/2016/08/kansas-republicans-rebuke-their-conservative-governor-brown-back/494405/*

Berry, William D., Richard C. Fording, Evan J. Ringquist, Russell L. Hanson, and Carl Klarner. 2013. "A New Measure of State Government Ideology, and Evidence That Both the New Measure and an Old Measure Are Valid." *State Politics & Policy Quarterly* 13(2):164–182.

Bertelli, Anthony M. and Laurence E. Lynn. 2006. *Madison's Managers: Public Administration and The Constitution*. Baltimore, MD: Johns Hopkins University Press.

Binder, Sarah A. and Forrest Maltzman. 2009. *Advice and Dissent: The Struggle to Shape the Federal Judiciary*. Washington, DC: Brookings Institution Press.

Binker, Mark. 2017. "Cooper Rejects Bill to Make NC Judicial Elections Partisan." WRAL.com. *www.wral.com/cooper-rejects-bill-to-make-nc-judicial-elections-partisan-/16588679/*

Black, Ryan C. and Ryan J. Owens. 2016. "Courting the President: How Circuit Court Judges Alter Their Behavior for Promotion to the Supreme Court." *American Journal of Political Science* 60(1):30–43.

Blythe, Ann. 2016. "NC Lawmakers Create Partisan Election Process for Courts That Review Their Laws." *The News & Observer*, December 16. *www.news observer.com/news/politics-government/state-politics/article121449157.html*

Blythe, Ann. 2018. "We're Voting for Judges This Year, but Are Lawmakers Done Changing the Rules for Those Elections?" *The News & Observer*, June 8. *www.newsobserver.com/news/politics-government/article212835994.html*

Bonica, Adam. 2014. "Mapping the Ideological Marketplace." *American Journal of Political Science* 58(2):367–387.

Bonica, Adam. 2016a. "Avenues of influence: On the political expenditures of corporations and their directors and executives." *Business and Politics* 18(4):367–394.

Bonica, Adam. 2016b. "Database on Ideology, Money in Politics, and Elections: Public Version 2.0." [Computer file]. Stanford, CA: Stanford University Libraries [distributor]. http://data.stanford.edu/dime

Bonica, Adam. 2019. "Are Donation-Based Measures of Ideology Valid Predictors of Individual-Level Policy Preferences?" *The Journal of Politics* 81(1):327–333.

Bonica, Adam, Adam S. Chilton, Kyle Rozema, and Maya Sen. 2018. "The Legal Academy's Ideological Uniformity." *Journal of Legal Studies* 47(1):1–43.

Bonica, Adam, Adam S. Chilton, and Maya Sen. 2016. "The Political Ideologies of American Lawyers." *Journal of Legal Analysis* 8(2):277–335.

Bonica, Adam, Chen Jowei, Johnson Tim et al. 2015. "Senate Gate-Keeping, Presidential Staffing of 'Inferior Offices,' and the Ideological Composition of Appointments to the Public Bureaucracy." *Quarterly Journal of Political Science* 10(1):5–40.

Bonica, Adam, Nolan McCarty, Keith T. Poole, and Howard Rosenthal. 2013. "Why Hasn't Democracy Slowed Rising Inequality?" *The Journal of Economic Perspectives* 27(3):103–123.

Bonica, Adam, Nolan McCarty, Keith T. Poole, and Howard Rosenthal. 2015. "Congressional Polarization and Its Connection to Income Inequality: An Update." *American Gridlock: The Sources, Character, and Impact of Political Polarization* pp. 357–77.

Bonica, Adam, Howard L. Rosenthal, Kristy Blackwood, and David Rothman. Forthcoming. "Ideological Sorting of Physicians in both Geography and the Workplace." *Journal of Health Politics, Policy and Law* .

Bonica, Adam and Maya Sen. 2017a. "A Common-Space Scaling of the American Judiciary and Legal Profession." *Political Analysis* 25(1):114–121.

Bonica, Adam and Maya Sen. 2017b. "Judicial Reform as a Tug of War: How Ideological Differences Between Politicians and the Bar Explain Attempts at Judicial Reform." *Vanderbilt Law Review* 70(6):1781–1811.

Bonica, Adam and Maya Sen. 2017c. "The Politics of Selecting the Bench from the Bar: The Legal Profession and Partisan Incentives to Introduce Ideology into Judicial Selection." *The Journal of Law & Economics* 60(4):559–595.

Bonica, Adam and Michael J. Woodruff. 2015. "A Common-Space Measure of State Supreme Court Ideology." *Journal of Law, Economics, & Organization* 31(3):472–498.

Bonneau, Chris W. and Damon M. Cann. 2015. "Party Identification and Vote Choice in Partisan and Nonpartisan Elections." *Political Behavior* 37(1):43–66.

Bonneau, Chris W. and Melinda Gann Hall. 2009. *In Defense of Judicial Elections*. Routledge Press.

Boughton, Melissa. 2017. "House Republicans Pass Committee Hurdle to Make Last Judicial Elections Partisan Again." *The Progressive Pulse*. *http://pulse.nc policywatch.org/2017/02/21/house-republicans-pass-committee-hurdle-make-last-judicial-elections-partisan/*

Boyd, Christina L. 2011. "Federal District Court Judge Ideology Data." University of Georgia. *http://cLboyd.net/ideology.html*

Brace, Paul, Laura Langer, and Melinda Gann Hall. 2000. "Measuring the Preferences of State Supreme Court Judges." *The Journal of Politics* 62(2):387–413.

Brace, Paul R. and Melinda Gann Hall. 1997. "The Interplay of Preferences, Case Facts, Context, and Rules in the Politics of Judicial Choice." *The Journal of Politics* 59(4):1206–1231.

Brandeis, Louis Dembitz. 1914. *Business: A Profession*. Boston: Small, Maynard.

Brandenburg, Bert. 2008. "What's the Best Way to Pack a Court?" *Slate*, November 14. *https://slate.com/news-and-politics/2008/11/the-attack-on-merit-select ion-for-judges.html*

Bratton, Kathleen A. and Rorie L. Spill. 2002. "Existing Diversity and Judicial Selection: The Role of the Appointment Method in Establishing Gender Diversity in State Supreme Courts." *Social Science Quarterly* 83(2): 504–518.

Brill, Howard W. 2009. "The Arkansas Code of Judicial Conduct of 2009." *Arkansas Law Notes*. Fayetteville, AR: University of Arkansas Law School, pp. 1–27. *http://media.law.uark.edu/arklawnotes/files/2011/03/Brill-The-Arka nsas-Code-of-Judial-Conduct-of-2009-Arkansas-Law-Notes-2009.pdf*

Brockman, Norbert C. 1962. "The History of the American Bar Association: A Bibliographic Essay." *The American Journal of Legal History* 6(3):269–285.

Bump, Philip. 2017. "How Unusual Are Trump's 'Not Qualified' Judicial Nominations?" *The Washington Post*, December 15. *www.washingtonpost.com/ news/politics/wp/2017/11/10/how-unusual-are-trumps-not-qualified-judicial-nominations/?utm_term=.c5a69ad48c3a*

Burnett, Craig M. and Lydia Tiede. 2015. "Party Labels and Vote Choice in Judicial Elections." *American Politics Research* 43(2):232–254.

Burns, James MacGregor. 2009. *Packing the Court: The Rise of Judicial Power and the Coming Crisis of the Supreme Court*. New York: Penguin Books.

Byrd, Johnnie. 2001. "JNC Reform is Timely." *www.aif.com/information/2001/ sno10101.html*

Caldeira, Gregory A., John R. Wright, and Christopher J.W. Zorn. 1999. "Sophisticated Voting and Gate-Keeping in the Supreme Court." *Journal of Law, Economics, & Organization* 15(3):549–572.

California Bar Association. 2011. "Survey of Members of The State Bar of California, December 2011." www.calbar.ca.gov/Portals/0/documents/reports/ 2011-12_SBCdemosurvey_sumandfacts.pdf

Cameron, Charles M., Albert D. Cover, and Jeffrey A. Segal. 1990. "Senate Voting on Supreme Court Nominees: A Neoinstitutional Model." *American Political Science Review* 84(2):525–534.

Campbell, Tom. 2018. "2018: The Year of Judicial Reform?" *The News Reporter*. *https://docplayer.net/150064722-The-news-reporter-monday-january-1-2018.html*

Canes-Wrone, Brandice and Tom S. Clark. 2009. "Judicial Independence and Nonpartisan Elections." *Wisconsin Law Review* 2009(1):21–65.

Canes-Wrone, Brandice, Tom S. Clark, and Jason P. Kelly. 2014. "Judicial Selection and Death Penalty Decisions." *American Political Science Review* 108(1):23–39.

Caplan, Lincoln. 2016. "The Political War Against the Kansas Supreme Court." *The New Yorker*, February 5. *www.newyorker.com/news/news-desk/the-political-war-against-the-kansas-supreme-court*

Carnahan, Seth and Brad N. Greenwood. 2018. "Managers' Political Beliefs and Gender Inequality Among Subordinates: Does His Ideology Matter More Than Hers?" *Administrative Science Quarterly* 63(2):287–322.

Carnes, Nicholas. 2012. "Does the Numerical Underrepresentation of the Working Class in Congress Matter?" *Legislative Studies Quarterly* 37(1):5–34.

Carnes, Nicholas. 2013. *White-Collar Government: The Hidden Role of Class in Economic Policy Making*. Chicago, IL: University of Chicago Press.

Carpenter, Tim. 2015. "Ex-Senator Tim Owens: Ideology Drives Sam Brownback's Push for Judicial Reform." *The Topeka Capital-Journal*, February 9. *www.cjonline.com/article/20150209/NEWS/302099695*

Carter, Stephen L. 1994. *The Confirmation Mess*. New York: Basic Books.

Caulder, Matt. 2016. "Non-Partisan Judicial Elections ... Aren't." NC Capitol Connection. *http://nccapitolconnection.com/2016/10/21/non-partisan-judicial-elections-arent//*

Chamber of Commerce of the State of New York. 1937. "Law Organization Demands Better Method of Selecting State Judges." *American Bar Association Journal* 23(7):528–531.

Chen, Jowei and Tim Johnson. 2015. "Federal Employee Unionization and Presidential Control of the Bureaucracy: Estimating and Explaining Ideological Change in Executive Agencies." *Journal of Theoretical Politics* 27(1):151–174.

Chilton, Adam S. and Eric A. Posner. 2015. "An Empirical Study of Political Bias in Legal Scholarship." *The Journal of Legal Studies* 44(2):277–314.

Choi, Stephen J., Mitu Gulati, and Eric A. Posner. 2010. "Professionals or Politicians: The Uncertain Empirical Case for an Elected Rather Than Appointed Judiciary." *Journal of Law, Economics, & Organization* 26(2):290–336.

Clark, Tom S. 2009. "Measuring Ideological Polarization on the United States Supreme Court." *Political Research Quarterly* 62(1):146–157.

Clark, Tom S. and Benjamin Lauderdale. 2010. "Locating Supreme Court Opinions in Doctrine Space." *American Journal of Political Science* 54(4):871–890.

Clinton, Joshua D., Simon Jackman, and Douglas Rivers. 2004. "The Statistical Analysis of Roll Call Data." *American Political Science Review* 98(2):355–70.

Cody, Carl. 2014. "Majority in Congress Are Millionaires." *National Public Radio*, January 10. *www.npr.org/sections/itsallpolitics/2014/01/10/2613982 05/majority-in-congress-are-millionaires*

Cohen, Andrew. 2013. "'A Broken System': Texas's Former Chief Justice Condemns Judicial Elections." *The Atlantic*, October 18. *www.theatlantic .com/national/archive/2013/10/a-broken-system-texass-former-chief-justice-co ndemns-judicial-elections/280654/*

Cohen, Michael. 1969. "Lawyers and Political Careers." *Law & Society Review* 3(4):563–574.

Corasaniti, Nick. 2016. "At Debate, Donald Trump Calls on Republicans to 'Delay, Delay, Delay'." *The New York Times*, February 13. *www.nytimes.com/ live/supreme-court-justice-antonin-scalia-dies-at-79/at-debate-trump-calls-on-republicans-to-delay-delay-delay/*

Corriher, Billy. 2018. "The North Carolina Legislature Is Attacking Judges Who Rule Against It." *ABA Journal*, March 22.

Crandall, Robert W., Vikram Maheshri, and Clifford Winston. 2011. *First Thing We Do, Let's Deregulate All The Lawyers*. Brookings Institution Press.

Cruz, Ted. 2015. "Constitutional Remedies to a Lawless Supreme Court." *National Review*. *www.nationalreview.com/2015/06/ted-cruz-supreme-court-constitutional-amendment/*

Davis, Kearns. 2016. "Statement Addresses Campaign Advertising." North Carolina Bar Association. *www.ncbar.org/news/statement-addresses-campaign-ad vertising/*

Derge, David R. 1959. "The Lawyer As Decision-Maker in the American State Legislature." *The Journal of Politics* 21(3):408–433.

Devins, Neal and Lawrence Baum. 2016. "Split Definitive: How Party Polarization Turned the Supreme Court into a Partisan Court." *The Supreme Court Review* 2016(9):301–365.

Downes, William Jacob. 2013. "Does The ABA Promote Democracy in America." *Georgetown Journal of Legal Ethics* 26(4):645–659.

Dwyer, Devin. 2019. "Chief Justice John Roberts Touts Nonpartisan Supreme Court as Impeachment Battle Begins." *ABC News*, September 24. *https://abcne ws.go.com/Politics/chief-justice-john-roberts-touts-nonpartisan-supreme-court /story?id=65806237*

Eckholm, Erik. 2016. "Outraged by Kansas Justices? Rulings, Republicans Seek to Reshape Court." *The New York Times*, April 2. *www.nytimes.com/ 2016/04/02/us/outraged-by-kansas-justices-rulings-gop-seeks-to-reshape-court .html*

Ely, James W. 1979. "The Legal Practice of Andrew Jackson." *Tennessee Historical Quarterly* 38(4):421.

Epstein, Lee, Andrew D. Martin, Jeffrey A. Segal, and Chad Westerland. 2007. "The Judicial Common Space." *Journal of Law, Economics, & Organization* 23(2):303–325.

Epstein, Lee and Eric Posner. 2018. "If the Supreme Court Is Nakedly Political, Can It Be Just?" *The New York Times*, September 7. *www.nytimes.com/ 2018/07/09/opinion/supreme-court-nominee-trump.html*

Epstein, Lee and Jack Knight. 1998. *The Choices Justices Make*. Washington, DC: CQ Press.

Epstein, Lee, William M. Landes, and Richard A. Posner. 2013. *The Behavior of Federal Judges: A Theoretical and Empirical Study of Rational Choice*. Cambridge, MA: Harvard University Press.

Esteban, Joan-María and Debraj Ray. 1994. "On the Measurement of Polarization." *Econometrica* 62(4):819–851.

Eulau, Heinz and John D. Sprague. 1964. *Lawyers in Politics: A Study in Professional Convergence.* Indianapolis, IN: Bobbs-Merrill Company.

Facundo, Alvaredo, Anthony B. Atkinson, Thomas Piketty, Emmanuel Saez, and Gabriel Zucman. 2016. "The World Wealth and Income Database." *www.wid.world*

Farhang, Sean. 2010. *The Litigation State: Public Regulation and Private Lawsuits in the U.S.* Princeton, NJ: Princeton University Press.

Feerick, John D., Sandra Day O'Connor, and Judith S. Kaye. 2012. "A Conversation with Justice Sandra Day O'Connor and Judge Judith S. Kaye." *Fordham Law Review* 81(3):1149–1167.

Feinberg, Andrew. 2018. "'This Is All Bogus, and It's to Take Control Over the Judiciary': A Veteran Administrative Law Judge Slams Trump's Order Making ALJs Political Appointees." Beltway Breakfast. *www.beltwaybreakfast.com/courts/2018/07/11/this-is-all-bogus-and-its-to-take-control-over-the-judiciary-a-veteran-administrative-law-judge-slams-trumps-order-making-aljs-political-appointees/*

Feinstein, Brian D. and Daniel J. Hemel. 2017. "Partisan Balance With Bite." *Columbia Law Review* 118(1):9–82.

Fiorina, Morris P. and Samuel J. Abrams. 2008. "Political Polarization in the American Public." *Annual Review of Political Science* 11:563–588.

Firestone, David. 2000. "Contesting the Vote: The Overview; Florida Court Backs Recount; Bush Appealing to U.S. Justices." *The New York Times*, December 9. *www.nytimes.com/2000/12/09/us/contesting-vote-overview-florida-court-backs-recount-bush-appealing-us-justices.html*

Fitzpatrick, Brian T. 2009. "The Politics of Merit Selection." *Missouri Law Review* 74(3):675–710.

Fletcher, Michael A. and Charles Babington. 2005. "Miers, Under Fire From Right, Withdrawn As Court Nominee." *The Washington Post*, October 27. *www.washingtonpost.com/wp-dyn/content/article/2005/10/27/AR2005102700547.html*

Fowler, Linda L. and Robert D. McClure. 1990. *Political Ambition: Who Decides to Run for Congress.* New Haven, CT: Yale University Press.

Fox, Lawrence J. 2004. The Academics Have It Wrong: Hysteria Is No Substitute for Sound Public Policy Analysis. In *Enron: Corporate Fiascos and Their Implications*, ed. Nancy B. Rapoport and Bala G. Dharan. New York: Foundation Press.

Franck, Raphaël. 2013. "The Lawyers' Comparative Advantage in Parliamentary Elections." Unpublished Manuscript.

Frank, Jerome. 1930. *Law and the Modern Mind.* New York: Anchor Books.

Friedman, Lawrence M. 1985. *Total Justice.* New York: Russell Sage Foundation.

Fukuyama, Francis. 2014. *Political Order and Political Decay: From the Industrial Revolution to the Globalization of Democracy.* New York: Farrar, Straus and Giroux.

Gallagher, Eileen C. 2005. "The ABA Revisits the Model Code of Judicial Conduct." *The Judges' Journal* 44(1):7–12.

Gallup. 2015. "Honesty/Ethics in Professions." Gallup Poll. *www.gallup.com/poll/1654/honesty-ethics-professions.aspx*

George, Tracey E. 1999. "The Dynamics and Determinants of the Decision to Grant *En Banc* Review." *Washington Law Review* 74:213–274.

Ghitza, Yair and Andrew Gelman. 2014. "The Great Society, Reagan's Revolution, and Generations of Presidential Voting." Working Paper.

Gibson, James. 2008. "Challenges to the Impartiality of State Supreme Courts: Legitimacy Theory and 'New-Style' Judicial Campaigns." *American Political Science Review* 102(1):59–75.

Gibson, James L. 2009. "'New-style' Judicial Campaigns and the Legitimacy of State High Courts." *The Journal of Politics* 71(4):1285–1304.

Gibson, James L., Jeffrey A. Gottfried, Michael X. Delli Carpini, and Kathleen Hall Jamieson. 2011. "The Effects of Judicial Campaign Activity on the Legitimacy of Courts: A Survey-Based Experiment." *Political Research Quarterly* 64(3):545–558.

Giles, Micheal W., Virginia A. Hettinger, and Todd Peppers. 2001. "Picking Federal Judges: A Note on Policy and Partisan Selection Agendas." *Political Research Quarterly* 54(3):623–641.

Global Witness. 2016. "Lowering the Bar." Global Witness. www.globalwitness.org/documents/18208/Lowering-the-Bar.pdf

Goldman, Sheldon. 1997. *Picking Federal Judges: Lower Court Selection from Roosevelt through Reagan.* New Haven, CT: Yale University Press.

Goldstein, Amy. 2001. "Bush Curtails ABA Role in Selecting U.S. Judges." *The Washington Post*, March 23.

Gonzales, Alberto. 2001. "Letter from Alberto Gonzales, U.S. Attorney General, to Martha Barnett, President of the American Bar Association."

Grassley, Charles E, Orrin G. Hatch, and Jeff Sessions et al. 2016. "Letter to Mitch McConnell." United States Senate Committee on the Judiciary.

Green, Justin J., John R. Schmidhauser, Larry L. Berg, and David Brady. 1973. "Lawyers in Congress: A New Look at Some Old Assumptions." *Western Political Quarterly* 26(3):440–452.

Greenhouse, Linda. 2017. "Will Politics Tarnish the Supreme Court's Legitimacy?" *The New York Times*, October 26. *www.nytimes.com/2017/10/26/opinion/politics-supreme-court-legitimacy.html*

Gross, Ariela. 2001. The Law and the Culture of Slavery: Natchez, Mississippi. In *Local Matters: Race, Crime, and Justice in the Nineteenth-Century South*, ed. Christopher Waldrep and Donald G. Nieman. Athens, GA: University of Georgia Press, pp. 92–124.

Gross, Ariela J. 2000. *Double Character: Slavery and Mastery in the Antebellum Southern Courtroom.* Princeton, NJ: Princeton University Press.

Guthrie, William D. 1934. "The Child Labor Amendment." *American Bar Association Journal* 20(7):404–406. *www.jstor.org/stable/25710434*

Hadfield, Gillian K. 2008. "Legal Barriers to Innovation: The Growing Economic Cost of Professional Control Over Corporate Legal Markets." *Stanford Law Review* 60(6):101–146.

Hadfield, Gillian K. 2010. "Higher Demand, Lower Supply? A Comparative Assessment of the Legal Resource Landscape for Ordinary Americans." *Fordham Urban Law Journal* 37(1):129.

Hafner-Burton, Emilie M., Thad Kousser, and David G. Victor. 2014. Firms, Pluralism, and Congressional Foreign Policy Lobbying. In 2014 *Meetings of the American Political Science Association*, pp. 1–47.

Hall, Kermit L. 1983. "The Judiciary on Trial: State Constitutional Reform and the Rise of an Elected Judiciary, 1876–1860." *Historian* 45(3):337–354.

Hall, Kermit L. 1984. "Progressive Reform and the Decline of Democratic Accountability: The Popular Election of State Supreme Court Judges, 1850–1920." *Law & Social Inquiry* 9(2):345–369.

Hamilton, Alexander, James Madison, and John Jay. 1787. *The Federalist Papers.*

Hanssen, F. Andrew. 1999. "The Effect of Judicial Institutions on Uncertainty and the Rate of Litigation: The Election Versus Appointment of State Judges." *The Journal of Legal Studies* 28(1):205–232.

Harris, Adam. 2018. "America Is Divided by Education." *The Atlantic*, November 7. *www.theatlantic.com/education/archive/2018/11/education-gap-explains-american-politics/575113/*

Harris, Allison P. and Maya Sen. 2019. "Bias and Judging." *Annual Review of Political Science* 22:241–259.

Helland, Eric and Alexander Tabarrok. 2002. "The Effect of Electoral Institutions on Tort Awards." *American Law and Economics Review* 4(2):341–370.

Henderson, Bill. 2015. "Size of the US Legal Market by Type of Client." The Legal Whiteboard Network. *http://lawprofessors.typepad.com/legalwhiteboard/2015/01/size-of-the-us-legal-market-by-type-of-client.html*

Hendricks, Valeria. 2001. "'Fixing' the Unbroken Judicial Nominating Commissions: View from a Survivor of the 2001 Legislative Session." *The Record: Journal of the Appellate Practice Section of the Florida Bar* 9(4):7–8.

Herszenhorn, David. 2016. "G.O.P. Senators Say Obama Supreme Court Pick Will Be Rejected." *The New York Times*, February 24. *www.nytimes.com/2016/02/24/us/politics/supreme-court-nomination-obama.html*

Hetherington, Marc J. 2001. "Resurgent Mass Partisanship: The Role of Elite Polarization." *American Political Science Review* 95(3):619–631.

Hicks, George W. Jr. 2005. "The Conservative Influence of the Federalist Society on the Harvard Law School Student Body." *Harvard Journal of Law & Public Policy* 29(2):623–718.

Hollibaugh, Gary E. and Lawrence S. Rothenberg. 2019. "Appointments and Attrition: Time and Executive Disadvantage in the Appointments Process." *Journal of Public Policy:* 1–19.

Hollis-Brusky, Amanda. 2015. *Ideas with Consequences: The Federalist Society and the Conservative Counterrevolution.* New York: Oxford University Press.

Horwitz, Morton J. 1992. *The Transformation of American Law, 1870-1960: The Crisis of Legal Orthodoxy.* New York: Oxford University Press.

Huber, Gregory A. and Sanford C. Gordon. 2004. "Accountability and Coercion: Is Justice Blind When It Runs for Office?" *American Journal of Political Science* 48(2):247–263.

Hunter, Elmo B. 1991. "Revisiting the History and Success of Merit Selection in Missouri and Elsewhere." *UMKC Law Review* 60(1):69–71.

Hurwitz, Mark S. and Drew Noble Lanier. 2003. "Explaining Judicial Diversity: The Differential Ability of Women and Minorities to Attain Seats on State Supreme and Appellate Courts." *State Politics & Policy Quarterly* 3(4):329–352.

Hutcheson, Elwood. 1937. "The Administration of Justice as Affected by Insecurity of Tenure of Judicial and Administrative Officers." *American Bar Association Journal* 23(12):930–987.

Inter-Parliamentary Union: PARLINE Database on National Parliaments. 2017. *http://archive.ipu.org/parline-e/parlinesearch.asp*

Jackson, Jeffrey D. 2000. "The Selection of Judges in Kansas: A Comparison of Systems." *Kansas Bar Association Journal* 69(1):32–42.

Jarvis, Craig and Ann Blythe. 2017. "Veto Override Means Voters Will Know Judges' Party Affiliations." *The News & Observer*, March 23. *www.news observer.com/news/politics-government/state-politics/article140327188.html*

Jefferson, Thomas. 1790. "Letter From Thomas Jefferson to Thomas Mann Randolph, Jr." *https://founders.archives.gov/documents/Jefferson/01-16-02-0264*

Judicial Selection in the States. 2018. Ballotpedia.org. Retrieved August 11, 2018 https://ballotpedia.org/Judicial_selection_in_the_states.

Kagan, Elena. 1995. "Confirmation Messes, Old and New." *The University of Chicago Law Review* 62(2):919–942.

Kagan, Robert A. 2009. *Adversarial Legalism: The American Way of Law*. Cambridge, MA: Harvard University Press.

Kales, Albert M. 1927. "Methods of Selecting and Retiring Judges." *Journal of the American Judicature Society* 11(5):133–144.

Karmasek, Jessica M. 2013. "Kansas Court of Appeals Judges Now Picked by Governor, with Senate Confirmation." *Legal News Line. https://legalnewsline .com/stories/510514947-kansas-court-of-appeals-judges-now-picked-by-gover nor-with-senate-confirmation*

Kastellec, Jonathan P., Jeffrey R. Lax, and Justin H. Phillips. 2010. "Public Opinion and Senate Confirmation of Supreme Court Nominees." *The Journal of Politics* 72(3):767–784.

Kay, John and John Vickers. 1988. "Regulatory Reform in Britain." *Economic Policy* 3(7):285–351.

Kerr, Orrin S. 2018. "Trump Picked Kavanaugh: How Will He Change the Supreme Court?" *POLITICO*, July 9. *www.politico.com/magazine/story/20 18/07/09/donald-trump-brett-kavanaugh-supreme-court-218963*

Kessler, Amalia D. 2017. *Inventing American Exceptionalism: The Origins of American Adversarial Legal Culture, 1800-1877*. New Haven, CT: Yale University Press.

Khalid, Asma. 2018. "Trump Changes How Federal Agency In-House Judges Are Hired." National Public Radio, July 10. *www.npr.org/2018/07/10/627826602/ trump-changes-how-federal-agency-in-house-judges-are-hired*

Kim, Seung Min. 2019. "Democratic Presidential Candidates Come Under Pressure to Release Supreme Court Picks." *The Washington Post*, October 15. *www.washingtonpost.com/politics/democratic-presidential-candidates-come-under-pressure-to-release-supreme-court-picks/2019/10/15/2bf3bd34-eefb-11 e9-b2da-606ba1ef30e3_story.html*

Klein, Michael. 2014. "American 'Hypocrisy': Why the US Is Now the Focus of Transparency Efforts." *The Cayman Islands Journal*, June 1. *www.journal .ky/2016/06/01/american-hypocrisy-why-the-us-is-now-the-focus-of-transpare ncy-efforts/*

Krehbiel, Keith. 2007. "Supreme Court Appointments As a Move-the-Median Game." *American Journal of Political Science* 51(2):231–240.

Kritzer, Herbert M. 2015. *Justices on the Ballot: Continuity and Change in State Supreme Court Elections.* Cambridge: Cambridge University Press.

Kroft, Steve. 2016. "Anonymous, Inc." CBS News, August 28. *www.cbsnews .com/news/hidden-camera-investigation-money-laundering-60-minutes/*

Laffont, Jean-Jacques and Jean Tirole. 1991. "The Politics of Government Decision-Making: A Theory of Regulatory Capture." *Quarterly Journal of Economics* 106(4):1089–1127.

Lanier, Drew Noble and Roger Handberg. 2001. "In the Eye of the Hurricane: Florida Courts, Judicial Independence, and Politics." *Fordham Urban Law Journal* 29(3):1029–1052.

Lauderdale, Benjamin E. and Tom S. Clark. 2014. "Scaling Politically Meaningful Dimensions Using Texts and Votes." *American Journal of Political Science* 58(3):754–771.

Layman, Geoffrey C. and Thomas M. Carsey. 2002. "Party Polarization and 'Conflict Extension' in the American Electorate." *American Journal of Political Science* 46(4):786–802.

Lefler, Dion. 2016. "Kansas Senate Passes Judicial-Impeachment Bill." *The Wichita Eagle*, March 22. *www.kansas.com/news/politics-government/ article67506877.html*

Legal Executive Institute. 2016. "The Size of the US Legal Market." Legal Executive Institute *http://legalexecutiveinstitute.com/the-size-of-the-us-legal-market-shrinking-piece-of-a-bigger-pie-an-lei-graphic/).*

Lerner, Joshua Y. 2018. "Getting the Message Across: Evaluating Think Tank Influence in Congress." *Public Choice* 175(3):347–366.

Leubsdorf, John and William H. Simon. 2015. "RE: Professional Responsibility Assessment of Lawyer Interview Transcripts." Global Witness.

Lewis, Neil A. 2001. "A Conservative Legal Group Thrives in Bush's Washington." *The New York Times*, April 18. *www.nytimes.com/2001/04/18/ us/a-conservative-legal-group-thrives-in-bush-s-washington.html*

Lewis, Steve. 2016. "Capitol Updates: No Less Than 20 Measures Filed to Change Oklahoma's Judicial System This Year." Oklahoma Policy Institute. *https://okpolicy.org/no-less-20-measures-filed-change-oklahomas-judicial-syst em-year-capitol-updates*

Lim, Claire S.H. 2013. "Preferences and Incentives of Appointed and Elected Public Officials: Evidence from State Trial Court Judges." *American Economic Review* 103(4):1360–1397.

Lincoln, Abraham. 1865. "Letter to Isham Reavis."

Lott, John R. 2005. "The Judicial Confirmation Process: The Difficulty with Being Smart." *Journal of Empirical Legal Studies* 2(3):407–447.

Lyall, Sarah. 2017. "Liberals Are Still Angry, but Merrick Garland Has Reached Acceptance." *The New York Times*, February 19. *www.nytimes.com/ 2017/02/19/us/politics/merrick-garland-supreme-court-obama-nominee.html*

Mann, Fred. 2014. "Families of Carr Brothers' Victims Seek Removal of Two Kansas Supreme Court Justices." *The Wichita Eagle*, October 10. *www.kansas .com/news/local/crime/article2651289.html*

Manno, Lizzie. 2018. "After a Pennsylvania Supreme Court Decision on Gerry-mandering, Republicans Threaten Impeachment." *Paste Magazine*, February 6. *www.pastemagazine.com/articles/2018/02/after-a-state-supreme-court-decision -on-gerrymande.html*

Martin, Andrew D. and Kevin M. Quinn. 2002. "Dynamic Ideal Point Estimation via Markov Chain Monte Carlo for the U.S. Supreme Court, 1953–1999." *Political Analysis* 10(2):134–153.

Martin, Gregory J. and Zachary Peskowitz. 2018. "Agency Problems in Polit-ical Campaigns: Media Buying and Consulting." *American Political Science Review* 112(2):231–248.

Matter, Ulrich and Alois Stutzer. 2015. "The Role of Lawyer-Legislators in Shap-ing the Law: Evidence from Voting on Tort Reforms." *The Journal of Law & Economics* 58(2):357–384.

Maute, Judith L. 2008. "Bar Associations, Self-Regulation and Consumer Pro-tection: Whither Thou Goest." *Journal of the Professional Lawyer* (1):53–87.

McCarthy, Justin. 2014. "Americans Losing Confidence in All Branches of U.S. Gov't." Gallup Poll. *https://news.gallup.com/poll/171992/americans-losing-co nfidence-branches-gov.aspx*

McCarty, Nolan, Keith T. Poole, and Howard Rosenthal. 2001. "The Hunt for Party Discipline in Congress." *American Political Science Review* 95(3):673–687.

McCarty, Nolan M., Keith T. Poole, and Howard Rosenthal. 2016. *Polarized America: The Dance of Ideology and Unequal Riches*. Cambridge, MA: MIT Press.

McConnell, Mitch. 2016. "Sen. Mitch McConnell Speech at Fancy Farm, 2016." Kentucky Educational Television. *https://youtu.be/kP1G45maN4A*

McConnell, Mitch Lindsey Graham, Charles E. Grassley et al. 2019. "Letter to Scott M. Harris In Re: New York State Rifle & Pistol Association v. City of New York, No. 18-280." U.S. Senate.

McGinnis, John O., Matthew A. Schwartz, and Benjamin Tisdell. 2004. "The Patterns and Implications of Political Contributions by Elite Law School Faculty." *Georgetown Law Journal* 93(4):1167–1213.

McKenna, Marian Cecilia, and Joseph McKenna. 2002. *Franklin Roosevelt and the Great Constitutional War: The Court-Packing Crisis of 1937*. New York: Fordham University Press.

McKnight, David L. and Paul J. Hinton. 2013. "International Comparisons of Litigation Costs: Canada, Europe, and the United States." U.S. Chamber of Commerce Institute for Legal Reform.

Merrill, Thomas W. 1996. "Capture Theory and the Courts: 1967–1983." *Chicago-Kent Law Review* 72(4):1039–1117.

Messenger, Tony. 2010. "Missouri Plan for Selecting Judges Faces New Chal-lenge." *St. Louis Post-Dispatch*, November 27. *www.stltoday.com/news/local/ govt-and-politics/missouri-plan-for-selecting-judges-faces-new-challenge/article _7fb91810-c4da-5957-951d-daec4f112746.html*

Michelson, Ethan. 2013. "Women in the Legal Profession, 1970-2010: A Study of the Global Supply of Lawyers." *Indiana Journal of Global Legal Studies* 20(18):1071–1137.

Miller, Mark C. 1995. *The High Priests of American Politics: The Role of Lawyers in American Political Institutions.* Knoxville, TN: University of Tennessee Press.

Moliterno, James E. 2012. "The Trouble with Lawyer Regulation." *Emory Law Journal* 62(4):885–908.

Moraski, Bryon J. and Charles R. Shipan. 1999. "The Politics of Supreme Court Nominations: A Theory of Institutional Constraints and Choices." *American Journal of Political Science* 43(4):1069–1095.

Nixon, David C. and David L. Goss. 2001. "Confirmation Delay for Vacancies on the Circuit Courts of Appeals." *American Politics Research* 29(3):246–274.

Nomination of Neil M. Gorsuch. 2017. "Nomination of Neil M. Gorsuch to be an Associate Justice of the Supreme Court of the United States." Senate Hearings.

Obama, Barack. 2016. "Merrick Garland Deserves a Vote—For Democracy's Sake." *The Wall Street Journal*, July 17. *www.wsj.com/articles/merrick-gar land-deserves-a-votefor-democracys-sake-1468797686*

O'Connor, Sandra Day. 2004. Foreword. In *America's Lawyer-Presidents*, ed. Norman Gross. Evanston, IL: Northwestern University Press, pp. ix–xi.

O'Connor, Sandra Day. 2007. "Justice for Sale." *Wall Street Journal*, November 15. *www.wsj.com/articles/SB119509262956693711*

Oliver, Dawn L. 2009. "Landing a Legal Job in the Federal Government." American Bar Association, Young Lawyers Division.

Olson, Elizabeth. 2016. "Women Make Up Majority of U.S. Law Students for First Time." *The New York Times*, December 16. *www.nytimes.com/2016/12/ 16/business/dealbook/women-majority-of-us-law-students-first-time.html*

Ornstein, Norman J. Ornstein, Thomas E. Mann, Michael J. Malbin et al. 2017. "Vital Statistics on Congress." The Brookings Institution.

Pero, Dan. 2013. "Op-ed: Judicial Merit Selection Is the Wrong Choice for Pennsylvania." *Penn Live*, February 19. *www.pennlive.com/opinion/2013/02/ judicial_merit_selection_is_the_wrong_choice_for_pennsylvania.html*

Pew Research Center. 2013. "Public Esteem for Military Still High, Clergy in the Middle, Lawyers at the Bottom." *www.pewforum.org/2013/07/11/pub lic-esteem-for-military-still-high/*

Pew Research Center. 2016. "2016 Campaign: Strong Interest, Widespread Dissatisfaction." *http://assets.pewresearch.org/wp-content/uploa ds/sites/5/2016/07/07-07-16-Voter-attitudes-release.pdf*

Poole, Keith T. and Howard Rosenthal. 1985. "A Spatial Model for Legislative Roll Call Analysis." *American Journal of Political Science* 29(2):357–384.

Posner, Richard. 2010. *How Judges Think.* Cambridge, MA: Harvard University Press.

Pound, Roscoe. 1906. "The Causes of Popular Dissatisfaction with the Administration of Justice." *Remarks to Twentieth Annual Meeting of the American Bar Association.*

Pound, Roscoe. 1938. "Report of the Special Committee on Administrative Law." *Annual Report of the American Bar Association* (63):331–362.

Pound, Roscoe. 1953. *The Lawyer from Antiquity to Modern Times.* Eagan, MN: West Publishing Company.

Pound, Roscoe. 1964. "The Causes of Popular Dissatisfaction with the Administration of Justice." *Crime & Delinquency* 10(4):355–371.

Presser, Stephen B. John L. Dodd, Christopher Murray et al. 2003. "The Case for Judicial Appointments." The Federalist Society Judicial Appointments White Paper Task Force. *https://fedsoc.org/commentary/publications/the-case-for-judicial-appointments*

Prior, Markus. 2013. "Media and Political Polarization." *Annual Review of Political Science* 16:101–127.

Pritchett, C Herman. 1948. *The Roosevelt Court: A Study in Judicial Politics and Values, 1937-1947.* New Orleans: Quid Pro Books.

Provine, Doris Marie. 1986. *Judging Credentials: Nonlawyer Judges and the Politics of Professionalism.* Chicago, IL: University of Chicago Press.

Ramsey, Ross. 2017. "Analysis: Rising Criticism Threatens One-Punch Voting in Texas." *The Texas Tribune*, February 3. *www.texastribune.org/2017/02/03/analysis-rising-criticism-threatens-one-punch-voting-texas/*

Ramseyer, J. Mark. 2013. "Liability for Defective Products: Comparative Hypotheses and Evidence from Japan." *American Journal of Comparative Law* 61(3):617–655.

Rankin, Bill. 2013. "Ex-Justice Says Contested Elections Threaten Fair Judiciary." *The Atlanta Journal-Constitution*, August 12. *www.ajc.com/news/local/justice-says-contested-elections-threaten-fair-judiciary/gCmODxkhBtiamG8U8PRpiI/*

Reid, Harry. 2016. "Press Release of Harry Reid." *The New York Times*, February 17. *www.nytimes.com/interactive/2016/02/17/upshot/scalia-supreme-court-senate-nomination.html*

Rhode, Deborah L. 1981. "Policing the Professional Monopoly: A Constitutional and Empirical Analysis of Unauthorized Practice Prohibitions." *Stanford Law Review* 34(1):1–112.

Rhode, Deborah L. 2004. *Access to Justice.* New York: Oxford University Press.

Rhode, Deborah L. 2015. *The Trouble with Lawyers.* New York: Oxford University Press.

Robbins, Laila and Alicia Bannon. 2019. "State Supreme Court Diversity." Brennen Center for Justice.

Roberts, John. 2016. "Interview with John Roberts at New England Law School." Politico, February 3. *www.c-span.org/video/?404131-1/discussion-chief-justicejohn-roberts*

Robinson, Nick. 2015. "The Declining Dominance of Lawyers in U.S. Federal Politics." HLS Center on the Legal Profession Research Paper No. 2015-10.

Rock, Emily and Lawrence Baum. 2010. "The Impact of High-Visibility Contests for U.S. State Court Judgeships: Partisan Voting in Nonpartisan Elections." *State Politics & Policy Quarterly* 10(4):368–396.

Roosevelt, Franklin D. 1940. "Veto of a Bill Regulating Administrative Agencies, December 8, 1940." Online by Gerhard Peters and John T. Woolley, The American Presidency Project. *www.presidency.ucsb.edu/ws/?pid=15914*

Roosevelt, Theodore. 1906. *A Compilation of The Messages and Speeches of Theodore Roosevelt, 1901-1905*. Vol. 1. Bureau of National Literature and Art.

Rose, Steve. 2016. "Attempt to Oust Kansas Supreme Court Judges Is Likely Doomed." *Kansas City Star*, June 18. *www.kansascity.com/opinion/opn-co lumns-blogs/steve-rose/article84456322.html*

Ruger, Theodore W., Pauline T. Kim, Andrew D. Martin, and Kevin M. Quinn. 2004. "The Supreme Court Forecasting Project: Legal and Political Science Approaches to Predicting Supreme Court Decisionmaking." *Columbia Law Review* 104(4):1150–1210.

Russomanno, Herman J. 2001. "Protecting the Independence of Florida Lawyers." *The Florida Bar Journal* 75(4):6.

Salokar, Rebecca Mae. 2007. "Endorsements in Judicial Campaigns: The Ethics of Messaging." *Justice System Journal* 28(3):342–357.

Salokar, Rebecca Mae and Kimberly A. Shaw. 2002. "The Impact of National Politics on State Courts: Florida After Election 2000." *Justice System Journal* 23(1):57–74.

Sample, James, Adam Skaggs, Jonathan Blitzer, and Linda Casey. 2010. "The New Politics of Judicial Elections, 2000-2009." Brennan Center for Justice Report. *www.justiceatstake.org/media/cms/JASNPJEDecadeONLINE_8E7F D3FEB83E3.pdf*

Sarokin, H. Lee. 2014. "For Sale—Going Fast: An Independent Judiciary— Buy a Judge Today." *The Huffington Post*, August 7. *www.huffpost .com/entry/judicial-elections_b_5655959*

Scherer, Nancy, Brandon L. Bartels, and Amy Steigerwalt. 2008. "Sounding the Fire Alarm: The Role of Interest Groups in the Lower Federal Court Confirmation Process." *The Journal of Politics* 70(4):1026–1039.

Schubert, Glendon A. 1974. *The Judicial Mind Revisited: Psychometric Analysis of Supreme Court Ideology*. Oxford: Oxford University Press.

Segal, Jeffrey and Harold J. Spaeth. 2002. *The Supreme Court and the Attitudinal Model Revisited*. Cambridge: Cambridge University Press.

Semple, Noel. 2017. "Legal Services Regulation in Canada: Plus Ça Change?" Working Paper, University of Windsor.

Sen, Maya. 2014a. "How Judicial Qualification Ratings May Disadvantage Minority and Female Candidates." *Journal of Law and Courts* 2(1):33–65.

Sen, Maya. 2014b. "Minority Judicial Candidates Have Changed: The ABA Ratings Gap Has Not." *Judicature* 98:46.

Sen, Maya. 2017a. "Diversity, Qualifications, and Ideology: How Female and Minority Judges Have Changed, or Not Changed, over Time." *Wisconsin Law Review* 2017(2):367–400.

Sen, Maya. 2017b. "How Political Signals Affect Public Support for Judicial Nominations: Evidence from a Conjoint Experiment." *Political Research Quarterly* 70(2):374–393.

Severino, Carrie. 2013. "Governor Brownback Signs Judicial-Selection Reform." *The National Review*, March 27. *www.nationalreview.com/bench-memos/ governor-brownback-signs-judicial-selection-reform-carrie-severino/*

Shamir, Ronen. 1995. *Managing Legal Uncertainty: Elite Lawyers in the New Deal.* Durham, NC: Duke University Press.

Shapiro, Bruce. 1997. "Sleeping Lawyer Syndrome." *The Nation,* April 7.

Shaw, Gwyneth K. 2001. "Republicans Try to Cut Influence of Florida Bar." *Orlando Sentinel,* April 23. *http://articles.orlandosentinel.com/2001-04-23/news/0104230194_1_florida-bar-brummer-bar-officials*

Shepherd, George B. 2003. "No African-American Lawyers Allowed: The Inefficient Racism of the ABA's Accreditation of Law Schools." *Journal of Legal Education* 53(1):103–156.

Sherman, Mark. 2018. "Roberts, Trump Spar in Extraordinary Scrap Over Judges." Associated Press, November 21.

Shorman, Jonathan. 2016. "Kansas Lawmakers Send Judicial Funding Fix to Governor." *The Topeka Capital-Journal,* January 28. *http://cjonline.com/news/2016-01-28/kansas-lawmakers-send-judicial-funding-fix-governor*

Shortell, David. 2017. "As Judiciary Nominees Come Quick, Democrats Cry Foul." CNN, November 15. *www.cnn.com/2017/11/15/politics/trump-federal-judge-nominees-scrutinized/index.html*

Shugerman, Jed Handelsman. 2009. "Economic Crisis and the Rise of Judicial Elections and Judicial Review." *Harvard Law Review* 123(5):1061–1150.

Shugerman, Jed Handelsman. 2012. *The People's Courts.* Cambridge, MA: Harvard University Press.

Siebenmark, Jerry. 2014. "Brownback Speaks at Rally Opposing Same-sex Marriage in Summit Church Lot." *The Wichita Eagle,* October 18. *www.kansas.com/news/politics-government/article3000547.html*

Simon, Ammon. 2012. "Kansas Update." National Review Online. *www.nationalreview.com/bench-memos/kansas-update-ammon-simon/*

Simon, Ammon. 2013. "The Battle for Judicial Selection Reform in Kansas." National Review Online. *www.nationalreview.com/bench-memos/336925/battle-judicial-selection-reform-kansas-ammon-simon*

Smelcer, Susan Navarro, Amy Steigerwalt, and Richard L. Vining Jr. 2012. "Bias and the Bar: Evaluating the ABA Ratings of Federal Judicial Nominees." *Political Research Quarterly* 65(4):827–840.

Snyder, James M., Jr. and Tim Groseclose. 2000. "Estimating Party Influence in Congressional Roll-Call Voting." *American Journal of Political Science* 44(2):193–211.

Snyder, Laura. 2016. *Democratizing Legal Services: Obstacles and Opportunities.* Lanham, MD: Lexington Books.

Songer, Donald R. 1982. "The Policy Consequences of Senate Involvement in the Selection of Judges in the United States Courts of Appeals." *Western Political Quarterly* 35(1):107–119.

Songer, Donald R., Jeffrey A. Segal, and Charles M. Cameron. 1994. "The Hierarchy of Justice: Testing a Principal-Agent Model of Supreme Court-Circuit Court Interactions." *American Journal of Political Science* 38(4):673–696.

Spahn, Bradley. 2017. "Before The American Voter." Working Paper, Stanford University.

Stephen, Frank H. and James H. Love. 2000. "Regulation of the Legal Profession." *Encyclopedia of Law and Economics* 3:987–1017.

Stern, Mark Joseph. 2018. "North Carolina Republicans' Latest Judicial Power Grab May Have Backfired Spectacularly." *Slate*, July 17. *https://slate.com/news -and-politics/2018/07/north-carolina-republicans-plan-to-steal-a-state-supre me-court-seat-from-anita-earls-is-backfiring.html*

Stevens, Robert. 1967. *Law School: Legal Education in America from 1850 to the 1980s*. Chapel Hill, NC: University of North Carolina Press.

Stigler, George J. 1971. "The Theory of Economic Regulation." *The Bell Journal of Economics and Management Science* 2(1):3–21.

Stone, Harlan F. 1934. "The Public Influence of the Bar." *Harvard Law Review* 48(1):1–14.

Sunstein, Cass R., David Schkade, Lisa M. Ellman, and Andres Sawicki. 2006. *Are Judges Political?* Washington, DC: Brookings Institution Press.

Tabarrok, Alexander and Eric Helland. 1999. "Court Politics: The Political Economy of Tort Awards." *The Journal of Law & Economics* 42(1):157–188.

Taft, William H. 1913. "The Selection and Tenure of Judges." *American Bar Association Annual Report* 38(1):418–435.

Taylor, Clifford. 2010. "Without Merit: Why 'Merit' Selection Is the Wrong Way for States to Choose Judges." The Heritage Foundation. *www.heritage.org/ courts/report/without-merit-why-merit-selection-the-wrong-way-states-choose -judges*

Teles, Steven M. 2012. *The Rise of the Conservative Legal Movement: The Battle for Control of the Law*. Princeton, NJ: Princeton University Press.

The Global 100. 2016. *www.americanlawyer.com/id=1202767838452/The-Glob al-100*

The UK 100. 2016. *http://reports.thelawyer.com/analysis/intelligence/uk-100- 2016*

The US 100. 2016. *http://reports.thelawyer.com/analysis/intelligence/uk-100- 2016*

Thieme, Sebastian. 2017. "Ideology and Extremism of Interest Groups: Evidence from Lobbyist Declarations in Iowa, Nebraska, and Wisconsin." *https://ssrn.com/abstract=2950719*

Tocqueville, Alexis de. 1835. *Democracy in America*. New York: Knopf.

Toobin, Jeffrey. 2008. *The Nine: Inside the Secret World of the Supreme Court*. New York: Anchor Books.

Toobin, Jeffrey. 2017. "The Conservative Pipeline To the Supreme Court." *The New Yorker*, April 17. *www.newyorker.com/magazine/2017/04/17/the-conse rvative-pipeline-to-the-supreme-court*

Trevor, Reece Alexa Graumlich, Elena Mercado et al. 2017. "Judicial Selection in California." Stanford University Law and Policy Lab. *https://law.stanford .edu/wp-content/uploads/2017/06/Judicial-Selection-in-California.pdf*

Trump, Donald J. 2018. "Interview with President Donald J. Trump." Fox News: Fox & Friends, May 24.

Under the Dome Blog. 2015. "NC House Votes for Partisan Judicial Elections." *Raleigh News and Observer*. *www.newsobserver.com/news/politics-gov ernment/politics-columns-blogs/under-the-dome/article18687441.html*

Vile, John R. and Mario Perez-Reilly. 1990. "U.S. Constitution and Judicial Qualifications: A Curious Omission." *Judicature* 74(4):198.

Wagner, Erich. 2019. "Bipartisan Bill Would Restore Administrative Law Judges to Competitive Service." *Government Executive.*

Wald, Eli. 2010. "Should Judges Regulate Lawyers?" *McGeorge Law Review* 42(1):149–175.

Wall Street Journal Editorial Board. 2008. "Without Judicial Merit." *The Wall Street Journal. www.wsj.com/articles/SB121944471520256513*

Walmsley, Roy. 2013. "World Prison Population List (2013)." International Centre for Prison Studies/University of Essex.

Ware, Stephen J. 2007. "Selection to the Kansas Supreme Court." *Kansas Journal of Law & Public Policy* 17(3):386–423.

Warren, Charles. 1980. *A History of the American Bar.* Cambridge: Cambridge University Press.

Washington State Bar Association. 2012. "The Washington State Bar Association Membership Study 2012." www.wsba.org/docs/default-source/about-wsba/diversity/wsba-membership-study-report-2012.pdf

Way, Dan. 2016. "Update: McCrory Signs Judicial Reform Bill." *The Carolina Journal,* December 15. *www.carolinajournal.com/news-article/senate-passes-judicial-election-reform-amid-protests-house-takes-it-up/*

Weiss, Debra Cassens. 2018. "ABA President Says Trump Order Could Politicize the Process of Hiring Administrative Law Judges." *ABA Journal,* July 16.

Whisner, Mary. 2014. "The 411 on Lawyer Directories." *Law Library Journal* 106(2):257–266.

Wilson, James. 1989. *Bureaucracy: What Government Agencies Do and Why They Do It.* New York: Basic Books.

Wilson, Woodrow. 1910. "The Lawyer and the Community." *The North American Review* 192(660):604–622.

Winters, Glenn R. 1965. "Selection of Judges: An Historical Introduction." *Texas Law Review* 44(6):1081–1087.

Woll, Peter. 1963. *Administrative Law: The Informal Process.* Berkeley: University of California Press.

World Justice Project. 2016. "WJP Rule of Law Index 2016." *http://data.worldjusticeproject.org/*

Yeoman, Barry. 2017. "Law and Disorder in North Carolina." *The American Prospect,* December 21. *http://prospect.org/article/law-and-disorder-north-carolina*

Yoder, Eric. 2018. "Trump Moves to Shield Administrative Law Judge Decisions in Wake of High Court Ruling." *The Washington Post,* July 10. *www.washingtonpost.com/news/powerpost/wp/2018/07/10/trump-moves-to-shield-administrative-law-judge-decisions-in-wake-of-high-court-ruling/*

Zeppos, Nicholas S. 1997. "The Legal Profession and the Development of Administrative Law." *Chicago-Kent Law Review* 72(4):1119.

Zorn, Christopher and Jennifer Barnes Bowie. 2010. "Ideological Influences on Decision Making in the Federal Judicial Hierarchy: An Empirical Assessment." *The Journal of Politics* 72(4):1212–1221.

Index

Other Books in the Series (Continued from page ii)